Learning PostgreSQL 11
Third Edition

A beginner's guide to building high-performance PostgreSQL database solutions

Salahaldin Juba
Andrey Volkov

BIRMINGHAM - MUMBAI

Learning PostgreSQL 11
Third Edition

Copyright © 2019 Packt Publishing

All rights reserved. No part of this book may be reproduced, stored in a retrieval system, or transmitted in any form or by any means, without the prior written permission of the publisher, except in the case of brief quotations embedded in critical articles or reviews.

Every effort has been made in the preparation of this book to ensure the accuracy of the information presented. However, the information contained in this book is sold without warranty, either express or implied. Neither the authors, nor Packt Publishing or its dealers and distributors, will be held liable for any damages caused or alleged to have been caused directly or indirectly by this book.

Packt Publishing has endeavored to provide trademark information about all of the companies and products mentioned in this book by the appropriate use of capitals. However, Packt Publishing cannot guarantee the accuracy of this information.

Commissioning Editor: Pravin Dhandre
Acquisition Editor: Joshua Nadar
Content Development Editors: Roshan Kumar, Pooja Parvatkar
Technical Editor: Nilesh Sawakhande
Copy Editor: Safis Editing
Project Coordinator: Namrata Swetta
Proofreader: Safis Editing
Indexer: Tejal Daruwale Soni
Graphics: Jisha Chirayil
Production Coordinator: Shraddha Falebhai

First published: November 2015
Second edition: December 2017
Third edition: January 2019

Production reference: 1310119

Published by Packt Publishing Ltd.
Livery Place
35 Livery Street
Birmingham
B3 2PB, UK.

ISBN 978-1-78953-546-4

www.packtpub.com

`mapt.io`

Mapt is an online digital library that gives you full access to over 5,000 books and videos, as well as industry leading tools to help you plan your personal development and advance your career. For more information, please visit our website.

Why subscribe?

- Spend less time learning and more time coding with practical eBooks and Videos from over 4,000 industry professionals

- Improve your learning with Skill Plans built especially for you

- Get a free eBook or video every month

- Mapt is fully searchable

- Copy and paste, print, and bookmark content

Packt.com

Did you know that Packt offers eBook versions of every book published, with PDF and ePub files available? You can upgrade to the eBook version at `www.packt.com` and as a print book customer, you are entitled to a discount on the eBook copy. Get in touch with us at `customercare@packtpub.com` for more details.

At `www.packt.com`, you can also read a collection of free technical articles, sign up for a range of free newsletters, and receive exclusive discounts and offers on Packt books and eBooks.

Contributors

About the authors

Salahaldin Juba has over a decade of experience in industry and academia, with a focus on database development for large-scale and enterprise applications. He holds an MSc in environmental management with a distinction, and a B.Eng in computer systems. He is also a Microsoft Certified Solution Developer (MCSD).

He has worked mainly with SQL server, PostgreSQL, and Greenplum databases. As a software engineer, he works mainly with defining ETL processes with external parties, promoting SQL best practices, designing OLTP and OLAP applications, and providing training and consultation services.

Andrey Volkov studied information systems in banking, and started his career as a financial analyst at a commercial bank. He joined a data warehouse team, and after some time, he lead the team by taking the position of the data warehouse architect.

There he worked mainly with Oracle database stack and used it to develop logical and physical models of financial and accounting data, implement them in the database, develop ETL processes, and perform analytical tasks.

Now Andrey works as a senior database developer at a telecommunication provider. There, he works mainly with PostgreSQL databases, being responsible for data modeling, developing a data warehouse, reporting, and billing systems.

About the reviewers

Alexey Lesovsky has worked in web development and worked with Linux and related stuff in his early career as a system administrator. His favorite topics were and are KVM virtualization, monitoring systems, and Linux itself.

Being a system administrator, he was exposed to PostgreSQL in its early years. His interests then moved from system administration to pure database administration for PostgreSQL databases.

He has been with Data Egret for close to five years and has been a great asset for developing new Postgres utilities, including the famous PGCenter.

He is also a frequent speaker at various PostgreSQL events, among them PGCon, *PGConf (dot) EU*, and others.

He has also authored *Getting Started with oVirt 3.3* by Packt Publishing.

Darren Douglas is Chief Instructor at *PostgresCourse (dot) com*. He has taught PostgreSQL for over 4 years and has trained professional DBAs from Fortune 500 companies as well as the US and Canadian federal governments.

Since first using PostgreSQL in 2008, he has since led database development and deployment with PostgreSQL across multiple industries including e-commerce, mining, mobile marketing, and insurance. He also consults on full-stack software development projects and DevOps initiatives.

He lives in Tucson, Arizona with his wife Joanah. Together they spend time in volunteer projects and are learning the Swahili language.

Packt is searching for authors like you

If you're interested in becoming an author for Packt, please visit `authors.packtpub.com` and apply today. We have worked with thousands of developers and tech professionals, just like you, to help them share their insight with the global tech community. You can make a general application, apply for a specific hot topic that we are recruiting an author for, or submit your own idea.

Table of Contents

Preface

Picking the right database management system is a difficult task due to the vast number of options on the market. Depending on the business model, you can pick a commercial database or an open source database with commercial support. In addition to this, there are several technical and non-technical factors to assess. When it comes to picking a relational database management system, PostgreSQL stands at the top for several reasons. The PostgreSQL slogan, *"The world's most advanced open source database,"* emphasizes the sophistication of its features and the high degree of community confidence.

PostgreSQL is an open source object relational database management system. It competes with major relational databases such as Oracle, MySQL, and SQL Server. Its licensing model allows commercial use without any limitations and there are a lot of companies offering commercial support of PostgreSQL. For this reason, start-ups often favor PostgreSQL. Due to its rich extensions, it is often used for research purposes. PostgreSQL code is also a base for a few open source and commercial database solutions such as Greenplum and Amazon Redshift.

PostgreSQL runs on most modern operating systems, including Windows, Mac, and Linux flavors. Its installation and configuration is fairly easy, as it is supported by most packaging tools, such as `apt`, `yum`, or Homebrew. Also, there are interactive installers for Windows and macOS. There are extensions and tools that help to manage and monitor PostgreSQL servers, such as pgAdmin and psql. PostgreSQL complies with ANSI SQL standards, which makes it easy to learn and use for database developers and database administrators. Other than this, there are a lot of resources helping developers to learn and troubleshootPosgreSQL; it has very good and well-structured documentation and a very active and organized community.

PostgreSQL can be used for both **online transaction processing (OLTP)** and **online analytical processing (OLAP)** applications. In addition to that, PostgreSQL supports both pessimistic and optimistic concurrency control, and the locking behavior can be chosen based on the use case. PostgreSQL provides a lot of features that help to handle very large amounts of data efficiently, such as partitioning and parallel execution. PostgreSQL is scalable thanks to its replication capabilities. All this makes PostgreSQL attractive because it can be used to set up highly available and performant data management solutions.

Who this book is for

This book is for readers interested in learning about PostgreSQL from scratch. Those looking to build solid database or data warehousing applications or wanting to get up to speed with the latest features of PostgreSQL 11 will also find this book useful. No prior knowledge of database programming or administration is required to get started.

What this book covers

Chapter 1, *Relational Databases*, discusses database management systems and covers relational databases as well.

Chapter 2, *PostgreSQL in Action*, guides the reader through the installation of PostgreSQL, establishing a connection to the server, and running very basic queries. Also, the reader will learn some general information about PostgreSQL's history and capabilities as well.

Chapter 3, *PostgreSQL Basic Building Blocks*, explores the basic building blocks of PostgreSQL. We'll also take a look at the hierarchy of the database objects in PostgreSQL. This will help you to understand how to configure the database cluster and tune its settings.

Chapter 4, *PostgreSQL Advanced Building Blocks*, discusses the more advanced PostgreSQL building blocks, including views, indexes, functions, triggers, and rules. In addition to that, the web car portal schema will be reviewed. Several **Data Definition Language** (**DDL**) commands will also be introduced in this chapter as well.

Chapter 5, *SQL Language*, explains the concept of SQL and the logic of SQL statements.

Chapter 6, *Advanced Query Writing*, discusses some more advanced SQL features supported by PostgreSQL, such as **common table expressions** (**CTEs**) and window functions. These features allow us to implement a logic that wouldn't be possible otherwise, that is, recursive queries.

Chapter 7, *Server-Side Programming with PL/pgSQL*, compares the SQL language and PL/pgSQL, and will also explain the function parameters of PostgreSQL.

Chapter 8, *OLAP and Data Warehousing*, discusses some features of PostgreSQL that will help you to implement a data warehouse solution based on a PostgreSQL database, and also covers the related theoretical concepts.

Chapter 9, *Beyond Conventional Data Types*, covers various data types, such as arrays, Hstore, JSON, and full-text search.

Chapter 10, *Transactions and Concurrency Control*, focuses on the basic concepts that guarantee the correct execution of transactions. It also discusses concurrency control problems, locking systems, deadlocks, and advisory locks.

Chapter 11, *PostgreSQL Security*, discusses authentication in PostgreSQL, including PostgreSQL host-based authentication and best practices.

Chapter 12, *The PostgreSQL Catalog*, discusses some tasks that developers and administrators need to do on a daily basis, for example, cleaning up database data and unused objects, building an index automatically, and monitoring database object access.

Chapter 13, *Optimizing Database Performance*, focuses on basic configuration and query rewriting. It also focuses on tuning performance for write and read, and also identifying and detecting problems in queries.

Chapter 14, *Testing*, discusses some techniques for testing database objects. They can be applied when implementing changes in the data structure of complex systems and when developing database interfaces.

Chapter 15, *Using PostgreSQL in Python Applications*, iscusses how to connect to a PostgreSQL database from applications written in Python.

Chapter 16, *Scalability*, discusses the problem of scalability and the CAP theorem. We will also learn about the different scaling scenarios and their implementation in PostgreSQL.

Chapter 17, *What's Next?*, summarizes the topics we've covered in this book, provides some tips, and points the reader in the right direction for further learning.

To get the most out of this book

In general, PostgreSQL server and client tools do not need exceptional hardware. PostgreSQL can be installed on almost all modern platforms, including Linux, Windows, and Mac. Also, when a certain library is needed, the installation instructions are given:

- You need PostgreSQL version 11; however, most of the examples can be executed on earlier versions as well. In order to execute the sample code, scripts, and examples provided in the book, you need to have at least a PostgreSQL client tool installed on your machine—preferably psql—and access to a remote server running the PostgreSQL server.

- In a Windows environment, the cmd.exe Command Prompt is not very convenient; thus, the user might consider using Cygwin (http:/ / www. cygwin. com/) or another alternative, such as PowerShell.

- Some chapters might require additional software. For example, in Chapter 15, *Using PostgreSQL in Python Applications*, you need to install Python and the required Python libraries to interact with PostgreSQL. In Chapter 16, *Scalability*, Docker is used to give the reader a better user experience.

- For other chapters, such as Chapter 9, *Beyond Conventional Data types*, and Chapter 11, *PostgreSQL Security*, it is better to use Linux because some of the software used is not very convenient on Windows, such as NGINX and GnuPG. To run a Linux distribution on your Windows machine, you can use Virtual Box (https://www.virtualbox.org/).

Download the example code files

You can download the example code files for this book from your account at www.packt.com. If you purchased this book elsewhere, you can visit www.packt.com/support and register to have the files emailed directly to you.

You can download the code files by following these steps:

1. Log in or register at www.packt.com.
2. Select the **SUPPORT** tab.
3. Click on **Code Downloads & Errata**.
4. Enter the name of the book in the **Search** box and follow the onscreen instructions.

Once the file is downloaded, please make sure that you unzip or extract the folder using the latest version of:

- WinRAR/7-Zip for Windows
- Zipeg/iZip/UnRarX for Mac
- 7-Zip/PeaZip for Linux

The code bundle for the book is also hosted on GitHub at
`https://github.com/PacktPublishing/Learning-PostgreSQL-11-Third-Edition`. In case
there's an update to the code, it will be updated on the existing GitHub repository.

We also have other code bundles from our rich catalog of books and videos available at
`https://github.com/PacktPublishing/`. Check them out!

Download the color images

We also provide a PDF file that has color images of the screenshots/diagrams used in this
book. You can download it here:
`http://www.packtpub.com/sites/default/files/downloads/9781789535464_ColorImages`
`.pdf`.

Conventions used

There are a number of text conventions used throughout this book.

`CodeInText`: Indicates code words in text, database table names, folder names, filenames,
file extensions, pathnames, dummy URLs, user input, and Twitter handles. Here is an
example: "PostgreSQL provides the `CREATE EXTENSION` command to load extensions to
the current database."

A block of code is set as follows:

```
log_destination = 'csvlog'
logging_collector = on
log_filename = 'postgresql.log'
log_statement = 'all'
```

When we wish to draw your attention to a particular part of a code block, the relevant lines
or items are set in bold:

```
postgres=# CREATE FOREIGN TABLE postgres_log
( log_time timestamp(3) with time zone,
  user_name text,
  database_name text,
```

Any command-line input or output is written as follows:

```
sudo service postgresql restart
```

Bold: Indicates a new term, an important word, or words that you see onscreen. For example, words in menus or dialog boxes appear in the text like this. Here is an example: "Select **System info** from the **Administration** panel."

 Warnings or important notes appear like this.

 Tips and tricks appear like this.

Get in touch

Feedback from our readers is always welcome.

General feedback: If you have questions about any aspect of this book, mention the book title in the subject of your message and email us at customercare@packtpub.com.

Errata: Although we have taken every care to ensure the accuracy of our content, mistakes do happen. If you have found a mistake in this book, we would be grateful if you would report this to us. Please visit www.packt.com/submit-errata, selecting your book, clicking on the Errata Submission Form link, and entering the details.

Piracy: If you come across any illegal copies of our works in any form on the Internet, we would be grateful if you would provide us with the location address or website name. Please contact us at copyright@packt.com with a link to the material.

If you are interested in becoming an author: If there is a topic that you have expertise in and you are interested in either writing or contributing to a book, please visit authors.packtpub.com.

Reviews

Please leave a review. Once you have read and used this book, why not leave a review on the site that you purchased it from? Potential readers can then see and use your unbiased opinion to make purchase decisions, we at Packt can understand what you think about our products, and our authors can see your feedback on their book. Thank you!

For more information about Packt, please visit packt.com.

1
Relational Databases

This chapter, and the ones following, will provide a high-level overview of topics related to database development. These topics will cover the theoretical aspects of relational databases. The first two chapters try to summarize theoretical topics that are seen on a daily basis. Understanding these theoretical concepts will enable developers to not only come up with clean designs but also to master relational databases.

This chapter is not restricted to learning PostgreSQL, but covers all relational databases. The topics covered in this chapter include the following:

- Database management systems
- Relational algebra
- Data modeling

Database management systems

Different **database management systems (DBMS)** support diverse application scenarios, use cases, and requirements. DBMS have a long history. First, we will quickly take a look at the recent history, and then explore the market-dominant database management system categories.

A brief history

Broadly, the term database can be used to present a collection of things. Moreover, this term brings to mind many other terms including data, information, data structure, and management. A database can be defined as a collection or repository of data, which has a certain structure, managed by a DBMS. Data can be structured as tabular data, semi-structured as XML documents, or unstructured data that does not fit a predefined data model.

In the early days, databases were mainly aimed at supporting business applications; this led us to the well-defined relational algebra and relational database systems. With the introduction of object-oriented languages, new paradigms of DBMS appeared, such as object-relational databases and object-oriented databases. Also, many businesses, as well as scientific applications, use arrays, images, and spatial data; thus, new models such as raster, map, and array algebra are supported. Graph databases are used to support graph queries such as the shortest path from one node to another, along with supporting traversal queries easily.

With the advent of web applications such as social portals, it is now necessary to support a huge number of requests in a distributed manner. This has led to another new paradigm of databases called **Not Only SQL (NoSQL)**, which has different requirements, such as performance over fault tolerance and horizontal scaling capabilities. In general, the timeline of database evolution was greatly affected by many factors, such as the following:

- **Functional requirements**: The nature of the applications using a DBMS led to the development of extensions on top of relational databases such as PostGIS (for spatial data), or even a dedicated DBMS such as SciDB (for scientific data analytics).
- **Nonfunctional requirements**: The success of object-oriented programming languages has created new trends such as object-oriented databases. Object-relational DBMS have appeared to bridge the gap between relational databases and the object-oriented programming languages. Data explosion and the necessity to handle terabytes of data on commodity hardware have led to database systems that can easily scale up horizontally.

Database categories

Many database models have appeared and vanished, such as the network model and the hierarchical model. The predominant categories now in the market are relational, object-relational, and NoSQL databases. One should not think of NoSQL and SQL databases as rivals; they are complementary to each other. By utilizing different database systems, one can overcome many limitations and get the best of different technologies.

NoSQL databases can provide great benefits such as availability, schema-free, and horizontal scaling, but they also have limitations such as performance, data retrieval constraints, and learning time. Relational databases often adhere to SQL as defined by ISO. SQL is a very expressive and extremely powerful tool for retrieving data in different forms. Many NoSQL databases such as Cassandra lack the capability to retrieve data as in relational databases.

NoSQL databases

NoSQL databases are affected by the CAP theorem, also known as Brewer's theorem. In 2002, S. Gilbert and N. Lynch published a formal proof of the CAP theorem in their article *Brewer's conjecture and the feasibility of consistent, available, partition-tolerant web services*. In 2009, the NoSQL movement began. Currently, there are over 150 NoSQL databases (`nosql-database.org`).

The CAP theorem

The CAP theorem states that it is impossible for a distributed computing system to simultaneously provide all three of the following guarantees:

- **Consistent**: All clients see (immediately) the latest data even in the case of updates.
- **Available**: All clients can find a replica of some data even in the case of a node failure. This means that even if some part of the system goes down, the clients can still access consistent and valid data.
- **Partition tolerance**: The system continues to work regardless of arbitrary message loss or failure of part of the system.

The choice of which features to discard determines the nature of the system. For example, one could sacrifice consistency to get a scalable, simple, and high-performance database management system. Often, the main difference between a relational database and a NoSQL database is consistency. A relational database enforces **atomicity**, **consistency**, **isolation**, and **durability (ACID)** properties. In contrast, many NoSQL databases adopt the **basically available, soft-state, eventual consistency (BASE)** model.

NoSQL motivation

A NoSQL database does not entity relation model for data storage, manipulation, and retrieval. NoSQL databases are often distributed, open source, and horizontally scalable. NoSQL often adopts the base model, which prizes availability over consistency, and informally guarantees that if no new updates are made on a data item, eventually all access to that data item will return the latest version of that data item. The advantages of this approach include the following:

- Simplicity of design
- Horizontal scaling and easy replication

- Schema-free
- A huge amount of data support

We will now explore a few types of NoSQL databases.

Key-value databases

The key-value store is the simplest database store. In this database model, the storage, as its name suggests, is based on maps or hash tables. Some key-value databases allow complex values to be stored as lists and hash tables. Key-value pairs are extremely fast for certain scenarios but lack the support for complex queries and aggregation. Some of the existing open source key-value databases are Riak, Redis, Couchbase Server, and MemcacheDB.

Columnar databases

Columnar or column-oriented databases are based on columns. Data in a certain column in a two-dimensional relation is stored together.

Unlike relational databases, adding columns is inexpensive and is done on a row-by-row basis. Rows can have a different set of columns. Tables can benefit from this structure by eliminating the storage cost of the null values. This model is best suited for distributed databases.

HBase is one of the most famous columnar databases. It is based on the Google Bigtable storage system. Column-oriented databases are designed for huge data scenarios, so they scale up easily. For example, Facebook uses HBase to power their message infrastructure. For small datasets, HBase is not a suitable architecture. First, the recommended hardware topology for HBase is a five-node server deployment. Also, it needs a lot of administration and is difficult to learn and master.

Document databases

A document-oriented database is suitable for documents and semi-structured data. The central concept of a document-oriented database is the notion of a document. Documents encapsulate and encode data (or information) in some standard formats or encodings such as XML, JSON, and BSON. Documents do not adhere to a standard schema or have the same structure, so they provide a high degree of flexibility. Unlike relational databases, changing the structure of the document is simple and does not lock the clients from accessing the data.

Document databases merge the power of relational databases and column-oriented databases. They provide support for ad hoc queries and can be scaled up easily. Depending on the design of the document database, MongoDB is designed to handle a huge amount of data efficiently. On the other hand, CouchDB provides high availability even in the case of hardware failure.

Graph databases

Graph databases are based on graph theory, where a database consists of nodes and edges. The nodes, as well as the edges, can be assigned data. Graph databases allow traversing between the nodes using edges. As a graph is a generic data structure, graph databases are capable of representing different data. A famous implementation of an open source, commercially supported graph database is Neo4j.

Relational and object-relational databases

Relational DBMS are one of the most widely used DBMSes in the world. It is highly unlikely that any organization, institution, or personal computer today does not have or use a piece of software that relies on RDBMS.

Software applications can use relational databases via dedicated database servers or via lightweight RDBMS engines, embedded in the software applications as shared libraries.

The capabilities of a relational database management system vary from one vendor to another, but most of them adhere to the **American National Standards Institute (ANSI)** SQL standards. A relational database is formally described by relational algebra, and is based on the relational model. **Object-relational databases (ORDs)** are similar to relational databases. They support the following object-oriented model concepts:

- User-defined and complex data types
- Inheritance

ACID properties

In a relational database, a single logical operation is called a **transaction**. The technical translation of a transaction is a set of database operations, which are **create**, **read**, **update**, and **delete (CRUD)**. An example of explaining a transaction is a budget assignment to several projects in the company assuming we have a fixed amount of money. If we increase a certain project budget, we need to deduct this amount of increase from another project. The ACID properties in this context could be described as follows:

- **Atomicity**: All or nothing, which means that if a part of a transaction fails, then the transaction fails as a whole.
- **Consistency**: Any transaction gets the database from one valid state to another valid state. Database consistency is governed normally by data constraints and the relation between data and any combination thereof. For example, imagine if someone would like to completely purge his account on a shopping service. In order to purge his account, his account details, such as a list of addresses, will also need to be purged. This is governed by foreign key constraints, which will be explained in detail in the coming chapter.
- **Isolation**: Concurrent execution of transactions results in a system state that would be obtained if the transactions were executed serially.
- **Durability**: The transactions that are committed—that is, executed successfully—are persistent even with power loss or some server crashes. In PostgreSQL, this is done normally by a technique called **Write-Ahead Logging (WAL)**. Another database refers to this as a transaction log such as in Oracle.

The SQL language

Relational databases are often linked to **Structured Query Language** (**SQL**). SQL is a declarative programming language and is the standard relational database language. The ANSI and the **International Organization for Standardization** (**ISO**) published the SQL standard for the first time in 1986, followed by many versions such as SQL:1999, SQL:2003, SQL:2006, SQL:2008, SQL:2011, and SQL:2016.

The SQL language has several parts:

- **Data definition language** (**DDL**): It defines and amends the relational structure
- **Data manipulation language** (**DML**): It retrieves and extracts information from the relations
- **Data control language** (**DCL**): It controls the access rights to relations

Relational model concepts

A relational model is a first-order predicate logic that was first introduced by Edgar F. Codd in 1970 in his paper *A Relational Model of Data for Large Shared Data Banks*. A database is represented as a collection of relations. The state of the whole database is defined by the state of all the relations in the database. Different information can be extracted from the relations by joining and aggregating data from different relations and by applying filters on the data. In this section, the basic concepts of the relational model are introduced using the top-down approach by first describing the relation, tuple, attribute, and domain.

 The terms relation, tuple, attribute, and unknown, which are used in the formal relational model, are equivalent to table, row, column, and null in the SQL language.

Relation

Think of a relation as a table with a header, columns, and rows. The table name and the header help in interpreting the data in the rows. Each row represents a group of related data, which points to a certain object.

A relation is represented by a set of tuples. Tuples should have the same set of ordered attributes. Attributes have a domain, that is, a type and a name:

	customer_id	first_name	last_name	email
Tuple →	1	thomas	sieh	thomas@example.com
Tuple →	2	wang	kim	kim@example.com
	Attribute ↑	**Attribute ↑**	**Attribute ↑**	**Attribute ↑**

The relation schema is denoted by the relation name and the relation attributes. For example, customer (customer_id, first_name, last_name, and email) is the relation schema for the customer relation. **Relation state** is defined by the set of relation tuples; thus, adding, deleting, and amending a tuple will change the relation to another state.

Tuple order or position in the relation is not important, and the relation is not sensitive to tuple order. The tuples in the relation could be ordered by a single attribute or a set of attributes. Also, a relation cannot have duplicate tuples.

A relation can represent entities in the real world, such as a customer, or can be used to represent an association between relations. For example, the customer could have several services and a service can be offered to several customers. This could be modeled by three relations: customer, service, and customer_service. The customer_service relation associates the customer and the service relations. Separating the data in different relations is a key concept in relational database modeling, and is called normalization. Normalization is the process of organizing relation columns and relations to reduce data redundancy. For example, assume that a collection of services is stored in the customer relation. If a service is assigned to multiple customers, this would result in data redundancy. Also, updating a certain service would require updating all its copies in the customer table.

Tuple

A tuple is a set of ordered attributes. They are written by listing the elements within parentheses () and separated by commas, such as (john, smith, 1971). Tuple elements are identified via the attribute name. Tuples have the following properties:

- $(a_1, a_2, a_3, ..., a_n) = (b_1, b_2, b_3, ..., b_n)$ *if and only if* $a_1 = b_1$, $a_2 = b_2$, ..., $a_n = b_n$

- A tuple is not a set; the order of attributes matters as well as duplicate members:
  - $(a_1, a_2) \neq (a_2, a_1)$
  - $(a_1, a_1) \neq (a_1)$
- A tuple has a finite set of attributes

In the formal relational model, multi-valued attributes, as well as composite attributes, are not allowed. This is important to reduce data redundancy and increase data consistency. This isn't strictly true in modern relational database systems because of the utilization of complex data types such as JSON and key-value stores.

There is a lot of debate regarding the application of normalization; the rule of thumb is to apply normalization unless there is a good reason not to do so.

The null value

Predicates in relational databases use **three-valued logic (3VL)**, where there are three truth values: `true`, `false`, and `null`,. In a relational database, the third value, `null`, can be interpreted in many ways, such as unknown data, missing data, not applicable, or will be loaded later. The 3VL is used to remove ambiguity. For example, no two `null` values are equal.

In the next chapter, you will learn how to connect to the database and run queries. Now, I would like to show how a logical OR/AND truth table can be generated by the SQL language:

Logical AND and OR operators are commutative, that is, *A AND B = B AND A*.

```
\pset null null
WITH data (v) as (VALUES (true), (false),(null))
    SELECT DISTINCT
        first.v::TEXT as a,
        second.v::TEXT as b,
        (first.v AND second.v)::TEXT AS "a and b",
        (first.v OR second.v)::TEXT as "a or b"
    FROM
        data as first cross join
        data as second
    ORDER BY a DESC nulls last, b DESC nulls last;
```

```
    a    |  b      | a and b | a or b
-------+-------+---------+--------
  true   | true   | true    | true
  true   | false  | false   | true
  true   | null   | null    | true
  false  | true   | false   | true
  false  | false  | false   | false
  false  | null   | false   | null
  null   | true   | null    | true
  null   | false  | false   | null
  null   | null   | null    | null
(9 rows)
```

The following table, which is generated by SQL, shows the NOT truth operator:

```
WITH data (v) as (VALUES (true), (false),(null)) SELECT v::text as a, (NOT
v)::text as "NOT a" FROM data order by a desc nulls last;
   a    | NOT a
-------+-------
  true  | false
  false | true
  null  | null
(3 rows)
```

Attribute

Each attribute has a name and a domain, and the name should be distinct within the relation. The domain defines the possible set of values that the attribute can have. One way to define the domain is to define the data type and a constraint on this data type. For example, the hourly wage should be a positive real number and bigger than five if we assume that the minimum hourly wage is five dollars. The domain could be continuous, such as salary, which is any positive real number, or discrete, such as gender.

The formal relational model puts a constraint on the domain: the value should be atomic. Atomicity means that each value in the domain is indivisible. For instance, the name attribute domain is not atomic because it can be divided into first name and last name. Some examples of domains are as follows:

- **Phone number**: Numeric text with a certain length.
- **Country code**: Defined by ISO 3166 as a list of two-letter codes (ISO alpha-2) and three-letter codes (ISO alpha-3). The country codes for Germany are DE and DEU for alpha-2 and alpha-3 respectively.

In real-life applications, it is better to use ISO and international standards for lookup tables such as country and currency. This enables you to expose your data much more easy to third-party software and increases your data quality.

Constraint

The relational model defines many constraints in order to control data integrity, redundancy, and validity. Here are some examples of checking for data:

- **Redundancy**: Duplicate tuples are not allowed in the relation.
- **Validity**: Check constraints and domain constraints are used to validate the data input, for example, the date of birth should be a date that occurred in the past.
- **Integrity**: The relations within a single database are linked to each other. An action on a relation such as updating or deleting a tuple might leave the other relations in an invalid state.

We could classify the constraints in a relational database roughly into two categories:

- **Inherited constraints from the relational model**: Domain integrity, entity integrity, and referential integrity constraints.
- **Semantic constraint, business rules, and application-specific constraints**: These constraints cannot be expressed explicitly by the relational model. However, with the introduction of procedural SQL languages such as PL/pgSQL for PostgreSQL, relational databases can also be used to model these constraints.

Domain integrity constraint

The domain integrity constraint ensures data validity. The first step in defining the domain integrity constraint is to determine the appropriate data type. The domain data types could be an `integer`, `real`, `boolean`, `character`, `text`, `inet`, and so on. For example, the data type of the first name and email address is `text`. After specifying the data type, check constraints, such as the mail address pattern, need to be defined:

- **Check constraint**: A check constraint can be applied to a single attribute or a combination of many attributes in a tuple. Let's assume that the `customer_service` schema is defined as `customer_id`, `service_id`, `start_date`, `end_date`, and `order_date`. For this relation, we can have a check constraint to make sure that `start_date` and `end_date` are entered correctly by applying the following check: `start_date` is less than `end_date`.

- **Default constraint**: The attribute can have a default value. The default value could be a fixed value such as the default hourly wage of the employees, for example, $10. It may also have a dynamic value based on a function such as random, current time, and date. For example, in the `customer_service` relation, `order_date` can have a default value, which is the current date.
- **Unique constraint**: A unique constraint guarantees that the attribute has a distinct value in each tuple. It allows null values. For example, let's assume that we have a relation player defined as a player (`player_id`, `player_nickname`). The player uses his ID to play with others; he can also pick up a nickname, which is also unique to identify himself.
- **Not null constraint**: By default, the attribute value can be `null`. The not null constraint prevents an attribute from having a `null` value. For example, each person in the birth registry record should have a name.

Entity integrity constraint

In the relational model, a relation is defined as a set of tuples. This means that all the tuples in a relation must be distinct. The entity integrity constraint is enforced by having a primary key, which is an attribute/set of attributes with the following characteristics:

- The attribute should be unique
- The attributes should be not null

Each relation must have only one primary key, but can have many unique keys. A candidate key is a minimal set of attributes that can identify a tuple. All unique, not null attributes can be candidate keys. The set of all attributes form a super key. In practice, we often pick up a single attribute to be a primary key instead of a compound key (a key that consists of two or more attributes that uniquely identify a tuple) to simplify the joining of the relations with each other.

If the primary key is generated by the DBMS, then it is called a **surrogate key** or **synthetic key**. Otherwise, it is called a **natural key**. The surrogate key candidates can be sequences and **universal unique identifiers** (**UUIDs**). A surrogate key has many advantages such as performance, requirement change tolerance, agility, and compatibility with object-relational mappers. The chief disadvantage of surrogate keys is that it makes redundant tuples possible.

A sequence is a number generator that is used to generate a series of numbers based on the current number's value. This term is used mainly in PostgreSQL and Oracle databases. PostgreSQL also has an `identity` column, which is mainly used to generate series of numbers. More about this topic is explained in `Chapter 4`, *PostgreSQL Advanced Building Blocks*.

Referential integrity constraints

Relations are associated with each other via common attributes. Referential integrity constraints govern the association between two relations and ensure data consistency between tuples. If a tuple in one relation references a tuple in another relation, then the referenced tuple must exist. In the customer service example, if a service is assigned to a customer, then the service and the customer must exist, as shown in the following example:

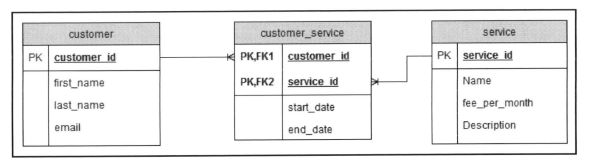

For instance, in the `customer_service` relation, we cannot have a tuple with values (`5, 1,01-01-2014, NULL`), because we do not have a customer with `customer_id` equal to `5`.

The lack of referential integrity constraints can lead to many problems:

- Invalid data in the common attributes
- Invalid information during joining of data from different relations
- Performance degradation either due to bad execution plans generated by the PostgreSQL planner or by a third-party tool

Foreign keys can increase performance in reading data from multiple tables. The query execution planner will have a better estimation of the number of rows that need to be processed. Temporarily disabling foreign keys in special cases such as bulk uploading will lead to a performance boost, since integrity checks are not performed.

Referential integrity constraints are achieved via foreign keys. A **foreign key** is an attribute or a set of attributes that can identify a tuple in the referenced relation. As the purpose of a foreign key is to identify a tuple in the referenced relation, foreign keys are generally primary keys in the referenced relation. Unlike a primary key, a foreign key can have a `null` value. It can also reference a unique attribute in the referenced relation. Allowing a foreign key to have a `null` value enables us to model different cardinality constraints. Cardinality constraints define the participation between two different relations. For example, a parent can have more than one child; this relation is called a one-to-many relationship because one tuple in the referenced relation is associated with many tuples in the referencing relation. Also, a relation could reference itself. This foreign key is called a **self-referencing** or **recursive foreign key**.

For example, a company acquired by another company:

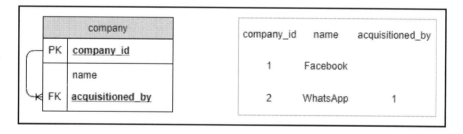

To ensure data integrity, foreign keys can be used to define several behaviors when a tuple in the referenced relation is updated or deleted. The following behaviors are called referential actions:

- **Cascade**: When a tuple is deleted or updated in the referenced relation, the tuples in the referencing relation are also updated or deleted
- **Restrict**: The tuple cannot be deleted or the referenced attribute cannot be updated if it is referenced by another relation
- **No action**: Similar to restrict, but it is deferred to the end of the transaction
- **Set default**: When a tuple in the referenced relation is deleted or the referenced attribute is updated, then the foreign key value is assigned the default value
- **Set null**: The foreign key attribute value is set to null when the referenced tuple is deleted

Semantic constraints

Integrity constraints or business logic constraints describe the database application constraints in general. These constraints are either enforced by the business logic tier of the application program or by SQL procedural languages. Trigger and rule systems can also be used for this purpose. For example, the customer should have at most one active service at a time. Based on the nature of the application, one could favor using an SQL procedural language or a high-level programming language to meet the semantic constraints, or mix the two approaches.

The advantages of using the SQL programming language are as follows:

- **Performance**: RDBMSes often have complex analyzers to generate efficient execution plans. Also, in some cases such as data mining, the amount of data that needs to be manipulated is very large. Manipulating the data using procedural SQL languages eliminates the network data transfer. Finally, some procedural SQL languages utilize clever caching algorithms.
- **Last-minute change**: For SQL procedural languages, one could deploy bug fixes without service disruption.

 Implementing business logic in the database tier has a lot of pros and cons and it is a highly contentious topic. For example, some disadvantages of implementing business logic in the database are visibility, developer efficiency in writing code due to a lack of proper tools and IDEs, and code reuse.

Relational algebra

Relational algebra is the formal language of the relational model. It defines a set of closed operations over relations, that is, the result of each operation is a new relation. Relational algebra inherits many operators from set algebra. Relational algebra operations can be categorized into two groups:

- The first one is a group of operations that are inherited from set theory such as UNION, intersection, set difference, and Cartesian product, also known as cross product.

- The second is a group of operations that are specific to the relational model such as SELECT and PROJECT. Relational algebra operations could also be classified as binary and unary operations.

The primitive operators are as follows:

- **SELECT (σ):** A unary operation written as $\sigma\phi_R$ where ϕ is a predicate. The selection retrieves the tuples in R, where ϕ holds.
- **PROJECT (π):** A unary operation used to slice the relation in a vertical dimension, that is, attributes. This operation is written as $\pi_{a1,a2,...,an} R()$, where $a1$, $a2$, ..., an are a set of attribute names.
- **Cartesian product ($\times$):** A binary operation used to generate a more complex relation by joining each tuple of its operands together. Let's assume that R and S are two relations, then $R \times S = (r_1, r_2, ..., r_n, s_1, s_2, ..., s_n)$ where $(r_1, r_2,...,r_n) \in R$ and $(s_1, s_2, ..., s_n) \in S$.
- **UNION ($\cup$):** Appends two relations together; note that the relations should be UNION-compatible, that is, they should have the same set of ordered attributes. Formally, $R \cup S = (r_1,r_2...r_n) \cup (s_1,s_2,...,s_n)$ where $(r_1, r_2,...,r_n) \in R$ and $(s_1, s_2, ..., s_n) \in S$.
- **Difference (-):** A binary operation in which the operands should be UNION-compatible. Difference creates a new relation from the tuples, which exist in one relation but not in the other. The set difference for the relation R and S can be given as $R\text{-}S = (r_1,r_2,...r_n)$ where $(r_1,r_2,...r_n) \in R$ and $(r_1,r_2,...r_n) \notin S$.
- **RENAME (ρ):** A unary operation that works on attributes. This operator is mainly used to distinguish the attributes with the same names but in different relation when joined together, or it is used to give a more user-friendly name for the attribute for presentation purposes. RENAME is expressed as $\varrho_{a/b}R$, where a and b are attribute names and b is an attribute of R.

In addition to the primitive operators, there are aggregation functions such as sum, count, min, max, and avg aggregates. Primitive operators can be used to define other relation operators such as left-join, right-join, equi-join, and intersection. Relational algebra is very important due to its expressive power in optimizing and rewriting queries. For example, the selection is commutative, so $\sigma_a\sigma_bR = \sigma_b\sigma_aR$. A cascaded selection may also be replaced by a single selection with a conjunction of all the predicates, that is, $\sigma_a\sigma_bR = \sigma_{a\ AND\ b}R$.

The SELECT and PROJECT operations

SELECT is used to restrict tuples from the relation. SELECT always returns a unique set of tuples; that is inherited from entity integrity constraint. For example, the query *give me the customer information where the customer_id equals 2* is written as follows:

$$\sigma_{customer\_id\,=2}\ customer$$

The selection, as mentioned earlier, is commutative; the query *give me all customers where the customer's email is known, and the customer's first name is kim* is written in three different ways, as follows:

$$\sigma_{email\ is\ not\ null}(\sigma_{first\_name\,=kim}\ customer)$$

$$\sigma_{first\_name\,=kim}(\sigma_{email\ is\ not\ null}\ customer)$$

$$\sigma_{first\_name\,=kim\ and\ email\ is\ not\ null}\ (customer)$$

The selection predicates are certainly determined by the data types. For numeric data types, the comparison operator might be ≠, =, <, >, ≥, or ≤. The predicate expression can also contain complex expressions and functions. The equivalent SQL statement for the SELECT operator is the SELECT * statement, and the predicate is defined in the WHERE clause.

> The * symbol means all the relation attributes; note that in a production environment, it is not recommended to use *. Instead, one should list all the relation attributes explicitly. Using * in production code could easily break the application since the order and the type of expected result is given implicitly. This situation can occur when one renames a table attribute field, or adds a new column.

The following SELECT statement is equivalent to the relational algebra expression $\sigma_{customer\_id\,=2}\ customer$:

```
SELECT * FROM customer WHERE customer_id = 2;
```

The PROJECT operation could be visualized as a vertical slicing of the table. The query *give me the customer names* is written in relational algebra as follows:

$$\pi_{first\_name,\ last\_name}\ customer$$

The following is the result of projection expression:

first_name	last_name
thomas	sieh
wang	kim

Duplicate tuples are not allowed in the formal relational model; the number of tuples returned from the PROJECT operator is always equal to or less than the number of total tuples in the relation. If a PROJECT operator's attribute list contains a primary key, then the resultant relation has the same number of tuples as the projected relation.

The projection operator also can be optimized, for example, cascading projections could be optimized as the following expression:

$$\pi_a(\pi_{a,}\pi_b(R)) = \pi_a(R)$$

The SQL equivalent for the PROJECT operator is SELECT DISTINCT. The DISTINCT keyword is used to eliminate duplicates. To get the result shown in the preceding expression, one could execute the following SQL statement:

```
SELECT DISTINCT first_name, last_name FROM customers;
```

The sequence of the execution of the PROJECT and SELECT operations can be interchangeable in some cases. The query *give me the name of the customer with customer_id equal to 2* could be written as follows:

$$\sigma_{customer\_id\,=2}\,(\pi_{\,first\_name,\,last\_name}\,customer)$$

$$\pi_{\,first\_name,\,last\_name}(\sigma_{customer\_id\,=2}\,customer)$$

In other cases, the PROJECT and SELECT operators must have an explicit order, as shown in the following example; otherwise, it will lead to an incorrect expression. The query *give me the last name of the customers where the first name is kim* could be written in the following way:

$$\pi_{\,last\_name}(\sigma_{first\_name=kim}\,customer)$$

The RENAME operation

The RENAME operation is used to alter the attribute name of the resultant relation or to give a specific name to the resultant relation. The RENAME operation is used to perform the following:

- Remove confusion if two or more relations have attributes with the same name
- Provide user-friendly names for attributes, especially when interfacing with reporting engines
- Provide a convenient way to change the relation definition and still be backward compatible

The AS keyword in SQL is the equivalent of the RENAME operator in relational algebra. The following SQL example creates a relation with one tuple and one attribute, which is renamed PI:

```
SELECT 3.14::real AS PI;
```

The set theory operations

The set theory operations are UNION, intersection, and minus (difference). Intersection is not a primitive relational algebra operator, because it can be written using the UNION and difference operators:

$$A \cap B = ((A \cup B)-(A-B))-(B-A)$$

The intersection and union are commutative:

$$A \cap B = B \cap A$$

$$A \cup B = B \cup A$$

For example, the query *give me all the customer IDs where the customer does not have a service assigned to him* could be written as follows:

$$\pi_{customer\_id} \; customer - \pi_{customer\_id} \; customer\_service$$

The Cartesian product operation

The Cartesian product operation is used to combine tuples from two relations into a single one. The number of attributes in the single relation equals the sum of the number of attributes of the two relations. The number of tuples in the single relation equals the product of the number of tuples in the two relations. Let's assume that A and B are two relations, and $C = A \times B$:

The number of attributes of C = the number of attributes of A + the number of attributes of B

*The number of tuples of C = the number of tuples of A * the number of tuples of B*

The following table shows the cross join of customer and customer service:

customer_id	first_name	las_name
1	thomas	sieh
2	wang	kim

X

customer_service_id	customer_id	start_date	end_date
1	1	2017-11-01	2018-11-01
2	1	2017-11-01	2018-11-01

=

customer_id	first_name	las_name	customer_service_id	customer_id	start_date	end_date
1	thomas	sieh	1	1	2017-11-01	2018-11-01
2	wang	kim	1	1	2017-11-01	2018-11-01
1	thomas	sieh	2	1	2017-11-01	2018-11-01
2	wang	kim	2	1	2017-11-01	2018-11-01

The equivalent SQL join for Cartesian product is `CROSS JOIN`; the query for the customer with `customer_id` equal to 1, retrieve the `customer_id`, name, and the customer service IDs can be written in SQL as follows:

```
SELECT DISTINCT customer_id, first_name, last_name, service_id FROM
customer AS c CROSS JOIN customer_service AS cs WHERE
c.customer_id=cs.customer_id AND c.customer_id = 1;
```

In the preceding example, one can see the relationship between relational algebra and the SQL language. For example, we have used `SELECT`, `RENAME`, `PROJECT`, and `Cartesian product`. The preceding example shows how relational algebra could be used to optimize query execution. This example could be executed in several ways:

Execution plan 1:

1. `SELECT` the customer where `customer_id = 1`
2. `SELECT` the customer service where `customer_id = 1`

1. CROSS JOIN the relations resulting from *Step 1* and *Step 2*
2. PROJECT customer_id, first_name, last_name, and service_id from the relation resulting from *Step 3*

Execution plan 2:

1. CROSS JOIN customer and customer_service
2. SELECT all the tuples where
   Customer_service.customer_id=customer.customer_id and
   customer.customer_id = 1
3. PROJECT customer_id, first_name, last_name, and service_id from the relation resulting from *Step 2*

> The SELECT query is written in this way to show how to translate relational algebra to SQL. In modern SQL code, we can PROJECT attributes without using DISTINCT. In addition to that, one should use a proper join instead of cross join.

Each execution plan has a cost in terms of CPU, **random access memory (RAM)**, and hard disk operations. The RDBMS picks the one with the lowest cost. In the preceding execution plans, the RENAME and DISTINCT operators were ignored for simplicity.

Data modeling

Data models describe real-world entities such as customer, service, products, and the relation between these entities. Data models provide an abstraction for the relations in the database. Data models aid the developers in modeling business requirements and translating business requirements to relations. They are also used for the exchange of information between the developers and business owners.

In the enterprise, data models play a very important role in achieving data consistency across interacting systems. For example, if an entity is not defined, or is poorly defined, then this will lead to inconsistent and misinterpreted data across the enterprise. For instance, if the semantics of the customer entity are not defined clearly, and different business departments use different names for the same entity such as customer and client, this may lead to confusion in the operational departments.

Data model perspectives

Data model perspectives are defined by ANSI as follows:

- **Conceptual data model**: Describes the domain semantics, and is used to communicate the main business rules, actors, and concepts. It describes the business requirements at a high level and is often called a high-level data model.
- **Logical data model**: Describes the semantics for a certain technology, for example, the UML class diagram for object-oriented languages.
- **Physical data model**: Describes how data is actually stored and manipulated at the hardware level, such as storage area network, table space, CPUs, and so on.

According to ANSI, this abstraction allows changing one part of the three perspectives without amending the other parts. One could change both the logical and the physical data models without changing the conceptual model. To explain, sorting data using bubble or quick sort is not of interest for the conceptual data model. Also, changing the structure of the relations could be transparent to the conceptual model. One could split one relation into many relations after applying normalization rules, or by using `enum` data types in order to model the lookup tables.

The entity-relation model

The **entity-relation** (**ER**) model falls into the conceptual data model category. It captures and represents the data model for both business users and developers. The ER model can be transformed into the relational model by following certain techniques.

Conceptual modeling is a part of the **software development life cycle** (**SDLC**). It is normally done after the functional and data requirement-gathering stage. At this point, the developer is able to make the first draft of the ER diagram as well as describe functional requirements using data flow diagrams, sequence diagrams, user stories, and many other techniques.

During the design phase, the database developer should give great attention to the design, run a benchmark stack to ensure performance, and validate user requirements. Developers modeling simple systems could start coding directly. However, care should be taken when making the design, since data modeling involves not only algorithms in modeling the application but also data. The change in design might lead to a lot of complexities in the future such as data migration from one data structure to another.

While designing a database schema, avoiding design pitfalls is not enough. There are alternative designs where one could be chosen. The following pitfalls should be avoided:

- **Data redundancy**: Bad database designs elicit redundant data. Redundant data can cause several other problems, including data inconsistency and performance degradation. When updating a tuple that contains redundant data, the changes on the redundant data should be reflected in all the tuples that contain this data.
- **Null saturation**: By nature, some applications have sparse data, such as medical applications. Imagine a relation called diagnostics, which has hundreds of attributes for symptoms such as fever, headache, sneezing, and so on. Most of them are not valid for certain diagnostics, but they are valid in general. This could be modeled by utilizing complex data types such as JSON.
- **Tight coupling**: In some cases, tight coupling leads to complex and difficult-to-change data structures. Since business requirements change with time, some requirements might become obsolete. Modeling generalization and specialization (for example, a part-time student is a student) in a tightly coupled way may cause problems.

Sample application

In order to explain the basics of the ER model, an online web portal to buy and sell cars will be modeled. The requirements of this sample application are as follows, and an ER model will be developed step by step:

1. The portal provides the facility to register users online and provides different services for users based on their categories.
2. Users might be sellers or normal users. The sellers can create new car advertisements; other users can explore and search for cars.
3. All users should provide their full name and a valid email address during registration. The email address will be used for logging in.
4. The seller should also provide an address.

5. The user can rate the advertisement and the seller's service quality.
6. All users' search history should be maintained for later use.
7. The sellers have ranks and this affects the advertisement search; the rank is determined by the number of posted advertisements and the user's rank.
8. The car advertisement has a date and the car can have many attributes such as color, number of doors, number of previous owners, registration number, pictures, and so on.

Entities, attributes, and keys

The ER diagram represents entities, attributes, and relationships. An entity is a representation of a real-world object such as a car or a user. An attribute is a property of an object and describes it. A relationship represents an association between two or more entities.

The attributes might be composite or simple (atomic). Composite attributes can be divided into smaller subparts. A subpart of a composite attribute provides incomplete information that is semantically not useful by itself. For example, the address is composed of a street name, building number, and postal code. Any one of them isn't useful alone, without its counterparts.

Attributes could also be single-valued or multi-valued. The color of a bird is an example of a multi-valued attribute. It can be red and black, or a combination of any other colors. A multi-valued attribute can have a lower and upper bound to constrain the number of values allowed. In addition, some attributes can be derived from other attributes. Age can be derived from the birth date. In our example, the final rank of a seller is derived from the number of advertisements and the user ratings.

Key attributes can identify an entity in the real world. A key attribute should be marked as a unique attribute, but not necessarily as a primary key, when physically modeling the relation. Finally, several attribute types could be grouped together to form a complex attribute:

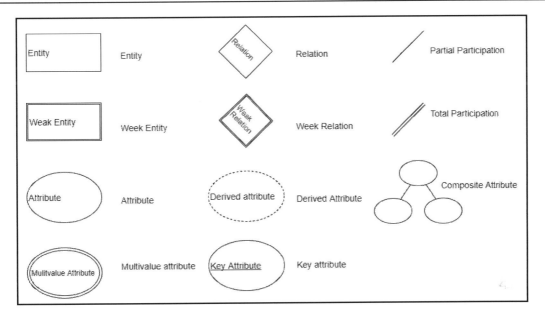

Entities should have a name and a set of attributes. They are classified into the following:

- **Weak entity**: Does not have key attributes of its own
- **Strong entity/regular entity**: Has a key attribute

A weak entity is usually related to a strong entity. This strong entity is called the **identifying entity**. Weak entities have a partial key, also known as a discriminator, which is an attribute that can uniquely identify the weak entity, and it is related to the identifying entity. In our example, if we assume that the search key is distinct each time the user searches for cars, then the search key is the partial key. The weak entity symbol is distinguished by surrounding the entity box with a double line.

The following diagram shows the preliminary design of a car portal application. The user entity has several attributes. The name attribute is a composite attribute, and email is a key attribute. The seller entity is a specialization of the user entity. The total rank is a derived attribute calculated by aggregating the user ratings and the number of advertisements. The color attribute of the car is multi-valued. The seller can be rated by the users for certain advertisements; this relation is a ternary relation, because the rating involves three entities, which are car, seller, and user.

The car picture is a subpart attribute of the advertisement. The following diagram shows that the car can be advertised more than once by different sellers. In the real world, this makes sense, because one could ask more than one seller to sell his car:

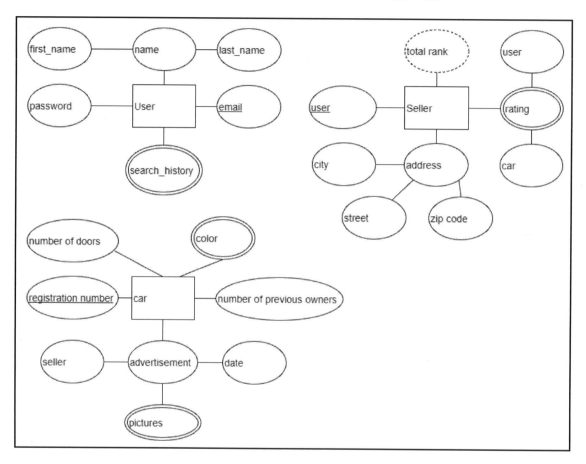

When an attribute of one entity refers to another entity, some relationships exist. In the ER model, these references should not be modeled as attributes but as relationships or weak entities. Similar to entities, there are two classes of relationships: weak and strong. Weak relationships associate the weak entities with other entities. Relationships can have attributes as entities. In our example, the car is advertised by the seller; the advertisement date is a property of the relationship.

Relationships have cardinality constraints to limit the possible combinations of entities that participate in a relationship. The cardinality constraint of car and seller is **1:N**; the car is advertised by one seller, and the seller can advertise many cars. The participation between seller and user is called total participation, and is denoted by a double line. This means that a seller cannot exist alone, and he must be a user.

The many-to-many relationship cardinality constraint is denoted by **N:M** to emphasize the different participation by the entities.

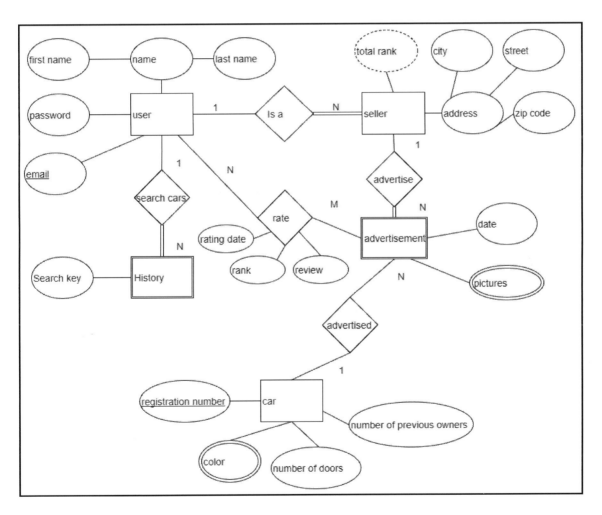

Up until now, only the basic concepts of ER diagrams have been covered. Some concepts, such as (min, max) cardinality notation, ternary/*n*-ary relationships, generalization, specialization, and **enhanced entity relation (EER)** diagrams, have not been discussed.

Mapping ER to relations

The rules to map an ER diagram to a set of relations (that is, the database schema) are almost straightforward, but not rigid. One could model an entity as an attribute, and then refine it to a relationship. An attribute that belongs to several entities can be promoted to be an independent entity. The most common rules are as follows (note that only basic rules have been covered, and the list is not exhaustive):

- Map regular entities to relations. If entities have composite attributes, then include all the subparts of the attributes. Pick one of the key attributes as a primary key.
- Map weak entities to relations. Include simple attributes and the subparts of the composite attributes. Add a foreign key to reference the identifying entity. The primary key is normally the combination of the partial key and the foreign key.
- If a relationship has an attribute and the relation cardinality is **1:1**, then the relation attribute can be assigned to one of the participating entities.
- If a relationship has an attribute and the relation cardinality is **1:N**, then the relation attribute can be assigned to the participating entity on the **N** side.
- Map many-to-many relationships, also known as **N:M**, to a new relation. Add foreign keys to reference the participating entities. The primary key is the composition of foreign keys.
- Map a multi-valued attribute to a relation. Add a foreign key to reference the entity that owns the multi-valued attribute. The primary key is the composition of the foreign key and the multi-valued attribute.

UML class diagrams

Unified Modeling Language (UML) is a standard developed by the **Object Management Group (OMG)**. UML diagrams are widely used in modeling software solutions, and there are several types of UML diagrams for different modeling purposes including class, use case, activity, and implementation diagrams.

A class diagram can represent several types of associations, that is, the relationship between classes. They can depict attributes as well as methods. An ER diagram can be easily translated into a UML class diagram. UML class diagrams also have the following advantages:

- **Code reverse-engineering**: The database schema can be easily reversed to generate a UML class diagram.
- **Modeling extended relational database objects**: Modern relational databases have several object types such as sequences, views, indexes, functions, and stored procedures. UML class diagrams have the capability to represent these object types.

The following class diagram is generated from reverse-engineering the SQL code of a `car_portal` database:

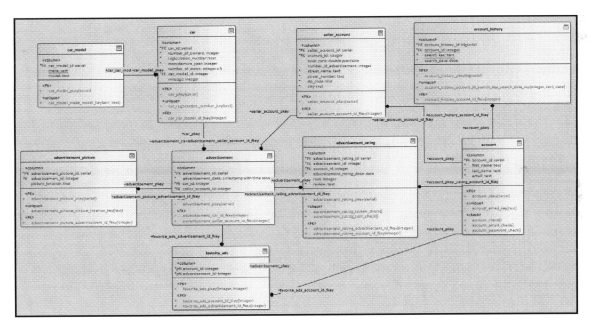

Summary

The design of a database management system is affected by the CAP theorem. Relational databases and NoSQL databases are not rivals, but are complementary. One can utilize different database categories in a single software application. In certain scenarios, one can use the key-value store as a cache engine on top of the relational database to gain performance.

Relational and object-relational databases are the dominant databases on the market. Relational databases are based on the concept of relations and have a very robust mathematical model. Object-relational databases such as PostgreSQL overcome the limitations of relational databases by introducing complex data types, inheritance, and rich extensions.

Relational databases are based on the relation, tuple, and attribute concepts. They ensure data validity and consistency by employing several techniques such as entity integrity, constraints, referential integrity, and data normalization.

The next chapter provides first-hand experience in installing the PostgreSQL server and client tools on different platforms, while also introducing PostgreSQL capabilities, such as out-of-the-box replication support and its very rich data types.

Questions

1. How does CAP theorem affect database general characteristics? Give an example of a database that complies with ACID properties and compare it with another database that utilizes BASE.
2. Describe ACID attributes briefly.
3. Think of a scenario where one can utilize different database categories to fulfill different business requirements.
4. What is the difference between tuple and set?
5. 3VL is used in the relational model; give examples of NULL value interpretation.
6. Why should the tuples in the relation be unique? Which constraint ensures tuple uniqueness?
7. Given two relations where both relations have 10 tuples and five attributes, assuming we have applied the Cartesian product on the two relations, what is the total number of attributes and tuples for the resultant relation?

8. What is a domain constraint? List domain constraint types. Assuming a relation, `client`, has an attribute, `phone_number`, define the domain constraint for this attribute.

9. Imagine that you have been assigned to a team that will be developing the online car portal system. As the team leader for the data design team, you have to provide a work plan that identifies the phases of data design. For each data model perspective phase, provide the following:

   - The scope of the data modeling phase
   - The inputs of the phase
   - The outputs of the phase

2
PostgreSQL in Action

PostgreSQL (pronounced Post-Gres-Q-L), or **postgres** for short, is an open source object-relational-database management system. It emphasizes extensibility and creativity as well as compatibility. It competes with the major relational database vendors, such as Oracle, MySQL, and **Microsoft SQL Server** (**MSSQL**). It's used by different sectors, including government agencies and the public and private sectors. It's a cross-platform DBMS, and it runs on most modern operating systems, including Windows, macOS, and Linux flavors. It conforms to SQL and is ACID-compliant.

By the end of this chapter, the user should be able to install PostgreSQL, establish a connection to the server, and run very basic queries. Also, the user will know general information about PostgreSQL's history and capabilities. In this chapter, we will explore the following topics:

- PostgreSQL history
- Selected PostgreSQL forks
- Companies utilizing PostgreSQL and success stories
- PostgreSQL usage patterns and application
- PostgreSQL architecture, capabilities, and features
- PostgreSQL installation on Linux as well as Windows
- PostgreSQL client tools with emphases on `psql` because it's often used on a daily basis

An overview of PostgreSQL

PostgreSQL (`http://www.PostgreSQL.org/`) has many useful features. It provides enterprise-level services, including performance, unique features, and scalability. It has a very supportive community and very good documentation.

PostgreSQL history

PostgreSQL was started as a project at the **University of California at Berkeley (UCB)**, then it was developed by the community in 1996.

So far, PostgreSQL is actively developed by the PostgreSQL community as well as universities. The following time frames show the history of PostgreSQL's development:

- **1977-1985, the Ingres project**: Michael Stonebraker created a **relational database management system (RDBMS)** based on the formal relational model.
- **1986-1994, Postgres**: Michael Stonebraker created Postgres in order to support complex data types and the object-relational model.
- **1995, Postgres95**: Andrew Yu and Jolly Chen changed the Postgres PostQUEL query language with an extended subset of SQL.
- **1996, PostgreSQL**: Several developers dedicated a lot of labor and time to stabilize Postgres95. The first open source version was released on January 29, 1997. With the introduction of new features, and enhancements, and due to it being an open source project, the Postgres95 name was changed to PostgreSQL.

  PostgreSQL began at version 6, with a very strong starting point due to the advantage of several years of research and development. Being an open source project with a very good reputation, PostgreSQL attracted hundreds of developers. Currently, PostgreSQL has an uncountable number of extensions and a very active community.

The advantages of PostgreSQL

PostgreSQL provides many features that attract developers, administrators, architects, and companies.

Business advantages of PostgreSQL

PostgreSQL is a free **open source software (OSS)**. It's released under the PostgreSQL license. The PostgreSQL license is highly permissive, and PostgreSQL is not subject to monopoly and acquisition—because of this, companies have the following advantages:

- No associated licensing cost to PostgreSQL.
- Unlimited number of deployments of PostgreSQL.
- More profitable business model.

- PostgreSQL is SQL-standards-compliant; thus, finding professional developers is not very difficult. PostgreSQL is easy to learn, and porting code from one database vendor to PostgreSQL is cost-efficient. Also, the PostgreSQL administrative tasks are easy to automate, thereby reducing the staffing cost significantly.
- PostgreSQL is cross-platform, and it has drivers for all modern programming languages; thus, there is no need to change the company policy regarding the software stack in order to use PostgreSQL.
- PostgreSQL is scalable and gives high performance.
- PostgreSQL is very reliable; it rarely crashes. Also, PostgreSQL is ACID-compliant, which means that it can tolerate some hardware failure. In addition, it can be configured and installed as a cluster to ensure **high availability (HA)**.

PostgreSQL user advantages

PostgreSQL is very attractive for developers, administrators, and architects. It has rich features that enable developers to perform tasks in an agile way. The following are some of the features that are attractive to developers:

- A new release almost every year; there have been 25 major releases so far, starting from Postgres 6.0.
- Very good documentation and an active community enables developers to find and solve problems quickly. The PostgreSQL manual is more than 2,500 pages.
- A rich extension repository enables developers to focus on business logic. Also, it enables developers to meet requirement changes easily.
- The source code is available free of charge. It can be customized and extended without much effort. There are many tools and utilities for PostgreSQL.
- Rich client and administrative tools enable developers to perform routine tasks, such as describing database objects, exporting and importing data, and dumping and restoring databases very quickly.
- Database-administration tasks don't require a lot of time and can be automated.
- PostgreSQL can be integrated easily with other database-management systems, giving the software architecture a good flexibility for implementing software designs.

PostgreSQL applications

PostgreSQL can be used with a variety of applications. The main PostgreSQL application domains can be classified into two categories:

- **Online transactional processing (OLTP)**: Characterized by a large amount of `SELECT`, `INSERT`, `UPDATE`, and `DELETE` operations, very fast processing of operations, and the maintaining of data integrity in a multi-access environment. Performance is measured in the number of transactions per second. The operations are often executed in a fraction of a second and often grouped in logical groups, also known as transactions.
- **Online analytical processing (OLAP)**: Characterized by a small amount of requests, complex queries that involve data aggregation, huge amounts of data from different sources with different formats, data mining, and historical data analysis.
- **Hybrid transactional/analytical processing (HTAP)**: A hybrid architecture to break the wall between OLTP and OLAP.

OLTP is used to model business operations, such as **customer relationship management (CRM)**. For instance, the car web portal example in `Chapter 1`, *Relational Databases*, is an example of an OLTP application. OLAP applications are used for business intelligence, decision support, reporting, and planning. An OLTP database's size is relatively small compared to an OLAP database. OLTP normally follows relational model concepts, such as normalization, when designing the database, while OLAP has less relation; the schema often has the shape of a star or a snowflake. Finally, the data is denormalized.

In the car web portal example, we could have had another database to store and maintain all the historical data of the *sellers* and *users*, which we could have used to analyze user preferences and seller activities. This database is an example of an OLAP application.

Unlike OLTP, OLAP's main operation is data analysis and retrieval. OLAP data is often generated by a process called **extract**, **transform**, and **load** (**ETL**). ETL is used to load data in to the OLAP database from different data sources and different formats. PostgreSQL can be used out of the box for OLTP applications. For OLAP, there are many extensions and tools to support it, such as **foreign data wrappers** (**FDW**), table partitioning, and, recently, parallel query execution.

Success stories

PostgreSQL is used in many application domains, including communication, medical, geographical, and e-commerce. Many companies provide consultation as well as commercial services, such as migrating proprietary RDBMSes to PostgreSQL in order to cut off the licensing costs. These companies often influence and enhance PostgreSQL by developing and submitting new features. The following are a few companies that have used PostgreSQL:

- Instagram, a social networking service that enables its user to share pictures and photos
- The **American Chemical Society** (**ACS**), which uses PostgreSQL to store more than one terabyte of data for the journal archive

In addition, PostgreSQL is used by HP, VMware, and Heroku. PostgreSQL is used by many scientific communities and organizations, such as NASA, due to its extensible and rich data types.

Forks

A fork is an independent development of a software project based on another project. There are more than 20 PostgreSQL forks; PostgreSQL-extensible APIs make PostgreSQL a great candidate for forking. Over the years, many groups forked PostgreSQL and contributed their findings to PostgreSQL.

HadoopDB is a hybrid between the PostgreSQL RDBMS and MapReduce technologies that targets analytical workload. The following is a list of popular PostgreSQL forks:

- **Greenplum**: A DBMS for OLAP applications built on the foundation of PostgreSQL. It utilizes the shared-nothing and **massively parallel processing** (**MPP**) architectures. It's used as a data warehouse and for analytical workloads. Greenplum started as proprietary software and open sourced in 2015.
- **EnterpriseDB Advanced Server**: A proprietary DBMS that provides Oracle with the capability to cap the Oracle fees.

- **Vertica**: A column-oriented database system that was started by Michael Stonebraker in 2005, and was acquired by HP in 2011. Vertica reused the SQL parser, semantic analyzer, and standard SQL rewrites from the PostgreSQL implementation.
- **Netezza**: A popular data-warehouse appliance solution.
- **Amazon Redshift**: A popular data-warehouse management system based on PostgreSQL 8.0.2. It is mainly designed for OLAP applications.
- **PostgreSQL extensions**: Several companies developed a data framework as an extension to PostgreSQL, such as Citus, PipelineDB, and TimeScaleDB. Developing a framework as extensions enables the developers to benefit from new PostgreSQL releases and features. Citus extends PostgreSQL and provides scaling capabilities for PostgreSQL. PipelineDB is a PostgreSQL extension for time-series aggregation, and real-time reporting. TimeScaleDB is a scalable data store for time-series data.

PostgreSQL architecture

PostgreSQL uses the client/server model, where the client and server programs can be on different hosts. The communication between the client and server is normally done via TCP/IP protocols or via Linux sockets. PostgreSQL can handle multiple connections from a client. A common PostgreSQL program consists of the following operating system processes:

- **Client process or program (frontend)**: The database frontend application performs a database action. The frontend can be a web server that wants to display a web page or a command-line tool to do maintenance tasks. PostgreSQL provides frontend tools such as `psql`, `createdb`, `dropdb`, and `createuser`.
- **Server process (backend)**: The server process manages database files, accepts connections from client applications, and performs actions on behalf of the client. The server process name is `postgres`. PostgreSQL's main server process forks a new process for each new connection; thus, client and server processes communicate with each other without the intervention of the main server process (`postgres`), and they have a certain lifetime, which is determined by accepting and terminating a client connection.

The aforementioned abstract conceptual PostgreSQL architecture gives an overview of the PostgreSQL capabilities and its interaction with the client and the operating system. The PostgreSQL server could be divided roughly into four subsystems, as follows:

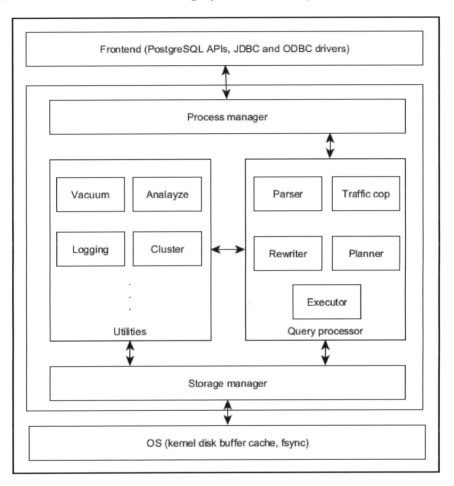

- **Process manager**: The process manager client connections, such as forking and the terminating process. It also handles background services, such as logger, and WAL writer processes.
- **Query processor**: When a client sends a query to PostgreSQL, the query is parsed by the parser, and then the traffic cop subsystem determines the query type. A utility query is passed to the utilities subsystem. SELECT, INSERT, UPDATE, and DELETE queries are rewritten by the rewriter, following which an execution plan is generated by the planner. Finally, the query is executed and the result is returned to the client.

- **Utilities**: The utilities subsystem provides a means to maintain the database, such as claiming storage, updating statistics, and exporting and importing data with a certain format or logging.
- **Storage manager**: The storage handles the memory cache, disk buffers, and storage allocation.

Almost all PostgreSQL components can be configured, including a logger, planner, statistical analyzer, and storage manager. PostgreSQL configuration is governed by the nature of the application, such as OLAP, OLTP, and HATP.

The PostgreSQL community

PostgreSQL has a very cooperative, active, and organized community. In the last eight years, the PostgreSQL community has published eight major releases.

There are dozens of mailing lists organized into categories, such as user, developer, and associations. Examples of user mailing lists are pgsql-general, psql-doc, and psql-bugs. pgsql-general is a very important mailing list for beginners. All non-bug-related questions regarding PostgreSQL installation, tuning, basic administration, PostgreSQL features, and general discussions are submitted to this list.

The PostgreSQL community runs a blog-aggregation service called **Planet PostgreSQL** (`planet.postgresql.org`). Several PostgreSQL developers and companies use this service to share their experience and knowledge.

PostgreSQL capabilities

PostgreSQL provides enterprise-level services that guarantee the continuation of the business. For example, PostgreSQL supports replication, which enables the developers to provide HA solutions. PostgreSQL can integrate data from different data sources; this makes it easy for developers to use it for **ETL** jobs. In addition, PostgreSQL security is treated as a first-class citizen. Security update patches are shipped in minor releases to make it easier for administrators to upgrade PostgreSQL.

Finally, the features of PostgreSQL are endless: PostgreSQL provides advanced SQL statements, very rich extensions, and interactive tools.

Replication

Replication allows data from one database server to be replicated to another server. Replication is used mainly to achieve the following:

- **High availability**: A second server can take over if the primary server fails.
- **Load balancing**: Several servers can serve the same requests.
- **Fast execution**: PostgreSQL is shipped with the tools to execute the queries efficiently, such as several kind of indexes and smart planner. In addition, the read load can be distributed on the replicas in streaming replication.

PostgreSQL supports replication out of the box via streaming and logical replication. **Streaming replication** is a master-standby replication that uses file-based log shipping. Streaming replication is a binary replication technique, because SQL statements aren't analyzed. It's based on taking a snapshot of the master node, and then shipping the changes—the WAL files—from the master node to the slave node and replaying them on the slave. The master can be used for read/write operations, and the slave can be used to serve read requests. Streaming replication is relatively easy to set up and configure; it can support synchronous and asynchronous replications as well as cascading replication.

A synchronous replication is the default streaming-replication mode. If the primary server crashes, transactions that were committed on the primary may not have been replicated to the standby server, leading to data inconsistency. In synchronous replication, a data-modifying operation must be committed on one or more synchronous servers in order to be considered successful. In cascading replication, one could add a replica to a slave. This allows PostgreSQL to scale horizontally for read operations.

PostgreSQL also supports **logical streaming replication**; unlike streaming replication, which replicates the binary data bit by bit, logical replication translates the WAL files back to logical changes. This gives us the freedom to have more control over the replication such as applying filters. For example, in logical replication, parts of data can be replicated, while in streaming replication the slave is a clone of the master. Another important aspect of logical replication is being able to write on the replicated server, such as extra indexes, as well as temporary tables. Finally, you can replicate data from several servers and combine it on a single server.

In addition to PostgreSQL replication techniques, there are several other open source solutions to target different workloads:

- **Slony-1**: This is a master-to-multiple-slave replication system. Unlike PostgreSQL, it can be used with different server versions. So, one could replicate the 9.6 server data to the 11 server. Slony is very useful for upgrading servers without downtime.
- **Bucardo**: An open source project for an asynchronous replication system that allows multi-master as well as multi-slave operations.
- **pgpool-II**: This is the middleware between PostgreSQL and the client. In addition to replication, it can be used for connection pooling, load balancing, and parallel query execution.
- **HA management tools**: Patroni, stolon, and repmgr are a set of management tools for HA for PostgreSQL. repmgr manages the replication and failover of PostgreSQL. stolon is a cloud-native PostgreSQL manager. Patroni is a template for PostgreSQL HA with ZooKeeper, etcd, or Consul.
- **Distributed Replicated Block Device (DRBD)**: A general solution for HA. It can be understood as a RAID-1 network. This solution requires advanced knowledge and may not be straightforward to set up.

Security

PostgreSQL supports several authentication methods, including password, LDAB, GSSAPI, SSPI, Kerberos, ident-based, RADUIS, certificate, and PAM authentication. All database vulnerabilities are listed in the PostgreSQL security information web page (`http://www.postgresql.org/support/security/`) with information about the affected version, the vulnerability class, and the affected component.

The PostgreSQL security updates are made available as minor updates. Also, known security issues are always fixed with the next major releases. Publishing security updates in minor updates makes it easy for a PostgreSQL administrator to keep PostgreSQL secure and up to date with minimal downtime.

PostgreSQL can control the database object access at several levels, including database, table, view, function, sequence, column, and row. This enables PostgreSQL to have great authorization control.

PostgreSQL can use encryption to protect data by hardware encryption. Also, you can encrypt certain information by utilizing the pgcrypto extension.

Extensions

PostgreSQL can be extended to support new data types and functionality. Extensions in PostgreSQL are a great way to add new functions, not being a core developer. PostgreSQL provides the CREATE EXTENSION command to load extensions to the current database. Also, PostgreSQL has a central distribution network (**PGXN**: www.pgxn.org) that allows users to explore and download extensions. When installing the PostgreSQL binaries, the postgresql-contib package contains many useful extensions, such as tablefunc, which allows table pivoting, and the pgcrypto extension; the README file in the installation directory contains the summary information.

The ability of PostgreSQL to support extensions is a result of the following features:

- **PostgreSQL data types**: PostgreSQL has very rich data types. It supports primitive data types as well as some primitive data structures, such as arrays, out of the box. In addition, it supports the following complex data types:
  - **Geometric data types**: Including point, line segment (lseg), path, polygon, and box.
  - **Network address types**: Including cidr, inet, and macaddr.
  - **tsvector and tsquery**: This is a sorted list of lexemes that enables Postgres to perform full text search.
  - **Universal unique identifiers (UUID)**: UUID solves many problems related to databases, such as offline data generation.
  - **NoSQL**: It supports several NoSQL data types, including XML, hstore, and JSON. Enum, range, and domain are user-defined data types with specific constraints, such as a set of allowed values, data range constraint, and check constraints.

    A composite data type is a user-defined data type, where an attribute is composed of several attributes.

- **Supported languages**: PostgreSQL allows functions to be written in several languages. The PostgreSQL community supports the following languages: SQL, C, Python, PL/pgSQL, Perl, and Tcl. In addition, there are many externally maintained procedural languages, including Java, R, PHP, Ruby, and Unix shell.

The following example shows you how to create a new composite type called phone_number. An equality operator is also created to check whether two phone numbers are equal by comparing the area code and the line number. The following example shows how to create a composite data type:

```
CREATE TYPE phone_number AS (
    area_code varchar(3),
    line_number varchar(7)
);
CREATE OR REPLACE FUNCTION phone_number_equal (phone_number,phone_number)
RETURNS boolean AS $$
BEGIN
    IF $1.area_code=$2.area_code AND $1.line_number=$2.line_number THEN
        RETURN TRUE ;
    ELSE
        RETURN FALSE;
    END IF;
END; $$ LANGUAGE plpgsql;
CREATE OPERATOR = (
LEFTARG = phone_number,
RIGHTARG = phone_number,
PROCEDURE = phone_number_equal
);
```

For test purpose:

```
SELECT row('123','222244')::phone_number = row('1','222244')::phone_number;
```

The preceding examples show how one can create new data types. A data type called phone_number is created. The phone_number data type is composed of two atomic data types, area_code and line_number. The = operator is overloaded to handle the equality of the new data type. To define the behavior of the = operator, you need to define the operator arguments and the function that handles the arguments. In this case, the function is phone_number_equal and the arguments are of the phone_number type.

NoSQL capabilities

PostgreSQL is more than a relational database and a SQL language. PostgreSQL is now home to different NoSQL data types. The power of PostgreSQL and schema less data stores enables developers to build reliable and flexible applications in an agile way.

PostgreSQL supports the **JavaScript Simple Object Notation (JSON)** data type, which is often used to share data across different systems in modern RESTful web applications. In PostgreSQL release 9.4, PostgreSQL introduced another structured binary format to save JSON documents instead of using the JSON format in prior versions. The new data type is called JSONB. This data type eliminates the need to parse a JSON document before it's committed to the database. In other words, PostgreSQL can ingest a JSON document at a speed comparable with document databases, while still maintaining compliance with ACID. In PostgreSQL version 9.5, several functions are added to make handling JSON documents much easier. In version 10, full text search is supported for JSON and JSONB documents.

Key/value pairs are also supported by the PostgreSQL hstore extension. hstore is used to store semi-structured data, and it can be used in several scenarios to decrease the number of attributes that are rarely used and often contain null values.

Finally, PostgreSQL supports the **Extensible Markup Language (XML)** data type. XML is very flexible and is often used to define document formats. XML is used in RSS, Atom, SOAP, and XHTML. PostgreSQL supports several XML functions to generate and create XML documents. Also, it supports XPath to find information in an XML document.

Foreign data wrappers

In 2011, PostgreSQL 9.1 was released with a read-only support for SQL/**Management of External Data (MED)** ISO/IEC 9075-9:2003 standard. SQL/MED defines **foreign data wrappers (FDWs)** to allow the relational database to manage external data. FDW can be used to achieve data integration in a federated database-system environment. PostgreSQL supports RDBMS, NoSQL, and foreign data wrapper files, including Oracle, Redis, MongoDB, and delimited files.

A simple use case for FDWs is to have one database server for analytical purposes, and then ship the result of this server to another server that works as a caching layer.

Also, FDW can be used to test data changes. Imagine you have two databases, one with different data due to applying a certain development patch. One could use FDW to assess the effect of this patch by comparing the data from the two databases.

PostgreSQL supports `postgres_fdw` starting from release 9.3. `postgres_fdw` is used to enable data sharing and access between different PostgreSQL databases. It supports the `SELECT`, `INSERT`, `UPDATE`, and `DELETE` operations on foreign tables.

The following example shows you how to read **comma-separated value** (**CSV**) files using FDW; you can read CSV files to parse logs. Let's assume that we want to read the database logs generated by PostgreSQL. This is quite useful in a production environment as you can have statistics about executed queries; the table structure can be found in the documentation at https://www.postgresql.org/docs/current/static/runtime-config-logging.html. To enable CSV logging, you need to change the following values in postgresql.conf. For simplicity, all statements will be logged, but this isn't recommended in a production environment since it'll consume a lot of server resources:

```
log_destination = 'csvlog'
logging_collector = on
log_filename = 'postgresql.log'
log_statement = 'all'
```

For the changes to take effect, you need to restart PostgreSQL from the Terminal as follows:

```
sudo service postgresql restart
```

To install the FDW file, we need to run the following command:

```
postgres=# CREATE EXTENSION file_fdw ;
CREATE EXTENSION
```

To access the file, we need to create the FDW server, as follows:

```
postgres=# CREATE SERVER fileserver FOREIGN DATA WRAPPER file_fdw;
CREATE SERVER
```

Also, we need to create an FDW table and link it to the log file; in our case, it's located in the log folder in the PostgreSQL cluster directory:

```
postgres=# CREATE FOREIGN TABLE postgres_log
( log_time timestamp(3) with time zone,
  user_name text,
  database_name text,
  process_id integer,
  connection_from text,
  session_id text,
  session_line_num bigint,
  command_tag text,
  session_start_time timestamp with time zone,
  virtual_transaction_id text,
  transaction_id bigint,
  error_severity text,
  sql_state_code text,
  message text,
  detail text,
```

```
    hint text,
    internal_query text,
    internal_query_pos integer,
    context text,
    query text,
    query_pos integer,
    location text,
    application_name text
) SERVER fileserver OPTIONS ( filename
'/var/lib/postgresql/11/main/log/postgresql.csv', header 'true', format
'csv' );
CREATE FOREIGN TABLE
```

To test our example, let's get one log line in JSON format, as follows:

```
postgres=# SELECT row_to_json(postgres_log, true) FROM postgres_log limit
1;
                                  row_to_json
------------------------------------------------------------------------
 {"log_time":"2018-12-10T00:35:19.768+01:00", +
  "user_name":null, +
  "database_name":null, +
  "process_id":25847, +
  "connection_from":null, +
  "session_id":"5c0da6b7.64f7", +
  "session_line_num":1, +
  "command_tag":null, +
  "session_start_time":"2018-12-10T00:35:19+01:00", +
  "virtual_transaction_id":null, +
  "transaction_id":0, +
  "error_severity":"LOG", +
  "sql_state_code":"00000", +
  "message":"database system was shut down at 2018-12-10 00:35:19 CET",+
  "detail":null, +
  "hint":null, +
  "internal_query":null, +
  "internal_query_pos":null, +
  "context":null, +
  "query":null, +
  "query_pos":null, +
  "location":null, +
  "application_name":""}
(1 row)
```

As we've seen, you can store the PostgreSQL logs in the PostgreSQL cluster. This allows the developer to search for certain user actions. Also, it allows the administrators to conduct statistical analysis on performance, such as finding the slowest queries to tune the PostgreSQL server configuration or rewriting slow queries.

 The creation of the foreign data wrapper table depends on the log format. This format changes from one version to another. This information can be found in the documentation
at `https://www.postgresql.org/docs/current/runtime-config-loggin g.html#RUNTIME-CONFIG-LOGGING-CSVLOG`.

Performance

PostgreSQL has a proven performance. It employs several techniques to improve concurrency and scalability, including the following:

- **PostgreSQL locking system**: PostgreSQL provides several types of locks at the table and row levels. PostgreSQL is able to use more granular locks that prevent locking/blocking more than necessary; this increases concurrency and decreases the blocking time.

- **Indexes**: PostgreSQL provides six types of indexes: btree, hash, Generalized Inverted Index (**GIN**), the **Generalized Search Tree** (**GiST**) index, SP-GiST, and **Block Range Indexes** (**BRIN**). Each index type can be used for a certain scenario. For example, btree can be used for efficient equality and range queries. GIST can be used for text search and for geospatial data. PostgreSQL supports partial, unique, and multicolumn indexes. It also supports indexes on expressions and operator classes.

- **Explain, analyze, vacuum, and cluster**: PostgreSQL provides several commands to boost performance and provide transparency. The `explain` command shows the execution plan of a SQL statement. You can change some parameter settings, such as memory settings, and then compare the execution plan before and after the change. The `analyze` command is used to collect the statistics on tables and columns. The `vacuum` command is used for garbage collection to reclaim unused hard disk space. The `cluster` command is used to arrange data physically on the hard disk. All these commands can be configured based on the database workload.

- **Table inheritance and constraint exclusion**: Table inheritance allows us to easily create tables with the same structure. Those tables are used to store subsets of data based on certain criteria. This allows a very fast retrieval of information in certain scenarios, because only a subset of data is accessed when answering a query.
- **Very rich SQL constructs**: PostgreSQL supports very rich SQL constructs. It supports correlated and uncorrelated subqueries. It supports **common table expression (CTE)**, window functions, and recursive queries. Once developers have learned these SQL constructs, they will be able to write a crisp SQL code very quickly. Moreover, they will be able to write complex queries with minimal effort. The PostgreSQL community keeps adding new SQL features in each release.

Installing PostgreSQL

PostgreSQL can be installed on almost all modern operating systems. It can be installed on all recent Linux distributions, Windows 2000 SP4 and later, FreeBSD, OpenBSD, macOS, AIX, and Solaris. Also, PostgreSQL can work on various CPU architectures, including x86, x86_64, and IA64. You can check whether a platform (operating system and CPU architecture combination) is supported by exploring the PostgreSQL build farm at http://buildfarm.postgresql.org/. You can compile and install

In order to automate PostgreSQL installation and to reduce server administrative tasks, it's recommended you use PostgreSQL binaries, which come with the operating system packaging system. This approach normally has one drawback: binaries that aren't up to date. However, PostgreSQL's official website maintains the binaries for the most common platforms, including BSD, Linux, macOS, Solaris, and Windows.

The instructions, as well as the binaries, to install PostgreSQL can be found on the official web page (https://www.postgresql.org/download/). The following screenshot shows the instruction to add the **apt** repository to the Ubuntu Bionic release.

Note that the installation instructions are generated based on the release name. The installation page URL for Ubuntu is `https://www.postgresql.org/download/linux/ubuntu/`:

To use the apt repository, follow these steps:

-

    Bionic (18.04)

- Create the file `/etc/apt/sources.list.d/pgdg.list` and add a line for the repository

    `deb http://apt.postgresql.org/pub/repos/apt/ bionic-pgdg main`

- Import the repository signing key, and update the package lists

    `wget --quiet -O - https://www.postgresql.org/media/keys/ACCC4CF8.asc | sudo apt-key add -`
    `sudo apt-get update`

Installing PostgreSQL on Linux via source

Installing PostgreSQL form source code is straightforward using `configure`, `make`, and `make install`. First, you need to make sure that all the prerequisite libraries, as well as the C++ compiler, are installed. The installation instruction might change based on the Linux version and installed libraries.

The following installation instructions are performed on a fresh installation of Ubuntu Bionic. On Ubuntu, you can get and install the prerequisites, including the compiler, zlib, and readline libraries, via the following command:

```
sudo apt-get install build-essential
sudo apt-get install zlib1g-dev libreadline6-dev
```

You can get the source code of PostgreSQL from the PostgreSQL server FTP site and extract it as follows:

```
wget https://ftp.postgresql.org/pub/source/v11.1/postgresql-11.1.tar.bz2
tar -xvf postgresql-11.1.tar.bz2
```

To configure PostgreSQL, run the `./configure` command; note that, if there are missing libraries, `configure` will raise an error:

```
cd postgresql-11.1
./configure
```

After a successful configuration, to build PostgreSQL run `make`:

```
make
```

To install PostgreSQL, switch to a privileged user account, such as root, and run `make install`:

```
sudo su
make install
```

At this point, PostgreSQL is installed. The binaries can be found at `/usr/local/pgsql`. PostgreSQL runs using the `postgres` user . In order to run the server, we need to create a user account, as follows:

```
adduser postgres
```

The last step of the installation is to create a database cluster and run PostgreSQL for this cluster. Perform the following steps:

1. Create a folder to store the database cluster information.
2. Change the folder permissions and make the owner the `postgres` user. The `postgres` user account will be used to run the PostgreSQL server.
3. Initialize the cluster using the `initdb` command. `initdb` needs the folder location of the cluster.
4. Run PostgreSQL using the `postgres` command. The `postgres` command needs the cluster folder location:

```
$mkdir /usr/local/pgsql/data chown postgres /usr/local/pgsql/data
$su - postgres /usr/local/pgsql/bin/initdb -D /usr/local/pgsql/data
/usr/local/pgsql/bin/postgres -D /usr/local/pgsql/data >logfile
2>&1 &
```

The previous installation instructions are quite minimal. PostgreSQL allows the user to configure the binary location, compiler flags, libraries, and so on. In the preceding code, the defaults are used. To verify our installation, you can connect to the server as follows:

```
/usr/local/pgsql/bin/psql postgres
psql (11.1)
Type "help" for help.
```

```
postgres=# SELECT version();
                                                   version
-------------------------------------------------------------------------------
------------------------------
 PostgreSQL 11.1 on x86_64-pc-linux-gnu, compiled by gcc (Ubuntu
7.3.0-27ubuntu1~18.04) 7.3.0, 64-bit
(1 row)
```

Finally, installing PostgreSQL from source code doesn't amend the system environment path or create a Linux service with `systemd`. To stop the PostgreSQL server, simply exit the Terminal. For production environments, it's better to use ready in binaries.

Installing PostgreSQL using Advanced Package Tool

Advanced Package Tool (APT) is used to handle the installation and removal of software on Debian and Debian-based distributions, such as the Ubuntu operating system.

As stated earlier, recent PostgreSQL binaries might not yet be integrated with the official Debian and Ubuntu repositories. To set up the PostgreSQL `apt` repository on Debian or Ubuntu, execute the following:

```
sudo sh -c 'echo "deb http://apt.postgresql.org/pub/repos/apt/
$(lsb_release -cs)-pgdg main" > /etc/apt/sources.list.d/pgdg.list'
wget --quiet -O - https://www.PostgreSQL.org/media/keys/ACCC4CF8.asc | sudo
apt-key add -
sudo apt-get update
```

After adding a new `apt` repository, it's good to upgrade your system as follows:

```
sudo apt-get upgrade
```

Client installation

If you have a PostgreSQL server already installed and you need to interact with it, you need to install the `postgresql-client` software package. In order to do so, open a Terminal and execute the following command:

```
sudo apt-get install postgresql-client-11
```

With the installation of `postgresql-client-11`, several tools are installed, including the PostgreSQL interactive Terminal (`psql`), which is a very powerful interactive frontend tool for PostgreSQL. To see the full list of installed programs, you can browse the installation directory. Note that the installation path might vary depending on the installed PostgreSQL version and the operating system:

```
$ls /usr/lib/postgresql/11/bin/
clusterdb createdb createuser dropdb dropuser pg_basebackup pg_dump
pg_dumpall pg_isready pg_receivewal pg_recvlogical pg_restore psql
reindexdb vacuumdb
```

To connect to an existing PostgreSQL server using `psql`, specify the connection string, which might include the host, the database, the port, and the username.

Another powerful frontend **graphical user interface** (**GUI**) tool is pgAdmin4, which is used for PostgreSQL administration and development. pgAdmin is favored by beginners, while `psql` can be used for shell scripting.

pgAdmin4 has many features, such as cross-platform, web-based, server, and desktop modes. To install pgAdmin in desktop mode, run the following command:

```
sudo apt-get install  pgadmin4
```

To run it, simply execute the following command in the Terminal:

```
pgadmin4
```

Server installation

If you've already installed the server using source code, you might not be able to start the server due to port conflict. To avoid errors, make sure to stop the PostgreSQL server installed via source and then run the following command:

```
sudo apt-get install postgresql-11
```

The installation will give you information about the location of the PostgreSQL configuration files, data location, locale, port, and PostgreSQL status, as shown in the following output:

```
Creating config file /etc/postgresql-common/createcluster.conf with new
version
Building PostgreSQL dictionaries from installed myspell/hunspell
packages...
  en_us
Removing obsolete dictionary files:
```

```
Created symlink /etc/systemd/system/multi-
user.target.wants/postgresql.service →
/lib/systemd/system/postgresql.service.
Processing triggers for man-db (2.8.3-2) ...
Setting up postgresql-11 (11.1-1.pgdg18.04+1) ...
Creating new PostgreSQL cluster 11/main ...
/usr/lib/postgresql/11/bin/initdb -D /var/lib/postgresql/11/main --auth-
local peer --auth-host md5
The files belonging to this database system will be owned by user
"postgres".
This user must also own the server process.

The database cluster will be initialized with locales
  COLLATE:  en_US.UTF-8
  CTYPE:    en_US.UTF-8
  MESSAGES: en_US.UTF-8
  MONETARY: de_DE.UTF-8
  NUMERIC:  de_DE.UTF-8
  TIME:     de_DE.UTF-8
The default database encoding has accordingly been set to "UTF8".
The default text search configuration will be set to "english".

Data page checksums are disabled.

fixing permissions on existing directory /var/lib/postgresql/11/main ... ok
creating subdirectories ... ok
selecting default max_connections ... 100
selecting default shared_buffers ... 128MB
selecting dynamic shared memory implementation ... posix
creating configuration files ... ok
running bootstrap script ... ok
performing post-bootstrap initialization ... ok
syncing data to disk ... ok

Success.
```

You can now start the database server using the following command:

```
/usr/lib/postgresql/11/bin/pg_ctl -D /var/lib/postgresql/11/main -l logfile
start
```

PostgreSQL initializes a storage area on the hard disk called a database cluster. A database cluster is a collection of databases managed by a single instance of a running database server. This means that one can have more than one instance of PostgreSQL running on the same server by initializing several database clusters. These instances can be of different PostgreSQL server versions or the same version.

The database cluster locale is `en_US.UTF-8` by default; when a database cluster is created, the database cluster will be initialized with the locale setting of its execution environment. This can be controlled by specifying the locale when creating a database cluster.

 Another important package is `postgresql-contrib`, which contains community-approved extensions. Often, this package is provided separately. However, in the PostgreSQL 10 APT repository, it has been integrated with the server package.

To check the installation, `grep` the `postgres` processes, as follows:

```
pgrep -a postgres
25565 /usr/lib/postgresql/11/bin/postgres -D /var/lib/postgresql/11/main -c
config_file=/etc/postgresql/11/main/postgresql.conf
25567 postgres: 11/main: checkpointer
25568 postgres: 11/main: background writer
25569 postgres: 11/main: walwriter
25570 postgres: 11/main: autovacuum launcher
25571 postgres: 11/main: stats collector
25572 postgres: 11/main: logical replication launcher
```

The preceding query shows the main server process with two options: the `-D` option specifies the database cluster, and the `-c` option specifies the configuration file. Also, it shows many utility processes, such as `autovacuum`, and statistics-collector processes.

Finally, install the server and client in one command, as follows:

```
sudo apt-get install postgresql-11 postgresql-client-11
```

Basic server configuration

In order to access the server, we need to understand the PostgreSQL authentication mechanism. On Linux systems, you can connect to PostgreSQL using a Unix-socket or TCP/IP protocol. Also, PostgreSQL supports many types of authentication methods.

When a PostgreSQL server is installed, a new operating system user, as well as a database user, with the name `postgres` is created. This user can connect to the database server using peer authentication. The peer authentication gets the client's operating system username and uses it to access the databases that can be accessed. Peer authentication is supported only by local connections—connections that use Unix sockets. Peer authentication is supported by Linux distribution but not by Windows.

Client authentication is controlled by a configuration file named `pg_hba.conf`, where `pg` stands for PostgreSQL and `hba` stands for host-based authentication. To take a look at peer authentication, let's display the content of `pg_hba.conf`:

```
$sudo su
grep -v '^#' /etc/postgresql/11/main/pg_hba.conf|grep 'peer'
local all postgres peer
local all all peer
local replication all peer
```

The interpretation of the first line of the `grep` result is shown in the preceding command. The `postgres` user can connect to all the databases using Unix-socket and the peer authentication method.

To connect to the database servers using the `postgres` user, first we need to switch the operating system's current user to `postgres` and then invoke `psql`. This is done via following Linux command:

```
$sudo -u postgres psql
psql (11.1 (Ubuntu 11.1-1.pgdg18.04+1))
Type "help" for help.

postgres=# SELECT version();
                                                              version
-----------------------------------------------------------------------
---------------------------------------------------------
 PostgreSQL 11.1 (Ubuntu 11.1-1.pgdg18.04+1) on x86_64-pc-linux-gnu,
compiled by gcc (Ubuntu 7.3.0-27ubuntu1~18.04) 7.3.0, 64-bit
(1 row)
```

The preceding query shows the `psql` interactive Terminal. The `SELECT version ();` `SELECT` statement was executed, and the PostgreSQL version information was displayed. As shown in the preceding result, the installed version is PostgreSQL 11.1.

Prior to PostgreSQL 10, the PostgreSQL version number had three digits. Major releases occur roughly on an annual basis and usually change the internal format of the data. This means that the stored data's backward compatibility between major releases isn't maintained. A major release is numbered by incrementing either the first or the second digit, such as 9.5 and 9.6. Minor releases are numbered by increasing the third digit of the release number, for example, 9.6.1 to 9.6.2. Minor releases are only bug fixes.

In PostgreSQL 10, the versioning policy has changed; major releases are numbered by incrementing the first number, that is, from 10 to 11. Minor releases are numbered by incrementing the second part of the number, for example, 10.0 to 10.1.

Installing PostgreSQL on Windows

The installation of PostgreSQL on Windows is easier than Linux for beginners. You can download the PostgreSQL binaries from EnterpriseDB at `https://www.enterprisedb.com/downloads/postgres-postgresql-downloads`. The installer wizard will guide the user through the installation process. The installation wizard gives the user the ability to specify the binaries' location, the database cluster location, the port, the `postgres` user password, and the locale. The following screenshot shows the installation directory of PostgreSQL:

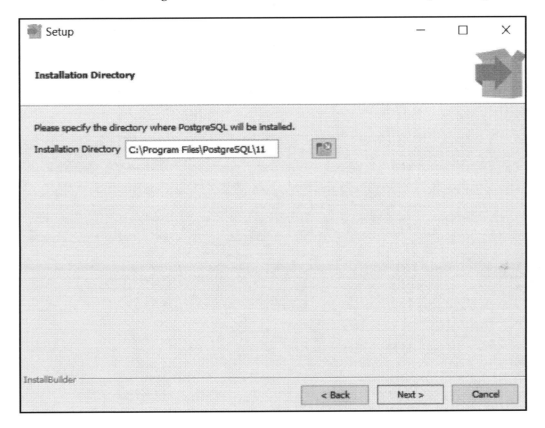

The following screenshot shows the components that will be installed:

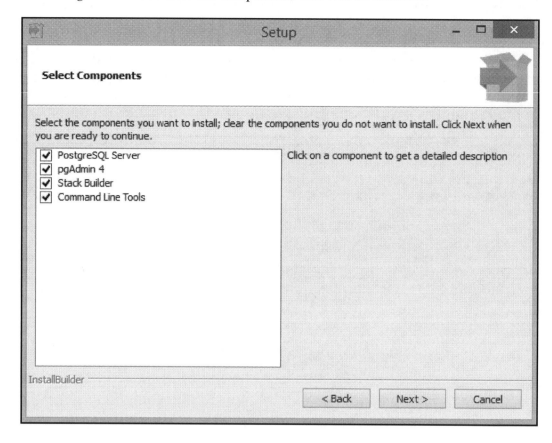

The installer will also launch the Stack Builder wizard, which is used to install the PostgreSQL drivers and many other utilities, as shown in the following screenshot:

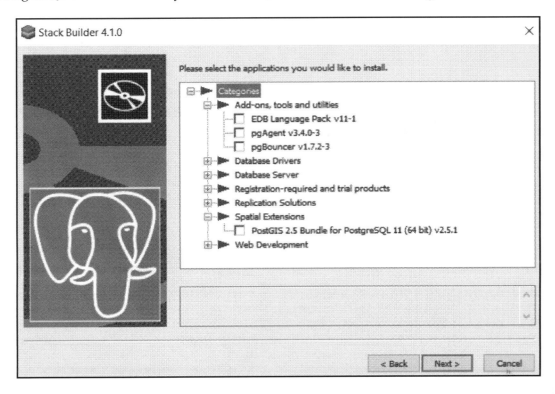

Using the `psql` client isn't very convenient in the latest version of Windows due to the lack of some capabilities, such as copying, pasting, and resizing, in Command Prompt (`CMD.exe`). pgAdmin is often used in the Windows operating system. Another option is to use a Command Prompt alternative, such as PowerShell, or a Linux emulator, such as Cygwin or MobaXterm.

PostgreSQL in Windows is installed as a service; in order to validate the installation, you can view the **Service** tab in the Task Manager utility.

PostgreSQL clients

In addition to PgAdmin4 and the `psql` client tools, there are a lot of vendors producing tools for PostgreSQL that cover different areas, such as database administration, modeling, development, reporting, ETL, and reverse-engineering. In addition to the `psql` tool, PostgreSQL is shipped with several client tools, including the following:

- **Wrappers**: The wrappers are built around SQL commands, such as CREATE USER. These wrappers facilitate the interaction between the database server and the developer, and automate daily routine tasks.
- **Backup and replication**: PostgreSQL supports physical and logical backups. The physical backup is performed by copying the database files and the WAL files accumulated while copying files. The physical backup can be combined with WAL in order to achieve streaming replication or a hot standby solution. Logical backup is used to dump the database in the form of SQL statements. Unlike physical backup, you can dump and restore a single database, a table, or even a specific dataset.

The PostgreSQL community unifies the look and feel of the client tools as much as possible; this makes it easy to use and learn. For example, the connection options are unified across all client tools. The following list shows the connection options for `psql`, which are common for other PostgreSQL clients, such as `createdb` and `createuser`:

- `-d`: The database name
- `-h`: The hostname or IP address
- `-u`: The username
- `-p`: The port

Also, most PostgreSQL clients can use the environment variables supported by `libpq`, such as PGHOST, PGDATABASE, and PGUSER. The `libpq` environment variables can be used to determine the default connection parameter values.

The psql client

The `psql` client is maintained by the PostgreSQL community, and it's part of the PostgreSQL binary distribution. `psql` has an overwhelming number of features, such as the following:

- **psql is configurable**: `psql` can be configured easily. The configuration might be applied to user-session behavior, such as `commit` and `rollback`, a `psql` prompt, history files, and even shortcuts for predefined SQL statements.
- **Integration with editor and pager tools**: The `psql` query result can be directed to your favorite pager, such as `less` or `more`. Also, `psql` doesn't come with an editor, but it can utilize several editors. The following example shows how to use the `nano` editor to edit a function:

```
postgres=# \setenv PSQL_EDITOR /bin/nano
postgres=# \ef
```

- **Autocompletion and SQL syntax help**: `psql` supports autocompletion for database object names and SQL constructs query result format control; `psql` supports different formats, such as HTML and latex. For example, when using the `\ef` meta command, a template is generated as follows:

```
CREATE FUNCTION ( )
 RETURNS
 LANGUAGE
 -- common options:  IMMUTABLE STABLE STRICT SECURITY DEFINER
AS $function$

$function$
```

- The `psql` client tool is very handy in shell scripting, information retrieval, and learning the PostgreSQL internals. The following are some of the `psql` meta commands that are used daily:
    - `\d+ [pattern]`: This describes all the relevant information for a relation. In PostgreSQL, the term relation is used for a table, view, sequence, or index.
    - `\df+ [pattern]`: This describes a function.
    - `\z [pattern]`: This shows the relation access privileges.
    - `\timing`: Displays the execution time.
    - `\h`: Gives syntax help on the specified SQL command.
    - `\c`: Connects to a database.

For shell scripting, there are several options and environment variables that make psql very convenient:

- −A: The output isn't aligned; by default, the output is aligned.
- −q: This option forces psql not to write a welcome message or any other informational output.
- −t: This option tells psql to write the tuples only, without any header information.
- −X: This option tells psql to ignore the psql configuration that's stored in the ~/.psqlrc file.
- −o: This option tells psql to output the query result to a certain location.
- −F: This option determines the field separator between columns. It can be used to generate CSV, which is useful in exporting data.
- PGOPTIONS: psql can use PGOPTIONS to add command-line options to send to the server at runtime. This can be used to control statement behavior, such as to allow index scans only or to specify the statement timeout.

Let's imagine we want to write a bash script to check the number of opened connection systems:

```bash
#!/bin/bash
proc_number='PGOPTIONS='--statement_timeout=0'
psql -AqXt -c"SELECT count(*) FROM pg_stat_activity"'
```

The result of the psql −AqXt −c "SELECT count(*) FROM pg_stat_activity" command is assigned to a bash variable. PGOPTIONS='--statement_timeout=100' is used for demonstration only and to show how to change the default execution behavior. statement _timeout is used to time out the query after a certain time in milliseconds; this is often used if the query is blocking and requires a lot of time, as a safety measure, to not block other processes. The −AqXt options, as discussed previously, cause psql to return only the result without any decoration, as follows:

```
psql -AqXt -c "SELECT count(*) FROM pg_stat_activity"
1
```

psql advanced settings

The psql client can be personalized. The .psqlrc file is used to store user preferences for later use. There are several aspects of psql personalization, including the following:

- Look and feel
- Behavior
- Shortcuts

You can change the psql prompt to show the connection string information including the server name, database name, username, and port. The psql variables—PROMPT1, PROMPT2, and PROMPT3—can be used to customize user preferences. PROMPT1 and PROMPT2 are issued when you create a new command and a command that expects more input, respectively. The following example shows some of the prompt options; by default, when you connect to the database, only the name of the database is shown.

The set meta-command is used to assign a psql variable to a value. In this case, it assigns PROMPT1 to (%n@%M:%>;) [%/]%R%#%x >;. The percent sign (%) is used as a placeholder for substitution. The substitutions in the example will be as follows:

```
postgres=# \set PROMPT1 '(%n@%M:%>) [%/]%R%#%x > '
(postgres@[local]:5432) [postgres]=# > BEGIN;
BEGIN
(postgres@[local]:5432) [postgres]=#* > SELECT 1;
 ?column?
----------
        1
(1 row)

(postgres@[local]:5432) [postgres]=#* > SELECT 1/0;
ERROR: division by zero
(postgres@[local]:5432) [postgres]=#! > ROLLBACK;
ROLLBACK
(postgres@[local]:5432) [postgres]=# > SELECT
postgres-# 1;
```

The following list of signs is used in the previous example; their meanings are as follows:

- %M: The full hostname. In the example, [local] is displayed, because we use the Linux socket.
- %>: The PostgreSQL port number.
- %n: The database session username.
- %/: The current database name.

- %R: Normally substituted with =;; if the session is disconnected for a certain reason, it's substituted with (!).
- %#: Used to distinguish superusers from normal users. The hash sign (#) indicates that the user is a superuser. For a normal user, the sign is (>).
- %x: The transaction status. The * sign is used to indicate the transaction block, and the (!) sign to indicate a failed transaction block.

Did you notice how PROMPT2 was issued when the SELECT 1 SQL statement was written over two lines? Finally, pay attention to the * sign, which indicates a transaction block.

In the psql tool, you can create shortcuts that can be used for a common query, such as showing the current database activities using variables assignment set meta-command. Again, the : symbol is used for substitution. The following example shows how you can add a shortcut for a query:

```
postgres=# \set activity 'SELECT pid, query, backend_type, state FROM
pg_stat_activity';
postgres=# :activity;
  pid  | query                                                                  |
backend_type          | state
-------+----------------------------------------------------------------------+---
------------------+--------
 3814  |                                                                        |
background worker    |
 3812  |                                                                        |
autovacuum launcher  |
 22827 |SELECT pid, query, backend_type, state FROM pg_stat_activity;           |
client backend        | active
 3810  |                                                                        |
background writer    |
 3809  |                                                                        |
checkpointer          |
 3811  |                                                                        |
WALwriter             |
(6 rows)
```

In `psql`, you can configure the transaction's execution behavior. `psql` provides three variables, ON_ERROR_ROLLBACK, ON_ERROR_STOP, and AUTOCOMMIT:

- ON_ERROR_STOP: By default, `psql` continues executing commands even after it encounters an error. This is useful for some operations, such as dumping and restoring the whole database, where some errors can be ignored, such as missing extensions. However, in developing applications, such as deploying new application, errors can't be ignored, and it's good to set this variable to ON. This variable is useful with the -f, \i, and \ir options, which are used to specify the file for the `psql` client, include a file from the `psql` client, and include the file from relative path in the `psql` client, respectively:

```
$ echo -e 'SELECT 1/0;\nSELECT 1;'>/tmp/test_rollback.sql
$ psql
Type "help" for help.

postgres=# \i /tmp/test_rollback.sql
psql:/tmp/test_rollback.sql:1: ERROR: division by zero
 ?column?
----------
 1
(1 row)

postgres=# \set ON_ERROR_STOP true
postgres=# \i /tmp/test_rollback.sql
psql:/tmp/test_rollback.sql:1: ERROR: division by zero
```

- ON_ERROR_ROLLBACK: When an error occurs in a transaction block, one of three actions is performed depending on the value of this variable. When the variable value is off, the whole transaction is rolled back—this is the default behavior. When the variable value is ON, the error is ignored, and the transaction is continued. The interactive mode ignores the errors in the interactive sessions, but not when reading files.
- AUTOCOMMIT: This option causes SQL statements outside an explicit transaction block to be committed implicitly. To reduce human error, you can turn this option off.

Disabling the AUTOCOMMIT setting is quite useful, because it allows the developer to rollback the unwanted changes. Note that when deploying or amending the database on life systems, it's recommended to make the changes within a transaction block and also prepare a rollback script.

Finally, the `timing` meta-command in `psql` shows the query execution time and is often used to quickly assess performance issues. The `pset` meta-command can also be used to control the output formatting.

PostgreSQL utility tools

Several PostgreSQL utility tools are wrappers around SQL constructs. These tools are used to create and drop databases, users, and languages. For example, the `dropdb` and `createdb` commands are wrappers around DROP DATABASE [IF EXISTS] and CREATE DATABASE, respectively.

PostgreSQL also provides tools to maintain the system objects, mainly `clusterdb` and `reindexdb`. `clusterdb` is a wrapper around the CLUSTER statement, which is used to physically reorder the table based on certain index information. This can increase database-performance read operations due to the locality of reference principles, mainly the spatial locality. Clustering the table helps to retrieve data from adjacent storage blocks and thus reduces the hard-disk-access cost.

The CLUSTER command is a blocking command, which means that querying the table will be blocked until the clustering is done. In production systems, blocking commands, such as CLUSTER, should be used wisely.

`reindexdb` is a wrapper around reindex SQL statement. There are several reasons to reindex an index, for example, the index might get corrupted—which rarely happens in practice—or bloated. Index bloat happens when the index size grows due to sparse deletion. Index bloat affects performance since index scans take more time due to reading more disk blocks than needed.

In addition to the previous tools, PostgreSQL also provides tools for the following:

- **Physical backup**: This is used to back up PostgreSQL's database files. This method is a very fast way to create a backup, but the backup can only be restored on compatible PostgreSQL versions. The `pg_basebackup` tool is used for this purpose. `pg_basebackup` is often used to set up streaming replication as the standby is a clone of a master.

- **Logical backup**: This is used to back up the database objects in the form of SQL statements, such as CREATE TABLE, CREATE VIEW, and COPY. The generated backup can be restored on different PostgreSQL cluster versions, but it's slow. The pg_dump and pg_dumpall tools are used to dump a single database or a database cluster, respectively. pg_dump also can be used to dump a specific relation or a set of relations and schemas. Also, it has a lot of features, such as dumping schemas only or data only. pg_dumpall internally uses pg_dump to dump all databases on the cluster. Finally, the pg_restore tool is used to restore the dumps generated by pg_dump or pg_dumpall.

pg_dump doesn't dump the CREATE DATABASE statement command. For example, you can dump a database called customer to another database called client. Due to this, if you have special privileges assigned to the database, such as CONNECT, you need to assign these privileges to the new database.

Summary

PostgreSQL is an open source, object-oriented relational database system. It supports many advanced features and complies with the ANSI-SQL standard. It has won industry recognition and user appreciation. The PostgreSQL slogan, *The world's most advanced open source database*, reflects the sophistication of PostgreSQL's features. It's a result of many years of research and collaboration between academia and industry. Start-up companies often favor PostgreSQL due to licensing costs, and it can aid profitable business models. PostgreSQL is also favored by many developers because of its capabilities and advantages.

PostgreSQL can be used for OLTP and OLAP applications. It is ACID-compliant; thus, it can be used out of the box for OLTP applications. For OLAP applications, PostgreSQL supports the Windows functions, FDW, table inheritance, declarative table partitioning, and parallel query execution. Also, it has many external extensions. Several proprietary DBMSes are based on PostgreSQL. In addition, there are several open source forks that add new features and technologies to PostgreSQL, such as MPP and MapReduce.

PostgreSQL has a very organized active community, including users, developers, companies, and associations. The community contributes to PostgreSQL on a daily basis; many companies have contributed to PostgreSQL by publishing best practices or articles, submitting feature requests to the development group, submitting new features, and developing new tools and software.

The first interaction with PostgreSQL is quick and easy, and you only need a few minutes to install it. PostgreSQL is shipped with many client tools to help user interactions. PostgreSQL is user-friendly; the psql meta-command, \h, \timing, \pset, auto completion, and comprehensive official documentation make it easy for developers to complete their tasks quickly.

In the next chapter, we'll take a look at the PostgreSQL building components. Also, you'll be able to create your first database and use some DDL statements, such as CREATE TABLE and CREATE VIEW. The next chapter will provide some advice regarding coding and coding styles for SQL, and will provide an overview of high-level component interactions.

Questions

1. What's the difference between logical and streaming replication?
2. Why do PostgreSQL security updates often require minimal downtime?
3. What's the name of the main process of the PostgreSQL server?
4. When installing PostgreSQL on Linux, you don't need to provide a password; what's the reason for this?
5. What is Greenplum?
6. What's meant by a physical backup and what utilities does PostgreSQL provide to achieve this?
7. A developer destroyed some data by mistake on a database cluster. Do you think the administrator can recover PostgreSQL to a specific point in time?
8. We briefly mentioned the CLUSTER and REINDEX statements. Use the psql tool's client meta-command to get the syntax for the CLUSTER and INDEX statements.
9. Why is the psql tool very handy in shell scripting?

3
PostgreSQL Basic Building Blocks

In this chapter, we'll build a PostgreSQL database, and explore the basic building blocks of PostgreSQL. The conceptual model of a car web portal, which was presented in Chapter 1, *Relational Databases*, will be translated into a physical model. Also, some data-modeling techniques, such as surrogate keys, will be discussed briefly and some coding best practices will be presented.

We'll also take a look at the hierarchy of the database objects in PostgreSQL. This will help you to understand how to configure the database cluster and tune its settings. More detailed information will be presented to show the usage of template databases, user databases, roles, tablespaces, schemas, configuration settings, and tables. We will cover the following topics in this chapter:

- Database coding
- PostgreSQL object hierarchy
- PostgreSQL database components
- Native PostgreSQL data types
- The car web portal database

Database coding

Software engineering principles should be applied to database coding. This is important to keep the code clean and to speed up development cycles. This section will address several issues, such as naming conventions, documentation, and version control.

If you're familiar with these concepts, feel free to skip this section.

Database naming conventions

A naming convention describes how names are to be formulated. Naming conventions allow some information to be derived based on patterns, which helps developers to easily search for and predict the database's object names. Database naming conventions should be standardized across the organization. There's a lot of debate on how to name database objects. For example, some developers prefer to have prefixes or suffixes to distinguish the database object type from the names. For example, you could suffix a table or a view with `tbl` and `vw`, respectively.

With regard to database object names, you should try to use descriptive names, and avoid acronyms and abbreviations if possible. Also, singular names are preferred, because a table is often mapped to an entity in a high-level programming language; thus, singular names lead to unified naming across the database tier and the business logic tier. Furthermore, specifying the cardinality and participation between tables is straightforward when the table names are singular.

In the database world, compound object names often use underscores, but not camel case, due to the ANSI SQL standard specifications regarding identifier quotation and case-sensitivity. In the ANSI SQL standard, non-quoted identifiers are case-insensitive.

In general, it's up to the developer to come up with a naming convention that suits their needs; in existing projects, don't invent any new naming conventions, unless the new naming conventions are communicated to the team members. In this book, we use the following conventions:

- The names of tables and views are not suffixed
- The database object names are unique across the database or within schemas
- The identifiers are singular, including table, view, and column names.
- Underscores are used for compound names
- The primary key is composed of the table name and the suffix ID
- A foreign key has the same name of the referenced primary key in the linked table
- The internal naming conventions of PostgreSQL are used to rename the primary keys, foreign keys, identity columns, and sequences

Don't use keywords to rename your database objects. The list of SQL keywords can be found at https://www.postgresql.org/docs/current/static/sql-keywords-appendix.html.

PostgreSQL identifiers

The length of PostgreSQL object names is 63 characters; PostgreSQL also follows ANSI SQL regarding case-sensitivity. If you wanted to use camel case or restricted symbols, such as dashes to name database objects, you could achieve that by putting the identifier name in double quotes. PostgreSQL identifier names have the following constraints:

- The identifier name should start with an underscore or a letter. Letters can be Latin or non-Latin.
- The identifier name can be composed of letters, digits, underscore, and the dollar sign. For compatibility reasons, the use of the dollar sign isn't recommended.
- The minimum length of the identifier is typically 1 character, and the maximum length is 63.

In addition to the preceding points, it isn't recommended to use keywords as table names.

Documentation

Documentation is essential for developers, as well as business owners, to understand the full picture. Documentation for the database schema, objects, and code should be maintained. ER and class diagrams are very useful in understanding the full picture. There are tons of programs that support UML and ER diagrams. You can generate ER and UML diagrams by using graph-editing tools, such as yEd, or an online tool, such as draw.io. Also, there are many commercial UML modeling tools that support reverse-engineering code.

Code documentation provides an insight into complex SQL statements. PostgreSQL uses -- and /**/ for single-line and multiline comments, respectively. The single-line comment, --, works on the rest of the line after the comment marker. Therefore, it can be used on the same line as the actual statement. Finally, PostgreSQL allows the developer to store the database object description via the COMMENT ON command.

Version control systems

It's recommended you maintain your code using a revision-control system, such as Git or SVN. When writing SQL code, it's better to create an installation script and execute it in one transaction. This approach makes it easy to clean up if an error occurs. Also, a good practice is to create a rollback script to quickly return schema to the previous state if something goes wrong at the application level.

Database objects have different properties: some are a part of the physical schema, and some control database access. The following is a proposal for organizing the database code in order to increase the **separation of concerns (SoC)**.

For each database in a PostgreSQL cluster, you should maintain the DDL script, for objects that are part of the physical schema, and the DML script, which populates the tables with static data, together. The state of an object, such as a table or index in the physical schema, is defined by the object structure and the data that is contained by this object; thus, the object can't be recreated without being dropped first. Also, the structure of the physical schema object doesn't change often. In addition, the refactoring of some of the physical schema objects, such as tables, might require data migration. In other words, changing the definition of a physical schema object requires some planning.

Store the DDL scripts for objects that aren't part of the physical schema, such as views and functions, separately. Keeping the definitions of views and functions together allows the developer to refactor them easily. Also, the developer will be able to extract the dependency trees between these objects.

Maintain the DCL script separately. This allows the developer to separate the security aspect from the functional requirements of the database. This means that the database developers and administrators can work closely without interfering in each other's work.

Database-migration tools

You can integrate a database-migration tool, such as Liquibase, Sqitch, or Flyway (`https://flywaydb.org/`), with Git. This gives the developer the ability to perform continuous integration. In addition, it gives the administrators a great overview of the database's activities. It's a good practice to deploy manual DML scripts using Flyway, as this increases visibility.

PostgreSQL object hierarchy

Understanding the organization of the PostgreSQL database's logical objects helps with the understanding of object relations and interactions. PostgreSQL databases, roles, tablespaces, settings, and template languages have the same level of hierarchy, as shown in the following diagram:

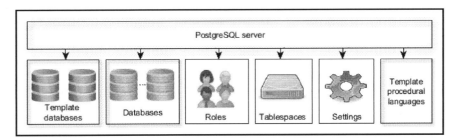

All objects in the hierarchy are explained in detail in the following section.

Template databases

By default, when a database is created, it's cloned from a template database called `template1`. The template database contains a set of tables, views, and functions that are used to model the relation between the user-defined database objects. These tables, views, and functions are part of the system catalog schema, called `pg_catalog`.

 The schema is very close to the namespace concept in object-oriented languages. It's often used to organize database objects, functionality, security access, or to eliminate name collision.

The PostgreSQL server has two template databases:

- `template1`: The default database to be cloned. It can be modified to allow global modification to all the newly-created databases. For example, if someone intends to use a certain extension in all the databases, they can install this extension in the `template1` database. Installing an extension in `template1` won't be cascaded to the already existing databases, but it will affect the databases that will be created after this installation.

- `template0`: A safeguard or version database that has several purposes:
  - If `template1` is corrupted by a user, this can be used to fix `template1`.
  - It's handy in restoring a database dump. When a developer dumps a database, all the extensions are also dumped. If the extension is already installed in `template1`, this will lead to a collision, because the newly-created database already contains the extensions. Unlike `template1`, `template0` doesn't contain encoding-specific or locale-specific data.

> You can create a database using a user database as a template. This is very handy for testing, database refactoring purposes, deployment plans, and so on.

User databases

You can have as many databases as you want in a database cluster. A client that connects to the PostgreSQL server can access only the data in a single database, which is specified in the connection string. That means data isn't shared between the databases unless the PostgreSQL foreign data wrapper or DB link extensions are used.

> It's recommended to use PostgreSQL foreign data wrapper to do cross-database querying. DB link, if not used carefully, might cause memory exhaustion issues.

Every database in the database cluster has an owner and a set of associated permissions to control the actions allowed for a particular role. The privileges on PostgreSQL objects, which include databases, views, tables, and sequences, are represented in the `psql` client as follows:

```
<user>=<privileges>/granted by
```

If the user part of the privileges isn't present, this means that the privileges are applied to PostgreSQL's special PUBLIC role.

The `psql` client tool's `\l` meta-command is used to list all the databases in the database cluster with the associated attributes:

```
postgres=# \l
                                     List of databases
        Name        |    Owner      | Encoding |  Collate    |   Ctype      |
Access privileges
--------------------+---------------+----------+-------------+-------------+-
--------------------------
  car_portal        | car_portal_app | UTF8    | en_US.UTF-8 | en_US.UTF-8 |
  postgres          | postgres       | UTF8    | en_US.UTF-8 | en_US.UTF-8 |
  template0         | postgres       | UTF8    | en_US.UTF-8 | en_US.UTF-8 |
=c/postgres +
                    |               |          |             |             |
postgres=CTc/postgres
  template1         | postgres       | UTF8    | en_US.UTF-8 | en_US.UTF-8 |
=c/postgres +
                    |               |          |             |             |
postgres=CTc/postgres
```

The database-access privileges are the following:

- CREATE (-C): The create access privilege allows the specified role to create new schemas in the database.
- CONNECT (-c): When a role tries to connect to a database, the connect permissions are checked.
- TEMPORARY (-T): The temporary access privilege allows the specified role to create temporary tables. Temporary tables are very similar to tables, but they aren't persistent, and they're destroyed after the user session is terminated.

In the preceding example, the postgres database has no explicit privileges assigned. Also notice that the PUBLIC role is allowed to connect to the template1 database by default.

Encoding allows you to store text in a variety of character sets, including one-byte character sets, such as SQL_ASCII, or multiple-byte characters sets, such as UTF-8. PostgreSQL supports a rich set of character encodings. For the full list of character encodings, visit http://www.postgresql.org/docs/current/static/multibyte.html.

In addition to these attributes, PostgreSQL has several other attributes for various purposes, including the following:

- **Maintenance**: The datfrozenxid attribute is used by autovaccum operations.
- **Storage management**: The dattablespace attribute is used to determine to which tablespace the database belongs.

- **Concurrency**: The `datconnlimit` attribute is used to determine the number of concurrent connections (`-1` means no limits).
- **Protection**: The `datallowconn` attribute disables the connection to a database. This is used mainly to protect `template0` from being altered.

The `psql` client tool's `\c` meta-command establishes a new connection to a database and closes the current one. It also accepts a connection string, such as a username and password.

```
postgres=# \c template0
FATAL: database "template0" is not currently accepting connections
Previous connection kept
```

`pg_catalog` tables are regular tables, thus you can use the SELECT, UPDATE, and DELETE operations to manipulate them. Doing so is not recommended, and needs the utmost attention. Manipulating catalog tables manually can lead to silent errors, database crashes, data integrity corruption, and unexpected behavior.

The catalog tables are very useful for automating some tasks; Chapter 12, *The PostgreSQL Catalog*, is dedicated to `pg_catalog`. The following example shows how you can alter the connection to limit the database property by using the ALTER database command. The following example changes the `datconnlimit` value from `-1` to `1`:

```
postgres=# SELECT datconnlimit FROM pg_database WHERE datname='postgres';
 datconnlimit
--------------
           -1
(1 row)

postgres=# ALTER DATABASE postgres CONNECTION LIMIT 1;
ALTER DATABASE
```

Roles

Roles belong to the PostgreSQL server cluster and not to a certain database. A role can either be a database user or a database group. The role concept subsumes the concepts of users and groups in the old PostgreSQL versions. For compatibility reasons, with PostgreSQL version 8.1 and later, the CREATE USER and CREATE GROUP SQL commands are still supported.

The roles have several attributes, which are as follows:

- SUPERUSER: A superuser role can bypass all permission checks except the LOGIN attribute.
- LOGIN: A role with the LOGIN attribute can be used by a client to connect to a database.
- CREATEDB: A role with the create database attribute can create databases.
- CREATEROLE: A role with this feature enabled can create, delete, and alter other roles.
- REPLICATION: A role with this attribute can be used to stream replication.
- PASSWORD: The PASSWORD role can be used with the md5 and scram-sha-256 authentication method. The password expiration can be controlled by specifying the validity period. Note that this password differs from the OS password. In newer versions of PostgreSQL server—mainly 10 and 11—it's recommended to use scram-sha-256, instead of md5, because it's more secure.
- CONNECTION LIMIT: This specifies the number of concurrent connections that the user can initiate. Connection creation consumes hardware resources; thus, it's recommended to use connection pooling tools such as **Pgpool-II**, **Yandex Odyssey**, **PgBouncer**, or some APIs, such as **Apache DBCP** or **c3p0**.
- INHERIT: If specified, the role will inherit the privileges assigned to the roles that it's a member of. If not specified, INHERIT is the default.
- BYPASSRLS: If specified, this role can bypass **row-level security (RLS)**.

During the installation of PostgreSQL, the postgres superuser role is created. CREATE USER is equivalent to CREATEROLE with the LOGIN option, and CREATE GROUP is equivalent to CREATEROLE with the NOLOGIN option.

A role can be a member of another role to simplify accessing and managing database permissions; for example, you can create a role with no login, also known as a group, and grant it permission to access the database objects. If a new role needs to access the same database objects with the same permissions as the group, the new role could be assigned a membership to this group. This is achieved by the GRANT and REVOKE SQL commands, which are discussed in detail in Chapter 11, *PostgreSQL Security*.

The roles of a cluster don't necessarily have privileges to access every database in the cluster.

Tablespaces

A **tablespace** is a defined storage location for a database or database objects. Tablespaces are used by administrators to achieve the following:

- **Maintenance**: If the hard disk partition runs out of space where the database cluster is created and can't be extended, a tablespace on another partition can be created to solve this problem by moving the data to another location.
- **Optimization**: Heavily-accessed data could be stored in fast media, such as a **solid-state drive (SSD)**. At the same time, tables that are not performance-critical could be stored on a slow disk.

The SQL statement to create a tablespace is `CREATE TABLESPACE`.

Template procedural languages

Template procedural languages are used to register a new language in a convenient way. There are two ways to create a programming language; the first is by specifying only the name of the programming language. In this method, PostgreSQL consults the programming language template and determines the parameters. The second way is to specify the name as well as the parameters. The SQL command to create a language is `CREATE LANGUAGE`.

In PostgreSQL versions 9.1 and later, `CREATE EXTENSION` can be used to install a programming language. The template procedural languages are maintained in the `pg_pltemplate` catalog table. This table might be decommissioned in favor of keeping the procedural language information in their installation scripts.

Settings

The PostgreSQL settings control different aspects of the PostgreSQL server, including replication, write-ahead logs, resource consumption, query planning, logging, authentication, statistic collection, garbage collection, client connections, lock management, error handling, and debug options.

The following SQL command shows the number of PostgreSQL settings. Note that this number might differ slightly between different installations as well as customized settings:

```
postgres=# SELECT count(*) FROM pg_settings;
 count
-------
   289
(1 row)
```

Executing the preceding query on different machines can give different results.

The parameters can be as follows:

- **Boolean**: 0, 1, true, false, on, off, or any case-insensitive form of the previous values. The ENABLE_SEQSCAN setting falls into this category.
- **Integer**: An integer might specify a memory or time value; there is an implicit unit for each setting, such as seconds or minutes. In order to avoid confusion, PostgreSQL allows units to be specified. For example, you could specify 128 MB as a shared_buffers setting value.
- **Enum**: These are predefined values, such as ERROR and WARNING.
- **Floating point**: cpu_operator_cost has a floating point domain. cpu_operator_cost is used to optimize the PostgreSQL execution plans.
- **String**: A string might be used to specify the file location on a hard disk, such as the location of the authentication file.

The setting context determines how to change a setting's value and when the change can take effect. The setting contexts are as follows:

- internal: The setting cannot be changed directly. You might need to recompile the server source code or initialize the database cluster to change this. For example, the length of PostgreSQL identifiers is 63 characters.
- postmaster: Changing a setting value requires restarting the server. Values for these settings are typically stored in the PostgreSQL postgresql.conf file.
- sighup: No server restart is required. The setting change can be made by amending the postgresql.conf file, followed by sending a SIGHUP signal to the PostgreSQL server process.
- backend: No server restart is required. They can also be set for a particular session.

- `superuser`: Only a superuser can change this setting. This setting can be set in `postgresql.conf` or via the `SET` command.
- `user`: This is similar to superuser, and is typically used to change the session-local values.

PostgreSQL provides the `SET` and `SHOW` commands to change and inspect the value of a setting parameter, respectively. These commands are used to change the setting parameters in the superuser and user context. Typically, changing the value of a setting parameter in the `postgresql.conf` file makes the effect global.

PostgreSQL's `ALTER SYSTEM` command and `postgresql.conf.auto` provide a convenient way to change the configuration of the whole database cluster without editing the `postgresql.conf` file manually. It uses `postgresql.conf.auto` to overwrite the configuration parameters in `postgresql.conf`, so `postgresql.conf.auto` has a higher priority than `postgresql.conf`. For more information, have a look at the `Chapter 12`, *The PostgreSQL Catalog*.

The settings can also have a local effect, and can be applied to different contexts, such as sessions and tables. For example, let's assume that you would like some clients to be able to perform the read-only operation; this is useful for configuring tools such as Confluence (by Atlassian). In this case, you can achieve that by setting the `default_transaction_read_only` parameter:

```
postgres=# SET default_transaction_read_only to on;
SET
postgres=# CREATE TABLE test_readonly AS SELECT 1;
ERROR: cannot execute CREATE TABLE AS in a read-only transaction
```

In the preceding example, the creation of a table has failed within the opened session; however, if you open a new session and try to execute the `CREATE TABLE` command, it will be executed successfully because the default value of the `default_transaction_read_only` setting is `off`. Setting the `default_transaction_read_only` parameter in the `postgresql.conf` file will have a global effect, as mentioned earlier.

PostgreSQL also provides the `pg_reload_conf()` function, which is equivalent to sending the SIGHUP signal to the PostgreSQL process.

> In general, it's preferable to use `pg_reload_conf()` or reload the configuration settings via the `init` script because it's safer than the SIGHUP kill signal due to human error.

In order to force all new sessions into the read-only mode in a Debian Linux distribution, you can do the following:

1. Edit `postgresql.conf` and alter the value of `default_transaction_read_only`. This can be done in Ubuntu with the following commands:

```
$sudo su postgres
$CONF=/etc/postgresql/11/main/postgresql.conf
$sed -i "s/#default_transaction_read_only =
off/default_transaction_read_only = on/" $CONF
```

2. Reload the configuration by executing the `pg_reload_conf()` function:

```
$psql -U postgres -c "SELECT pg_reload_conf()"
```

You need to plan carefully for changing the settings' parameter values that require server downtime. For non-critical changes, you can change the `postgresql.conf` file in order to make sure that the change will take effect when the server is restarted due to security updates. For urgent changes, you should follow certain processes, such as scheduling downtime and informing the user of this downtime. Developers, in general, are concerned with two settings categories, which are as follows:

- **Client connection defaults**: These settings control the statement behaviors, locale, and formatting
- **Query planning**: These settings control the planner configuration, and give hints to the developer on how to rewrite SQL queries

PostgreSQL high-level object interaction

To sum up, a PostgreSQL server can contain many databases, programming languages, roles, and tablespaces. Each database has an owner and a default tablespace; a role can be granted permission to access or can own several databases. The settings can be used to control the behavior of the PostgreSQL server on several levels, such as the database and the session.

Finally, a database can use several programming languages:

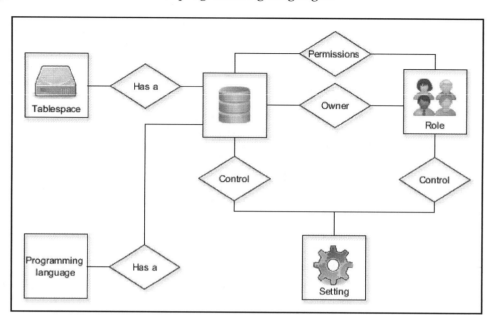

In order to create a database, you need to specify the owner and the encoding of the database; if the encoding of template1 doesn't match the required encoding, template0 should be used explicitly.

For the car-web high-level objects interaction-portal database, let's assume the database owner is the car_portal_role role and the encoding is UTF-8. To create this database on Linux, execute the following commands:

```
CREATE ROLE car_portal_app LOGIN;
CREATE DATABASE car_portal ENCODING 'UTF-8' LC_COLLATE 'en_US.UTF-8'
LC_CTYPE 'en_US.UTF-8' TEMPLATE template0 OWNER car_portal_app;
```

On Windows, the CREATE DATABASE syntax is a bit different due to locale:

```
CREATE DATABASE car_portal ENCODING 'UTF-8' LC_COLLATE 'English_United
States' LC_CTYPE 'English_United States' TEMPLATE template0 OWNER
car_portal_app;
```

PostgreSQL database components

A PostgreSQL database could be considered a container for database schemas; the database must contain at least one schema. A database schema is used to organize the database objects in a manner similar to namespaces in high-level programming languages.

Schemas

Object names can be reused in different schemas without conflict. The schema contains all the database-named objects, including tables, views, functions, aggregates, indexes, sequences, triggers, data types, domains, and ranges:

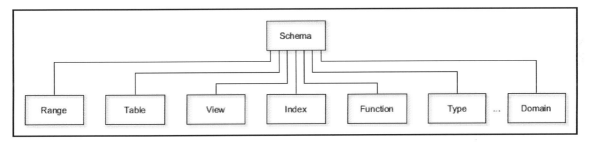

By default, there is a schema called *public* in the template databases. That means all the newly-created databases also contain this schema. All users, by default, can access this schema implicitly. Again, this is inherited from the template databases. Allowing this access pattern simulates a situation where the server is not schema-aware. This is useful in small companies where there's no need to have complex security. Also, this enables a smooth transition from non-schema-aware databases.

In a multi-user and multi-database environment setup, remember to revoke the ability for all users to create objects in the public schema. This is done with the `REVOKE CREATE ON SCHEMA public FROM PUBLIC;` command in the newly-created database, or in the `template1` database.

When a user wants to access a certain object, they need to specify the schema name and the object name separated by a period (.). If the search_path database setting doesn't contain this name, or if the developer likes to use fully-qualified names (for example, to select all the entries in pg_database in the pg_catalog schema), you need to write the following command:

```
SELECT * FROM pg_catalog.pg_database;
--Alternatively you can also use the following command:
TABLE pg_catalog.pg_database;
```

Qualified database-object names are sometimes tedious to write, so most developers prefer to use the unqualified object name, which is composed of the object name without the schema. PostgreSQL provides a search_path setting that's similar to the using directive in the C++ language. search_path is composed of schemas that are used by the server to search for the object. The default search_path, as shown in the following code, is $user, public. If there's a schema with the same name as the user, it will be used first to search for objects or to create new objects. If the object isn't found in the schemas specified in the search_path, an error will be thrown as follows:

```
postgres=# SHOW search_path;
    search_path
-----------------
 "$user", public
(1 row)
```

 Generally speaking, you shouldn't rely on implicit conventions and information such as SELECT *, NATURAL JOIN, or JOIN USING. In this context, it's recommended to use fully-qualified names.

Schema usages

Schemas are used for the following reasons:

- **Control authorization**: In a multi-user database environment, you can use schemas to group objects based on roles.

- **Organize database objects**: You can organize the database objects in groups based on business logic. For example, historical and auditing data could be logically grouped and organized in a specific schema.

- **Maintain third-party SQL code**: The extensions available in the contribution package can be used with several applications. Maintaining these extensions in separate schemas enables the developer to reuse these extensions and to update them easily.

In the car web portal, let's assume that we would like to create a schema named `car_portal_app`, owned by the `car_portal_app` role. This can be done as follows:

```
CREATE SCHEMA car_portal_app AUTHORIZATION car_portal_app;
```

The schema owner is the same as the schema name, if not provided:

```
CREATE SCHEMA AUTHORIZATION car_portal_app;
```

For more information about the syntax of the `CREATE SCHEMA` command, you can use the `psql \h` meta-command, which displays the `psql` client tool's inline help, or take a look at the PostgreSQL manual at `http://www.postgresql.org/docs/current/static/sql-createschema.html`.

Tables

Tables are a core database object. The `CREATE TABLE` statement is very rich. It can be used for several purposes, such as cloning a table, which is handy for database refactoring to create an uninstall script to roll back changes. Also, it can be used to materialize the result of the `SELECT` statement to boost performance, or for temporarily storing the intermediate data and results.

The PostgreSQL tables are used internally to model views and sequences. In PostgreSQL, tables can be of different types:

- **Ordinary table**: The table lifespan starts with table creation and ends with table dropping.
- **Temporary table**: The table lifespan is the user session. This is often used with procedural languages to model business logic.
- **Unlogged table**: Unlogged tables are faster than ordinary tables, because data isn't written into the WAL files. Unlogged tables aren't crash-safe. Also, since streaming replication is based on shipping the WAL files, unlogged tables can't be replicated to the standby node.
- **Child table**: A child table is an ordinary table that inherits one or more tables. The inheritance is often used with constraint exclusion to physically partition the data on the hard disk and to improve performance by retrieving a subset of data that has a certain value.

The CREATE TABLE syntax is quite long; it's full syntax can be found at http://www. postgresql.org/docs/current/static/sql-createtable.html. The CREATE TABLE SQL command normally requires the following input:

- Table name of the created table.
- The table type.
- The table's storage parameters. These parameters are used to control the table's storage allocation and several other administrative tasks.
- The table columns, including the data type, default values, and constraint.
- The cloned table name and the options to clone the table.

To create a table, you can write a query as simple as the following:

```
CREATE TEMP TABLE temp  AS SELECT 1 AS one;
```

The preceding SQL command creates a temporary table with one column and one tuple. The column name and type are 1 and integer, respectively.

PostgreSQL native data types

When designing a database table, you should take care to pick the appropriate data type. When the database goes to production, changing the data type of a column can become a very costly operation, especially for heavily-loaded tables. The cost often comes from locking the table, and in some cases, rewriting it. When picking a data type, consider a balance between the following factors:

- **Extensibility**: Can the maximum length of a type be increased or decreased without a full table rewrite and a full table scan?
- **Data type size**: Going for a safe option, such as choosing big integers instead of integers, will cause more storage consumption.
- **Support**: This factor is important for rich data types, such as XML, JSON, and hstore. If the drivers, such as JDBC drivers, don't support rich types, you need to write your own code to serialize and deserialize the data.

PostgreSQL provides a very extensive set of data types. Some of the native data type categories are as follows:

- Numeric type
- Character type
- Date and time types

These data types are common for most relational databases. Moreover, they are often sufficient for modeling traditional applications.

Numeric types

The following table shows the various numeric types:

Name	Comments	Size	Range
smallint	SQL equivalent: Int2	2 bytes	-32,768 to +32,767.
integer	SQL equivalent: Int4 Integer is an alias for INT.	4 bytes	-2,147,483,648 to +2,147,483,647.
bigint	SQL equivalent: Int8 8 bytes	8 bytes	-9,223,372,036,854,775,808 to +9,223,372,036,854,775,807.
numeric or decimal	No difference in PostgreSQL	Variable	Up to 131,072 digits before the decimal point; up to 16,383 digits after the decimal point.
real	Special values: Infinity, Infinity, NaN	4 bytes	Platform-dependent, at least six-digit precision. Often, the range is 1E-37 to 1E+37.
double precision	Special values: Infinity, Infinity, NaN	8 bytes	Platform dependent, at least 15-digit precision. Often, the range is 1E-307 to 1E+308.

PostgreSQL supports various mathematical operators and functions, such as geometric functions and bitwise operations. The smallint data type can be used to save disk space, while bigint can be used if the integer range isn't sufficient.

Similar to the C language, the result of an integer expression is also an integer. So, the results of the mathematical operations 3/2 and 1/3 are 1 and 0, respectively. Thus, the fractional part is always truncated. Unlike in the C language, PostgreSQL uses the round-half-to-even algorithm when casting a double value to INT:

```
postgres=# SELECT
        CAST(5.9 AS INT) AS "CAST (5.9 AS INT)",
        CAST(5.1 AS INT) AS "CAST(5.1 AS INT)",
        CAST(-23.5 AS INT) AS "CAST(-23.5 AS INT)" ,
        5.5::INT AS "5.5::INT";

  CAST (5.9 AS INT) | CAST(5.1 AS INT) | CAST(-23.5 AS INT) | 5.5::INT
 -------------------+------------------+--------------------+----------
```

```
                      6 | 5                    | -24                    | 6
  (1 row)

postgres=# SELECT 2/3 AS "2/3", 1/3 AS "1/3", 3/2 AS "3/2";
  2/3 | 1/3 | 3/2
 -----+-----+-----
    0 | 0   | 1
  (1 row)
```

The `numeric` and `decimal` types are recommended for storing monetary and other amounts where precision is required. There are three forms of definition for a numeric or decimal value:

- Numeric (precision, scale)
- Numeric (precision)
- Numeric

Precision is the total number of digits, while scale is the number of digits of the fraction part. For example, the number 12.344 has a precision of 5 and a scale of 3. If a `numeric` type is used to define a column type without precision or scale, the column can store any number with any precision and scale.

If precision isn't required, don't use the `numeric` and `decimal` types. Operations on `numeric` types are slower than floats and double precision.

Floating-point and double precision are inexact; this means that the values in some cases can't be represented in the internal binary format, and are stored as approximations. The full documentation about numeric data types can be found at `https://www.postgresql.org/docs/current/static/datatype-numeric.html`.

Serial types, namely `smallserial`, `serial`, and `bigserial`, are wrappers on top of `smallint`, `integer`, and `bigint`, respectively. `serial` types aren't true data types. They're often used as surrogate keys, and by default, they aren't allowed to have a `null` value. The `serial` type utilizes the sequences behind the scene. A sequence is a database object that's used to generate sequences by specifying the minimum, maximum, and increment values. For example, the following code creates a table customer with a `customer_id` column as `serial`:

```
CREATE TABLE customer (
  customer_id SERIAL
);
```

The preceding code create a sequence and a table. It will set the default value of the `customer_id` column to the sequence's `next` function. Finally, it will change the ownership of the sequence to the column. To verify this, let's describe the created objects:

```
postgres=# \d customer
 Table "public.customer"
 Column      | Type    | Collation | Nullable | Default
-------------+---------+-----------+----------+---------------------------
-------------------
 customer_id | integer |           | not null |
nextval('customer_customer_id_seq'::regclass)
postgres=# \d customer_customer_id_seq
 Sequence "public.customer_customer_id_seq"
 Type    | Start | Minimum | Maximum     | Increment | Cycles? | Cache
---------+-------+---------+-------------+-----------+---------+-------
 integer | 1     | 1       | 2147483647  | 1         | no      | 1
Owned by: public.customer.customer_id
```

The preceding code will generate the following code behind the scenes:

```
CREATE SEQUENCE customer_customer_id_seq;
CREATE TABLE customer (
  customer_id integer NOT NULL DEFAULT nextval('customer_customer_id_seq')
);
ALTER SEQUENCE customer_customer_id_seq OWNED BY customer.Customer_id;
```

When creating a column with the serial type, remember the following things:

- A sequence will be created with the name `tableName_columnName_seq`. In the preceding example, the sequence name is `customer_customer_id_seq`.
- The column will have a `NOT NULL` constraint.
- The column will have a default value generated by the `nextval()` function.
- The sequence will be owned by the column, which means that the sequence will be dropped automatically if the column is dropped.

> The preceding example shows how PostgreSQL names an object if the object name isn't specified explicitly. PostgreSQL names objects using the `{tablename}_{columnname(s)}_{suffix}` pattern, where the `pkey`, `key`, `excl`, `idx`, `fkey`, and `check` suffixes stand for a primary key constraint, a unique constraint, an exclusion constraint, an index, a foreign key constraint, and a check constraint, respectively. A common mistake when using the serial type is forgetting to grant proper permissions to the generated sequence.

In PostgreSQL, you can insert a value other than the default value into a column. When using the sequence's `nextval()` function as a default value, you should respect that and use the sequence. This is important if the sequence is used as a default value for a primary column.

Serial types and identity columns

Serial types and identity columns are used to define surrogate keys. The synopsis for defining a column as an identity column is as follows:

```
GENERATED { ALWAYS | BY DEFAULT } AS IDENTITY [ ( sequence_options ) ]
```

It's better to use identity columns, which were introduced in PostgreSQL 10, rather than serial, because this overcomes some of the serial type's limitations:

- **Compatibility**: The identity column adheres to SQL standards, this makes it easier to migrate PostgreSQL to other relational databases and vice versa.
- **Permissions**: The permissions of the sequence object that was created by using the serial column is managed separately. Often, developers tend to forget to assign proper permissions to the sequence object when changing the permissions of the table that contains the defined serial type.
- **Sequence value and user data precedence**: The serial type uses default constrain to assign the value of the column. That means you can override the default values. The identity column can control this behavior. The BY DEFAULT option allows the user to insert data into the column. If ALWAYS is specified, the user value won't be accepted unless the INSERT statement specifies OVERRIDING SYSTEM VALUE. Note that this setting is ignored by the COPY statement.
- **Managing table structure**: It's easier, from a syntactical point view, to manage the identity column. It's also easier to alter existing columns' default values if they're defined as an identity.

Both identity columns and serial types use sequence objects behind the scenes. In most cases, it's straightforward to replace a serial type with an identity column, because both behave similarly.

The following examples shows how to define surrogate keys using an identity column and a serial type. They also show the limitations of the serial type:

- Create a table of the SERIAL type and perform an INSERT operation:

```
postgres=# CREATE TABLE test_serial (id SERIAL PRIMARY KEY, payload
text);
CREATE TABLE
postgres=# INSERT INTO test_serial (payload) SELECT 'a' RETURNING
*;
 id | payload
----+---------
  1 | a
(1 row)
postgres=# INSERT INTO test_serial (id, payload) SELECT 2, 'a'
RETURNING *;
 id | payload
----+---------
  2 | a
(1 row)
postgres=# INSERT INTO test_serial (payload) SELECT 'a' RETURNING
*;
ERROR: duplicate key value violates unique constraint
"test_serial_pkey"
DETAIL: Key (id)=(2) already exists.
```

- Create a table with IDENTITY and perform an INSERT operation:

```
postgres=# CREATE TABLE test_identity ( id INTEGER generated by
default as identity PRIMARY KEY, payload text);
CREATE TABLE
postgres=# INSERT INTO test_identity (payload) SELECT 'a' RETURNING
*;
 id | payload
----+---------
  1 | a
(1 row)
postgres=# INSERT INTO test_identity (id, payload) SELECT 1, 'a'
RETURNING *;
ERROR: duplicate key value violates unique constraint
"test_identity_pkey"
DETAIL: Key (id)=(1) already exists.
postgres=# INSERT INTO test_identity (id, payload) SELECT 100000,
'a' RETURNING *;
   id | payload
--------+---------
 100000 | a
(1 row)
```

- IDENTITY and SERIAL internal implementation depends on sequence:

```
postgres=# \ds
                 List of relations
 Schema |        Name          |   Type    |  Owner
--------+----------------------+-----------+----------
 public | test_identity_id_seq | sequence  | postgres
 public | test_serial_id_seq   | sequence  | postgres
(2 rows)
```

- Create an IDENTITY column with the ALWAYS option:

```
postgres=# CREATE TABLE test_identity2 ( id INTEGER generated
always as identity PRIMARY KEY, payload text);
CREATE TABLE
postgres=# INSERT INTO test_identity2 (id, payload) SELECT 1, 'a'
RETURNING *;
ERROR: cannot insert into column "id"
DETAIL: Column "id" is an identity column defined as GENERATED
ALWAYS.
HINT: Use OVERRIDING SYSTEM VALUE to override.
```

IDENTITY columns are developed to overcome known limitations of the SERIAL type; mainly, permission issues and comparability.

Character types

The following table shows the various character types:

Name	Comments	Trailing spaces	Maximum length
char	Equivalent to char(1), it must be quoted as shown in the name.	Semantically insignificant	1
name	Equivalent to varchar(64). Used by Postgres for object names.	Semantically significant	64
char(n)	Alias: character(n). Fixed-length character where the length is n. Internally called **blank padded character (bpchar)**.	Semantically insignificant	1 to 10485760
varchar(n)	Alias: character varying(n). Variable-length character where the maximum length is n.	Semantically significant	1 to 10485760
text	Variable-length character.	Semantically significant	Unlimited

PostgreSQL provides two general text types—the `char(n)` and `varchar(n)` data types—where n is the number of characters allowed. In the `char` data type, if a value is less than the specified length, trailing spaces are padded at the end of the value. Operations on the `char` data types ignore the trailing spaces. Take a look at the following example:

```
postgres=#SELECT 'a'::CHAR(2) = 'a '::CHAR(2) AS "Trailing space is
ignored" ,length('a'::CHAR(10));
 Trailing space is ignored | length
---------------------------+--------
 t                         | 1
(1 row)
```

It isn't recommended to perform binary operations on `varchar`, `text`, and `char` strings due to trailing spaces.

For both the `char` and `varchar` data types, if the string is longer than the maximum allowed length, an error will be raised in the case of INSERT or UPDATE unless the extra characters are all spaces. In the latter case, the string will be truncated. In the case of casting, extra characters will be truncated automatically without raising an error. The following example shows how mixing different data types might cause problems:

```
postgres=# SELECT
        'a '::VARCHAR(2) = 'a '::TEXT AS "Text and varchar",
        'a '::CHAR(2) = 'a '::TEXT AS "Char and text",
        'a '::CHAR(2) = 'a '::VARCHAR(2) AS "Char and varchar";
 Text and varchar | Char and text | Char and varchar
------------------+---------------+------------------
 t                | f             | t
(1 row)
postgres=# SELECT length ('a '::CHAR(2)), length ('a '::VARCHAR(2));
 length | length
--------+--------
      1 | 2
(1 row)
```

The preceding example shows that `'a '::CHAR(2)` equals `'a '::VARCHAR(2)`, but both have different lengths, which isn't logical. Also, it shows that `'a '::CHAR(2)` isn't equal to `'a '::text`. Finally, `'a '::VARCHAR(2)` equals `'a'::text`. The preceding example causes confusion because if variable a is equal to b, and b is equal to c, a should be equal to c according to mathematics.

The PostgreSQL text-storage size depends on several factors, namely, the length of the text value and the text decoding and compression. The `text` data type can be considered an unlimited `varchar()` type. The maximum text size that can be stored is 1 GB, which is the maximum column size.

For fixed-length strings, the `character` data type and the `character varying` data type consume the same amount of hard disk space. For variable-length strings, the `character varying` data type consumes less space, because the `character` type appends the string with space. The following code shows the storage consumption for fixed- and variable-length texts for the character and `character varying` data types. It simply creates two tables, populates the tables with fictional data using fixed- and variable-length strings, and gets the table size in a human-readable form:

```
CREATE TABLE char_size_test (
 size CHAR(10)
);
CREATE TABLE varchar_size_test(
 size varchar(10)
);
WITH test_data AS (
 SELECT substring(md5(random()::text), 1, 5) FROM generate_series (1,
1000000)
),char_data_insert AS (
 INSERT INTO char_size_test SELECT * FROM test_data
) INSERT INTO varchar_size_test SELECT * FROM test_data;
```

Use this code to get the table size:

```
postgres=# \dt+ varchar_size_test
                        List of relations
   Schema | Name              | Type  | Owner    | Size  | Description
 ---------+-------------------+-------+----------+-------+-------------
   public | varchar_size_test | table | postgres | 35 MB |
 (1 row)

postgres=# \dt+ char_size_test
                        List of relations
   Schema | Name           | Type  | Owner    | Size  | Description
 ---------+----------------+-------+----------+-------+-------------
   public | char_size_test | table | postgres | 42 MB |
 (1 row)
```

The `varchar` data type can be emulated by the `text` data type and a check constraint to check the text length. For example, the following code snippets are semantically equivalent:

```
CREATE TABLE emulate_varchar(
 test VARCHAR(4)
);
--semantically equivalent to
CREATE TABLE emulate_varchar (
 test TEXT,
 CONSTRAINT test_length CHECK (length(test) <= 4)
);
```

In PostgreSQL, there's no difference in performance between the different character types, so it's recommended you use the `text` data type. This allows the developer to react quickly to the changes in business requirements. For example, one common business case is changing the text length, such as changing the length of a customer ticket number from six to eight characters due to length limitation, or changing how certain information is stored in the database. In such a scenario, if the data type is `text`, this could be done by amending the check constraint without altering the table structure. The full documentation of character datatypes can be found at `https://www.postgresql.org/docs/current/static/datatype-character.html`.

Date and time types

The `date` and `time` data types are commonly used to describe the occurrence of events, such as birth dates. PostgreSQL supports the following `date` and `time` types:

Name	Size in bytes	Description	Low value	High value
Timestamp without time zone	8	Date and time without time zone, equivalent to timestamp	4713 BC	294276 AD
Timestamp with time zone	8	Date and time with time zone, equivalent to timestamptz	4713 BC	294276 AD
Date	4	Date only	4713 BC	294276 AD
Time without time zone	8	Time of day	00:00:00	24:00:00
Time with time zone	12	Time of day with time zone	00:00:00+1459	24:00:00-1459
Interval	16	Time interval	-178,000,000 years	+178,000,000 years

PostgreSQL stores the timestamp with and without the time zone in the **Coordinated Universal Time** (UTC) format, and only the time is stored without the time zone. This explains the identical storage size for both the timestamp with the time zone and the timestamp without the time zone.

There are two approaches for handling the timestamp correctly. The first approach is to use the timestamp without the time zone, and let the client side handle the time zone differences. This is useful for in-house development, applications with only one-time zone, and when the clients know the time zone differences.

The other approach is to use the timestamp with the time zone. In PostgreSQL, this is given the `timestamptz` extension. The following are some of the best practices to avoid the common pitfalls when using `timestamptz`:

- Make sure to set the default time zone for all connections. This is done by setting the time zone configuration in the `postgresql.conf` file. Since PostgreSQL stores the timestamp with the time zone in UTC format internally, it's a good practice to set the default connection to UTC as well. Also, UTC helps us to overcome the potential problems due to **Daylight Savings Time (DST)**.
- The time zone should be specified in each `CRUD` operation.
- Don't perform operations on the timestamp without time zone and the timestamp with time zone, this will normally lead to the wrong results due to implicit conversion.
- Don't invent your own conversion; instead, use the database server to convert between the different time zones.
- Investigate the data types of high-level languages to determine which type could be used with PostgreSQL without extra handling.

PostgreSQL has two important settings: `timezone` and `DATESTYLE`. `DATESTYLE` has two purposes:

- **Setting the display format**: `DATESTYLE` specifies the timestamp and `timestamptz` rendering style
- **Interpreting ambiguous data**: `DATESTYLE` specifies how to interpret timestamp and `timestamptz`

The `pg_timezone_names` and `pg_timezone_abbrevs` views provide a list of the time zone names and abbreviations, respectively. They also provide information regarding the time offset from UTC, and whether the time zone observes DST. For example, the following code snippet sets the `timezone` setting to Jerusalem, and then retrieves the local date and time in `Jerusalem`:

```
postgres=# SET timezone TO 'Asia/jerusalem';
SET
postgres=# SELECT now();
              now
-------------------------------
 2018-08-19 19:33:06.806009+03
(1 row)
```

The PostgreSQL `AT TIME ZONE` statement converts the timestamp with or without the `timezone` to a specified time zone; its behavior depends on the converted type. The following example clarifies this construct:

```
postgres=# SHOW timezone;
   TimeZone
----------------
 Asia/Jerusalem
(1 row)

postgres=# \x
Expanded display is on.
postgres=#SELECT
now() AS "Return current timestap in Jerusalem",
now()::timestamp AS "Return current timestap in Jerusalem with out time
zone information",
now() AT TIME ZONE 'CST' AS "Return current time in Central Standard Time
without time zone information",
'2018-08-19:00:00:00'::timestamp AT TIME ZONE 'CST' AS "Convert the time in
CST to Jerusalem time zone";

[ RECORD 1 ]----------------------------------------------------------------
+-------------------------------
Return current timestamp in Jerusalem
| 2018-08-19 20:19:20.126501+03
Return current timestamp in Jerusalem with out time zone information
| 2018-08-19 20:19:20.126501
Return current time in Central Standard Time without time zone information
| 2018-08-19 11:19:20.126501
Convert the time in CST to Jerusalem time zone
| 2018-08-19 09:00:00+03
```

The `now()` function returns the current timestamp with the time zone in the Asia/Jerusalem time zone. Notice that the time zone offset is `+03` because it's summer in Jerusalem. The time zone offset can change due to DST. In winter, the time zone offset in Jerusalem is two hours.

When casting the `timestamp` with the `time zone` to timestamp as in `now()::timestamp`, the time zone offset is truncated. This can be useful for developers who are developing applications in-house in one site.

The `now() AT TIME ZONE 'CST'` expression converts the `timestamp` with the Jerusalem `time zone` to the timestamp in the specified time zone, `CST`. Since the central standard time offset is `-6` from UTC, nine hours are deducted, since Jerusalem is offset three hours from UTC.

The last expression, `'2018-08-19:00:00:00'::timestamp AT TIME ZONE 'CST'`, is reinterpreted as a timestamp as being in that time zone, `CST`, for the purposes of converting it to the connection default time zone, `Asia/jerusalem`.

You can summarize the conversion between the timestamp with and without the time zone as follows:

- The `'y'::TIMESTAMP WITHOUT TIMEZONE AT TIME ZONE 'x'` expression is interpreted as follows: the `y` value of the `TIMESTAMP` type will be converted from the `x` time zone to the session time zone.
- The `'y'::TIMESTAMP WITH TIMEZONE AT TIME ZONE 'x'` expression converts the `'y'` value of the `timestamptz` time to a value of the `TIMESTAMP` type at the specified time zone, `x`.

PostgreSQL is intelligent in handling timestamps with time zones. The following example shows how PostgreSQL handles DST:

```
postgres=# SET timezone TO 'Europe/Berlin';
SET
postgres=# SELECT '2017-03-26 2:00:00'::timestamptz;
      timestamptz
------------------------
 2017-03-26 03:00:00+02
(1 row)
```

The date is recommended when there is no need to specify the time, such as birthdays, holidays, and absence days. Time with time-zone storage is 12 bytes: 8 bytes are used to store the time, and 4 bytes are used to store the time zone. The time without a time zone consumes only 8 bytes. Conversions between time zones can be made using the AT TIME ZONE construct.

Finally, the interval data type is very important in handling timestamp operations, as well as describing some business cases. From the point of view of functional requirements, the interval data type can represent a period of time, such as estimation time for the completion of a certain task.

The result type of the basic arithmetic operations such as + and - on timestamp, timestamptz, time, and time with time zone is of the interval type. The result of the same operations on the date type is an integer. The following example shows timestamptz and date subtraction. Notice the format of the specifying intervals:

```
postgres=#SELECT'2014-10-11'::date -'2014-10-10'::date = 1 AS "date
Subtraction",
'2014-09-01 23:30:00'::timestamptz -'2014-09-01 22:00:00'::timestamptz=
Interval '1 hour, 30 minutes' AS "Time stamp subtraction";

 date Subtraction | Time stamp subtraction
------------------+------------------------
 t                | t
(1 row)
```

The car web portal database

At this stage, you can convert the business model of the car web portal presented in Chapter 1, *Relational Databases*, into a logical model. To help the developer to create a table, follow this minimal checklist:

- What is the primary key?
- What is the default value for each column?
- What is the type of each column?
- What are the constraints on each column or set of columns?
- Are permissions set correctly on tables, sequences, and schemas?
- Are foreign keys specified with the proper actions?
- What is the data life cycle?
- What are the operations allowed on the data?

To create the car web portal schema, the formal relational model won't be applied strictly. Also, surrogate keys will be used instead of natural keys. The advantages of using surrogate keys are as follows:

- Natural keys can change; you can change the current email address to another one. On the one hand, you could argue that if a *natural key* can change, what has been identified is, in fact, *not* an actual natural key. On the other hand, what *is* the natural key to identify a person? Using a surrogate key guarantees that if a row is referenced by another row, this reference isn't lost, because the surrogate key hasn't changed.

- Consider some incorrect assumptions about natural keys. Let's take an email address as an example. The general assumption about an email address is that it identifies a person uniquely. This isn't true; some email service providers set policies, such as email expiration based on activity. Private companies might have general email addresses, such as `contact@...` or `support@....` This is also applicable to phone numbers.

- Surrogate keys can be used to support a temporal database design within the relational database world. For example, some companies have very strict security requirements, and data should be versioned for each operation.

- Surrogate keys often use compact data types such as integers. This enables better performance than composite natural keys.

- Surrogate keys can be used in PostgreSQL to eliminate the effects of cross-column statistic limitation. PostgreSQL collects statistics per single column by default. In some cases, this isn't convenient because columns might be correlated. In this case, PostgreSQL gives a wrong estimation to the planner, and thus, imperfect execution plans are generated. To overcome this limitation, the developer can educate PostgreSQL about cross-column statistics.

- Surrogate keys are better supported than natural keys by object-relational mappers, such as Hibernate.

Despite all the advantages of surrogate keys, they also have a few disadvantages:

- A surrogate key is auto-generated, and the generation of the value might give different results. For example, you insert data in a test database and a staging database, and after comparing the two, you see the data isn't identical.

- A surrogate key isn't descriptive. From a communication point of view, it's easier to refer to a person by a name instead of an auto-generated number.

- Surrogate keys can lead to data redundancy and can generate duplicate tuples if not handled carefully.

In the web car portal ER diagram, there's an entity with the name user. Since `user` is a reserved keyword, the name `account` will be used to create the table. Note that to create a database object using a PostgreSQL keyword, the name should be quoted. The following example shows how to create a `user` table:

```
postgres=# \set VERBOSITY 'verbose'
postgres=# CREATE TABLE user AS SELECT 1;
ERROR: 42601: syntax error at or near "user"
LINE 1: CREATE TABLE user AS SELECT 1;
                     ^
LOCATION: scanner_yyerror, scan.1:1086
postgres=# CREATE TABLE "user" AS SELECT 1;
SELECT 1
```

In the preceding example, the VERBOSITY setting for `psql` can be used to show error codes. Error codes are useful in detecting errors and trapping exceptions.

> `\set` is a psql meta-command that's used to control the `psql` command-line tool's behavior; SET is a PostgreSQL SQL command to change a runtime parameter.

To create an `account` table, execute the following command:

```
CREATE TABLE account (
  account_id INT PRIMARY KEY GENERATED BY DEFAULT AS IDENTITY,
  first_name TEXT NOT NULL,
  last_name TEXT NOT NULL,
  email TEXT NOT NULL UNIQUE,
  password TEXT NOT NULL,
  CHECK(first_name !~ '\s' AND last_name !~ '\s'),
  CHECK (email ~* '^\w+@\w+[.]\w+$'),
  CHECK (char_length(password)>=8)
);
```

The following is a summary of the `user` table:

- `account_id` is defined as the primary key, and identity is used to auto-generate default values. `account_id` is naturally unique and not null.
- The `first_name`, `last_name`, `email`, and `password` attributes aren't allowed to have null values.
- `password` should be at least eight characters in length. In reality, the password length is handled in business logic, since passwords shouldn't be stored in a plain text format in the database. For more information about securing data, have a look at `Chapter 11`, *PostgreSQL Security*.

- email should match a certain regex expression. Note that the email regular expression is really simplistic.

Behind the scenes, the following objects are created:

- A sequence to emulate the identity columns.
- Two indices, both unique. The first one is used to validate the primary key, account_id. The second is used to validate the email address.

To create seller_account, execute the following statement:

```
CREATE TABLE seller_account (
    seller_account_id INT PRIMARY KEY GENERATED BY DEFAULT AS IDENTITY,
    account_id INT NOT NULL REFERENCES account(account_id),
    total_rank FLOAT,
    number_of_advertisement INT,
    street_name TEXT NOT NULL,
    street_number TEXT NOT NULL,
    zip_code TEXT NOT NULL,
    city TEXT NOT NULL
);
```

As we can see, the seller account has a one-to-one relationship with the account. This is enforced by account_id, which consists of NOT NULL and UNIQUE constraints. Also, in this case, you can model the seller account as follows, by marking account_id as the PRIMARY KEY:

```
CREATE TABLE seller_account (
    account_id INT PRIMARY KEY REFERENCES account(account_id)
    ...
);
```

The first design is more flexible and less ambiguous. First of all, the requirements might change, and the user account and the seller account relation might change from one-to-one to one-to-many. For example, the user concept might be generalized to handle companies where the company has several seller accounts.

To model the car table, we need to create a car model. This is quite important because it will help the application user, mainly the seller, to pick up a model instead of entering the model information. In addition to that, the seller might not have all the information about the car model. Finally, allowing the seller to enter the model information might lead to data inconsistency due to human error. In real applications, lookup information, such as currency, countries, and car models, can be downloaded from certain providers. For example, country information is provided by ISO: https://www.iso.org/iso-3166-country-codes.html.

To model a one-to-many relationship, let's have a look at the relation between the advertisement and seller account. The seller can put several advertisements online. Assuming the `car` table already exists, this can be modeled as follows:

```
CREATE TABLE advertisement(
 advertisement_id INT PRIMARY KEY GENERATED BY DEFAULT AS IDENTITY,
 advertisement_date TIMESTAMP WITH TIME ZONE NOT NULL,
 car_id INT NOT NULL REFERENCES car(car_id),
 seller_account_id INT NOT NULL REFERENCES seller_account
(seller_account_id)
);
```

`seller_account_id` has a `NOT NULL` constraint, that means the advertisement has a full-participation relationship with a seller account. It's impossible to create an advertisement without specifying the seller account. Also, the foreign key action option is not specified. The default option, `NO ACTION`, will be applied implicitly. If you try to delete an account, an error will be raised if it's referenced in the advertisement table.

An example of many-to-many relationships is shown by the `favorite_advertisement` table, where the user marks a certain advertisement as a favorite. Also, it can be seen in `advertisement_rating`, where the user rates a certain advertisement.

The `favorite_advertisement` table is modeled as follows:

```
CREATE TABLE favorite_advertisement(
   PRIMARY KEY (account_id,advertisement_id),
   account_id INT NOT NULL REFERENCES account(account_id),
   advertisement_id INT NOT NULL REFERENCES advertisement(advertisement_id)
);
```

The `favorite_advertisement` table associates advertisements and users; the primary key is defined as a composite key of the foreign keys.

The car portal schema shows common patterns, such as one-to-one, one-to-many and many-to-many. In cases of ambiguous business requirements or specifications, you could work around this by using rich datatypes and then iterate and refactor the model after getting more input.

The data modeling explained in this chapter is suitable for **online transaction processing (OLTP)**; data consistency has been handled implicitly. To get a better picture, it's advisable to have a look at database normalization.

Analytical systems and OLAP applications have different data-modeling techniques due to data size and data-access patterns. For more information, have a look at `Chapter 8`, *OLAP and Data Warehousing*.

A database is often the base tier in an application; it's important to take special care of the database model. Bad designs in the data tier affect the business and presentation tiers. Also, the bad design might affect developer productivity because developers can't use technologies such as **object-relational mappers (ORMs)** directly.

Summary

In this chapter, we explored the basic building blocks of PostgreSQL. There are several shared objects across the database cluster. These shared objects are roles, tablespaces, databases, including template databases, template procedural languages, and some setting parameters. The tablespace is a defined storage normally used by the database administrator for optimization or maintenance purposes.

The `template1` database is cloned each time a database is created. It can be loaded with extensions that should be available for all new databases. The `template0` database provides a fallback strategy in case the `template1` database is corrupted. Also, it can be used if the `template1` locale isn't the required locale.

The role has several attributes, such as login, superuser, and createdb. The role is called a user in the older PostgreSQL version if it can log into the database, and a group if it can't. Roles can be granted to other roles; this allows database administrators to manage permissions easily.

PostgreSQL has more than 200 settings that control database behavior. These settings can have different contexts, such as internal, postmaster, backend, user, superuser, and SIGHUP. To take a quick look at these settings, you can use the `pg_settings` view.

The user database is the container for schemas, tables, views, functions, ranges, domain, sequences, and indexes. The database-access permissions can be controlled via the create, temporary, and connect access privileges. Several aspects of database behavior can be controlled by the `ALTER DATABASE` statement. The `pg_database` catalog table describes all the databases in the PostgreSQL cluster.

PostgreSQL provides a rich set of data types, including numeric, text, and date/time data types. Choosing a data type is an important task; thus, you should seek a balance between between extensibility, storage consumption, and performance when choosing a data type. You should be careful when performing operations on a mixture of different data types due to implicit conversion. For example, you should know how the system behaves when comparing the text data type with the `varchar` data type. This also applies to the time and date data types.

Tables are the major building blocks in PostgreSQL; they're used internally to implement views and sequences. A table can be categorized as temporary or permanent. In streaming replication, `unlogged` tables aren't replicated to the slave nodes.

In the next chapter, more building blocks will be explored, such as indexes and views. By the end of the next chapter, you should have the basic knowledge to design and implement the physical data structure of an application.

Questions

1. What's the purpose of the `template1` and `template0` databases?
2. What are the database-access privileges?
3. How can we use tablespace to tune the database server's performance?
4. What's the difference between a user and a group in PostgreSQL?
5. What's the name of the schema that already exists in the template database?
6. Give the usages of arranging database objects in schema.
7. What are the table types in PostgreSQL?
8. The `SHOW` command shows the setting value—how can you get more information about a certain setting, such as context?
9. List the basic data types in PostgreSQL.
10. Is there a performance difference when dealing with the `VARCHAR` and `TEXT` data types?
11. How can you represent `VARCHAR(20)` in another data type in PostgreSQL?
12. Describe the `TIMESTAMP` and `TIMESTAMP WITH ZONE` data types.
13. Which numeric data types should be used when we want to store data accurately?
14. Translate the following ER diagram into a relational schema:

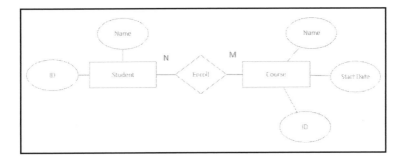

4
PostgreSQL Advanced Building Blocks

This chapter will introduce the remainder of the PostgreSQL building blocks, including views, indexes, functions, triggers, and rules. In addition to that, the web car portal schema will be revised. Several **Data Definition Language (DDL)** commands, such as CREATE and ALTER, will also be introduced. Since the lexical structure and several **Data Manipulation Language (DML)** commands haven't been introduced yet, we will try to use simple DML commands.

In this chapter, the following topics will be covered:

- **Views**: Views are an important part of database modeling because they act as an interface or as an abstraction layer. The *Views* section will cover view synopsis and usages, and an updatable view example will be demonstrated.
- **Indexes**: Indexes are the secret sauce for ensuring consistency and performance. Index types will be discussed.
- **Functions**: Functions can be used to perform very complex logic in the database. Also, they can be used to return scalar values or datasets. Functions will be discussed briefly here, since functions are discussed in detail in Chapter 07, *Server-Side Programming with PL/pgSQL*.
- **User-defined data types**: One big advantage of PostgreSQL is being able to define and use new, different data types; this section will show several use cases, wherein user-defined data types will be used to solve some issues.
- **Triggers and rule systems**: Triggers and rule systems allow developers to handle events triggered by INSERT, UPDATE, DELETE, and so on. The trigger system is used to model complex business requirements that are difficult to achieve using plain SQL.

Views

A **view** can be considered a named query or a wrapper around a SELECT statement. Views are the essential building blocks of relational databases from a UML modeling perspective; a view can be thought of as a method for a UML class. Views share several advantages with functions; the following benefits are shared between views and stored procedures. Views can be used for the following purposes:

- Simplifying complex queries and increasing code modularity
- Tuning performance by caching the view results for later use
- Decreasing the amount of SQL code
- Bridging the gap between relational databases and object-oriented languages, especially updatable views
- Implementing authorization at the row level, by leaving out rows that do not meet a certain predicate
- Implementing interfaces and the abstraction layer between high-level languages and relational databases
- Implementing last-minute changes

A view should meet the current business needs, instead of potential future business needs. It should be designed to provide certain functionality or service. Note that the more attributes there are in a view, the more effort will be required to refactor the view. In addition to that, when a view aggregates data from many tables and is used as an interface, there might be a degradation in performance, due to many factors (for example, bad execution plans due to outdated statistics for some tables, execution plan time generation, and so on).

When implementing complex business logic in a database using views and stored procedures, database refactoring, especially for base tables, might turn out to be very expensive. To solve this issue, consider migrating the business logic to the application business tier.

Some frameworks, such as object-relational mappers, might have specific needs, such as a unique key. This limits the usage of views in these frameworks; however, we can mitigate these issues by faking the primary keys, via window functions such as row_number.

In PostgreSQL, a view is internally modeled as a table with an _RETURN rule. So, in theory, we can create a table and convert it into a view.

However, this is not a recommended practice. The VIEW dependency tree is well maintained; this means that we cannot drop a view or amend its structure if another view depends on it, as follows:

```
postgres=# CREATE VIEW test AS SELECT 1 as v;
CREATE VIEW
postgres=# CREATE VIEW test2 AS SELECT v FROM test;
CREATE VIEW
postgres=# CREATE OR REPLACE VIEW test AS SELECT 1 as val;
ERROR: cannot change name of view column "v" to "val"
```

View synopsis

In the following view synopsis, the CREATE VIEW statement is used to create a view; if the REPLACE keyword is used, the view will be replaced (if it already exists). View attribute names can be given explicitly or they can be inherited from the SELECT statement:

```
CREATE [ OR REPLACE ] [ TEMP | TEMPORARY ] [ RECURSIVE ] VIEW name [ (
column_name [, ...] ) ]
    [ WITH ( view_option_name [= view_option_value] [, ... ] ) ]
    AS query
    [ WITH [ CASCADED | LOCAL ] CHECK OPTION ]
```

The synopses of materialized views differ from view synopsis. Please refer to the *Materialized views* section later in this chapter for the materialized view synopsis.

The following example shows how to create a view that only lists the user information, without the password. This might be useful for implementing data authorization to restrict applications from accessing the password. Note that the view column names are inherited from the SELECT list, as shown by the \d metacommand:

```
car_portal=> CREATE VIEW car_portal_app.account_information AS SELECT
account_id, first_name, last_name, email FROM car_portal_app.account;
CREATE VIEW
car_portal=> \d car_portal_app.account_information
        View "car_portal_app.account_information"
   Column    |  Type   | Collation | Nullable | Default
-------------+---------+-----------+----------+---------
 account_id  | integer |           |          |
 first_name  | text    |           |          |
 last_name   | text    |           |          |
 email       | text    |           |          |
```

The view column names can be assigned explicitly, as shown in the following example. This might be useful when we need to change the view column names:

```
CREATE OR REPLACE VIEW car_portal_app.account_information
(account_id,first_name,last_name,email) AS SELECT account_id, first_name,
last_name, email FROM car_portal_app.account;
```

When replacing the view definition using the REPLACE keyword, the column list should be identical before and after the replacement, including the column type, name, and order. The following example shows what happens when you try to change the view column order:

```
car_portal=> CREATE OR REPLACE VIEW account_information AS SELECT
account_id, last_name, first_name, email FROM car_portal_app.account;
ERROR: cannot change name of view column "first_name" to "last_name"
```

View categories

Views in PostgreSQL can be categorized into one of the following categories on the basis of their uses:

- **Temporary views**: A temporary view is automatically dropped at the end of a user session. If the TEMPORARY or TEMP keywords are not used, then the life cycle of the view starts with the view creation and ends with the action of dropping it.
- **Recursive views**: A recursive view is similar to the recursive functions in high-level languages. The view column list should be specified in recursive views. The recursion in relational databases, such as in recursive views or recursive **Common Table Expressions** (**CTEs**), can be used to write very complex queries, specifically for hierarchical data.
- **Updatable views**: Updatable views allow the user to see the view as a table. This means that the developer can perform INSERT, UPDATE, and DELETE operations on views, similar to tables. Updatable views can help to bridge the gap between an object model and a relational model (to some extent), and they can help to overcome problems such as polymorphism.
- **Materialized views**: A materialized view is a table whose contents are periodically refreshed, based on a certain query. Materialized views are useful for boosting the performance of queries that require a longer execution time and are executed frequently on static data. We could perceive materialized views as a caching technique. Since recursion will be covered in later chapters, we will focus on the updatable and materialized views.

Materialized views

The materialized view synopsis differs a little bit from the normal view synopsis. Materialized views are a PostgreSQL extension, but several databases, such as Oracle, support them. As shown in the following synopsis, a materialized view can be created in a certain TABLESPACE, as well as a storage_parameter, which is logical, since materialized views are physical objects:

```
CREATE MATERIALIZED VIEW [ IF NOT EXISTS ] table_name
    [ (column_name [, ...] ) ]
    [ WITH ( storage_parameter [= value] [, ... ] ) ]
    [ TABLESPACE tablespace_name ]
    AS query
    [ WITH [ NO ] DATA ]
```

At the time of the creation of a materialized view, it can be populated with data or left empty. If it is not populated, retrieving data from the unpopulated materialized view will raise ERROR. The REFRESH MATERIALIZED VIEW statement can be used to populate a materialized view. The synopsis for the REFRESH command is as follows:

```
REFRESH MATERIALIZED VIEW [ CONCURRENTLY ] name   [ WITH [ NO ] DATA ]
```

The following example shows an attempt to retrieve data from an unpopulated materialized view:

```
car_portal=> CREATE MATERIALIZED VIEW test_mat AS SELECT 1 WITH NO DATA;
CREATE MATERIALIZED VIEW
car_portal=> TABLE test_mat;
ERROR: materialized view "test_mat" has not been populated
HINT: Use the REFRESH MATERIALIZED VIEW command.
```

To refresh the view, as the hint suggested, need to refresh the view, as follows:

```
car_portal=> REFRESH MATERIALIZED VIEW test_mat;
REFRESH MATERIALIZED VIEW
car_portal=> TABLE test_mat;
 ?column?
----------
        1
(1 row)
```

 Refreshing materialized view is a blocking statement; this means that concurrent selects will be blocked for a specific time period until the refresh is done. This can be solved by refreshing the materialized view concurrently. To be able to use this option, the materialized view should have a unique index.

Materialized views are often used with **data warehousing**. In data warehousing, several queries are required for business analysis and decision support. The data in these kinds of applications does not usually change, but the calculation and aggregation of that data is often a costly operation. In general, a materialized view can be used for the following:

- Generating summary reports
- Caching the results of recurring queries
- Optimizing performance by processing data only once

Since materialized views are tables, they can also be indexed, leading to a great performance boost.

Updatable views

By default, simple PostgreSQL views are auto-updatable. **Auto-updatable** means that you can use the view with the DELETE, INSERT, and UPDATE statements, in order to manipulate the data of the underlying table. If the view is not updatable (which is not simple) due to the violation of one of the following constraints, the trigger and rule systems can be used to make it updatable. The view is automatically updatable if the following conditions are met:

- The view must be built on top of one table or an updatable view.
- The view definition must not contain the following clauses and set operators at the top level: DISTINCT, WITH, GROUP BY, OFFSET, HAVING, LIMIT, UNION, EXCEPT, and INTERSECT.
- The view's select list must be mapped to the underlying table directly, without using functions and expressions. Moreover, the columns in the select list shouldn't be repeated.
- The security_barrier property must not be set. The preceding conditions promise that the view attributes can be mapped directly to the underlying table attributes.

In the web car portal, let's assume that we have an updatable view that only shows the accounts that are not seller accounts, as follows:

```
CREATE VIEW car_portal_app.user_account AS SELECT account_id, first_name,
last_name, email, password  FROM car_portal_app.account WHERE account_id
NOT IN (SELECT account_id FROM car_portal_app.seller_account);
```

To test the `user_account` view, let's insert a row, as follows:

```
car_portal=> INSERT INTO car_portal_app.user_account VALUES
(default,'first_name1','last_name1','test@email.com','password');
INSERT 0 1
```

In the case of an auto-updatable view, we cannot modify data that isn't returned by the view. For example, let's insert an account with a seller account and then try to delete it, as follows:

```
car_portal=> WITH account_info AS ( INSERT INTO car_portal_app.user_account
VALUES (default,'first_name2','last_name2','test2@email.com','password')
RETURNING account_id)
INSERT INTO  car_portal_app.seller_account (account_id, street_name,
street_number, zip_code, city) SELECT account_id, 'street1', '555', '555',
'test_city' FROM account_info;
INSERT 0 1
```

In the preceding example, notice that the `INSERT` command to the user account was successful. However, even though the account was inserted successfully, we cannot delete it using the updatable view, since the check constraint will be effective, as follows:

```
car_portal=> DELETE FROM car_portal_app.user_account WHERE first_name =
'first_name2';
DELETE 0
car_portal=> SELECT * FROM account where first_name like 'first_name%';
 account_id | first_name  | last_name  | email            | password
------------+-------------+------------+------------------+----------
        482 | first_name1 | last_name1 | test@email.com   | password
        483 | first_name2 | last_name2 | test2@email.com  | password
(2 rows)
```

The `WITH CHECK OPTION` view is used to control the behavior of automatically updatable views. If `WITH CHECK OPTION` is not specified, we can `UPDATE` or `INSERT` a record, even if it is not visible in the view, which might cause a security risk. The following is a simple example to demonstrate this feature.

To demonstrate `WITH CHECK OPTION`, let's create a table, as follows:

```
CREATE TABLE check_option (val INT);
CREATE VIEW test_check_option AS SELECT * FROM check_option WHERE val > 0
WITH CHECK OPTION;
```

To test `WITH CHECK OPTION`, let's insert a row that violates the `check` condition, as follows:

```
car_portal=> INSERT INTO test_check_option VALUES (-1);
ERROR: new row violates check option for view "test_check_option"
DETAIL: Failing row contains (-1).
```

For more information about views, take a look at https://www.postgresql.org/docs/current/static/sql-createview.html. If you are uncertain whether a view is auto-updatable, you can verify this information by using information_schema, checking the value of the is_insertable_into flag, as follows:

```
car_portal=# SELECT table_name, is_insertable_into FROM
information_schema.tables WHERE table_name = 'user_account';
 table_name | is_insertable_into
------------+--------------------
 user_account | YES
(1 row)
```

Views can be used to protect data and provide different representations, by projecting columns and filtering rows. They can be used to tweak performance, in some cases. Also, they are very helpful in refactoring the database without changing the business logic tier. In the next section, we will present indexes, which are also very critical for data integrity and performance.

Indexes

An index is a physical database object that's defined in a table column or a list of columns. In PostgreSQL, there are many types of indexes and several ways to use them. Indexes can be used, in general, to do the following:

- **Optimize performance**: An index allows for the efficient retrieval of a small number of rows from the table. Whether the number of rows is considered small is determined by the total number of rows in the table and the execution planner settings.
- **Validate constraints**: An index can be used to validate the constraints on several rows. For example, the UNIQUE check constraint creates a unique index on the column behind the scenes.

The following example shows how to use GIST to forbid overlapping between date ranges. Checking for date overlapping is very important in reservation systems, such as car and hotel reservation systems. For more information, take a look at https://www.postgresql. org/docs/current/static/rangetypes.html:

```
CREATE TABLE no_date_overlap (
    date_range daterange,
    EXCLUDE USING GIST (date_range WITH &&)
);
```

To test for date range overlapping, let's insert some data, noting the syntax of the date range. The parentheses (or brackets) indicate whether the lower and upper bounds are exclusive or inclusive:

```
INSERT INTO no_date_overlap values('[2010-01-01, 2020-01-01)');
INSERT 0 1
INSERT INTO no_date_overlap values('[2010-01-01, 2017-01-01)');
ERROR: conflicting key value violates exclusion constraint
"no_date_overlap_date_range_excl"
DETAIL: Key (date_range)=([2010-01-01,2017-01-01)) conflicts with existing
key (date_range)=([2010-01-01,2020-01-01)).
```

Index synopses

Indexes can be created using the CREATE INDEX statement. Since an index is a physical database object, you can specify the TABLESPACE and storage_parameter options. An index can be created on columns or expressions. Index entries can be sorted in an ASC or DESC order. Also, you can specify the sort order for NULL values. If an index is created for text fields, you can also specify the collation. The ONLY option, as shown in the following synopsis, is used to handle table inheritance and partitioning. If a table is partitioned, the index will also be created in partitions, by default, when the ONLY option is not specified.

The following is the synopsis for the index:

```
CREATE [ UNIQUE ] INDEX [ CONCURRENTLY ] [ [ IF NOT EXISTS ] name ] ON [
ONLY ] table_name [ USING method ]
    ( { column_name | ( expression ) } [ COLLATE collation ] [ opclass ] [
ASC | DESC ] [ NULLS { FIRST | LAST } ] [, ...] )
    [ INCLUDE ( column_name [, ...] ) ]
    [ WITH ( storage_parameter = value [, ... ] ) ]
    [ TABLESPACE tablespace_name ]
    [ WHERE predicate ]
```

Indexes are created for primary and unique keys automatically.

Index selectivity

Let's take a look at the `account_history` table in the car web portal example, as follows:

```
CREATE TABLE account_history (
  account_history_id BIGINT PRIMARY KEY GENERATED BY DEFAULT AS IDENTITY,
  account_id INT NOT NULL REFERENCES account(account_id),
  search_key TEXT NOT NULL,
  search_date DATE NOT NULL,
  UNIQUE (account_id, search_key, search_date)
);
```

The unique constraint, `UNIQUE (account_id, search_key, search_date)`, has two purposes. The first purpose is to define the validity constraint for inserting the search key into the table only once each day, even if the user searches for the key several times. The second purpose is to retrieve data quickly. Let's assume that we would like to show the last 10 searches for a user. The query for performing this would be as follows:

```
SELECT search_key FROM account_history WHERE account_id = <account> GROUP
BY search_key ORDER BY max(search_date) limit 10;
```

The preceding query returns a maximum of ten records, containing different `search_key` instances, ordered by `search_date`. If we assume that the search `account_history` contains millions of rows, then reading all of the data would take a lot of time. In this case, this is not true, because the unique index will help us to read the data for only this particular customer.

Indexes are not used on tables if the table size is small. The PostgreSQL planner will scan the complete table, instead. To show this, `account_history` was populated with a very small dataset, generated as follows:

```
WITH test_account AS(
    INSERT INTO car_portal_app.account
        VALUES (1000, 'test_first_name',
'test_last_name','test3@email.com', 'password') RETURNING account_id
),car AS (
    SELECT i as car_model FROM (VALUES('brand=BMW'), ('brand=VW')) AS
foo(i)
),manufacturing_date AS (
```

```
        SELECT 'year='|| i as date FROM generate_series (2015, 2014, -1) as
foo(i)
)INSERT INTO car_portal_app.account_history (account_id, search_key,
search_date)
        SELECT account_id, car.car_model||'&'||manufacturing_date.date,
current_date
        FROM test_account, car, manufacturing_date;
VACUUM ANALYZE;
```

To test whether the index is used, let's run the query, as follows:

```
car_portal=> SELECT search_key FROM account_history WHERE account_id = 1000
GROUP BY search_key ORDER BY max(search_date) limit 10;
        search_key
---------------------
 brand=VW&year=2014
 brand=BMW&year=2014
 brand=VW&year=2015
 brand=BMW&year=2015
(4 rows)

car_portal=# EXPLAIN SELECT search_key FROM car_portal_app.account_history
WHERE account_id = 1000 GROUP BY search_key ORDER BY max(search_date) limit
10;
                               QUERY PLAN
-----------------------------------------------------------------------------
-------
 Limit (cost=1.15..1.16 rows=4 width=23)
   -> Sort (cost=1.15..1.16 rows=4 width=23)
         Sort Key: (max(search_date))
        -> HashAggregate (cost=1.07..1.11 rows=4 width=23)
              Group Key: search_key
              -> Seq Scan on account_history (cost=0.00..1.05 rows=4
width=23)
                    Filter: (account_id = 1000)
(7 rows)
```

The index in the preceding example is not used; the PostgreSQL planner decides whether to use an index based on the execution plan cost. For the same query with different parameters, the planner might pick a different plan, based on the data histogram. So, even if we have a big dataset and the predicate used in the query does not filter a lot of data, the index will not be used. To create such a scenario, let's insert some entries for another account and rerun the query, as follows:

```
WITH test_account AS(
   INSERT INTO car_portal_app.account
     VALUES (2000, 'test_first_name', 'test_last_name','test4@email.com',
'password') RETURNING account_id
```

```
),car AS ( SELECT i as car_model FROM (VALUES('brand=BMW'), ('brand=VW'),
('brand=Audi'), ('brand=MB')) AS foo(i)
),manufacturing_date AS (
  SELECT 'year='|| i as date FROM generate_series (2017, 1900, -1) as
foo(i)
) INSERT INTO account_history (account_id, search_key, search_date)
  SELECT account_id, car.car_model||'&'||manufacturing_date.date,
current_date
  FROM test_account, car, manufacturing_date;
```

To check whether the index will be chosen, let's run the query for the second account, which has more data, such as follows:

```
car_portal=# EXPLAIN SELECT search_key FROM account_history WHERE
account_id = 2000 GROUP BY search_key ORDER BY max(search_date) limit 10;
                                 QUERY PLAN
---------------------------------------------------------------------------
----------
 Limit (cost=27.10..27.13 rows=10 width=23)
   -> Sort (cost=27.10..28.27 rows=468 width=23)
         Sort Key: (max(search_date))
         -> HashAggregate (cost=12.31..16.99 rows=468 width=23)
             Group Key: search_key
             -> Seq Scan on account_history (cost=0.00..9.95 rows=472
width=23)
                 Filter: (account_id = 2000)
(7 rows)
```

Again, the index is not used, because we would like to read the whole table. The index selectivity here is very low, since account 2000 has 427 records, whereas account 1000 only has 4 records, as shown in the following snippet:

```
car_portal=> SELECT count(*), account_id FROM
car_portal_app.account_history group by account_id;
 count | account_id
-------+------------
 472   | 2000
 4     | 1000
(2 rows)
```

Finally, let's rerun the query for account 1000. In this case, the selectivity is high; hence, the index will be used:

```
EXPLAIN SELECT search_key FROM car_portal_app.account_history WHERE
account_id = 1000 GROUP BY search_key ORDER BY max(search_date) limit 10;
                                 QUERY PLAN
---------------------------------------------------------------------------
----------------------------------------------------------------------
```

```
Limit (cost=8.71..8.72 rows=4 width=23)
   -> Sort (cost=8.71..8.72 rows=4 width=23)
         Sort Key: (max(search_date))
         -> GroupAggregate (cost=8.60..8.67 rows=4 width=23)
               Group Key: search_key
               -> Sort (cost=8.60..8.61 rows=4 width=23)
                     Sort Key: search_key
                     -> Bitmap Heap Scan on account_history
(cost=4.30..8.56 rows=4 width=23)
                           Recheck Cond: (account_id = 1000)
                           -> Bitmap Index Scan on
account_history_account_id_search_key_search_date_key (cost=0.00..4.30
rows=4 width=0)
                                 Index Cond: (account_id = 1000)
(11 rows)
```

Index types

PostgreSQL supports different indexes; each index can be used for a certain scenario or data type, as follows:

- **B-tree index**: This is the default index in PostgreSQL when the index type is not specified with the CREATE INDEX command. The **B** stands for **balanced**, which means that the data on both sides of the tree is roughly equal. A B-tree can be used for equality, ranges, and null predicates. The B-tree index supports all PostgreSQL data types.

- **Hash index**: Prior to PostgreSQL 10, hash indexes are not well supported. They are not transaction-safe and are not replicated to the slave nodes in streaming replication. With PostgreSQL 10, the hash index limitations have been tackled. It is useful for equality predicates (=).

- **Generalized Inverted Index (GIN)**: The GIN index is useful when several values need to map to one row. It can be used with complex data structures, such as arrays and full-text searches.

- **Generalized Search Tree (GiST)**: The GiST indexes allow for the building of general balanced tree structures. They are useful in indexing geometric data types, as well as full-text searches.

- **Space-Partitioned GiST (SP-GiST)**: These are similar to GIST and support partitioned search trees. Generally speaking, GIST, GIN, and SP-GIST are designed to handle complex user-defined data types.

- **Block Range Index (BRIN)**: This was introduced in PostgreSQL 9.5. The BRIN index is useful for very large tables, where the size is limited. A BRIN index is slower than a B-tree index, but requires less space than the B-tree.

Index categories

We can classify indexes for several categories; not that these categories can be mixed up, which enables us to model very complex logic. For example, we could have a unique partial index, to make sure that only part of the data was unique, based on a certain condition. The index categories are as follows:

- **Partial indexes**: A partial index only indexes a subset of the table data that meets a certain predicate; the WHERE clause is used with the index. The idea behind a partial index is to decrease the index size, making it more maintainable and faster to access.

- **Covering indexes**: These were introduced in PostgreSQL 11. They allow some queries to be executed only using an index-only scan. Currently, this is only supported by B-tree indexes.

- **Unique indexes**: A unique index guarantees the uniqueness of a certain value in a row across the whole table. In the account table, the email column has a unique check constraint. This is implemented by the unique index, as shown by the \d metacommand:

```
car_portal=# \d car_portal_app.account
                       Table "car_portal_app.account"
     Column      |  Type   | Collation | Nullable | Default
-----------------+---------+-----------+----------+-------------------
-----------------
 account_id      | integer |           | not null | generated by
default as identity
 first_name      | text    |           | not null |
 last_name       | text    |           | not null |
 email           | text    |           | not null |
 password        | text    |           | not null |
Indexes:
    "account_pkey" PRIMARY KEY, btree (account_id)
    "account_email_key" UNIQUE CONSTRAINT, btree (email)
```

- **Multicolumn indexes**: These can be used for a certain pattern of query conditions. Suppose that a query has a pattern similar to the following: SELECT * FROM table WHERE $column_1$ = $constant_1$ and $column_2$= $constant_2$ AND ... $column_n$ = $constant_n$;. In this case, an index can be created on $column_1$, $column_2$, ..., and $column_n$, where n is less than or equal to 32.

- **Indexes on expressions**: As we stated earlier, an index can be created on a table column or multiple columns. One can also be created on expressions and function results.

You can also mix different categories together; for example, you can create a unique partial index. This gives the developer greater flexibility to meet business requirements or to optimize for speed. For example, as will be shown in later chapters, you can use indexes to optimize a case-insensitive search, by simply creating an index using the functions lower() or upper(), as follows:

```
car_portal=> CREATE index on car_portal_app.account(lower(first_name));
CREATE INDEX
```

The preceding index will speed up the performance of searching an account by names in a case-insensitive way, as follows:

```
SELECT * FROM car_portal_app.account WHERE lower(first_name) =
lower('foo');
```

 Indexes on expressions will only be chosen if precisely the same functional expression is used in the WHERE clause of the query.

Another use for expression indexes is to filter rows by casting a data type to another data type. For example, the departure time of a flight can be stored as timestamp; however, we often search for a date and not a time.

As we mentioned earlier, you can also use unique and partial indexes together. For example, let's assume that we have a table called employee, where each employee must have a supervisor, except for the company head. We can model this as a self-referencing table, as follows:

```
CREATE TABLE employee (employee_id INT PRIMARY KEY, supervisor_id INT);
ALTER TABLE employee ADD CONSTRAINT supervisor_id_fkey FOREIGN KEY
(supervisor_id) REFERENCES employee(employee_id);
```

To guarantee that only one row is assigned to a supervisor, we can add the following unique index:

```
CREATE UNIQUE INDEX ON employee ((1)) WHERE supervisor_id IS NULL;
```

The unique index on the constant expression, (1), will only allow one row with a null value. With the first insert of a null value, a unique index will be built, using the value 1. A second attempt to add a row with a null value will cause an error, because the value 1 is already indexed:

```
car_portal=> INSERT INTO employee VALUES (1, NULL);
INSERT 0 1
car_portal=> INSERT INTO employee VALUES (2, 1);
INSERT 0 1
car_portal=> INSERT INTO employee VALUES (3, NULL);
ERROR: duplicate key value violates unique constraint "employee_expr_idx"
DETAIL: Key ((1))=(1) already exists.
```

Currently, only B-tree, GIN, GIST, and BRIN support multicolumn indexes. When creating a multicolumn index, the column order is important. Since the multicolumn index size is often big, the planner might prefer to perform a sequential scan, rather than reading the index.

Covering index is a new feature that was introduced in PostgreSQL 11; this feature allows the developer to use index-only scans. You can use multicolumn indexes to achieve index-only scans also, but the size of the index is a bit larger than a covering index. Also, the maintenance of multicolumn indexes is higher than for covering indexes. This feature is very useful in OLAP applications when the developer would like to have access to a certain set of columns using certain search criteria; so, in principle, it is similar to vertical partitioning.

In addition, this feature can be used when multicolumn indexes cannot be used. PostgreSQL supports rich data types, and many of these data types do not have B-tree operators; see the following example:

```
car_portal=# CREATE TABLE bus_station(id INT, name TEXT , location POINT);
CREATE TABLE
car_portal=# CREATE INDEX ON bus_station(name, location);
ERROR: data type point has no default operator class for access method "btree"
HINT: You must specify an operator class for the index or define a default operator class for the data type.
```

If the developer is interested in retrieving the location of the bus station using an index-only scan when searching for bus stations by name, a solution could be as follows:

```
car_portal=# CREATE INDEX ON bus_station(name) INCLUDE (location);
CREATE INDEX
```

To test this feature, let's create an index on `first_name`, which will be used as the search criteria, and include `last_name` in the index, as follows:

```
CREATE INDEX ON car_portal_app.account (first_name) INCLUDE (last_name);
```

The following example shows that an index-only scan is used to get `first_name` and `last_name` of a certain user:

```
car_portal=# EXPLAIN SELECT first_name, last_name FROM
car_portal_app.account where first_name = 'James';
                                        QUERY PLAN
------------------------------------------------------------------------
----------------------------
 Index Only Scan using account_first_name_last_name_idx on account
(cost=0.27..8.29 rows=1 width=13)
    Index Cond: (first_name = 'James'::text)
(2 rows)
```

Best practices for indexes

It is often useful to index columns that are used with predicates and foreign keys. This enables PostgreSQL to use an index scan instead of a sequential scan. The benefits of indexes are not limited to the SELECT statements; DELETE and UPDATE statements can also benefit from them. There are some cases where an index is not used, and this is often due to small table size. In big tables, we should plan the space capacity carefully, since the index size might be very big. Also, note that indexes have a negative impact on INSERT statements, since amending the index comes with a cost.

There are several catalog tables and functions that help to maintain indexes, such as `pg_stat_all_indexes`, which gives statistics about index usage. You can refer to Chapter 12, *The PostgreSQL Catalog*, for more on index maintenance.

When creating an index, make sure that the index does not exist; otherwise, you could end up with duplicate indexes. PostgreSQL does not raise a warning when duplicate indexes are created, as shown in the following example:

```
car_portal=# CREATE index on car_portal_app.account(first_name);
CREATE INDEX
car_portal=# CREATE index on car_portal_app.account(first_name);
CREATE INDEX
```

In rare cases, an index might be bloated; PostgreSQL provides the REINDEX command, which is used to rebuild the index. Note that the REINDEX command is a blocking command. To solve this, you can concurrently create another index, identical to the original index, in order to avoid locks. Creating an index concurrently is often preferred in a live system, but it requires more work than creating a normal index.

Moreover, creating an index concurrently has some caveats; in some cases, the index creation might fail, leading to an invalid index. An invalid index can be dropped or rebuilt by using the DROP and REINDEX statements, respectively. To reindex the index, account_history_account_id_search_key_search_date_key, you can run the following script. Note that this is a blocking statement:

```
car_portal=# REINDEX index
car_portal_app.account_history_account_id_search_key_search_date_key;
REINDEX
```

Alternatively, you can create a concurrent index, which is not blocking, as follows:

```
car_portal=# CREATE UNIQUE INDEX CONCURRENTLY ON
car_portal_app.account_history(account_id, search_key, search_date);
CREATE INDEX
```

Finally, to clean up, you will need to drop the original index. In this particular case, we cannot use the DROP INDEX statement, because the index was created via the unique constraint. To Drop the index, the constraint needs to be dropped, as follows:

```
car_portal=# ALTER TABLE car_portal_app.account_history DROP CONSTRAINT
account_history_account_id_search_key_search_date_key;
ALTER TABLE
```

Finally, the unique constraint can be added, as follows:

```
car_portal=> ALTER TABLE account_history ADD CONSTRAINT
account_history_account_id_search_key_search_date_key UNIQUE USING INDEX
account_history_account_id_search_key_search_date_idx;
NOTICE: ALTER TABLE / ADD CONSTRAINT USING INDEX will rename index
"account_history_account_id_search_key_search_date_idx" to
"account_history_account_id_search_key_search_date_key"
ALTER TABLE
```

Functions

A PostgreSQL **function** is used to provide a distinct service, and it is often composed of a set of declarations, expressions, and statements. PostgreSQL has very rich built-in functions for almost all existing data types. In this chapter, we will focus on user-defined functions. However, more details about the syntax and function parameters will be covered in later chapters.

The PostgreSQL native programming language

PostgreSQL supports out-of-the-box, user-defined functions, written in C, SQL, and PL/pgSQL. There are also three other procedural languages that come with the standard PostgreSQL distribution—PL/Tcl, PL/Python, and PL/Perl. However, you will need to create the languages in order to use them, via the CREATE EXTENSION PostgreSQL command or the createlang utility tool. The simplest way to create a language and make it accessible to all databases is to create it in template1, directly after the PostgreSQL cluster installation. Note that you do not need to perform this step for C, SQL, and PL/pgSQL.

For beginners, the most convenient languages to use are SQL and PL/pgSQL, since they are supported directly. Moreover, they are highly portable, and they do not need special care during the upgrading of the PostgreSQL cluster. Creating functions in C is not as easy as creating them in SQL or PL/pgSQL, but since C is a general programming language, you can use it to create very complex functions, in order to handle complex data types, such as images.

Creating a function in the C language

In the following example, we will create a factorial function in the C language. This can be used as a template for creating more complex functions. You can create a PostgreSQL C function in four steps, as follows:

1. Install the postgresql-server-development library.
2. Define your function in C, create a make file, and compile it as a shared library (.so).

3. Specify the location of the shared library that contains your function. The easiest way to do this is to provide the library's absolute path when creating the function or to copy the function-shared library that's created to the PostgreSQL library directory.

4. Create the function in your database by using the CREATE FUNCTION statement.

To install the PostgreSQL development library, you can use the apt tool, as follows:

```
sudo  apt-get install postgresql-server-dev-11
```

In C language development, the make tools are often used to compile C code. The following is a simple makefile to compile the factorial function. pg_config is used to provide information about the installed version of PostgreSQL:

```
MODULES = fact

PG_CONFIG = pg_config
PGXS = $(shell $(PG_CONFIG) --pgxs)
INCLUDEDIR = $(shell $(PG_CONFIG) --includedir-server)
include $(PGXS)

fact.so: fact.o
        cc -shared -o fact.so fact.o

fact.o: fact.c
        cc -o fact.o -c fact.c $(CFLAGS) -I$(INCLUDEDIR)
```

The source code of the factorial fact for the abbreviated C function is as follows:

```
#include "postgres.h"
#include "fmgr.h"
#ifdef PG_MODULE_MAGIC
PG_MODULE_MAGIC;
#endif
Datum fact(PG_FUNCTION_ARGS);
PG_FUNCTION_INFO_V1(fact);
Datum
fact(PG_FUNCTION_ARGS) {
int32 fact = PG_GETARG_INT32(0);
int32 count = 1, result = 1;
for (count = 1; count <= fact; count++)
    result = result * count;
PG_RETURN_INT32(result);
}
```

The last step is to compile the code, copy the library to the PostgreSQL libraries location, and create the function as `postgres` or a normal user. You can compile the code as follows:

```
$make -f makefile
cc -o fact.o -c fact.c -Wall -Wmissing-prototypes -Wpointer-arith -
Wdeclaration-after-statement -Wendif-labels -Wmissing-format-attribute -
Wformat-security -fno-strict-aliasing -fwrapv -fexcess-precision=standard -
g -g -O2 -fstack-protector-strong -Wformat -Werror=format-security -fPIC -
pie -fno-omit-frame-pointer -fPIC -I/usr/include/postgresql/11/server
cc -shared -o fact.so fact.o
```

Now, you need to copy the file, and this requires `sudo` privileges:

```
$sudo cp fact.so $(pg_config --pkglibdir)/
```

Finally, as a `postgres` user, create the function in the `template` library and test it:

```
$ psql -d template1 -c "CREATE FUNCTION fact(INTEGER) RETURNS INTEGER AS
'fact', 'fact' LANGUAGE C STRICT;"
CREATE FUNCTION
$ psql -d template1 -c "SELECT fact(5);"
 fact
------
  120
(1 row)
```

Writing C functions is quite complicated when compared to SQL and PL/pgSQL functions. They might even cause some complications when upgrading the database if they are not well maintained:

```
CREATE OR REPLACE FUNCTION is_updatable_view (text) RETURNS BOOLEAN AS $$
    SELECT is_insertable_into='YES' FROM information_schema.tables WHERE
table_type = 'VIEW' AND table_name = $1
$$ LANGUAGE SQL;
```

The body of the SQL function can be composed of several SQL statements; the result of the last SQL statement determines the function return type. An SQL PostgreSQL function cannot be used to construct dynamic SQL statements, since the function argument can only be used to substitute data values and not identifiers. The following snippet is not valid in an SQL function:

```
CREATE FUNCTION drop_table (text) RETURNS VOID AS $$
 DROP TABLE $1;
$$ LANGUAGE SQL;
ERROR: syntax error at or near "$1"
LINE 2: DROP TABLE $1;
```

The PL/pgSQL language is full-fledged and is the preferable choice for use on a daily basis. It can contain a variable declaration, conditional and looping constructs, exception trapping, and so on. The following function returns the factorial of an integer:

```
CREATE OR REPLACE FUNCTION fact(fact INT) RETURNS INT AS
$$
DECLARE
    count INT = 1;
    result INT = 1;
BEGIN
    FOR count IN 1..fact LOOP
        result = result* count;
    END LOOP;
    RETURN result;
END;
$$ LANGUAGE plpgsql;
```

Function usage

PostgreSQL can be used in several different scenarios. For example, some developers use functions as an abstract interface with higher programming languages to hide the data model. Additionally, functions have several other uses, as follows:

- Performing complex logic that's difficult to perform with SQL
- Performing actions before or after the execution of an SQL statement, via the trigger system
- Cleaning SQL code by reusing the common code and bundling the SQL code in modules
- Automating common tasks related to a database by utilizing dynamic SQL

Function dependencies

When using PostgreSQL functions, you need to be careful not to end up with dangling functions, since the dependency between functions is not well maintained in the PostgreSQL system catalog. The following example shows how you can end up with a dangling function:

```
CREATE OR REPLACE FUNCTION test_dep (INT) RETURNS INT AS $$
BEGIN
            RETURN $1;
END;
$$
```

```
LANGUAGE plpgsql;
CREATE OR REPLACE FUNCTION test_dep_2(INT) RETURNS INT AS $$
BEGIN
    RETURN test_dep($1);
END;
$$
LANGUAGE plpgsql;
DROP FUNCTION test_dep(int);
```

The `test_dep_2` function is dangling. When this function is invoked, an error will be raised, as follows:

```
SELECT test_dep_2 (5);
ERROR: function test_dep(integer) does not exist
LINE 1: SELECT test_dep($1)
               ^
HINT: No function matches the given name and argument types. You might
need to add explicit type casts.
QUERY: SELECT test_dep($1)
CONTEXT: PL/pgSQL function test_dep_2(integer) line 3 at RETURN
```

PostgreSQL function categories

When you are creating a function, it is marked as volatile by default if the volatility classification is not specified. If the created function is not volatile, it is important to mark it as stable or immutable, because this will help the optimizer to generate the optimal execution plans. PostgreSQL functions can fall into one of the following volatility classifications:

- **Volatile**: A volatile function can return different results for successive calls, even if the function argument didn't change; it can also change the data in the database. The `random()` function is a volatile function.
- **Stable and immutable**: These functions cannot modify the database, and they are guaranteed to return the same results for the same arguments. A `stable` function provides this guarantee within the statement scope, while an `immutable` function provides this guarantee globally, without any scope.

For example, the `random()` function is volatile, since it will give a different result for each call. The `round()` function is immutable, because it will always give the same result for the same argument.

The `now()` function is stable, since it will always give the same result within the statement or transaction, as shown in the following code snippet:

```
car_portal=# BEGIN;
BEGIN
car_portal=# SELECT now();
              now
-------------------------------
 2019-01-24 12:20:47.126353+01
(1 row)

car_portal=# SELECT 'Some time has passed', now();
      ?column? | now
--------------------+-------------------------------
 Some time has passed | 2019-01-24 12:20:47.126353+01
(1 row)

car_portal=#
```

PostgreSQL anonymous functions

PostgreSQL provides the `DO` statement, which can be used to execute anonymous code blocks. The `DO` statement reduces the need to create shell scripts for administration purposes. However, note that all PostgreSQL functions are transactional; so, if you would like to create indexes, for example, shell scripting is a better alternative, or procedures, which are introduced in PostgreSQL 11. For more details, take a look at Chapter 7, *Server-Side Programming with PL/pgSQL*. In the car portal schema, let's assume that we would like to have another user who can only perform `select` statements. You can create a role, as follows:

```
CREATE user select_only;
```

Now, you need to grant `select` permission on each table for the newly created role. This can be done using dynamic SQL, as follows:

```
DO $$
 DECLARE r record;
BEGIN
 FOR r IN SELECT table_schema, table_name FROM information_schema.tables
WHERE table_schema = 'car_portal_app' LOOP
  EXECUTE 'GRANT SELECT ON ' || quote_ident(r.table_schema) || '.'||
quote_ident(r.table_name) || ' TO select_only';
 END LOOP;
END$$;
```

PostgreSQL provides developers with the ability to define custom user data types. There are two ways to implement a user data type, as follows:

- Use PostgreSQL C and C++ APIs to create new types and functions, as shown in the documentation at `https://www.postgresql.org/docs/current/xtypes.html`. This allows developers to create very complex data types.
- Use PostgreSQL SQL statements, such as `CREATE DOMAIN` and `CREATE TYPE`.

In the next section, we will focus on the SQL statements required to create types.

User-defined data types

PostgreSQL provides two methods to implement user-defined data types, via the following commands:

- `CREATE DOMAIN`: The `CREATE DOMAIN` command allows developers to create a user-defined data type with constraints. This helps to make the source code more modular.
- `CREATE TYPE`: The `CREATE TYPE` command is often used to create a composite type, which is useful in procedural languages, and is used as the return data type. Also, we can use the `CREATE TYPE` to create the `ENUM` type, which is useful to decrease the number of joins, specifically for lookup tables.

Often, developers decide not to use user-defined data types and to use flat tables instead, due to a lack of support on the driver side, such as JDBC and ODBC. Nonetheless, in JDBC, the composite data types can be retried as Java objects and parsed manually.

Domain objects, as with other database objects, should have a unique name within the schema scope. The first use case of domains is to use them for common patterns. For example, a text type that does not allow for null values and does not contain spaces is a common pattern. In the web car portal, the `first_name` and `last_name` columns in the account table are not null. They also should not contain spaces, and they can be defined as follows:

```
first_name TEXT NOT NULL,
last_name TEXT NOT NULL,
CHECK(first_name !~ 's' AND last_name !~ '\s'),
```

You can replace the text data type and the constraints by creating a domain and using it to define the `first_name` and `last_name` data types, as follows:

```
CREATE DOMAIN text_without_space_and_null AS TEXT NOT NULL CHECK (value!~
'\s');
```

In order to test `text_without_space_and_null` domain, let's use it in a table definition and execute several `INSERT` statements, as follows:

```
CREATE TABLE test_domain (
test_att text_without_space_and_null
);
```

Finally, let's insert several values into the `test_domain` table:

```
postgres=# INSERT INTO test_domain values ('hello');
INSERT 0 1
postgres=# INSERT INTO test_domain values ('hello world');
ERROR: value for domain text_without_space_and_null violates check
constraint "text_without_space_and_null_check"
postgres=# INSERT INTO test_domain values (null);
ERROR: domain text_without_space_and_null does not allow null values
```

Another good use case for creating domains is to create distinct identifiers across several tables, since some people tend to use numbers instead of names to retrieve information. You can do this by creating a sequence and wrapping it with a domain, as follows:

```
CREATE SEQUENCE global_id_seq;
CREATE DOMAIN global_serial INT DEFAULT NEXTVAL('global_id_seq') NOT NULL;
```

Finally, you can alter the domain by using the `ALTER DOMAIN` command. If a new constraint is added to a domain, it will cause all of the attributes using that domain to be validated against the new constraint. You can control this by suppressing the constraint validation on old values and then cleaning up the tables individually. For example, let's suppose that we would like to have a constraint on the text length of `text_without_space_and_null` domain; this can be done as follows:

```
ALTER DOMAIN text_without_space_and_null ADD CONSTRAINT
text_without_space_and_null_length_chk check (length(value)<=15);
```

The preceding SQL statement will fail due to a data violation if an attribute is using this domain and the attribute value length is more than 15 characters. So, to force the newly created data to adhere to the domain constraints and to leave the old data without validation, you can still create it, as follows:

```
ALTER DOMAIN text_without_space_and_null ADD CONSTRAINT text_without_
space_and_null_length_chk check (length(value)<=15) NOT VALID;
```

After data cleanup, you can also validate the constraint for old data by invoking the ALTER DOMAIN ... VALIDATE CONSTRAINT statement. Finally, the \dD+ psql metacommand can be used to describe the domain.

Composite data types are very useful for creating functions, especially when the return type is a row of several values. For example, let's suppose that we would like to have a function that returns seller_id, seller_name, the number of advertisements, and the total rank for a certain customer account. The first step is to create TYPE, as follows:

```
CREATE TYPE car_portal_app.seller_information AS (seller_id INT,
seller_name TEXT,number_of_advertisements BIGINT, total_rank float);
```

Then, we can use the newly created data TYPE as the return type of the function, as follows:

```
CREATE OR REPLACE FUNCTION car_portal_app.seller_information (account_id
INT ) RETURNS car_portal_app.seller_information AS $$
SELECT seller_account.seller_account_id, first_name || last_name as
seller_name, count(*), sum(rank)::float/count(*)
FROM car_portal_app.account INNER JOIN
  car_portal_app.seller_account ON account.account_id =
seller_account.account_id LEFT JOIN
  car_portal_app.advertisement ON advertisement.seller_account_id =
seller_account.seller_account_id LEFT JOIN
  car_portal_app.advertisement_rating ON advertisement.advertisement_id =
advertisement_rating.advertisement_id
WHERE account.account_id = $1
GROUP BY seller_account.seller_account_id, first_name, last_name
$$
LANGUAGE SQL;
```

CREATE TYPE can also be used to define ENUM; an ENUM type is a special data type that enables an attribute to be assigned one of the predefined constants. The usage of the ENUM data types reduces the number of joins needed to create some queries; hence, it makes SQL code more compact and easier to understand. In the advertisement_rating table, we have a column with the rank name, which is defined as follows:

```
-- This is a part of advertisement_rating table def.
rank INT NOT NULL,
CHECK (rank IN (1,2,3,4,5)),
```

In the preceding example, the given code is not semantically clear. For example, some people might consider 1 to be the highest rank, while others might consider 5 to be the highest rank. To solve this, you can use the lookup table, as follows:

```
CREATE TABLE rank (
    rank_id SERIAL PRIMARY KEY,
    rank_name TEXT NOT NULL
);
INSERT INTO rank VALUES (1, 'poor') , (2, 'fair'), (3, 'good') , (4,'very
good') ,( 5, 'excellent');
```

In the preceding approach, the user can explicitly see the rank table entries. Moreover, the rank table entries can be changed to reflect new business needs (for example, to make the ranking from 1 to 10). Additionally, in this approach, changing the rank table entries will not lock the advertisement_rating table, since the ALTER TABLE command will not be needed to change the check constraint, CHECK (rank IN (1, 2, 3, 4, 5)). The disadvantage of this approach lies in retrieving the information of a certain table that's linked to several lookup tables, since the tables need to be joined together. In our example, you need to join advertisement_rating and the rank table to get the semantics of rank_id. The more lookup tables, the more lengthy the queries are.

Another approach to modeling the rank is to use the ENUM data types, as follows:

```
CREATE TYPE rank AS ENUM ('poor', 'fair', 'good', 'very good','excellent');
```

The psql \dT metacommand is used to describe the ENUM data type. You can also use the enum_range function, as follows:

```
postgres=# SELECT enum_range(null::rank);
  enum_range
-----------------------------------------
 {poor,fair,good,"very good",excellent}
```

The ENUM data type order is determined by the order of the values in ENUM at the time of its creation:

```
postgres=# SELECT unnest(enum_range(null::rank)) order by 1 desc;
 unnest
-----------
 excellent
 very good
 good
 fair
 poor
(5 rows)
```

The ENUM PostgreSQL data types are type-safe, and different ENUM data types cannot be compared with each other. Moreover, ENUM data types can be altered and new values can be added. Note that adding a new value to ENUM might lock user activities, since this operation is blocking.

In the next section, we will discuss triggers and rule systems. These systems are used to implement very complex business logic, by applying actions based on data events.

Trigger and rule systems

PostgreSQL provides triggers and rule systems to automatically perform a certain function when an event, such as INSERT, UPDATE, or DELETE, is performed. Triggers and rules cannot be defined on SELECT statements, except for _RETURN, which is used in the internal implementation of PostgreSQL views.

From a functionality point of view, the trigger system is more generic; it can be used to implement complex actions more easily than rules. However, both trigger and rule systems can be used to implement the same functionalities in several cases. From a performance point of view, rules tend to be faster than triggers, but triggers tend to be simpler and more compatible with other RDBMs, since the rule system is a PostgreSQL extension.

Rule system

Creating a rule will either rewire the default rule or create a new rule for specific action on a specific table or view. In other words, a rule on an `insert` action can change the `insert` action's behavior or create a new action for `insert`. When using the rule system, note that it is based on the C macro system. This means that you can get strange results when it is used with volatile functions, such as `random()`, and sequence functions, such as `nextval()`. The following example shows how tricky the rule system can be. Let's suppose that we would like to audit the table for `car`. For this reason, a new table, called `car_log`, will be created to keep a track of all of the actions on the `car` table, such as `UPDATE`, `DELETE`, and `INSERT`. You can achieve this by using the trigger system, as follows:

```
CREATE TABLE car_portal_app.car_log (LIKE car_portal_app.car);
ALTER TABLE car_portal_app.car_log ADD COLUMN car_log_action varchar (1)
NOT NULL, ADD COLUMN car_log_time TIMESTAMP WITH TIME ZONE NOT NULL;

CREATE RULE car_log AS ON INSERT TO car_portal_app.car DO ALSO
 INSERT INTO car_portal_app.car_log (car_id, car_model_id,
number_of_owners, registration_number, number_of_doors,
manufacture_year, car_log_action, car_log_time)
 VALUES (new.car_id, new.car_model_id, new.number_of_owners,
new.registration_number, new.number_of_doors, new.manufacture_year, 'I',
now());
```

The preceding code creates the `car_log` table, which has a structure similar to the `car` table. The `car_log` table has two additional attributes to log the actions: such as insert (indicated in the example as `I`) and the action time. The preceding code also creates a rule on the `car` table to cascade the insert on the `car` table to the `car_log` table. To test the code, let's insert a record, as follows:

```
INSERT INTO car (car_id, car_model_id, number_of_owners,
registration_number, number_of_doors, manufacture_year) VALUES (100000, 2,
2, 'x', 3, 2017);
```

You can examine the contents of the `car_log` table, as follows:

```
car_portal=# \x
Expanded display is on.
car_portal=# SELECT to_json(car_log) FROM car_portal_app.car_log where
registration_number ='x';
-[ RECORD 1 ]---------------------------------------------------------------
----------------------------------------------------------------------------
------------------------------------------------------------------
to_json |
{"car_id":100000,"number_of_owners":2,"registration_number":"x","manufactur
```

```
e_year":2017,"number_of_doors":3,"car_model_id":2,"mileage":null,"car_log_a
ction":"I","car_log_time":"2019-01-24T13:32:29.462636+01:00"}

car_portal=# SELECT to_json(car) FROM car_portal_app.car where
registration_number ='x';
-[ RECORD 1 ]----------------------------------------------------------
-----------------------------------------------------------------------
to_json |
{"car_id":100000,"number_of_owners":2,"registration_number":"x","manufactur
e_year":2017,"number_of_doors":3,"car_model_id":2,"mileage":null}
```

As the preceding example shows, everything has gone as expected. One record is inserted into the `car_log` table, and that record is identical to the one inserted in the `car` table. However, as mentioned earlier, the rules system is built on macros, which cause some issues. For example, if we use the default value, it will create a problem, as shown in the following code snippet:

```
INSERT INTO car (car_id, car_model_id, number_of_owners,
registration_number, number_of_doors, manufacture_year) VALUES (default, 2,
2, 'y', 3, 2017);
```

Now, we can test the contents of the two tables, as follows:

```
car_portal=> SELECT to_json(car) FROM car where registration_number ='y';
                                                            to_json
-----------------------------------------------------------------------
---------------------------------------------------------------
{"car_id":230,"number_of_owners":2,"registration_number":"y","manufacture_y
ear":2017,"number_of_doors":3,"car_model_id":2,"mileage":null}
(1 row)

car_portal=> SELECT to_json(car_log) FROM car_log where registration_number
='y';
to_json
-----------------------------------------------------------------------
-----------------------------------------------------------------------
--------------------------------------------------------------
{"car_id":231,"number_of_owners":2,"registration_number":"y","manufacture_y
ear":2017,"number_of_doors":3,"car_model_id":2,"mileage":null,"car_log_acti
on":"I","car_log_time":"2017-11-20T20:14:49.820841+01:00"}
(1 row)
```

Note that the records in the `car` table and the `car_log` table are not identical. `car_id` in the `car` table is less than `car_id` in the `car_log` table, by one. We can see that the `DEFAULT` keyword is used to assign `car_id` the default value, which is `nextval('car_car_id_seq'::regclass)`.

When you are creating a rule, you can have a conditional rule (that is, you can rewrite the action if a certain condition is met), as shown in the following rule synopsis. However, you cannot have conditional rules for INSERT, UPDATE, and DELETE on views without having unconditional rules. To solve this problem, you can create an unconditional dummy rule. Having rules on views is one way of implementing updatable views.

Trigger system

PostgreSQL triggers a function when a certain event occurs on a table, view, or foreign table. Triggers are executed when a user tries to modify the data through any of the DML events, including INSERT, UPDATE, DELETE, or TRUNCATE. The trigger synopsis is as follows:

```
CREATE [ CONSTRAINT ] TRIGGER name { BEFORE | AFTER | INSTEAD OF } { event
[ OR ... ] }
    ON table_name
    [ FROM referenced_table_name ]
    [ NOT DEFERRABLE | [ DEFERRABLE ] [ INITIALLY IMMEDIATE | INITIALLY
DEFERRED ] ]
    [ REFERENCING { { OLD | NEW } TABLE [ AS ] transition_relation_name } [
... ] ]
    [ FOR [ EACH ] { ROW | STATEMENT } ]
    [ WHEN ( condition ) ]
    EXECUTE PROCEDURE function_name ( arguments )

where event can be one of:
    INSERT
    UPDATE [ OF column_name [, ... ] ]
    DELETE
    TRUNCATE
```

The trigger time context is one of the following:

- BEFORE: This is only applied to tables and is fired before the constraints are checked and the operation is performed. It is useful for checking data constraints on several tables, when it is not possible to model using referential integrity constraints.
- AFTER: This is also only applied on tables and is fired after the operation is performed. It is useful for cascading changes to other tables. An example use case would be data auditing.
- INSTEAD OF: This is applied on views and is used to make views updatable.

When a trigger is marked for each row, then the trigger function will be executed for each row that has been affected by the CRUD operation. A statement trigger is only executed once per operation. When the WHEN condition is supplied, only the rows that fulfill the condition will be handled by the trigger.

Finally, triggers can be marked as CONSTRAINT, to control when they can be executed; a trigger can be executed after the end of the statement or at the end of the transaction. The constraint trigger must be the AFTER or FOR EACH ROW trigger, and the firing time of the constraint trigger is controlled by the following options:

- DEFERRABLE: This marks the trigger as deferrable, which can be used to cause the trigger firing to be postponed till the end of the transaction.
- INITIALLY DEFERRED: This specifies the time when the trigger is to be executed. This means that the trigger will be executed at the end of the transaction. The trigger should be marked as DEFERRABLE.
- NOT DEFERRABLE: This is the default behavior of the trigger, which will cause the trigger to be fired after each statement in the transaction.
- INITIALLY IMMEDIATE: This specifies the time when the trigger is to be executed. This means that the trigger will be executed after each statement. The trigger should be marked as DEFERRABLE.

> Trigger names define the execution order of the triggers, which have the same firing time context alphabetically.

The firing time options (DEFERRABLE, INITIALLY DEFERRED, NOT DEFERRABLE, and INITIALLY IMMEDIATE) can also be applied to constraint triggers. These options are very useful when PostgreSQL interacts with external systems, such as memcached. For example, let's suppose that we have a trigger on a table, and this table is cached; whenever the table is updated, the cache is also updated. Since the caching system is not transactional, we can postpone the update until the end of the transaction in order to guarantee data consistency.

To explain the trigger system, let's redo the car_log table example using triggers. First of all, notice that the trigger type is the AFTER trigger, since the data should first be checked against the car table constraint before inserting it into the new table. To create a trigger, you need to create a function, as follows:

```
CREATE OR REPLACE FUNCTION car_portal_app.car_log_trg () RETURNS TRIGGER AS
$$
BEGIN
IF TG_OP = 'INSERT' THEN
```

```
        INSERT INTO car_portal_app.car_log SELECT NEW.*, 'I', NOW();
ELSIF TG_OP = 'UPDATE' THEN
        INSERT INTO car_portal_app.car_log SELECT NEW.*, 'U', NOW();
ELSIF TG_OP = 'DELETE' THEN
        INSERT INTO car_portal_app.car_log SELECT OLD.*, 'D', NOW();
END IF;
RETURN NULL; --ignored since this is after trigger
END;
$$
LANGUAGE plpgsql;
```

To create TRIGGER, we need to execute the following statement:

```
CREATE TRIGGER car_log AFTER INSERT OR UPDATE OR DELETE ON
car_portal_app.car FOR EACH ROW EXECUTE PROCEDURE
car_portal_app.car_log_trg ();
```

The trigger function should fulfill the following requirements:

- **Return type**: The TRIGGER function should return the TRIGGER pseudotype.
- **Return value**: The TRIGGER function must return a value. The value is often NULL for AFTER ... EACH ROW and for statement-level triggers, a row with the exact structure of the table that fired the trigger.
- **No arguments**: The TRIGGER function must be declared without an argument, even if you need to pass an argument to it. The passing of an argument is achieved via the TG_ARG variable. When the trigger function is created, several variables, such as TG_ARG and NEW, are created automatically. Other variables that are created are listed in the following table:

Trigger variable	Data type	Description
NEW	RECORD	This holds the row that is inserted or updated. In the case of the statement-level trigger, it is NULL.
OLD	RECORD	This holds the old row that is updated or deleted. In the case of the statement-level trigger, it is NULL.
TG_NAME	NAME	This is the trigger name.
TG_OP	NAME	This is the trigger operation, which can have one of the following values—INSERT, UPDATE, DELETE, or TRUNCATE.
TG_WHEN	NAME	This is the time when the trigger is fired, which can have one of the following values—AFTER or BEFORE.
TG_RELID	OID	This is the relation OID. You can get the relation name by casting it to text, using regclass::text.

Trigger variable	Data type	Description
TG_TABLE_NAME	NAME	This is the trigger table name.
TG_TABLE_SCHEMA	NAME	This is the trigger table schema name.
TG_ARG[]	TEXT array	This is the trigger argument. The indexing starts from zero, and a wrong index returns NULL.
TG_NARG	INTEGER	This is the number of arguments passed to the trigger.

A row-level trigger, which is fired BEFORE the actual operation, returning null values, will cancel the operation. This means that the next trigger will not be fired, and the affected row will not be deleted, updated, or inserted. For a trigger that's fired AFTER the operation or for a statement-level trigger, the return value will be ignored; however, the operation will be aborted if the trigger function raises an exception or an error, due to the relational database's transactional behavior.

In the preceding auditing example, if we change the car table definition (for example, by adding or dropping a column), the trigger function on the car table will fail, leading to the ignoring of the newly inserted or updated row. You can solve this by using exception trapping in the trigger definition.

Triggers with arguments

In the following example, another general auditing technique will be presented, which can be applied to several tables, while some table columns can be excluded from auditing. The new editing techniques use the hstore extension. hstore defines a hash map data type and provides a set of functions and operators to handle this data type. In the new auditing technique, the table rows will be stored as a hash map. The first step is to create the hstore extension and a table where the audited data will be stored, as follows:

```
SET search_path to car_portal_app;
CREATE extension hstore;
CREATE TABLE car_portal_app.log
(
    schema_name text NOT NULL,
    table_name text NOT NULL,
    old_row hstore,
    new_row hstore,
    action TEXT check (action IN ('I','U','D')) NOT NULL,
    created_by text NOT NULL,
    created_on timestamp without time zone NOT NULL
);
```

The second step is to define the TRIGGER function, as follows:

```
CREATE OR REPLACE FUNCTION car_portal_app.log_audit() RETURNS trigger AS $$
DECLARE
    log_row car_portal_app.log;
    excluded_columns text[] = NULL;
BEGIN
    log_row = ROW (TG_TABLE_SCHEMA::text,
TG_TABLE_NAME::text,NULL,NULL,NULL,current_user::TEXT,
current_timestamp);

    IF TG_ARGV[0] IS NOT NULL THEN excluded_columns = TG_ARGV[0]::text[];
END IF;

    IF (TG_OP = 'INSERT') THEN
        log_row.new_row = hstore(NEW.*) - excluded_columns;
        log_row.action ='I';
    ELSIF (TG_OP = 'UPDATE' AND (hstore(OLD.*) - excluded_columns !=
hstore(NEW.*)-excluded_columns)) THEN
        log_row.old_row = hstore(OLD.*) - excluded_columns;
        log_row.new_row = hstore(NEW.* )- excluded_columns;
        log_row.action ='U';
    ELSIF (TG_OP = 'DELETE') THEN
        log_row.old_row = hstore (OLD.*) - excluded_columns;
        log_row.action ='D';
    ELSE
        RETURN NULL; -- update on excluded columns
    END IF;
    INSERT INTO car_portal_app.log SELECT log_row.*;
    RETURN NULL;
END;
$$ LANGUAGE plpgsql;
```

The preceding function defines a variable, log_row, of the log type, and populates this variable with the trigger table name, the trigger table schema, the current user, and the current timestamp, using the row construct. Moreover, the preceding trigger function parses TG_ARGV to determine whether some columns need to be excluded from auditing. Note that the excluded columns are passed as a text array. Finally, the trigger function populates log.action, log.old_row, and log.new_row, based on the TG_OP variable.

To apply the preceding trigger to the car table, assuming that the number_of_doors attribute should be excluded from tracking, we can create the trigger as follows:

```
CREATE TRIGGER car_log_trg AFTER INSERT OR UPDATE OR DELETE ON
car_portal_app.car FOR EACH ROW EXECUTE PROCEDURE
log_audit('{number_of_doors}');
```

The array literal, `{number_of_doors}`, is passed to the `log_audit` function and accessed via the `TG_ARG` variable. Finally, the `hstore(NEW.*) - excluded_columns` expression is used to convert the `NEW` variable into the `hstore` type and then delete the keys specified in the `excluded_columns` array from the converted `hstore` type. The following example shows the trigger behavior for the `insert` statement:

```
car_portal=# INSERT INTO car (car_id, car_model_id, number_of_owners,
registration_number, number_of_doors, manufacture_year) VALUES (default, 2,
2, 'z', 3, 2017);
INSERT 0 1
```

To display the results, let's retrieve the contents of the `log` table in a JSON format, as follows:

```
car_portal=# SELECT jsonb_pretty((to_json(log))::jsonb) FROM
car_portal_app.log WHERE action = 'I' and
new_row->'registration_number'='z';
                 jsonb_pretty
-------------------------------------------------
 {                                              +
     "action": "I",                            +
     "new_row": {                              +
         "car_id": "235",                      +
         "mileage": null,                      +
         "car_model_id": "2",                  +
         "manufacture_year": "2017",           +
         "number_of_owners": "2",              +
         "registration_number": "z"            +
     },                                         +
     "old_row": null,                          +
     "created_by": "postgres",                 +
     "created_on": "2017-11-20T20:42:41.132194",+
     "table_name": "car",                      +
     "schema_name": "car_portal_app"           +
 }
(1 row)
```

Triggers and updatable views

For views that are not automatically updatable, the trigger system can be used to make them updatable. The `seller_account_information` view, which shows the information about the seller account, is not automatically updatable because it has `INNER JOIN`:

```
CREATE OR REPLACE VIEW car_portal_app.seller_account_info AS
    SELECT account.account_id, first_name, last_name, email, password,
```

```
seller_account_id,
    total_rank, number_of_advertisement, street_name, street_number,
zip_code , city
  FROM car_portal_app.account INNER JOIN
    car_portal_app.seller_account ON (account.account_id =
seller_account.account_id);
```

To verify that the preceding view, `seller_account_information`, is not updatable, we can check the information schema, as follows:

```
car_portal=# SELECT is_insertable_into FROM information_schema.tables WHERE
table_name = 'seller_account_info';
 is_insertable_into
--------------------
 NO
(1 row)
```

The following trigger function assumes that `account_id` and `seller_account_id` are always generated using the default values, which are the sequences generated automatically when creating a serial data type. This is often a good approach, and it relieves the developer from checking the table for a unique constraint before inserting new rows; it keeps primary key values without big gaps. Furthermore, the trigger function assumes that primary keys cannot be changed, for the same reason. Changing the primary keys might also cause problems when the default foreign key options, `cascade delete` and `cascade update`, are not used.

Finally, note that the trigger functions return `NEW` for the `INSERT` and `UPDATE` operations, `OLD` for the `DELETE` operation, and `NULL` in the case of an exception. Returning the proper value is important for detecting the number of rows that are affected by the operation. It is also very important to return the proper value. The `RETURNING` keyword, as shown in the following function, is used to assign the value for `NEW.account_id` and `NEW.seller_account_id`. Note that if the IDs are not assigned properly, it might lead to issues and difficult to trace problems for object-relational mappers, such as Hibernate:

```
CREATE OR REPLACE FUNCTION car_portal_app.seller_account_info_update ()
RETURNS TRIGGER AS $$
DECLARE
    acc_id INT;
    seller_acc_id INT;
BEGIN
    IF (TG_OP = 'INSERT') THEN
        WITH inserted_account AS (
            INSERT INTO car_portal_app.account (account_id, first_name,
last_name, password, email) VALUES (DEFAULT, NEW.first_name, NEW.last_name,
NEW.password, NEW.email) RETURNING account_id
```

```
        ), inserted_seller_account AS (
        INSERT INTO car_portal_app.seller_account(seller_account_id,
account_id, total_rank, number_of_advertisement, street_name,
street_number, zip_code, city)
        SELECT
nextval('car_portal_app.seller_account_seller_account_id_seq'::regclass),
account_id, NEW.total_rank, NEW.number_of_advertisement, NEW.street_name,
NEW.street_number, NEW.zip_code, NEW.city FROM inserted_account RETURNING
account_id, seller_account_id)
        SELECT account_id, seller_account_id INTO acc_id, seller_acc_id FROM
inserted_seller_account;
     NEW.account_id = acc_id;
     NEW.seller_account_id = seller_acc_id;
     RETURN NEW;
  ELSIF (TG_OP = 'UPDATE' AND OLD.account_id = NEW.account_id AND
OLD.seller_account_id = NEW.seller_account_id) THEN
     UPDATE car_portal_app.account SET first_name = new.first_name,
last_name = new.last_name, password= new.password, email = new.email WHERE
account_id = new.account_id;
     UPDATE car_portal_app.seller_account SET total_rank = NEW.total_rank,
number_of_advertisement= NEW.number_of_advertisement, street_name=
NEW.street_name, street_number = NEW.street_number, zip_code =
NEW.zip_code, city = NEW.city WHERE seller_account_id =
NEW.seller_account_id;
     RETURN NEW;
  ELSIF (TG_OP = 'DELETE') THEN
     DELETE FROM car_portal_app.seller_account WHERE seller_account_id =
OLD.seller_account_id;
     DELETE FROM car_portal_app.account WHERE account_id = OLD.account_id;
     RETURN OLD;
  ELSE
     RAISE EXCEPTION 'An error occurred for % operation', TG_OP;
     RETURN NULL;
  END IF;
END;
$$ LANGUAGE plpgsql;
```

To make the view updatable, you need to create an INSTEAD OF trigger and define the actions, as follows:

```
CREATE TRIGGER seller_account_info_trg INSTEAD OF INSERT OR UPDATE OR
DELETE ON car_portal_app.seller_account_info FOR EACH ROW EXECUTE PROCEDURE
car_portal_app.seller_account_info_update ();
```

To test `INSERT` on the view, we can run the following code:

```
car_portal=# INSERT INTO car_portal_app.seller_account_info
(first_name,last_name, password, email, total_rank,
number_of_advertisement, street_name, street_number, zip_code, city) VALUES
('test_first_name', 'test_last_name', 'test_password',
'test_email@test.com', NULL, 0, 'test_street_name', 'test_street_number',
'test_zip_code','test_city') RETURNING account_id, seller_account_id;
 account_id | seller_account_id
------------+-------------------
        485 | 148
(1 row)
```

Notice the return value; the primary keys are returned to the user correctly. To test `DELETE` and `UPDATE`, we simply run the following snippet:

```
car_portal=# UPDATE car_portal_app.seller_account_info set email =
'test2@test.com' WHERE seller_account_id=147 RETURNING seller_account_id;
 seller_account_id
-------------------
               147
(1 row)

UPDATE 1
car_portal=# DELETE FROM car_portal_app.seller_account_info WHERE
seller_account_id=147;
DELETE 1
```

Finally, if we try to delete all seller accounts, it will fail due to a referential integrity constraint, as follows:

```
car_portal=# DELETE FROM car_portal_app.seller_account_info;
ERROR: update or delete on table "seller_account" violates foreign key
constraint "advertisement_seller_account_id_fkey" on table "advertisement"
DETAIL: Key (seller_account_id)=(57) is still referenced from table
"advertisement".
CONTEXT: SQL statement "DELETE FROM car_portal_app.seller_account WHERE
seller_account_id = OLD.seller_account_id"
PL/pgSQL function seller_account_info_update() line 21 at SQL statement
car_portal=#
```

Summary

In this chapter, indexes, views, functions, user-defined data types, and rule and trigger systems were discussed. A view is a named query or a wrapper around a SELECT statement. They can be used as a data access layer, provide an abstraction level, and control data privileges and permissions. A view in PostgreSQL can be categorized as temporary, materialized, updatable, or recursive. Simple views in PostgreSQL are automatically updatable. To make complex views updatable, you can use the rule and trigger systems.

Indexes are physical database objects defined in a table column, a set of columns, and expressions. Indexes are often used to optimize performance or to validate data. There are several techniques for building indexes, including B-tree, hash, GIN, GIST, and BRIN. B-tree is the default indexing method. GIN and GIST are useful for indexing complex data types and for full-text searches. There are several types of indexes; each type can be used for a different use case. For example, partial indexes only index a subset of the data that meets a certain predicate. The unique index is often used to validate data, such as the uniqueness of primary keys. Finally, a multicolumn index can be used for specific data retrieval scenarios.

The information about indexes can be retrieved from the pg_catalog statistics and can be used for maintenance purposes. When an index is bloated, we can create a concurrent index, instead of re-indexing it. Note that the creation of concurrent indexes will not lock the database table.

PostgreSQL functions provide distinct services and are used similarly to views. Functions can be written in C, SQL, and PL/pgSQL, without extra extensions. One important use of functions is to assist in maintaining a database. This can be done easily, without using external scripting, such as Bash, by utilizing anonymous functions.

Specifying the function category as stable, volatile, or immutable is very important because it helps the optimizer to generate the optimal execution plan. Unfortunately, the interdependency between functions is not recorded in the database catalog. This means that you should take great care when writing complex logic using functions. User-defined data types can be created using the CREATE DOMAIN and CREATE TYPE commands. Some user-defined data types, such as ENUM, can greatly reduce the number of joins, leading to more understandable and efficient SQL code. PostgreSQL triggers and rules are used to execute an action when a certain event occurs. They can be used in different ways in several scenarios. You should be careful when using rules with volatile functions because they can have some side effects.

In the next chapter, we will introduce the SQL language. You will be able to write your own SQL queries and manipulate data with this expressive language.

Questions

1. Briefly describe the differences between a view, an updatable view, and a materialized view.
2. List the index types supported by PostgreSQL.
3. For range operators, such as > and <, which index type can be used?
4. For the equality operator (=), which index type can be used?
5. Which programming languages can be used to implement user-defined functions in PostgreSQL? Which languages are supported out of the box?
6. What are function volatility classifications?
7. What are the advantages of using trigger systems overrule systems in PostgreSQL?
8. Suppose that a developer would like to write a function to perform sanity checks for data. Which trigger event is suitable for this task?
9. Create a domain for positive integers.
10. How can ENUM be used to reduce the number of joins when writing SQL code?

5
SQL Language

Structured Query Language (SQL) is used to set up the structure of the database, to manipulate the data in a database, and to query the database. This chapter is dedicated to the **Data Manipulation Language (DML)** that is used to create data in a database, change or delete it, and retrieve it from the database.

After reading this chapter, you will understand the concept of SQL and the logic of SQL statements. You will be able to write your own SQL queries and manipulate data using this language. A complete reference for SQL can be found in the official PostgreSQL documentation at `http://www.postgresql.org/docs/current/static/sql.html`.

The topics that we will cover in this chapter are as follows:

- SQL fundamentals
- Lexical structure
- Querying data with `SELECT` statements
- Changing data in a database

The code examples in this chapter are based on the prototype of a car portal database described in the previous chapters. The scripts to create the database and fill it with sample data can be found in the attached media. They are called `schema.sql` and `data.sql`. All of the code examples from this chapter can be found in the `examples.sql` file.

Refer to `Chapter 2`, *PostgreSQL in Action*, for details on how to use the `psql` utility.

SQL fundamentals

SQL is used to manipulate the data in a database and to query the database. It's also used to define and change the structure of the data—in other words, to implement the data model. You already know this from the previous chapters.

In general, SQL has three parts:

- **Data Definition Language (DDL)**
- DML
- **Data Control Language (DCL)**

The first part is used to create and manage the structure of the data, the second part is used to manage the data itself, and the third part controls access to the data. Usually, the data structure is defined only once, and then it's rarely changed. However, data is constantly inserted into the database, changed, or retrieved. For this reason, the DML is used more often than the DDL.

SQL is not an imperative programming language, which makes it different from many other languages. To be more specific, you cannot define a detailed algorithm of how the data should be processed. This might give the impression of a lack of control over the data. When using imperative languages, the developer usually specifies the processing logic on a very detailed level: where to take the data from and how to do it, how to iterate through the array of records, and when and how to process them. If it's necessary to process the data from multiple sources, the developer should implement the relationship between them in the application layer rather than in the database.

SQL, in contrast, is a declarative language. In other words, to get the same result in other languages, the developer must write a whole story. In SQL, the developer writes only one main sentence and leaves details for the database. To develop SQL statements, you just define the format in which they are needed to get the data from the database, specify the tables where the data is stored, and state the rules for processing the data. All of the necessary operations, their exact order, and actual data-processing algorithms are chosen by the database, so the developer doesn't need to care about that.

This black-box behavior should not be treated as something bad. First, the box is not completely black: there are ways to find out how the data is processed by the database engine, and there are ways to control it. Second, the logic of SQL statements is very deterministic. Even if it isn't clear how the database is processing a query on a low level, the logic of the process and the result of the query is entirely determined by the SQL statement.

This determines the size of a statement (the smallest standalone element of execution). In Java, for example, every operation, such as assigning a value to a variable, is logically processed as a separate item of an algorithm. In contrast, the logic of SQL implies that the whole algorithm is executed all at once, as one statement. There is no way to get the state of the data at any intermediate step of the execution of the query. This doesn't limit the complexity of the query though. It's possible to implement a very sophisticated algorithm in a single SQL statement. Usually, it takes less time to implement complex logic in SQL than in any lower-level language. Developers operate with logical relational data structures and don't need to define their own algorithms for data processing on a physical level. This is what makes SQL so powerful.

> PostgreSQL does not define a maximum length for a SQL statement or any part of a statement. They can be very long and complex; they will work as long as the database backend has enough memory to process them.

Another good thing about SQL is that there is a standard for the language, so almost every modern relational database supports SQL. Although different databases might support different features and implement their own dialect of SQL, the basics of the language are the same. PostgreSQL also has its own SQL dialect, and we will point out some differences to the other RDBMSes. By the way, at the beginning of its history, Postgres did not support SQL. Support was added in 1994 and, after a while, the database was renamed PostgreSQL to indicate this fact.

SQL lexical structure

The minimum SQL instruction that can be executed by the database engine is a statement. It can also be called a command or query. For example, each of the following is a statement:

```
SELECT car_id, number_of_doors FROM car_portal_app.car;
DELETE FROM car_portal_app.a;
SELECT now();
```

SQL commands are terminated by a semicolon, ; .

> The end of input also terminates a command, but that depends on the tools being used; for example, `psql` would not execute a command when the user presses *Enter* if there is no semicolon, it would just move to a new line. However, when `psql` executes a SQL script from a file, the last command is always executed, even without a semicolon.

The following elements form the lexical structure of SQL:

- **Keywords**: Determine what exactly is required from the database to be done
- **Identifiers**: Refer to the objects in the database, such as tables, their fields, and functions
- **Constants (or literals)**: Parts of expressions whose values are specified directly in the code
- **Operators**: Determine how the data is processed in expressions
- **Special characters (such as parenthesis, brackets, and commas)**: Have meanings other than simply being an operator
- **Whitespaces**: Separate words from each other
- **Comments**: Used to describe a particular piece of code and are ignored by the database

Keywords are words such as `SELECT` or `UPDATE`. They have special meanings in SQL. For example, the names of statements or parts of statements are keywords. The full list of keywords can be found in the documentation at `http://www.postgresql.org/docs/current/static/sql-keywords-appendix.html`.

Identifiers are the names of database objects. Objects such as tables or views can be referred to by the name of the schema they belong to (see `Chapter 3`, *PostgreSQL Basic Building Blocks*) followed by the dot symbol, `.`, and the name of the object. This is called a **qualified object name**. If the name of the schema is included in the `search_path` setting, or if the object belongs to the current user's schema, then it isn't necessary to use the schema name when referring to the object. In that case, it is called an **unqualified object name**.

SQL is not case-sensitive. Both keywords and identifiers can contain any letters (`a-z`), digits (`0-9`), underscores (`_`), or dollar signs (`$`). However, they cannot start with a digit or a dollar sign. That makes them similar to each other and, without knowing the language, sometimes it's difficult to say whether a word is a keyword or an identifier. Usually, keywords are typed in uppercase.

In identifiers, it's still possible to use symbols other than those mentioned earlier, by double-quoting them. Note that double-quoted identifiers are case-sensitive. It's also possible to create objects with the same names as keywords, but this isn't recommended.

Constants in SQL are also called **literals**. PostgreSQL supports three types of implicitly-typed constants: numbers, strings, and bit strings. To use the constant values of any other data type, implicit or explicit conversion should be performed.

Numeric constants contain digits and, optionally, a decimal point and an exponent sign. These are examples of selecting valid numeric constants:

```
SELECT 1, 1.2, 0.3, .5, 1e15, 12.65e-6;
```

String constants should be quoted. There are two kinds of syntax for string constants in PostgreSQL: single quoted constants, such as in the SQL standard, and PostgreSQL-specific dollar-quoted constants. Putting the letter e before a string constant makes it possible to use C-style backslash-escaped characters, such as \n for a new-line or \t for tabulation. A single quote character (') inside a literal should be doubled ('') or used with an escape string \'. Putting the letter U with an ampersand (&) before the string without any spaces in between allows you to specify Unicode characters by their code after a backslash. Here is an example:

```
car_portal=> SELECT 'a', 'aa''aa', E'aa\naa', $$aa'aa$$, U&'41C418420';
 ?column? | ?column? | ?column? | ?column? | ?column?
----------+----------+----------+----------+----------
 a        | aa'aa    | aa      +| aa'aa    | МИР
          |          | aa       |          |
```

The first is simple: the letter a. The second will have a single quote in the middle. The third has a C-style new-line sequence: \n. The next string is dollar-quoted. The last has Unicode characters (the word means *peace* in Russian).

dollar-quoted string constants always have the same value as it is written in the code. No escape sequences are recognized and any kind of quotes will become part of the string. Dollar-quoted strings can have their names specified between the $ signs, which makes it possible to use one dollar-quoted string inside another, like this:

```
car_portal=> SELECT $str1$SELECT $$dollar-quoted string$$;$str1$;
 ?column?
----------------------------------
 SELECT $$dollar-quoted string$$;
```

Here, the $str1$ sequences are taking the role of quotes, and another $$ inside the literal does not terminate the string. That's why it's very common to use dollar-quoted string to define a function body that is usually given to the PostgreSQL server as a string literal.

Bit strings are preceded by the letter B and can contain only the digits 0 or 1. Alternatively, they can be preceded by the letter X and contain any digits, along with the letters A-F. In that case, they are hexadecimal strings. Most of the time, bit strings are converted into a numeric data type:

```
car_portal=> SELECT B'01010101'::int, X'AB21'::int;
 int4 | int4
------+-------
   85 | 43809
```

Operators are basic elements of data processing. They are used in SQL expressions. They take one or two arguments and return a value. Examples of operators include addition, +, and subtraction –. PostgreSQL supports a wide range of operators for all data types. In the statements, the operators look like a single character or a short sequence of characters from this list: + – * / < > = ~ ! @ # % ^ & | ` ?.

When several operators are used in the same expression, they are executed in a specific order. Some operators, such as multiplication, *, or division, /, have higher precedence among others, and some other operators, such as logical or comparison operators, have lower precedence. Operators with the same precedence are executed from left to right. A short list of operators and their precedence can be found in the documentation: https://www.postgresql.org/docs/current/static/sql-syntax-lexical.html#SQL-PRECEDENCE.

Special characters in SQL include the following:

- **Parentheses (())**: These are used to control the precedence of operations or to group expressions. They can also be used to identify tuples or attributes in a composite type, or as part of a function name. Some SQL commands have parentheses in their syntax.
- **Brackets ([])**: These are used to select elements from an array.
- **Colons (:)**: These are used to access parts of arrays.
- **Double colons (::)**: These are used for type-casing.
- **Commas (,)**: These are used to separate elements of a list.
- **Periods (.)**: These are used to separate schema, table, and column names from each other.
- **Semicolon (;)**: This is used to terminate a statement.
- **Asterisk (*)**: This is used to refer to all the fields of a table or all the elements of a composite value.

Whitespaces separate words from each other. In SQL, any number of spaces, new lines, or tabulations are considered a single whitespace.

Comments can be used in any part of SQL code. The server ignores comments, treating them as whitespace. Comments are quoted in pairs of `/*` and `*/`. Also, a whole line of code can be commented by using double dash `--`. In this case, a comment starts from the double dash and ends at the end of the line.

Simply speaking, DML has only four types of statements:

- `INSERT`: Used to put new data into the database
- `UPDATE`: Used to change the data
- `DELETE`: Used to delete the data
- `SELECT`: Used to retrieve the data

The structure of every statement is strict and human-readable, though the syntax of each statement is different. A complete list of detailed syntax diagrams can be found in the PostgreSQL documentation: `http://www.postgresql.org/docs/current/static/sql-commands.html`. Later in this chapter, the main elements of each statement will be described.

`SELECT` will be the first because it is the most-commonly used command and, often, it's used as an element of other commands. SQL allows us to nest commands, using a result of one command as an input for another command. These nested queries are called **subqueries**.

Querying data with SELECT statements

`SELECT` statements, `SELECT` queries, or just *queries* are used to retrieve data from a database. `SELECT` queries can have different sources: tables, views, functions, or the `VALUES` command. All of them are relations or can be treated as relations or return relations, which functions can do. The output of `SELECT` is also a relation that, in general, can have multiple columns and contain many rows. Since the result and the source of a query have the same nature in SQL, it is possible to use one `SELECT` query as a source for another statement. In this case, both queries are considered parts of one bigger query. The source of the data, output format, filters, grouping, ordering, and required transformations of the data are specified in the code of the query.

In general, SELECT queries do not change the data in the database and could be considered read-only, but there is an exception. If a volatile function is used in the query, then the data can be changed by the function.

Structure of a SELECT query

Let's start with a simple example.

We will use the sample database of a car web portal, which was mentioned in previous chapters. Assuming you have already installed a PostgreSQL server on your local machine and you have superuser access to the database, navigate to the directory where the schema.sql file is located and execute the following command to create the sample database:

```
> psql -h localhost -d postgres -f schema.sql
CREATE ROLE
psql:schema.sql:3: NOTICE: database "car_portal" does not exist, skipping
DROP DATABASE
CREATE DATABASE
psql (11.0)
You are now connected to database "car_portal" as user "postgres".
CREATE SCHEMA
SET
SET
CREATE TABLE
...
```

The output might be different depending on the operating system and particular versions of PostgreSQL and psql that are used. Please note, the script removes the car_portal database if it existed already. The error message in the output is caused by a Windows-specific locale name in the script file. It isn't a problem since the script has two commands, both for Windows and Linux.

Now, to connect to the sample database, the following command is used:

```
> psql -h localhost car_portal
```

What do we do if the connection fails with a `FATAL: no pg_hba.conf entry for host` message?

PostgreSQL uses the `pg_hba.conf` configuration file to specify which users can connect to which databases, from where, and how to authenticate them. By default, the file is located in `/etc/postgresql/11/main/pg_hba.conf` in Linux, and in `C:\Program Files\PostgreSQL\11\data\pg_hba.conf` in Windows.

For the sake of simplicity, to proceed with the examples in the book, edit the file and add the following two lines at the beginning:

```
host all all 127.0.0.1/32 trust
host all all ::1/128 trust
```

This will allow every user to connect to all the databases on the local machine without a password. Never use such settings in production, because this may be a serious security vulnerability!

For more about authentication and other security topics in PostgreSQL, check out `Chapter 11`, *PostgreSQL Security*.

There is a `car` table that contains information about cars registered in the system. Imagine the `car_portal` application needs to query the database to get information about cars that have three doors (counting the boot door). They should be sorted by their ID. The output should be limited to five records due to pagination in the user interface. The query will look like this:

```
SELECT car_id, registration_number, manufacture_year
  FROM car_portal_app.car
  WHERE number_of_doors=3
  ORDER BY car_id
  LIMIT 5;
```

This is the result:

```
 car_id | registration_number | manufacture_year
--------+---------------------+------------------
      2 | VSVW4565            |             2014
      5 | BXGK6290            |             2009
      6 | ORIU9886            |             2007
      7 | TGVF4726            |             2009
      8 | JISW6779            |             2013
(5 rows)
```

Let's see the syntax and the logic of the query. The query starts from the `SELECT` keyword, which determines the type of the statement. Therefore, this keyword is always required. The keyword is followed by the comma-separated list of the fields to be retrieved from the database. Instead of the list, it's possible to use an asterisk, *, which would mean that all the fields from the table are selected.

The name of the table is specified after the `FROM` keyword. It's possible to get the data from several tables at the same time. The filter criteria--predicate--is after the `WHERE` keyword. The sorting rule is at the end after `ORDER BY`. The `LIMIT` keyword makes the database return no more than five rows, even if the number of records retrieved from the database is greater.

These parts of the query—the keywords and the following expressions—are called clauses, such as the `FROM` clause and the `WHERE` clause. All of these clauses have their own purpose and logic. They must follow each other in a specific order. None of them are mandatory. The simplified syntax diagram for the `SELECT` statement is as follows:

```
SELECT [DISTINCT | ALL] <expression>[[AS] <output_name>][, ...]
[FROM <table>[, <table>... | <JOIN clause>...]
[WHERE <condition>]
[GROUP BY <expression>|<output_name>|<output_number> [,...]]
[HAVING <condition>]
[ORDER BY <expression>|<output_name>|<output_number> [ASC | DESC] [NULLS
FIRST | LAST] [,...]]
[OFFSET <expression>]
[LIMIT <expression>];
```

Some elements were not included here, such as the `WINDOW` clause, the `WITH` clause, or `FOR UPDATE`. A complete syntax diagram can be found in the documentation: `http://www.postgresql.org/docs/current/static/sql-select.html`.

Some of the omitted elements will be described in later chapters.

There is no part of the `SELECT` statement that is always mandatory. For example, the query might be simpler if no ordering or filtering is needed:

```
SELECT * FROM car_portal_app.car;
```

Even the `FROM` clause isn't mandatory. When you need to evaluate an expression that doesn't take any data from the database, the query takes this form:

```
car_portal=> SELECT 1;
 ?column?
----------
        1
```

This can be considered as Hello world in SQL.

 The FROM clause is optional in PostgreSQL, but in other RDBMSes, such as Oracle, the FROM keyword may be required.

Logically, the sequence of the operations performed by the SELECT query is as follows:

1. Take all the records from all the source tables. If there are subqueries in the FROM clause, they are evaluated beforehand.
2. Build all possible combinations of those records and discard the combinations that do not follow the JOIN conditions or set some fields to NULL in the case of outer joins.
3. Filter out the combinations that don't match the condition of the WHERE clause.
4. Build groups based on the values of the expressions of the GROUP BY list.
5. Filter the groups that match the HAVING conditions.
6. Evaluate expressions of the SELECT-list.
7. Eliminate duplicated rows if DISTINCT is specified.
8. Apply the UNION, EXCEPT, or INTERSECT set operations.
9. Sort rows according to the ORDER BY clause.
10. Discard records according to OFFSET and LIMIT.

In fact, PostgreSQL optimizes that algorithm by performing the steps in a different order or even simultaneously. For example, if LIMIT 1 is specified, then it doesn't make sense to retrieve all the rows from the source tables, but only the first one that matches the WHERE condition. In this case, PostgreSQL would scan the rows one by one and evaluate the condition for each of them in a loop, and stop once a matching row is found.

SELECT-list

After the SELECT keyword, you should specify the list of fields (or expressions) to retrieve from the database. This list is called SELECT-list. It defines the structure of the query result: the number, names, and types of the selected values.

Every expression in SELECT-list has a name in the output of the query. The names, when not provided by the user, are assigned automatically by the database and, in most cases, the name reflects the source of the data: a name of a column when a field from a table is selected, or the name of a function when one is used. In other cases, the name will look like ?column?. It's possible, and in many cases it totally makes sense, to provide a different name for a selected expression. This is done using the AS keyword, like this:

```
SELECT car_id AS identifier_of_a_car ...
```

In the result, the car_id column from the car table will be named identifier_of_a_car. The AS keyword is optional. The output column name follows the rules for any SQL identifier. It's possible to use the same name for several columns in a single SELECT query. Double-quoted names could be used, for example, when a report is generated by a SELECT query without any further processing. In that case, it may make sense to use more human-readable column names:

```
SELECT car_id "Identifier of a car" ...
```

In many cases, it is convenient to use an asterisk (*) instead of a SELECT-list. An asterisk represents all the fields from all the tables specified in the FROM clause. It's possible to use an asterisk for each table separately, like this:

```
SELECT car.*, car_model.make ...
```

In this example, all fields are selected from the car table and only one make field from car_model.

It's considered a bad practice to use * in situations where the query is used in other code, such as in applications, stored procedures, and view definitions. It isn't recommended because in the case of using *, the output format depends not on the code of the query but on the structure of the data. If the data structure changes, the output format also changes, which will break the application using it. However, if you explicitly specify all the output fields in the query and add another column to the input table afterward, this will not change the output of the query and will not break the application.

So, in our example, instead of SELECT * ..., it would be safer to use the following:

```
SELECT car_id, number_of_owners, registration_number, number_of_doors,
car_model_id, mileage ...
```

SQL expressions

Expressions in the SELECT-list are called **value expressions** or **scalar expressions**. This is because each expression in the SELECT-list always returns only one value (though the value can be an array).

Scalar expressions can also be called SQL expressions or simply expressions. Each expression in SQL has its data type. It's determined by the data type(s) of the input. In many cases, it's possible to explicitly change the type of the data. Each item of the SELECT-list becomes a column in the output dataset, of a type that the corresponding expression has.

SQL expressions can contain the following:

- Column names (in most cases)
- Constants
- Operator invocations
- Parentheses to control operations/precedence
- Function calls
- Aggregate expressions (we will discuss these later in the section "Grouping and aggregation")
- Scalar subqueries
- Type casts
- Conditional expressions

This list is not complete. There are several other cases for using SQL expressions that are not covered in this chapter.

Column names can be qualified and unqualified. **Qualified** means that the name of the column is preceded by the table name, and optionally, the schema name, all separated by a period, (.), symbol. **Unqualified** indicates just the names of the fields without table references. Qualified column names must be used when several tables in the FROM clause have columns with the same name. Unqualified naming in this case will cause an error: `column reference is ambiguous`. This means that the database can't understand which column is being referred to. It's possible to use a table alias instead of a table name, and in the case of using subqueries or functions, the alias must be used.

An example of using qualified names in a SELECT-list is as follows:

```
SELECT car.car_id, car.number_of_owners FROM car_portal_app.car;
```

SQL supports all common operators as most of the other programming languages do, such as logical, arithmetic, string, binary, and date/time. We will discuss logical operators later in reference to SQL conditions in the section "The WHERE clause". An example of using arithmetic operators in expressions would be as follows:

```
car_portal=> SELECT 1+1 AS two, 13%4 AS one, -5 AS minus_five,
  5! AS factorial, |/25 AS square_root;
 two | one | minus_five | factorial | square_root
-----+-----+------------+-----------+-------------
   2 |   1 |         -5 |       120 |           5
```

In PostgreSQL, it is also possible to create user-defined operators.

Function calls can also be part of a SQL expression. To call a SQL function, use its name and the arguments in parentheses:

```
car_portal=> SELECT substring('this is a string constant',11,6);
 substring
-----------
 string
```

A built-in function named substring was executed here. Three arguments were passed to the function: a string and two integers. This function extracts a part from the given string, starting from the character specified by the second argument and having a specified length. By default, PostgreSQL assigns to the output column the same name as the function.

If a function has no arguments, it's still necessary to use parentheses to indicate that it's a function name and not a field name or another identifier or keyword.

Another thing that makes SQL very flexible and powerful is scalar subqueries, which can be used as part of a value expression. This allows the developer to combine the results of different queries. **Scalar subqueries** or **scalar queries** are queries that return exactly one column and one or zero records. They have no special syntax and their difference from non-scalar queries is nominal.

Consider the following example:

```
car_portal=> SELECT (SELECT 1) + (SELECT 2) AS three;
 three
----------
     3
```

Here, the result of one scalar query that returns the value of 1 is added to the result of another scalar query that returns 2. The result of the whole expression is 3.

Type-casting means changing the data type of a value. Type casts have several syntax patterns, which all have the same meaning:

- CAST (<value> AS <type>)
- <value>::<type>
- <type> '<value>'
- <type> (<value>)

The first is a common SQL syntax that is supported in most databases. The second is PostgreSQL-specific. The third is only applicable for string constants and is usually used to define constants of other types apart from string or numeric. The last is function-like and can be applied only to types whose names are also existing function names, which is not very convenient. That's why this syntax is not widely used.

In many cases, PostgreSQL can do implicit type conversion. For example, the concatenation operator, || (double vertical bar), takes two operands of the string type. If one tries to concatenate a string with a number, PostgreSQL will convert the number to a string automatically:

```
car_portal=> SELECT 'One plus one equals ' || (1+1) AS str;
          str
------------------------
 One plus one equals 2
```

A conditional expression is an expression that returns different results depending on some condition. It's similar to an IF - THEN - ELSE statement in other programming languages. The syntax is as follows:

```
CASE WHEN <condition1> THEN <expression1> [WHEN <condition2> THEN
<expression2> ...] [ELSE <expression n>] END
```

The behavior is understandable from the syntax: if the first condition is met, the result of the first expression is returned; if the second condition is met, the second expression is used; and so on. If no condition is met, the expression specified in the ELSE part is evaluated. Each <condition> is itself an expression that returns a Boolean (true or false) result. All expressions used after the THEN keyword should return a result of the same type or at least of compatible types.

The number of condition-expression pairs should be one or more. ELSE is optional and when ELSE is not specified and there were no conditions evaluated to true, the whole CASE expression returns NULL.

CASE can be used in any place where an SQL expression is used. CASE expressions can be nested, that is, they can be put inside each other as both a condition part or an expression part. The order of evaluating conditions is the same as specified in the expression. This means, for any condition, it's known that all preceding conditions are evaluated as false. If any condition returns true, subsequent conditions are not evaluated at all.

There is a simplified syntax for CASE expressions. When all conditions check the same expression, whether it is equal to certain values, it is possible to do it like this:

```
CASE <checked_expression> WHEN <value1> THEN <result1>
[WHEN <value2> THEN <result2> ...] [ELSE <result_n>] END
```

This means that when the value of checked_expression is equal to value1, result1 is returned, and so on.

Here is an example of using a CASE expression:

```
car_portal=> SELECT CASE WHEN now() > date_trunc('day', now()) +
interval '12 hours' THEN 'PM' ELSE 'AM' END;
 case
------
 PM
```

Here, the current time is compared to midday (the current time is truncated to day, which gives midnight, and then a time interval of 12 hours is added). When the current time is after (the > operator) noon, the expression returns the PM string, otherwise it returns AM.

A single SQL expression can have many operators, functions, type casts, and so on. The length of a SQL expression has no limit in language specification. The SELECT-list is not the only place where SQL expressions can be used. In fact, they are used almost everywhere in SQL statements. For example, you can order the results of a query based on a SQL expression, as a sorting key. In an INSERT statement, they are used to calculate values of the fields for newly-inserted records. SQL expressions that return Boolean values are often used as conditions in the WHERE clause.

PostgreSQL supports the short-circuit evaluation of expressions and, sometimes, it skips the evaluation of some parts of an expression when they don't affect the result. For example, when evaluating the false AND z() expression, PostgreSQL will not call the z() function because the result of the AND operator is determined by its first operand, the false constant, and it is always false, regardless of what the z() function returns.

DISTINCT

Also related to the SELECT-list is a pair of keywords, DISTINCT and ALL, that can be used right after the SELECT keyword. When DISTINCT is specified, only unique rows from the input dataset will be returned. ALL returns all the rows—this is the default.

Consider the following example:

```
car_portal=> SELECT ALL make FROM car_portal_app.car_model;
      make
---------------
 Audi
 Audi
 Audi
 Audi
 BMW
 BMW
 . . .
(99 rows)
```

Consider the second example:

```
car_portal=> SELECT DISTINCT make FROM car_portal_app.car_model;
      make
---------------
 Ferrari
 GMC
 Citroen
 UAZ
 Audi
 Volvo
 . . .
(25 rows)
```

The input in both cases is the same: the table with the car models. However, the first query returned 99 records while the second only returned 25. This is because the first returned all the rows that were in the input table. The second query selected only the unique rows. DISTINCT removes duplicate records based on the expressions of the SELECT-list, not on the data in the input table. For example, if only the first letter of the name of the manufacturer is selected, the result will be even shorter because some names start with the same letter:

```
SELECT DISTINCT substring(make, 1, 1) FROM car_portal_app.car_model;
 substring
-----------
 H
 S
```

```
C
J
L
I
...
(21 rows)
```

DISTINCT also works when several columns are selected. In that case, DISTINCT will remove duplicated combinations of all the column values.

The FROM clause

The source of the rows for a query is specified after the FROM keyword. It's called the FROM clause. The query can select rows from zero, one, or more sources. When no source is specified, the FROM keyword should be omitted. A source of the rows for a query can be any combination of the following:

- Tables
- Views
- Functions
- Subqueries
- VALUES clauses

When multiple sources are specified, they should be separated by a comma or the JOIN clause should be used.

It's possible to set aliases for tables in the FROM clause. The optional AS keyword is used for that:

```
car_portal=> SELECT a.car_id, a.number_of_doors
  FROM car_portal_app.car AS a;
 car_id | number_of_doors
--------+-----------------
      1 |               5
      2 |               3
      3 |               5
...
```

In the preceding example, the `car_portal_app.car` table was substituted with its alias, `a`, in the SELECT-list. If an alias is used for a table or view in the FROM clause, in the SELECT-list (or anywhere else), it's no longer possible to refer to the table by its name. Subqueries, when used in the FROM clause, must have an alias. Aliases are often used when a self-join is performed, which means using the same table several times in the FROM clause.

Selecting from multiple tables

It's possible to select records from several sources at a time. Consider the following examples. There are two tables, each with three rows:

```
car_portal=> SELECT * FROM car_portal_app.a;
 a_int | a_text
-------+--------
     1 | one
     2 | two
     3 | three
(3 rows)

car_portal=> SELECT * FROM car_portal_app.b;
 b_int | b_text
-------+--------
     2 | two
     3 | three
     4 | four
(3 rows)
```

When records are selected from both of them, we get all the possible combinations of all their rows:

```
car_portal=> SELECT * FROM car_portal_app.a, car_portal_app.b;
 a_int | a_text | b_int | b_text
-------+--------+-------+--------
     1 | one    |     2 | two
     1 | one    |     3 | three
     1 | one    |     4 | four
     2 | two    |     2 | two
     2 | two    |     3 | three
     2 | two    |     4 | four
     3 | three  |     2 | two
     3 | three  |     3 | three
     3 | three  |     4 | four
(9 rows)
```

All of the possible combinations of records from several tables is called a **Cartesian product** and, in many cases, it doesn't make much sense. In most cases, the user is interested in certain combinations of rows, when rows from one table match rows from another table based on some criteria. For example, it may be necessary to select only the combinations when the integer fields of both the tables have equal values. To get this, the query should be changed:

```
car_portal=> SELECT * FROM car_portal_app.a, car_portal_app.b
  WHERE a_int=b_int;
 a_int | a_text | b_int | b_text
-------+--------+-------+--------
     2 | two    |     2 | two
     3 | three  |     3 | three
(2 rows)
```

The `a_int=b_int` condition joins the tables. The joining conditions could be specified in the WHERE clause, but in most cases, it's better to put them into the FROM clause to make it explicit that they are there for joining and not for filtering the result of the join, though there is no formal difference.

The JOIN keyword is used to add join conditions to the FROM clause. The following query has the same logic and the same results as the previous one:

```
SELECT * FROM car_portal_app.a JOIN car_portal_app.b ON a_int=b_int;
```

The JOIN condition can be specified in any of the following three ways:

- Using the ON keyword:

  ```
  <first table> JOIN <second table> ON <condition>
  ```

  The condition can be any SQL expression that returns a Boolean result. It isn't even necessary to include fields of the joined tables in the condition.

- Using the USING keyword:

  ```
  <first table> JOIN <second table> USING (<field list>)
  ```

  The join is based on the equality of all the fields specified in the comma-separated <field list>. The fields should exist in both tables with the same name. So this syntax may be not flexible enough.

- Performing a NATURAL JOIN:

  ```
  <first table> NATURAL JOIN <second table>
  ```

Here, the join is based on the equality of all the fields that have the same name in both tables.

 Usage of the USING or NATURAL JOIN syntax has a drawback that is similar to the usage of * in the SELECT-list. It's possible to change the structure of the tables, for example, by adding another column or renaming them, in a way that does not make the query invalid, but changes the logic of the query. This will cause errors that are very difficult to find.

What if not all of the rows from the first table can be matched to rows in the second table?

In our example, only rows with integer values of 2 and 3 exist in both tables. When we join on the a_int=b_int condition, only those two rows are selected from the tables. The rest of the rows are not selected. This kind of join is called an **inner join**.

It is shown as the filled area in the following diagram:

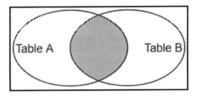

Inner join

When all the records from one table are selected, regardless of the existence of matching records in the other table, it's called an **outer join**. There are three types of outer joins. Check out at the following diagrams.

If all of the records are selected from the first table, along with only those records that match the joining condition from the second, it's a **left outer join**:

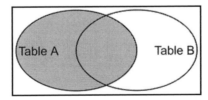

Left outer join

When all records from the second table are selected, along with only the matching records from the first table, it's a **right outer join**:

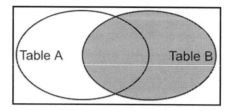

Right outer join

And when all the records from both tables are selected, it's a **full outer join**:

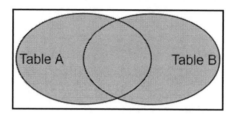

Full outer join

In SQL syntax, the words INNER and OUTER are optional. Consider the following code examples:

```
car_portal=> SELECT * FROM car_portal_app.a
  JOIN car_portal_app.b ON a_int=b_int;
 a_int | a_text | b_int | b_text
-------+--------+-------+--------
     2 | two    |     2 | two
     3 | three  |     3 | three
(2 rows)

car_portal=> SELECT * FROM car_portal_app.a
  LEFT JOIN car_portal_app.b ON a_int=b_int;
 a_int | a_text | b_int | b_text
-------+--------+-------+--------
     1 | one    |       |
     2 | two    |     2 | two
     3 | three  |     3 | three
(3 rows)

car_portal=> SELECT * FROM car_portal_app.a
  RIGHT JOIN car_portal_app.b ON a_int=b_int;
```

```
 a_int | a_text | b_int | b_text
-------+--------+-------+--------
     2 | two    |     2 | two
     3 | three  |     3 | three
       |        |     4 | four
(3 rows)

car_portal=> SELECT * FROM car_portal_app.a
  FULL JOIN car_portal_app.b ON a_int=b_int;
 a_int | a_text | b_int | b_text
-------+--------+-------+--------
     1 | one    |       |
     2 | two    |     2 | two
     3 | three  |     3 | three
       |        |     4 | four
(4 rows)
```

Note that the Cartesian product is not the same as the result of the full outer join. Cartesian product means all possible combinations of all records from the tables without any specific matching rules. A full outer join returns pairs of records when they match the join conditions. The records that don't have a pair in the other table are returned separately. Outer joins return empty values, NULL, in columns that correspond to the table from where no matching record is found.

As it's possible to query not only tables but also views, functions, and subqueries, it's also possible to join them using the same syntax as when joining tables:

```
car_portal=> SELECT *
 FROM car_portal_app.a
 INNER JOIN (SELECT * FROM car_portal_app.b WHERE b_text = 'two') subq
   ON a.a_int=subq.b_int;
 a_int | a_text | b_int | b_text
-------+--------+-------+--------
     2 | two    |     2 | two
```

In the example, the subquery got the `subq` alias and it was used in the join condition.

It's also possible to join more than two tables. In fact, every `JOIN` clause joins all the tables before the `JOIN` keyword with the table right after the keyword.

For example, this is correct:

```
SELECT *
  FROM table_a
    JOIN table_b ON table_a.field1=table_b.field1
    JOIN table_c ON table_a.field2=table_c.field2
      AND table_b.field3=table_c.field3;
```

At the point of joining the `table_c` table, the `table_a` table has been mentioned already in the `FROM` clause, therefore it is possible to refer to that table.

However, this is not correct:

```
SELECT *
  FROM table_a
    JOIN table_b ON table_b.field3=table_c.field3
    JOIN table_c ON table_a.field2=table_c.field2
```

The code will cause an error because at `JOIN table_b`, the `table_c` table has not been there yet.

The Cartesian product can also be implemented using the `JOIN` syntax. The CROSS `JOIN` keywords are used for that. Take a look at the following code:

```
SELECT * FROM car_portal_app.a CROSS JOIN car_portal_app.b;
```

The preceding code is equivalent to the following:

```
SELECT * FROM car_portal_app.a, car_portal_app.b;
```

The join condition in `INNER JOIN` in the logic of the query has the same meaning as a condition to filter the rows in the `WHERE` clause. So, the following two queries are, in fact, the same:

```
SELECT * FROM car_portal_app.a
  INNER JOIN car_portal_app.b ON a.a_int=b.b_int;

SELECT * FROM car_portal_app.a, car_portal_app.b
  WHERE a.a_int=b.b_int;
```

However, this is not the case for outer joins. There is no way to implement an `OUTER JOIN` with the `WHERE` clause in PostgreSQL, though it may be possible in other databases.

Self-joins

It's possible to join a table with itself. This is called a **self-join**. A self-join has no special syntax. In fact, all the data sources in a query are independent, even though they could be the same physically. Imagine you want to find out for the `a` table, for every record, if there are other records with a bigger value of the `a_int` field . The following query can be used for this:

```
car_portal=> SELECT t1.a_int AS current, t2.a_int AS bigger
  FROM car_portal_app.a t1
```

```
INNER JOIN car_portal_app.a t2 ON t2.a_int > t1.a_int;
current | bigger
--------+--------
      1 |      2
      1 |      3
      2 |      3
(3 rows)
```

The a table is joined to itself. From the logic of the query, it doesn't matter whether two different tables are joined or the same table is used twice. To be able to reference the fields and distinguish the instances of the table, the table aliases are used. The first instance in the preceding example is called t1 and the second t2. From the results, it is visible that for the value of 1, there are two bigger values: 2 and 3; and for the value 2, only one bigger value exists, which is 3. The examined value is in the current column and the larger values are in the bigger column.

The value of 3 does not appear in the current column because there are no values greater than 3. However, if you want to explicitly show that, LEFT JOIN could be used:

```
car_portal=> SELECT t1.a_int AS current, t2.a_int AS bigger
 FROM car_portal_app.a t1
 LEFT JOIN car_portal_app.a t2 ON t2.a_int > t1.a_int;
current | bigger
--------+--------
      1 |      2
      1 |      3
      2 |      3
      3 |
(4 rows)
```

The WHERE clause

In many cases, after the rows are taken from the input tables, they should be filtered. This is done via the WHERE clause. The filtering condition is specified after the WHERE keyword. The condition is a SQL expression that returns a Boolean value. That's why the syntax of the WHERE condition is the same as in the expressions in the SELECT-list. This is specific to PostgreSQL. In other databases, it may not be possible to use Boolean values in the SELECT-list, which makes SQL conditions different from SQL expressions. In PostgreSQL, the difference is only in the data type of a returned value.

Simple examples of WHERE conditions are as follows:

```
SELECT * FROM car_portal_app.car_model WHERE make='Peugeot';
SELECT * FROM car_portal_app.car WHERE mileage < 25000;
SELECT * FROM car_portal_app.car
   WHERE number_of_doors > 3 AND number_of_owners <= 2;
```

Although there is no formal difference between SQL expressions and SQL conditions in PostgreSQL, usually, all expressions that return a Boolean type are called conditional expressions or just conditions. They are mostly used in WHERE clauses; in conditional expressions, such as CASE; or in the JOIN clause.

Logical operators are commonly used in conditional expressions. They are AND, OR, and NOT. They take Boolean arguments and return Boolean values. Logical operators are evaluated in the following order: NOT, AND, OR, but they have a lower priority than any other operators. PostgreSQL tries to optimize the evaluation of logical expressions. For example, when the OR operator is evaluated, and it's known that the first operand is True, PostgreSQL may not evaluate the second operand at all, because the result of OR is already known. For that reason, PostgreSQL may change the actual order of evaluating expressions on purpose to get the results faster.

Sometimes, this might cause problems. For example, it's not possible to divide by zero, and if you wanted to filter rows based on the result of a division, this would not be correct:

```
SELECT * FROM t WHERE b/a>0.5 and a<>0;
```

It's not guaranteed that PostgreSQL will evaluate the a<>0 condition before the other one, b/a>0.5, and if a has a value of 0, this could cause an error. To be safe, you should use a CASE statement because the order of evaluation of CASE conditions is determined by the statement, as follows:

```
SELECT * FROM t WHERE CASE WHEN a=0 THEN false ELSE b/a>0.5 END;
```

There are some other operators and expressions that return Boolean values that are used in conditional expressions:

- Comparison operators
- Pattern-matching operators
- The OVERLAPS operator

- Row and array comparison constructs
- Subquery expressions
- Any function that returns a Boolean or is convertible to Boolean values

As in the SELECT-list, functions can be used in the WHERE clause as well as anywhere in expressions. Imagine you want to search for car models whose name is four letters long. This can be done using a length() function:

```
car_portal=> SELECT * FROM car_portal_app.car_model WHERE length(model)=4;
 car_model_id |    make    | model
--------------+------------+-------
           47 | KIA        | Seed
           57 | Nissan     | GT-R
           70 | Renault    | Clio
...
```

Comparison operators

Comparison operators are less (<), more (>), less or equal (<=), more or equal (>=), equal (=), and not equal (<> or !=—these two are synonyms). These operators can compare not only numbers but any values that can be compared, for example, dates or strings. There is a BETWEEN construct that also relates to comparing. Consider the following:

```
x BETWEEN a AND b
```

The preceding code is equivalent to the following:

```
x >= a AND x <= b
```

The OVERLAPS operator checks to see whether two ranges of dates overlap. Here is an example:

```
car_portal=> SELECT 1 WHERE (date '2018-10-15', date '2018-10-31')
  OVERLAPS (date '2018-10-25', date '2018-11-15');
 ?column?
----------
        1
```

 Formally, comparison operators have different precedence: >= and <= have the highest priority. Then comes BETWEEN, then OVERLAPS, then < and >. = has the lowest priority. However, it's difficult to come up with a practical example of using several comparison operators in the same expression without any parentheses.

Pattern matching

Pattern matching is always about strings. There are two similar operators: LIKE and ILIKE. They check whether a string matches a given pattern. Only two wildcards can be used in a pattern: an underscore, _, for exactly one character (or number) and a percent sign, %, for any number of any characters, including an empty string.

LIKE and ILIKE are the same, except that the first is case-sensitive and the second is not.

Apart from LIKE and ILIKE, there are the ~~ and ~~* operators, which are equivalent to LIKE and ILIKE, respectively. The LIKE operator belongs to the SQL standard; the others don't. There are also the !~~ and !~~* operators, which behave like NOT LIKE and NOT ILIKE, respectively, and they are PostgreSQL-specific.

For example, to get car models whose names start with s and have exactly four characters, you can use the following query:

```
car_portal=> SELECT * FROM car_portal_app.car_model
  WHERE model ILIKE 's___';
 car_model_id |     make    | model
--------------+-------------+-------
           47 | KIA         | Seed
```

There are two other pattern matching operators: SIMILAR and ~ (the tilde sign). They check for pattern matching using regular expressions. The difference between them is that SIMILAR uses regular expression syntax defined in SQL standard, while ~ uses **Portable Operating System Interface (POSIX)** regular expressions.

In the following example, we select all car models whose names consist of exactly two words:

```
car_portal=> SELECT * FROM car_portal_app.car_model
  WHERE model ~ '^\w+\W+\w+$';
 car_model_id |      make     |    model
--------------+---------------+--------------
           21 | Citroen       | C4 Picasso
           33 | Ford          | C-Max
           34 | Ford          | S-Max
  . . .
```

Row and array comparison constructs

Row and array comparison constructs are used to make multiple comparisons between values, groups of values, and arrays.

The `IN` expression is used to check whether a value equals any of the values from a list. The expression is as follows:

```
a IN (1, 2, 3)
```

The preceding code will return true if `a` is equal to `1`, `2`, or `3`. It's a shorter and cleaner way of implementing the logic than using comparison operators, as follows:

```
(a = 1 OR a = 2 OR a = 3)
```

SQL allows the use of array types, which are several elements as a whole in one single value. You will learn more about arrays in `Chapter 9`, *Beyond Conventional Data Types*. Arrays can be used to enrich comparison conditions. For example, this checks whether `a` is bigger than any of `x`, `y`, or `z`:

```
a > ANY (ARRAY[x, y, z])
```

The preceding code is equivalent to the following:

```
(a > x OR a > y OR a > z)
```

This checks whether `a` is bigger than `x`, `y`, and `z`:

```
a > ALL (ARRAY[x, y, z])
```

The preceding code is equivalent to the following:

```
(a > x AND a > y AND a > z )
```

The `IN`, `ALL`, and `ANY` (which has a synonym: `SOME`) keywords can also be used with subquery expressions to implement the same logic. The result of a subquery can be used in any place where it's possible to use a set of values or an array. This makes it possible, for instance, to select records from one table, when some values exist in another table.

For example, in the `car_portal` database, we have the tables with car models and cars separated for the sake of normalization. To get a list of all car models when there is a car of that model, the following query can be used:

```
car_portal=> SELECT * FROM car_portal_app.car_model
 WHERE car_model_id IN (SELECT car_model_id FROM car_portal_app.car);
 car_model_id |     make     | model
--------------+--------------+--------------
```

```
                   2 | Audi          | A2
                   3 | Audi          | A3
                   4 | Audi          | A4
   ...
   (86 rows)
```

Sometimes an IN expression can be replaced by INNER JOIN, but not always. Consider the following example:

```
car_portal=> SELECT car_model.*
  FROM car_portal_app.car_model
    INNER JOIN car_portal_app.car USING (car_model_id);
 car_model_id |     make      |    model
--------------+---------------+--------------
            2 | Audi          | A2
            2 | Audi          | A2
            2 | Audi          | A2
            3 | Audi          | A3
            3 | Audi          | A3
            4 | Audi          | A4
            4 | Audi          | A4
   ...
   (229 rows)
```

Although the same table is queried and the same columns are returned, the number of records is greater. This is because there are many cars of the same model, and for them, the model is selected several times.

> The NOT IN construct with a subquery is sometimes very slow, because the check for the nonexistence of a value is more expensive than the opposite. This construct can be replaced with NOT EXISTS or, sometimes, with a LEFT JOIN and a negative predicate in the WHERE clause.

Grouping and aggregation

In all of the previous examples, the number of records returned by the SELECT query was the same as the number of rows from the input table (or tables) after filtering. In other words, every row from any of the source tables (or joined tables) becomes exactly one row in the query result. Rows are processed one by one.

SQL provides a way to get aggregated results of processing several records at a time and then get the results in a single row. The easiest example would be counting the total number of records in a table. The input is all the records of a table. The output is a single record. Grouping and aggregation is used for this.

The GROUP BY clause

The GROUP BY clause is used for grouping. **Grouping** means splitting the whole input set of records into several groups, with a view to having only one result row for each group. Grouping is performed on the basis of a list of expressions. All records that have the same combination of values of grouping expressions are grouped together. This means that the groups are identified by the values of expressions defined in the GROUP BY clause. Usually, it makes sense to include these expressions in the SELECT-list to indicate which group is represented by the result row.

For example, let's group the cars by make and model and select the groups:

```
car_portal=> SELECT make, model
  FROM car_portal_app.car a
    INNER JOIN car_portal_app.car_model b ON a.car_model_id=b.car_model_id
  GROUP BY make, model;
    make        |      model
----------------+---------------
 Opel           | Corsa
 Ferrari        | 458 Italia
 Peugeot        | 308
 Opel           | Insignia
 ...
(86 rows)
```

Here, the list of all the car models that are used in the car table is selected. Each record in the result set represents a group of records from the source tables that relates to the same car model. In fact, this query gives the same result as SELECT DISTINCT make, model..., without GROUP BY, but the logic is different. DISTINCT removes duplicated values, but GROUP BY groups duplicated values together.

It's almost useless just to group rows. Usually, some computing is performed on the groups. As for the last example, it would be interesting to know how many cars of which model are in the system. This is done using aggregation. **Aggregation** means performing a calculation on a group of records that returns a single value for the whole group. This is done by the special aggregating functions that are used in SELECT-list. To get the number of cars, you need to use the `count` function:

```
car_portal=> SELECT make, model, count(*)
  FROM car_portal_app.car a
    INNER JOIN car_portal_app.car_model b ON a.car_model_id=b.car_model_id
  GROUP BY make, model;
   make         |     model      | count
---------------+----------------+-------
 Opel          | Corsa          |     6
 Ferrari       | 458 Italia     |     4
 Peugeot       | 308            |     3
 Opel          | Insignia       |     4
 ...
(86 rows)
```

There are several aggregating functions available in PostgreSQL. The most-frequently used are `count`, `sum`, `max`, `min`, and `avg` to compute, respectively, the number of records in a group, the total sum of a numeric expression for all the records in a group, to find the biggest and the smallest value, and to calculate the average value of an expression. There are some other aggregating functions, such as `corr`, which computes the correlation coefficient of the two given arguments: `stddev` for standard deviation, and `string_agg`, which concatenates the string values of an expression.

When grouping and aggregation is used, records are grouped. This means that several records become one. Therefore, no other expressions except the aggregation functions and expressions from the GROUP BY list can be included in the SELECT-list. If this is done, the database will raise an error:

```
car_portal=> SELECT a_int, a_text FROM car_portal_app.a GROUP BY a_int;
ERROR: column "a.a_text" must appear in the GROUP BY clause or be used in
an aggregate function
```

It's possible to create new expressions based on the expressions from the GROUP BY list. For example, if we have GROUP BY a, b, it's possible to use SELECT a + b.

What if we need to group all of the records of the table together, not on the basis of the values of some field, but the whole table? To do this, you should include aggregating functions in the SELECT-list (and only them!) and not use the GROUP BY clause:

```
car_portal=> SELECT count(*) FROM car_portal_app.car;
 count
-------
   229
(1 row)
```

If all of the records of a table are grouped without any GROUP BY expressions, then exactly one group is created. Note that the SQL queries that have aggregating functions in the SELECT-list and don't have the GROUP BY clause always return exactly one row, even if there are no rows in the input tables, or if all of them are filtered out:

```
car_portal=> SELECT count(*) FROM car_portal_app.car
  WHERE number_of_doors = 15;
 count
-------
     0
(1 row)
```

There are no cars with 15 doors. If the records were selected with this WHERE condition, no rows would be returned. However, if you used count(*), the aggregating function would return a row with a value of 0.

It's possible to count the number of unique values of the expression with count(DISTINCT <expression>):

```
car_portal=> SELECT count(*), count(DISTINCT car_model_id)
  FROM car_portal_app.car;
 count | count
-------+-------
   229 |    86
(1 row)
```

In the preceding example, the first column has the total number of cars. The second column is number of the car models to which the cars belong. As some cars are of the same model, the number of models is lower than the total number of cars.

The HAVING clause

Aggregating functions are not allowed in the WHERE clause, but it's possible to filter groups that follow a certain condition. This is different from filtering in the WHERE clause, because WHERE filters input rows, and groups are calculated afterward.

The filtering of groups is done in the HAVING clause. This is very similar to the WHERE clause, but only aggregating functions are allowed there. The HAVING clause is specified after the GROUP BY clause. Suppose you need to know which models have more than 5 cars entered in the system. This can be done using a subquery:

```
car_portal=> SELECT make, model FROM
(
  SELECT make, model, count(*) c
    FROM car_portal_app.car a
      INNER JOIN car_portal_app.car_model b
        ON a.car_model_id=b.car_model_id
    GROUP BY make, model
) subq
WHERE c > 5;
  make   | model
---------+-------
 Opel    | Corsa
 Peugeot | 208
(2 rows)
```

A simpler and clearer way is to do it with a HAVING clause:

```
car_portal=> SELECT make, model
  FROM car_portal_app.car a
    INNER JOIN car_portal_app.car_model b ON a.car_model_id=b.car_model_id
  GROUP BY make, model
  HAVING count(*) > 5;
  make   | model
---------+-------
 Opel    | Corsa
 Peugeot | 208
```

Ordering and limiting results

The results of a query are not ordered by default. The order of the rows is not defined and may depend on their physical location on disk, the joining algorithm or on other factors. In many cases, it's required to sort the result set. This is done with the ORDER BY clause. The list of expressions whose values should be sorted is specified after the ORDER BY keyword. At the beginning, the records are sorted on the basis of the first expression of the ORDER BY list. If some rows have the same value for the first expression, they are sorted by the values of the second expression, and so on.

For each item of the ORDER BY list, it's possible to specify whether the order should be ascending or descending. This is done by specifying the ASC or DESC keywords after the expression. Ascending is the default. NULL values are considered greater than any other values by default, but it's possible to explicitly define that NULLS should precede other rows by specifying NULLS FIRST, or NULLS LAST if NULLS should be at the end.

It's not necessary for the ORDER BY clause to contain the same expressions as the SELECT-list, but it usually does. So, to make it more convenient, in the ORDER BY list, it's possible to use the output column names that are assigned to the expression in the SELECT-list instead of fully-qualified expressions. It's also possible to use the numbers of the columns.

So, these examples are equivalent:

```
#Example 1:
SELECT number_of_owners, manufacture_year, trunc(mileage/1000) as kmiles
FROM car_portal_app.car
ORDER BY number_of_owners, manufacture_year, trunc(mileage/1000) DESC;

#Example 2:
SELECT number_of_owners, manufacture_year, trunc(mileage/1000) as kmiles
FROM car_portal_app.car
ORDER BY number_of_owners, manufacture_year, kmiles DESC;

#Example 3:
SELECT number_of_owners, manufacture_year, trunc(mileage/1000) as kmiles
FROM car_portal_app.car
ORDER BY 1, 2, 3 DESC;
```

Sometimes, it's necessary to limit the output of a query to a certain number of rows and discard the rest. This is done by specifying that number after the `LIMIT` keyword:

```
car_portal=> SELECT * FROM car_portal_app.car_model LIMIT 5;
 car_model_id | make  | model
--------------+-------+-------
            1 | Audi  | A1
            2 | Audi  | A2
            3 | Audi  | A3
            4 | Audi  | A4
            5 | Audi  | A5
(5 rows)
```

The preceding code returns only five rows regardless of the fact that the actual number of records in the table is greater. This is sometimes used in scalar subqueries that should not return more than one record.

Another similar task is to skip several rows at the beginning of the output. This is done using the `OFFSET` keyword. The `OFFSET` and `LIMIT` keywords can be used together:

```
car_portal=> SELECT * FROM car_portal_app.car_model OFFSET 5 LIMIT 5;
 car_model_id | make  | model
--------------+-------+-------
            6 | Audi  | A6
            7 | Audi  | A8
            8 | BMW   | 1er
            9 | BMW   | 3er
           10 | BMW   | 5er
(5 rows)
```

The typical use case for `OFFSET` and `LIMIT` is the implementation of paginated output in web applications. For example, if 10 rows are displayed on a page, then on the third page, rows 21-30 should be shown. Then, the `OFFSET 20 LIMIT 10` construct is used. In most cases of using `OFFSET` and `LIMIT`, the rows should be ordered, otherwise, it's not clear which records are returned. The keywords are then specified after the `ORDER BY` clause.

> Note that using the `OFFSET` keyword for pagination with big tables has a performance drawback. Simply speaking, to skip the first X rows and return the others, PostgreSQL would need to read those X rows from disk, which might take a lot of time.

Subqueries

Subqueries are a very powerful feature of SQL. They can be used almost everywhere in queries. The most obvious way to use subqueries is in a FROM clause, as a source for the main query:

```
car_portal=> SELECT * FROM (
  SELECT car_model_id, count(*) c
  FROM car_portal_app.car
  GROUP BY car_model_id
) subq
WHERE c = 1;
 car_model_id | c
--------------+---
            8 | 1
           80 | 1
...
(14 rows)
```

When subqueries are used in a FROM clause, they must have an alias. In the preceding example, the subquery is given the name subq.

Subqueries are often used in SQL conditions in IN expressions:

```
car_portal=> SELECT car_id, registration_number
FROM car_portal_app.car
WHERE car_model_id IN (
  SELECT car_model_id FROM car_portal_app.car_model
    WHERE make='Peugeot');
 car_id | registration_number
--------+---------------------
      1 | MUWH4675
     14 | MTZC8798
     18 | VFZF9207
...
(18 rows)
```

Scalar subqueries can be used everywhere in expressions—in the SELECT-list, the WHERE clause, and the GROUP BY clause, for example. Even in LIMIT:

```
car_portal=> SELECT (SELECT count(*) FROM car_portal_app.car_model)
FROM car_portal_app.car
LIMIT (SELECT MIN(car_id)+2 FROM car_portal_app.car);
count
-------
    99
    99
```

```
        99
    (3 rows)
```

This is a PostgreSQL-specific feature. Not every RDBMS supports subqueries in every place where an expression is allowed.

It isn't possible to refer to the internal elements of one subquery from inside another. However, subqueries can refer to the elements of the main query. For example, if it's necessary to count cars for each car model and select the top 5 most popular models, it can be done using a subquery in this way:

```
car_portal=> SELECT make, model,
    (SELECT count(*) FROM car_portal_app.car
      WHERE car_model_id = main.car_model_id)
  FROM car_portal_app.car_model AS main
  ORDER BY 3 DESC
  LIMIT 5;
   make    |   model   | count
-----------+-----------+-------
 Peugeot   | 208       |     7
 Opel      | Corsa     |     6
 Jeep      | Wrangler  |     5
 Renault   | Laguna    |     5
 Peugeot   | 407       |     5
(5 rows)
```

In the example, the scalar subquery in the select-list refers to the table from the main query by its alias, `main`. The subquery is executed for each record received from the main table, using the value of `car_model_id` in its `WHERE` condition.

Subqueries can be nested. This means it's possible to use subqueries inside another subquery.

Set operations – UNION, EXCEPT, and INTERSECT

Set operations are used to combine the results of several queries. This is different from joining, although the same results can often be achieved with joining. Simply speaking, joining means placing the records of two tables beside each other horizontally. The result of joining is that the number of columns equals the sum of the number of columns in the source tables, and the number of records will depend on the join conditions.

Combining, in contrast, means putting the result of one query on top of the result of another query vertically. The number of columns stays the same, but the number of rows is the sum of the rows from the sources.

There are three set operations:

- **UNION**: Appends the result of one query to the result of another query.
- **INTERSECT**: Returns the records that exist in the results of both queries, effectively performing an INNER JOIN operation.
- **EXCEPT**: Returns the records from the first query that don't exist in the result of the second query—the difference.

The syntax of the set operations is as follows:

```
#Syntax for UNION operator:
<query1> UNION <query2>;

#Syntax for INTERSECT operator:
<query1> INTERSECT <query2>;

#Syntax for EXCEPT operator:
<query1> EXCEPT <query2>;
```

It's possible to use several set operations in one statement:

```
SELECT a, b FROM t1
UNION
SELECT c, d FROM t2
INTERSECT
SELECT e, f FROM t3;
```

The priority of all set operations is the same. This means that, logically, they are executed in the same order as is used in the code. However, the order in which the records are returned is not predicted, unless the ORDER BY clause is used. In this case, the ORDER BY clause is applied after all of the set operations. For this reason, it doesn't make sense to put ORDER BY in the subqueries.

All set operations, by default, remove duplicated records as if SELECT DISTINCT is used. To avoid this and return all the records, the ALL keyword should be used, which is specified after the name of the set operation:

```
<query1> UNION ALL <query2>.
```

Set operations can be used to determine the difference between two tables:

```
car_portal=> SELECT 'a', * FROM
(
  SELECT * FROM car_portal_app.a
  EXCEPT ALL
  SELECT * FROM car_portal_app.b
) v1
UNION ALL
SELECT 'b', * FROM
(
  SELECT * FROM car_portal_app.b
  EXCEPT ALL
  SELECT * FROM car_portal_app.a
) v2;
 ?column? | a_int | a_text
----------+-------+--------
 a        |     1 | one
 b        |     4 | four
(2 rows)
```

From the results of that query, you can find out that row one exists in the a table, but doesn't exist in the b table. Row four exists in the b table, but not in a.

It's possible to append one set of records to another only when they have the same number of columns and they have, respectively, the same data types, or compatible data types. The output names for the columns are always taken from the first subquery, even if they are different in subsequent queries.

In other RDBMSes, set operations can have different names, for example, in Oracle, EXCEPT is called MINUS.

Dealing with NULLS

NULL is a special value that any field or expression can have, except for the fields when it's explicitly forbidden. NULL means the absence of any value. It can also be treated as an unknown value in some cases. In relation to logical values, NULL is neither true nor false. Working with NULL can be confusing, because almost all operators, when taking NULL as an argument, return NULL. If you try to compare some values and one of them is NULL, the result will also be NULL, which is not true.

For example, consider the following condition:

```
WHERE a > b
```

This will return NULL if a or b have a NULL value. This is expected, but for the following condition, this is not obvious:

```
WHERE a = b
```

Here, even if both a and b have a value of NULL, the result will still be NULL. The = operator always returns NULL if any of the arguments is NULL. Similarly, the following will also be evaluated as NULL, even if a has a NULL value:

```
WHERE a = NULL
```

To check the expression for a NULL value, a special predicate is used: IS NULL.

In the previous examples, when it's necessary to find records when a = b or both a and b are NULL, the condition should be changed this way:

```
WHERE a = b OR (a IS NULL AND b IS NULL)
```

There is a special construct that can be used to check the equivalence of expressions taking NULL into account: IS NOT DISTINCT FROM. The preceding example can be implemented in the following way, which has the same logic:

```
WHERE a IS NOT DISTINCT FROM b
```

Logical operators are different. They can sometimes return a NOT NULL value even if they take NULL as an argument. For logical operators, NULL means an unknown value.

The AND operator always returns false when any of the operands is false, even if the second is NULL. OR always returns true if one of the arguments is true. In all other cases, the result is unknown, therefore NULL:

```
car_portal=> SELECT true AND NULL, false AND NULL, true OR NULL,
  false OR NULL, NOT NULL;
 ?column? | ?column? | ?column? | ?column? | ?column?
----------+----------+----------+----------+----------
          | f        | t        |          |
```

The IN subquery expression deals with NULL in a way that might not seem obvious:

```
car_portal=> SELECT 1 IN (1, NULL) as in;
 in
----
 t

car_portal=> SELECT 2 IN (1, NULL) as in;
 in
----

(1 row)
```

When evaluating the IN expression and the value that is being checked doesn't appear in the list of values inside IN (or in the result of a subquery) but there is a NULL value, the result will be also NULL, not false. This is easy to understand if we treat the NULL value as unknown, just as logical operators do. In the first query from the preceding example, it's clear that 1 is included in the list inside the IN expression. Therefore, the result is true. In the second example, 2 is not equal to 1, but that is *unknown* whether 2 is equal to the NULL value. That's why the result is also unknown.

Functions can treat NULL values differently. Their behavior is determined by their code. Most built-in functions return NULL if any of the arguments are NULL.

Aggregating functions work with NULL values in a different way. They work with many rows and therefore many values. In general, they ignore NULL. sum calculates the total of all non-null values and ignores NULL. sum returns NULL only when all the received values are NULL. For avg, max, and min, it's the same. But for count, it's different. count returns the number of non-null values. So, if all the values are NULL, count returns 0.

The count function can be used with a start (*) argument, like this: count(*). This would make it count rows themselves, not a particular field or expression. In that case, it doesn't matter whether there are NULL values, the number of records will be returned.

In contrast to other databases, in PostgreSQL, an empty string is not NULL.

Consider the following example:

```
car_portal=> SELECT a IS NULL, b IS NULL, a = b
  FROM (SELECT ''::text a, NULL::text b) v;
 ?column? | ?column? | ?column?
----------+----------+----------
 f        | t        |
```

There are a couple of functions designed to deal with NULL values: COALESCE and NULLIF.

The COALESCE function takes any number of arguments of the same data type or compatible types. It returns the value of the first of its arguments that IS NOT NULL. The following two expressions are equivalent:

```
#Expression 1:
COALESCE(a, b, c)

#Expression 2:
CASE WHEN a IS NOT NULL THEN a WHEN b IS NOT NULL THEN b ELSE c END
```

NULLIF takes two arguments and returns NULL if they are equal. Otherwise, it returns the value of the first argument.

This is somehow the opposite of COALESCE. The following expressions are equivalent:

```
#Expression 1:
NULLIF (a, b)

#Expression 2:
CASE WHEN a = b THEN NULL ELSE a END
```

Another aspect of NULL values is that they are ignored by unique constraints. This means that if a field of a table is defined as UNIQUE, it's still possible to create several records with a NULL value in that field. Additionally, B-tree indexes, which are commonly used, do not index NULL values. Consider the following query:

```
SELECT * FROM t WHERE a IS NULL
```

The preceding query would not use an index on the a column if it existed.

Changing the data in a database

Data can be inserted into database tables, updated, or deleted from a database. Respectively, the statements used for this are INSERT, UPDATE, and DELETE.

The INSERT statement

The INSERT statement is used to insert new data into tables in the database. Records are always inserted into only one table.

The INSERT statement has the following syntax:

```
INSERT INTO <table_name> [(<field_list>)]
{VALUES (<expression_list>)[,...]}|{DEFAULT VALUES}|<SELECT query>;
```

The name of the table the records are inserted into is specified after the INSERT INTO keywords. There are two options when using the INSERT statement, which has a different syntax: to insert one or several individual records, or to insert a set of records produced by an SQL query.

To insert one or several records, the VALUES clause is used. The list of the field values of a new record to insert is specified after the VALUES keyword. Items in the list correspond to the fields of the table according to their order. When it isn't necessary to set values for all the fields of a new record, the names of the fields whose values should be set should be given in parentheses after the table name. The missing fields will then get their default values, if defined, or they will be set to NULL.

The number of items in the VALUES list must be the same as the number of fields after the table name:

```
car_portal=> INSERT INTO car_portal_app.a (a_int) VALUES (6);
INSERT 0 1
```

The output of the INSERT command ,when it has successfully executed, is the word INSERT followed by the OID of the row that has been inserted (when only one row is inserted and OIDs are enabled for the table, otherwise, it is zero) and the number of records inserted. To learn more about OIDs, refer to Chapter 12, *The PostgreSQL Catalog and System Administration Functions*.

Another way to set default values to a field is to use the DEFAULT keyword in the VALUES list. If a default is not defined for the field, a NULL value will be set:

```
INSERT INTO car_portal_app.a (a_text) VALUES (default);
```

It's also possible to set all of the fields of the new record to their default values using the DEFAULT VALUES keyword:

```
INSERT INTO car_portal_app.a DEFAULT VALUES;
```

It's possible to insert multiple records using the VALUES syntax, providing several lists of values, comma-separated:

```
INSERT INTO car_portal_app.a (a_int, a_text) VALUES (7, 'seven'),
(8,'eight');
```

This option is PostgreSQL-specific. Different databases might allow you to insert only one row at a time.

In fact, in PostgreSQL, the VALUES clause is a standalone SQL command. Therefore, it can be used as a subquery in a SELECT query:

```
car_portal=> SELECT * FROM (VALUES (7, 'seven'), (8, 'eight')) v;
 column1 | column2
---------+---------
       7 | seven
       8 | eight
(2 rows)
```

When the records to insert are taken from another table or view, a SELECT query is used instead of the VALUES clause:

```
INSERT INTO car_portal_app.a SELECT * FROM car_portal_app.b;
```

The result of the query should match the structure of the table: have the same number of columns of compatible types in the same order.

In the SELECT query, it's possible to use the table in which the records are inserted. For example, to duplicate records in a table, the following statement can be used:

```
INSERT INTO car_portal_app.a SELECT * FROM car_portal_app.a;
```

By default, the INSERT statement returns the number of inserted records. It's also possible to return the inserted records themselves or some of their fields. The output of the statement is then similar to the output of the SELECT query. The RETURNING keyword, with the list of fields to return, is used for this:

```
car_portal=> INSERT INTO car_portal_app.a
SELECT * FROM car_portal_app.b
RETURNING a_int;
 a_int
-------
     2
     3
     4
(3 rows)

INSERT 0 3
```

If a unique constraint is defined on the table where the rows are inserted, INSERT will fail if it tries to insert records that conflict with existing ones. However, it's possible to let INSERT ignore such records or update them instead.

Assuming that there is a unique constraint on the b table for the b_int field, consider the following example:

```
car_portal=> INSERT INTO b VALUES (2, 'new_two');
ERROR: duplicate key value violates unique constraint "b_b_int_key"
DETAIL: Key (b_int)=(2) already exists.
```

What if we want to change a record instead of inserting one, if it exists already:

```
car_portal=> INSERT INTO b VALUES (2, 'new_two')
  ON CONFLICT (b_int) DO UPDATE SET b_text = excluded.b_text
  RETURNING *;
 b_int | b_text
-------+---------
     2 | new_two
(1 row)

INSERT 0 1
```

Here, the ON CONFLICT clause specifies what has to happen if there is already a record with the same value in the b_int field. The syntax is straightforward. The table alias, excluded, refers to the values that are being inserted. When it's necessary to refer to the values that are in the table, the table name is used.

The SQL standard defines a special command, MERGE, for this functionality. However, in PostgreSQL, the ON CONFLICT clause is part of the syntax of the INSERT statement. In other RDBMSes, this functionality could also be implemented in different ways.

The UPDATE statement

The UPDATE statement is used to change the data or records of a table without changing their number. It has the following syntax:

```
UPDATE <table_name>
SET <field_name> = <expression>[, ...]
[FROM <table_name> [JOIN clause]]
[WHERE <condition>];
```

There are two ways of using the UPDATE statement. The first is similar to a simple SELECT statement and is called **sub-select**. The second is based on other tables and is similar to a SELECT statement with multiple tables. In most cases, the same result can be achieved using any of these methods.

In PostgreSQL, only one table can be updated at a time. Other databases may allow you to update multiple tables at the same time under certain conditions.

UPDATE using sub-select

The expression for a new value is the usual SQL expression. It's possible to refer to the same field in the expression. In that case, the old value is used:

```
UPDATE t SET f = f + 1 WHERE a = 5;
```

It's common to use a subquery in the UPDATE statements. To be able to refer to the table being updated from a subquery, the table should get an alias:

```
car_portal=> UPDATE car_portal_app.a updated SET a_text =
  (SELECT b_text FROM car_portal_app.b WHERE b_int = updated.a_int);
UPDATE 7
```

If the subquery returns no result, the field value is set to NULL.

Note that the output of the UPDATE command is the word UPDATE followed by the number of records that were updated.

The WHERE clause is similar to the one used in the SELECT statement. If the WHERE statement is not specified, all of the records are updated.

UPDATE using additional tables

The second way of updating rows in the table is to use the FROM clause in a similar manner as in the SELECT statement:

```
UPDATE car_portal_app.a SET a_int = b_int FROM car_portal_app.b
WHERE a.a_text=b.b_text;
```

Every row from a, when there are rows in b with the same value of the text field, will be updated. The new value for the numeric field is taken from the b table. Technically, it's nothing but an inner join of the two tables. However, the syntax here is different. As the a table is not a part of the FROM clause, using the usual JOIN syntax isn't possible and the tables are joined on the condition in the WHERE clause. If another table were used, it would be possible to join it to the b table using the join syntax, either inner or outer.

The FROM syntax of the UPDATE statement can seem more obvious in many cases. For example, the following statement performs the same changes to the table as the previous, but this is less clear:

```
UPDATE car_portal_app.a
  SET a_int = (SELECT b_int FROM car_portal_app.b
    WHERE a.a_text=b.b_text)
  WHERE a_text IN (SELECT b_text FROM car_portal_app.b);
```

Another advantage of the FROM syntax is that, in many cases, it's much faster. On the other hand, this syntax can have unpredictable results in cases when, for a single record of the updated table, there are several matching records from the tables of the FROM clause:

```
UPDATE car_portal_app.a SET a_int = b_int FROM car_portal_app.b;
```

This query is syntactically correct. However, we know that in the b table there is more than one record. Which of them will be selected for every updated row isn't determined, as no WHERE condition is specified. The same happens when the WHERE clause doesn't define the one-to-one matching rule:

```
car_portal=> UPDATE car_portal_app.a
SET a_int = b_int FROM car_portal_app.b WHERE b_int>=a_int;
UPDATE 6
```

For each record of the a table, there's more than one record from the b table where b_int is greater than or equal to a_int. That's why the result of this update is undefined. However, PostgreSQL will allow this to be executed.

For this reason, you should be careful when doing updates this way.

The UPDATE query can return the records that were changed if the RETURNING clause is used, just as it is in the INSERT statement:

```
car_portal=> UPDATE car_portal_app.a SET a_int = 0 RETURNING *;
 a_int | a_text
-------+--------
     0 | one
     0 | two
. . .
```

The DELETE statement

The DELETE statement is used to remove records from the database. As with UPDATE, there are two ways of deleting: using sub-select or using another table or tables. The sub-select syntax is as follows:

```
DELETE FROM <table_name> [WHERE <condition>];
```

Records that follow the condition will be removed from the table. If the WHERE clause is omitted, all of the records will be deleted.

DELETE based on another table is similar to using the FROM clause of the UPDATE statement. Instead of FROM, the USING keyword should be used because FROM is already used in the syntax of the DELETE statement:

```
car_portal=> DELETE FROM car_portal_app.a USING car_portal_app.b
WHERE a.a_int=b.b_int;
DELETE 6
```

The preceding statement will delete all the records from a when there is a record in b with the same value of the numeric field. The output of the command indicates the number of records that were deleted.

The previous command is equivalent to the following:

```
DELETE FROM car_portal_app.a
  WHERE a_int IN (SELECT b_int FROM car_portal_app.b);
```

As well as UPDATE and INSERT, the DELETE statement can return deleted rows when the RETURNING keyword is used:

```
car_portal=> DELETE FROM car_portal_app.a RETURNING *;
 a_int | a_text
-------+--------
     0 | one
     0 | two
. . .
```

The TRUNCATE statement

Another statement that can also change the data, but not the data structure, is `TRUNCATE`. It clears a table completely and almost instantly. It has the same effect as the `DELETE` statement without the `WHERE` clause. So, it's useful on large tables:

```
car_portal=> TRUNCATE TABLE car_portal_app.a;
TRUNCATE TABLE
```

The `TABLE` keyword is optional.

`TRUNCATE` can clear several tables at a time. To do so, use a list of tables in the command, as follows:

```
TRUNCATE car_portal_app.a, car_portal_app.b;
```

If there are sequences used to auto generate values that are owned by fields of the table being cleared, the `TRUNCATE` command can reset those sequences. To do this, the following command could be used:

```
TRUNCATE some_table RESTART IDENTITY;
```

If there are tables that have foreign keys that reference the table being cleared, those tables could also be cleared with the same command, as follows:

```
TRUNCATE some_table CASCADE;
```

Summary

SQL is used to interact with databases: to create and maintain data structures; to put data into a database; and to change it, to retrieve it, and delete it. SQL has commands related to DDL, DML, and DCL. In this chapter, we looked at the four SQL statements that form the basis of DML: `SELECT`, `INSERT`, `UPDATE`, and `DELETE`.

The `SELECT` statement was examined in detail to explain SQL concepts such as grouping and filtering, to show SQL expressions and conditions, and to explain how to use subqueries. Additionally, some relational algebra topics were covered in the section "Selecting from multiple tables".

In the next chapter, we will cover more complicated topics, such as some advanced SQL features and techniques, and the programming language PL/pgSQL, which can be used to implement functions in PostgreSQL.

Questions

1. What is SQL?
2. What are the three main parts of SQL?
3. What are keywords in SQL?
4. How do we specify a constant string value in SQL code?
5. How do we insert a single record into a table?
6. How to insert many records into a table by taking them from another table?
7. How do we change records in a table?
8. How do we change records in a table that takes new values from another table?
9. Is there a way to get the values of updated or inserted records right after a changing command?
10. How do we retrieve data from a table?
11. What is a table join?
12. What is the difference between an INNER JOIN and an OUTER JOIN?
13. What is a CROSS JOIN?
14. How do we filter rows when retrieving them from a table?
15. Is there a difference between SQL expressions and SQL conditions?
16. What are grouping and aggregation?
17. When using grouping, is there a way to filter groups?
18. How do we limit the result set to a certain number of records?
19. How do we remove records from a table?

Advanced Query Writing 6

In this chapter, we will discuss some more advanced SQL features supported by PostgreSQL that were not covered in the previous chapters. Some query-writing techniques will also be described.

In this chapter, we will cover the following topics:

- Common table expressions
- Window functions
- Advanced SQL techniques

The same sample database, `car_portal`, is used in the code examples here. It's recommended to recreate the sample database in order to get the same results as shown in the code examples. The scripts to create the database and fill it with data (`schema.sql` and `data.sql`) can be found in the attached code bundle for this chapter. All the code examples for this chapter can be found in the `examples.sql` file.

Common table expressions

Although SQL is a declarative language, it provides a way of implementing the logic of the sequential execution of code or reusing code.

Common table expressions (CTEs) are parts of a SQL statement that produce result sets, defined once, with a view to reuse it, possibly several times, in other parts of the statement.

The simplified syntax diagram for a CTE is as follows:

```
WITH <subquery name> AS (<subquery code>) [, ...]
SELECT <Select list> FROM <subquery name>;
```

In the preceding syntax, `subquery code` is a query whose results will be used later in the primary query, as if it were a real table. The subquery in parentheses after the `AS` keyword is a CTE. It can also be called a sub-statement or an auxiliary statement. The query after the `WITH` block is the primary or main query. The whole statement itself is called a `WITH` query.

It's possible to use not only the `SELECT` statements in a CTE, but also the `INSERT`, `UPDATE`, and `DELETE` statements.

It is also possible to use several CTEs in one `WITH` query. Every CTE has its name defined before the `AS` keyword. The main query can reference a CTE by its name. A CTE can also refer to another CTE by the name. A CTE can refer only to the CTEs that were defined before the referencing one.

The references to CTEs in the primary query can be treated as table names. In fact, PostgreSQL executes CTEs only once, caches the results, and reuses them instead of executing subqueries each time they occur in the main query. This makes them similar to tables.

CTEs can help developers to organize SQL code. Suppose we want to find the models of the cars in the sample database that were built after 2010, and have the least number of owners. Consider the following code:

```
car_portal=> WITH pre_select AS
(
 SELECT car_id, number_of_owners, car_model_id
 FROM car_portal_app.car WHERE manufacture_year >= 2010
),
joined_data AS
(
 SELECT car_id, make, model, number_of_owners
 FROM pre_select
 INNER JOIN car_portal_app.car_model
   ON pre_select.car_model_id = car_model.car_model_id
),
minimal_owners AS
(SELECT min(number_of_owners) AS min_number_of_owners FROM pre_select)
SELECT car_id, make, model, number_of_owners
 FROM joined_data INNER JOIN minimal_owners
 ON joined_data.number_of_owners = minimal_owners.min_number_of_owners;
 car_id |     make      |   model   | number_of_owners
--------+---------------+-----------+------------------
      2 | Opel          | Corsa     |                1
      3 | Citroen       | C3        |                1
     11 | Nissan        | GT-R      |                1
```

```
        36 | KIA              | Magentis   |                   1
...
(25 rows)
```

In the preceding example, the logical part of the query is presented as a sequence of actions—filtering in `pre_select` and then joining in `joined_data`. The other part, that is, calculating the minimal number of owners, is executed in a dedicated subquery, `minimal_owners`. This makes the implementation of the query logic similar to that of an imperative programming language.

The use of CTEs in the preceding example doesn't make the whole query faster. However, there are situations where the use of CTEs can increase performance. Moreover, sometimes it is not possible to implement the logic in any other way except than with CTEs. In the following sections, some of these situations are discussed in detail.

The order of execution of the CTEs is not defined. PostgreSQL aims to execute only the main query. If the main query contains references to the CTEs, then PostgreSQL will execute them first. If a `SELECT` sub-statement is not referenced by the main query, directly or indirectly, then it isn't executed at all. Data-changing CTEs are always executed.

Reusing SQL code with CTE

When the execution of a subquery takes a lot of time, and the subquery is used in the whole SQL statement more than once, it makes sense to put it into a `WITH` clause to reuse its results. This makes the query faster because PostgreSQL executes the subqueries from the `WITH` clause only once, caches the results in memory or on disk—depending on their size—and then reuses them.

For example, let's take the `car_portal` database. Suppose it's required to find newer car models. This would require it to calculate the average age of the cars of each model and then select the models with an average age lower than the average age of all the models.

This can be done in the following way:

```
car_portal=> SELECT make, model, avg_age FROM
(
  SELECT car_model_id,
      avg(EXTRACT(YEAR FROM now())-manufacture_year) AS avg_age
    FROM car_portal_app.car
    GROUP BY car_model_id
) age_subq1
INNER JOIN car_portal_app.car_model
  ON car_model.car_model_id = age_subq1.car_model_id
```

```
WHERE avg_age < (SELECT avg(avg_age) FROM
  (
    SELECT avg(EXTRACT(YEAR FROM now()) - manufacture_year) avg_age
      FROM car_portal_app.car
      GROUP BY car_model_id
  ) age_subq2
);
       make      |    model    |    avg_age
-----------------+-------------+------------------
  BMW            | 1er         |        1
  BMW            | X6          |       2.5
  Mercedes Benz  | A klasse    |       1.5
...
(41 rows)
```

The EXTRACT function used in the query returns the integer value of the given part of the date expression. In the preceding example, the function is used to retrieve the year from the current date. The difference between the current year and manufacture_year is the age of a car in years.

There are two subqueries that are almost the same, age_subq1 and age_subq2: the same table is queried and the same grouping and aggregation are performed. This makes it possible to use the same subquery twice by using a CTE:

```
car_portal=> WITH age_subq AS
(
  SELECT car_model_id,
      avg(EXTRACT(YEAR FROM now())-manufacture_year) AS avg_age
    FROM car_portal_app.car
    GROUP BY car_model_id
)
SELECT make, model, avg_age
  FROM age_subq
    INNER JOIN car_portal_app.car_model
      ON car_model.car_model_id = age_subq.car_model_id
  WHERE avg_age < (SELECT avg(avg_age) FROM age_subq);
       make      |    model    |    avg_age
-----------------+-------------+------------------
  BMW            | 1er         |        1
  BMW            | X6          |       2.5
  Mercedes Benz  | A klasse    |       1.5
...
(41 rows)
```

The result of both of the queries is the same. However, on the test system used to prepare the code samples, the first query took 1.9 milliseconds to finish and the second one took 1.0 milliseconds. Of course, in absolute values, the difference is nothing, but relatively, the WITH query is almost twice as fast. If the number of records in the tables was in the range of millions, the absolute difference would be substantial.

Another advantage of using a CTE, in this case, is that the code became shorter and easier to understand. That's another use case for the WITH clause. Long and complicated subqueries can be formatted as CTEs in order to make the whole query shorter and more understandable, even if it doesn't affect the performance.

Sometimes, though, it's better not to use a CTE. For example, you could try to preselect some columns from the table, thinking it would help the database to perform the query faster because of the reduced amount of information to process. In that case, the query could be as follows:

```
WITH car_subquery AS
(
    SELECT number_of_owners, manufacture_year, number_of_doors
      FROM car_portal_app.car
)
SELECT number_of_owners, number_of_doors FROM car_subquery
  WHERE manufacture_year = 2008;
```

This has the opposite effect. PostgreSQL does not push the WHERE clause from the primary query to the sub-statement. The database will retrieve all the records from the table, take three columns from them, and store this temporary dataset in memory. Then, the temporary data will be queried using the manufacture_year = 2008 predicate. If there was an index on manufacture_year, it would not be used because the temporary data is being queried and not the real table.

For this reason, the following query is executed five times faster than the preceding one, even though it seems to be almost the same:

```
SELECT number_of_owners, manufacture_year, number_of_doors
 FROM car_portal_app.car
 WHERE manufacture_year = 2008;
```

Recursive and hierarchical queries

It's possible to refer to the name of a CTE from the code of that CTE itself. These statements are called **recursive queries**. Recursive queries must have a special structure that tells the database that the subquery is recursive. The structure of a recursive query is as follows:

```
WITH RECURSIVE <subquery_name> (<field list>) AS
(
  <non-recursive term>
  UNION [ALL|DISTINCT]
  <recursive term>
)
[,...]
<main query>
```

Both non-recursive and recursive terms are subqueries that must return the same number of fields of the same types. The names of the fields are specified in the declaration of the whole recursive query; therefore, it does not matter which names are assigned to the fields in the subqueries.

A non-recursive term is also called an **anchor subquery**, while a recursive term is also known as an **iterating subquery**.

A non-recursive or anchor subquery is a starting point for the execution of a recursive query. It cannot refer to the name of the recursive subquery. It's executed only once. The results of the non-recursive term are passed again to the same CTE and then only the recursive term is executed. It can reference the recursive subquery. If the recursive term returns rows, they are passed to the CTE again. This is called iteration. Iteration is repeated as long as the result of the recursive term is not empty. The result of the whole query is all the rows returned by the non-recursive term and all the iterations of the recursive term. If the UNION ALL keywords are used, all the rows are returned. If UNION DISTINCT or just UNION is used, the duplicated rows are removed from the result set.

 The algorithm of a recursive subquery implies iterations but not recursion. However, in the SQL standard, queries of this kind are called recursive. In other databases, the same logic can be implemented in a similar manner, but the syntax can be slightly different.

For example, the following recursive query can be used to calculate the factorial values of numbers up to 5:

```
car_portal=> WITH RECURSIVE subq (n, factorial) AS
(
  SELECT 1, 1
  UNION ALL
```

```
      SELECT n + 1, factorial * (n + 1) from subq WHERE n < 5
)
SELECT * FROM subq;
 n | factorial
---+-----------
 1 |          1
 2 |          2
 3 |          6
 4 |         24
 5 |        120
(5 rows)
```

Here, SELECT 1, 1 is the anchor subquery. It returns one row (the n and factorial fields have values of 1 and 1), which is passed to the subsequent iterating subquery. The first iteration adds one to the value of the n field and multiplies the value of the factorial by (n+1), which gives the values 2 and 2. Then, it passes this row to the next iteration. The second iteration returns the values 3 and 6, and so on. The last iteration returns a row where the value of the n field equals 5.

This row is filtered out in the WHERE clause of the iterating subquery; that's why the following iteration returns nothing and the execution stops at this point. So, the whole recursive subquery returns a list of five numbers, from 1 to 5, and their factorial values.

If no WHERE clause was specified, the execution would never stop, which would cause an error in the end.

The preceding example is quite easy to implement without recursive queries. PostgreSQL provides a way to generate a series of numeric values and use them in subqueries. However, there's a task that cannot be solved without recursive queries: querying a hierarchy of objects.

There is no hierarchical data in the car portal database, so in order to illustrate the technique, we need to create some sample data. A typical hierarchy implies the existence of a parent-child relationship between objects, where an object can be a parent and a child at the same time.

Suppose there is a family—**Alan** has two children: **Bert** and **Bob**. **Bert** also has two children: **Carl** and **Carmen**. **Bob** has one child, **Cecil**, who has two children: **Dave** and **Den**. The relationships are shown in the following diagram, the arrows go from each person to their parent:

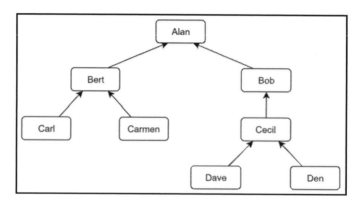

Hierarchical relationship

In the database, the hierarchy can be stored in a simple table with two columns: `person` and `parent`. The first will be the primary key and the second will be a foreign key that references the same table:

```
car_portal=>CREATE TABLE family (
  person text PRIMARY KEY,
  parent text REFERENCES family
);
CREATE TABLE
car_portal=> INSERT INTO family VALUES ('Alan', NULL),
  ('Bert', 'Alan'), ('Bob', 'Alan'), ('Carl', 'Bert'),
  ('Carmen', 'Bert'), ('Cecil', 'Bob'), ('Dave', 'Cecil'),
  ('Den', 'Cecil');
INSERT 0 8
```

The first inserted record with a `NULL` value for `parent` indicates that there's no information about Alan's parent.

Imagine you need to build a full bloodline for all the children in the family. It's not possible to do it by just joining tables, because each join will handle only one level of the hierarchy, but in general, the number of levels is not given.

The following recursive query will solve the problem:

```
car_portal=> WITH RECURSIVE genealogy (bloodline, person, level) AS
(
  SELECT person, person, 0 FROM family WHERE person = 'Alan'
  UNION ALL
  SELECT g.bloodline || ' -> ' || f.person, f.person, g.level + 1
    FROM family f, genealogy g WHERE f.parent = g.person
)
SELECT bloodline, level FROM genealogy;
          bloodline               | level
----------------------------------+-------
 Alan                             |   0
 Alan -> Bert                     |   1
 Alan -> Bob                      |   1
 Alan -> Bert -> Carl             |   2
 Alan -> Bert -> Carmen           |   2
 Alan -> Bob -> Cecil             |   2
 Alan -> Bob -> Cecil -> Dave     |   3
 Alan -> Bob -> Cecil -> Den      |   3
(8 rows)
```

In the non-recursive term, the start of the hierarchy is selected. We start from `Alan` because we know he has no parent defined in the table. His name is the initial value for the bloodline. On the first iteration, in the recursive term, his children are selected (the people whose parent is the person selected in the non-recursive term). Their names are added to the bloodline field with a separator, `->`. On the second iteration, the children of the children are selected, and so on. When no more children are found, the execution stops. The value in the field level is incremented on each iteration so that the number of iterations is visible in the results.

There is a potential problem with such hierarchical queries. If the data contained cycles, the recursive query would never stop if used in the same way as the preceding code. For example, let's change the starting record in the `family` table, as follows:

```
UPDATE family SET parent = 'Bert' WHERE person = 'Alan';
```

Now there's a cycle in the data: `Alan` is a child of his own child. If we run the previous bloodline query as is, it would process this cycle until it would eventually fail. To use the query, it's necessary to somehow make the query stop. This can be done by checking whether the person that is being processed by the recursive term was already included in the bloodline, as follows:

```
car_portal=> WITH RECURSIVE genealogy (bloodline, person, level, processed)
AS
(
```

```
    SELECT person, person, 0, ARRAY[person] FROM family WHERE person = 'Alan'
    UNION ALL
    SELECT g.bloodline || ' -> ' || f.person, f.person, g.level + 1,
        processed || f.person
      FROM family f, genealogy g
      WHERE f.parent = g.person AND NOT f.person = ANY(processed)
)
SELECT bloodline, level FROM genealogy;
           bloodline          | level
------------------------------+-------
 Alan                         |   0
 Alan -> Bert                 |   1
 Alan -> Bob                  |   1
 Alan -> Bert -> Carl         |   2
 Alan -> Bert -> Carmen       |   2
 Alan -> Bob -> Cecil         |   2
 Alan -> Bob -> Cecil -> Dave |   3
 Alan -> Bob -> Cecil -> Den  |   3
(8 rows)
```

The result is the same as in the previous example. The processed field that is used in the CTE, but not selected in the main query, is an array that contains the names of all the processed people. In fact, it has the same data as the field bloodline, but, in a way, this is more convenient to use in the WHERE clause. In each iteration, the name of the processed person is added to the array. Additionally, in the WHERE clause of the recursive term, the name of the person is checked so that it isn't equal to any element of the array.

There are some limitations to the implementation of recursive queries. The use of aggregation is not allowed in the recursive term. Moreover, the name of the recursive subquery can be referenced only once in the recursive term.

It's possible to combine recursive CTEs and non-recursive CTEs in one query. It's also possible to have several recursive CTEs. In this case, the RECURSIVE keyword should be used only once after the WITH keyword.

Changing data in multiple tables at a time

Another very useful application of CTEs is performing several data-changing statements at once. This is done by including the INSERT, UPDATE, and DELETE statements in CTEs. The results of any of these statements can be passed to the following CTEs or to the primary query by specifying the RETURNING clause. As well as for SELECT statements, the maximum number of common table expressions that change data is not defined.

For example, suppose you want to add a new car to the car portal database and there is no corresponding car model in the `car_model` table. To do this, you need to enter a new record in the `car_model` table, take the ID of the new record, and use this ID to insert the data into the `car` table:

```
car_portal=> INSERT INTO car_portal_app.car_model (make, model)
  VALUES ('Ford','Mustang') RETURNING car_model_id;
 car_model_id
--------------
          100
(1 row)
INSERT 0 1
car_portal=> INSERT INTO car_portal_app.car (
  number_of_owners, registration_number, manufacture_year,
  number_of_doors, car_model_id, mileage)
VALUES (1, 'GTR1231', 2014, 4, 100, 10423);
INSERT 0 1
```

Sometimes, it isn't convenient to perform two statements that store the intermediate ID number somewhere. `WITH` queries provide a way to make the changes in both tables at the same time:

```
car_portal=# WITH car_model_insert AS
(
  INSERT INTO car_portal_app.car_model (make, model) VALUES
('Ford','Mustang')
  RETURNING car_model_id
)
INSERT INTO car_portal_app.car (
  number_of_owners, registration_number, manufacture_year,
  number_of_doors, car_model_id, mileage)
SELECT 1, 'GTR1231', 2014, 4, car_model_id, 10423 FROM car_model_insert;
INSERT 0 1
```

CTEs that change the data are always executed. It doesn't matter whether they are referenced in the primary query directly or indirectly. However, the order of their execution isn't determined. You can influence that order by making them dependent on each other.

What if several CTEs change the same table or use the results produced by each other? Here are some principles of their isolation and interaction:

- For sub-statements:
    - All sub-statements work with the data as it was at the time of the start of the whole WITH query.
    - They don't see the results of each other's work. For example, it isn't possible for the DELETE sub-statement to remove a row that was inserted by another INSERT sub-statement.
    - The only way to pass information about the processed records from a data-changing CTE to another CTE is with the RETURNING clause.

- For triggers defined on the tables being changed:
    - **For BEFORE triggers**: Statement-level triggers are executed just before the execution of each sub-statement. Row-level triggers are executed just before the changing of every record. This means that a row-level trigger for one sub-statement can be executed before a statement-level trigger for another sub-statement even if the same table is changed.
    - **For AFTER triggers**: Both statement-level and row-level triggers are executed after the whole WITH query. They are executed in groups per every sub-statement: first at the row level and then at the statement level. This means that a statement-level trigger for one sub-statement can be executed before a row-level trigger for another sub-statement, even if the same table is changed.

    The statements inside the code of the triggers do see the changes in data that were made by other sub-statements.

- For the constraints defined on the tables being changed, assuming they are not set to DEFERRED:
    - PRIMARY KEY and UNIQUE constraints are validated for every record at the time the record is inserted or updated. They take into account the changes made by other sub-statements.
    - CHECK constraints are validated for every record at the time the record is inserted or updated. They don't take into account the changes made by other sub-statements.
    - FOREIGN KEY constraints are validated at the end of the execution of the whole WITH query.

Here is a simple example of dependency and interaction between CTEs:

```
car_portal=> CREATE TABLE t (f int UNIQUE);
CREATE TABLE
car_portal=> INSERT INTO t VALUES (1);
INSERT 0 1
car_portal=> WITH del_query AS (DELETE FROM t) INSERT INTO t VALUES (1);
ERROR: duplicate key value violates unique constraint "t_f_key"
```

The last query failed because PostgreSQL tried to execute the main query before the CTE. If you create a dependency that will make the CTE execute first, the record will be deleted and the new record will be inserted. In that case, the constraint will not be violated:

```
car_portal=> WITH del_query AS (DELETE FROM t RETURNING f)
INSERT INTO t SELECT 1 WHERE (SELECT count(*) FROM del_query) IS NOT NULL;
INSERT 0 1
```

In the preceding code snippet, the WHERE condition in the main query doesn't have any practical meaning because the result of count is never NULL. However, as the CTE is referenced in the query, it's executed before the execution of the main query.

Window functions

Apart from grouping and aggregation, PostgreSQL provides another way to perform computations based on the values of several records. It can be done using window functions. Grouping and aggregation mean one single output record for every group of several input records. Window functions can do similar things, but they are executed for every record, and the number of records in the output and the input is the same:

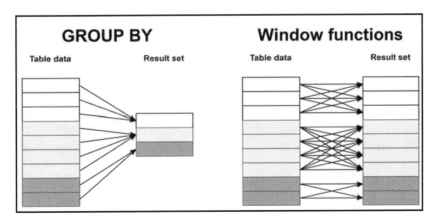

GROUP BY and window functions

In the preceding diagram, the rectangles represent the records of a table. Let's assume that the color of the rectangles indicates the value of a field used to group the records. When the GROUP BY operation is used in a query, each distinct value of that field will create a group and each group will become a single record in the results of the query. This was explained in Chapter 5, *SQL Language*. Window functions provide access to the values of all of the records of the group (which is called a partition, in this case), although the number of records in the result set stays the same. When window functions are used, no grouping is necessary, although it's possible.

Window functions are evaluated after grouping and aggregation. For this reason, the only places in the SELECT query where the window functions are allowed are select-list and the ORDER BY clause.

Window definitions

The syntax of the window functions is as follows:

```
<function_name> (<function_arguments>)
OVER (
  [PARTITION BY <expression_list>]
  [ORDER BY <order_by_list>]
  [<frame_clause>])
```

The construct in the parentheses after the OVER keyword is called the **window definition**.

Window functions, in general, work like aggregating functions. They process sets of records. These sets are built separately for each processed record and can overlap. That's why, unlike the normal aggregating functions, window functions are evaluated for each row.

For each record, a set of rows to be processed by a window function is built in the following way: at the beginning, the PARTITION BY clause is processed. All the records that have the same values after evaluating the expressions from expression_list as the current row is taken. The set of these rows is called the **partition**. The current row is also included in the partition. In fact, the PARTITION BY clause has the same logic and syntax as the GROUP BY clause of the SELECT statement, except that it isn't possible to refer to the output column names or numbers in PARTITION BY.

In other words, while processing each record, a window function will take a look at all the other records to check whether any of them fall into the same partition as the current one. If no PARTITION BY is specified, it means that all the rows will be included in a single partition at this step.

Next, the partition is sorted according to the ORDER BY clause, which has the same syntax and logic as the ORDER BY clause in the SELECT statement. Again, no references to the output column names or numbers are allowed here. If the ORDER BY clause is omitted, then all of the records of the set are considered to have the same position.

The last part of the window definition is called the **frame clause**. The frame clause can be one of the following:

```
ROWS | RANGE | GROUPS <frame_start> [<frame_exclusion>]
ROWS | RANGE | GROUPS BETWEEN <frame_start> AND <frame_end>
[<frame_exclusion>]
```

Processing the frame clause means taking a subset from the whole partition to pass it to the window function.

The subset is called the **window frame**. The frame has its start and end points. The definition of these points has different semantics depending on the type of the window frame. In the preceding syntax diagram, the start and end points are referenced by frame_start and frame_end, and can be any of the following:

- UNBOUNDED PRECEDING: The very first record of the partition
- <offset> PRECEDING: A record that is placed several records before the current one
- CURRENT ROW: The current row itself
- <offset> FOLLOWING: A record that is placed several records after the current record
- UNBOUNDED FOLLOWING: The very last record of the partition

These definitions make sense only when the partition is sorted, therefore, usage of the frame clause is only allowed when the ORDER BY clause is there.

The start point should precede the end point. That's why, for example, ROWS BETWEEN CURRENT ROW AND 1 PRECEDING is not correct.

A window frame can be defined using one of the three modes: the ROWS mode, the GROUPS mode, or the RANGE mode. The mode affects the meaning of the CURRENT ROW and the offset in the definition of the boundaries of the window frame, as follows:

- **The ROWS mode**: The CURRENT ROW points to the current row itself. The offset must be an expression that returns a non-negative integer. The offset then points to a row that's that number of rows before or after the current row.
- **The GROUPS mode**: The GROUPS mode deals with **peer groups**, which are groups of rows that have the same position in the ordered list according to the rule set by the ORDER BY clause. When defining the start point of the window frame, the CURRENT ROW points to the first row of the the same peer group where the current row belongs. The offset specifies the number of the preceding peer group, and the window would start from the first row of that group. When defining the end point, they would point to the last rows of the respective peer groups. The offset, again, must be an integer expression that returns a non-negative number.
- **The RANGE mode**: The CURRENT ROW points to the beginning or the end of the same peer group as the current row, just like in the GROUPS mode. The offset specifies a difference between the current row and the start or end point of the window frame. This works only when the ORDER BY clause has only one expression in its list. Depending on the type of that expression, the offset may also have a different type. For example, when the rows are ordered by a field of the date type, the offset should have the interval type. The offset should be non-negative.

If frame_end is omitted, CURRENT ROW is used by default.

If the whole frame clause is omitted, the frame will be built using the RANGE UNBOUNDED PRECEDING definition.

It's possible to exclude certain rows from the window frame, laying around the current row. The EXCLUDE construct is used for this. This is what was meant by frame_exclusion in the previous syntax diagram. The construct can be one of the following:

- EXCLUDE CURRENT ROW: Will remove the current row from the window frame
- EXCLUDE GROUP: Will remove the whole peer group of the current row
- EXCLUDE TIES: Excludes the peer group of the current row, but leaves the current row in
- EXCLUDE NO OTHERS: Doesn't exclude anything; this is the default

Look at the following example of a window definition:

```
OVER (
  PARTITION BY a
  ORDER BY b
  ROWS BETWEEN UNBOUNDED PRECEDING AND 5 FOLLOWING)
```

The preceding definition means that for every row, all the records with the same value of the a field will form the partition. Then, the partition will be ordered in an ascending manner by the values of the b field, and the frame will contain all the records from the beginning of the partition to the fifth one following the current row.

Here's another example: the rows are partitioned into two groups, having even or odd values of the a field. To build the window frame, the rows will be ordered by b, and all the rows that belong to the same peer group as the current row, and the previous and the next peer groups, will be included as follows:

```
OVER (
  PARTITION BY a % 2
  ORDER BY b
  GROUPS BETWEEN 1 PRECEDING AND 1 FOLLOWING)
```

 An empty window definition means that all the records will form a single partition. In this case, the behavior of a window function will be similar to aggregation without a GROUP BY clause, when all rows are aggregated.

The WINDOW clause

Window definitions can be quite long, and in many cases, it isn't convenient to use them in the select-list. Several window functions can use the same or similar window definitions. PostgreSQL provides a way to define windows and give them names that can be used in the OVER clause in window functions. This is done using the WINDOW clause of the SELECT statement, which is specified after the HAVING clause, as follows:

```
SELECT count() OVER w, sum(b) OVER w,
  avg(b) OVER (w ORDER BY c ROWS BETWEEN 1 PRECEDING AND 1 FOLLOWING)
FROM table1
WINDOW w AS (PARTITION BY a)
```

The predefined window can be used as is. In the preceding example, the `count` and `sum` window functions do so. The window definition can also be further detailed, like it is for the `avg` function in the example. The syntactical difference is the following: to reuse the same window definition, the window name should be specified after the `OVER` keyword without parentheses. To extend the window definition with the `ORDER BY` or frame clause, you should use the name of the window inside the parentheses.

When the same window definition is used several times, PostgreSQL will optimize the execution of the query by building partitions only once and then reusing the results.

Using window functions

Any aggregating function can be used as a window function, with the exception of ordered-set and hypothetical-set aggregates. User-defined aggregating functions can also be used as window functions. The presence of the `OVER` clause indicates that the function is used as a window function.

When the aggregating function is used as a window function, it will aggregate the rows that belong to the window frame of a current row. A typical use case for window functions are computing statistical values of different kinds. Take the `car_portal` database as an example. The `advertisement` table contains information about advertisements that users create. Suppose you need to analyze the quantity of advertisements that users create over a period of time. The report should contain monthly statistics. It should include the number of advertisements per month, a cumulative total showing the number of advertisements from the beginning of the year till each month, the moving average of the number of advertisements over five months, and the share of each month over the whole year. The query that generates the report would be as follows:

```
car_portal=> WITH monthly_data AS (
  SELECT date_trunc('month', advertisement_date) AS month, count(*) as cnt
    FROM car_portal_app.advertisement
    GROUP BY date_trunc('month', advertisement_date)
)
SELECT to_char(month,'YYYY-MM') as month, cnt,
  sum(cnt) OVER (w ORDER BY month) AS cnt_year,
  round(avg(cnt) OVER (
    ORDER BY month
    ROWS BETWEEN 2 PRECEDING AND 2 FOLLOWING), 1) AS mov_avg,
  round(cnt / sum(cnt) OVER w * 100,1) AS ratio_year
FROM monthly_data WINDOW w AS (PARTITION BY date_trunc('year',month));
  month  | cnt | cnt_year | mov_avg | ratio_year
---------+-----+----------+---------+------------
 2014-01 |  42 |       42 |    40.3 |        5.8
```

```
2014-02 |  49 |   91 |  44.5 |    6.7
2014-03 |  30 |  121 |  56.8 |    4.1
2014-04 |  57 |  178 |  69.0 |    7.8
2014-05 | 106 |  284 |  73.0 |   14.6
2014-06 | 103 |  387 |  81.0 |   14.2
2014-07 |  69 |  456 |  86.0 |    9.5
2014-08 |  70 |  526 |  74.0 |    9.6
2014-09 |  82 |  608 |  60.6 |   11.3
2014-10 |  46 |  654 |  54.2 |    6.3
2014-11 |  36 |  690 |  49.8 |    5.0
2014-12 |  37 |  727 |  35.2 |    5.1
2015-01 |  48 |   48 |  32.5 |   84.2
2015-02 |   9 |   57 |  31.3 |   15.8
```

(14 rows)

In the WITH clause, the data is aggregated on a monthly basis. In the main query, the w window is defined, which implies partitioning by year. This means that every window function that uses the w window will work with the records of the same year as the current record.

The first window function, sum, uses the w window. As ORDER BY is specified, each record has its place in the partition. The frame clause is omitted, therefore the default frame, RANGE BETWEEN UNBOUNDED PRECEDING AND CURRENT ROW, is applied. This means that the function calculates the sum of the values for the records from the beginning of each year till the current month. It's the cumulative total on a yearly basis.

The second function, avg, calculates the moving average. For each record, it calculates the average value over five records— the last two records before the current one, the current record itself, and first two records following the current one. It doesn't use a predefined window, because the moving average doesn't take the year into account. Only the order of the values matters.

The third window function, sum, uses the same window definition again. It calculates the total sum of the values for the whole year. This value is used as the denominator in the expression that calculates the share of the current month over the year.

There are several window functions that are not aggregating functions. They are used to get the values of other records within the partition, to calculate the rank of the current row among all rows, and to generate row numbers.

For example, let's change the report from the previous example. Suppose you need to calculate the difference in the quantity of advertisements for each month against the previous months and against the same month of the previous year. Suppose you also need to get the rank of the current month. The query would be as follows:

```
car_portal=> WITH monthly_data AS (
  SELECT date_trunc('month', advertisement_date) AS month, count(*) as cnt
    FROM car_portal_app.advertisement
    GROUP BY date_trunc('month', advertisement_date)
)
SELECT to_char(month,'YYYY-MM') as month, cnt,
    cnt - lag(cnt) OVER (ORDER BY month) as prev_m,
    cnt - lag(cnt, 12) OVER (ORDER BY month) as prev_y,
    rank() OVER (w ORDER BY cnt DESC) as rank
  FROM monthly_data
  WINDOW w AS (PARTITION BY date_trunc('year',month))
  ORDER BY month DESC;
```

month	cnt	prev_m	prev_y	rank
2015-02	9	-39	-40	2
2015-01	48	11	6	1
2014-12	37	1		10
2014-11	36	-10		11
2014-10	46	-36		8
2014-09	82	12		3
2014-08	70	1		4
2014-07	69	-34		5
2014-06	103	-3		2
2014-05	106	49		1
2014-04	57	27		6
2014-03	30	-19		12
2014-02	49	7		7
2014-01	42			9

```
(14 rows)
```

The lag function returns the value of a given expression for the record, which is the given number of records before the current one (the default is 1). In the first occurrence of the function in the example, it returns the value of the cnt field from the previous record, which corresponds to the previous month. You may notice that the number of advertisements for February 2015 is 9, which is lower than in January 2015, by 39.

The second lag returns the value of cnt for the record that is 12 records before the current one—meaning one year ago. The number for February 2015 is lower than the number for February 2014, by 40.

The `rank` function returns the rank of the current row within the partition. It returns the rank with gaps. This means that if two records have the same position according to the `ORDER BY` clause, both of them will get the same rank. The next record will get the rank after the next rank. For example, there may be two first records directly followed by a third one.

Here are some other window functions:

- `lead`: Similar to `lag`, but it returns the value of a given expression evaluated for the next record or for the record, that is, the given number of records after the current row.
- `first_value`, `last_value`, `nth_value`: These return the value of a given expression evaluated for the first record, last record, or n^{th} record of the frame, respectively.
- `row_number`: Returns the number of the current row within the partition.
- `dense_rank`: Returns the rank of the current row without gaps.
- `percent_rank` and `cume_dist`: Return the relative rank of the current row. The difference is that the first function uses rank and the second uses `row_number` as a numerator for the calculations.
- `ntile`: Divides the partition into the given number of equal parts and returns the number of the part where the current record belongs.

A more detailed description of these functions is available in the documentation at `http://www.postgresql.org/docs/current/static/functions-window.html`.

Window functions with grouping and aggregation

As window functions are evaluated after grouping, it's possible to use aggregating functions inside window functions, but not the other way around.

The code shown here is correct:

```
sum(count(*)) OVER()
```

The following approach will also work:

```
sum(a) OVER(ORDER BY count(*))
```

However, `sum(count(*) OVER())` is wrong.

For example, to calculate the rank of the seller accounts by the number of advertisements they make, the following query can be used:

```
car_portal=> SELECT seller_account_id, dense_rank() OVER(ORDER BY count(*)
DESC)
 FROM car_portal_app.advertisement
 GROUP BY seller_account_id;
 seller_account_id | dense_rank
-------------------+------------
                26 |          1
               128 |          2
                28 |          2
               126 |          2
 . . .
```

Advanced SQL techniques

In the following section, some other advanced SQL techniques will be introduced:

- The DISTINCT ON clause, which helps to group records and take the first record for each group
- Selecting sample data from a very big table
- Set-returning functions, which are functions that return relations
- LATERAL joins, which allow subqueries to reference each other
- Advanced grouping techniques that can be used to generate reports
- Some special aggregating functions

Selecting the first records

Quite often, it's necessary to find the first records based on some criteria. For example, let's take the car_portal database; suppose you need to find the earliest advertisement for each car_id in the advertisement table.

In this case, grouping can help. It requires a subquery to implement the logic:

```
SELECT advertisement_id, advertisement_date, adv.car_id, seller_account_id
 FROM car_portal_app.advertisement adv
 INNER JOIN (
   SELECT car_id, min(advertisement_date) min_date
   FROM car_portal_app.advertisement GROUP BY car_id
 ) first
   ON adv.car_id=first.car_id AND adv.advertisement_date = first.min_date;
```

However, if the ordering logic is complex and cannot be implemented using the `min` function, this approach won't work.

Although window functions can solve the problem, they aren't always convenient to use:

```
SELECT DISTINCT first_value(advertisement_id) OVER w AS advertisement_id,
    min(advertisement_date) OVER w AS advertisement_date,
    car_id, first_value(seller_account_id) OVER w AS seller_account_id
  FROM car_portal_app.advertisement
  WINDOW w AS (PARTITION BY car_id ORDER BY advertisement_date);
```

In the preceding code, `DISTINCT` is used to remove the duplicates that were grouped together in the previous example.

PostgreSQL provides an explicit way of selecting the first record within each group. The `DISTINCT ON` construct is used for this. The syntax is as follows:

```
SELECT DISTINCT ON (<expression_list>) <Select-List>
...
ORDER BY <order_by_list>
```

In the preceding code snippet, for each distinct combination of values of `expression_list`, only the first record will be returned by the `SELECT` statement. The `ORDER BY` clause is used to define a rule to determine which record is the first. The `expression_list` from the `DISTINCT ON` construct must be included in the `order_by_list` list.

For the task being discussed, this can be applied in the following way:

```
SELECT DISTINCT ON (car_id)
    advertisement_id, advertisement_date, car_id, seller_account_id
  FROM car_portal_app.advertisement
  ORDER BY car_id, advertisement_date;
```

This code is much clearer—easier to read and understand—and works faster in many cases.

Selecting a data sample

Suppose the `car_portal` database is huge and there is a task to collect some statistics about the data. The statistics don't have to be exactly accurate, estimated values would be good enough. It's important to collect the data quickly. PostgreSQL provides a way to query a random fraction of a table's records.

The syntax is as follows:

```
SELECT ... FROM <table>
  TABLESAMPLE <sampling_method> ( <argument> [, ...] )
  [ REPEATABLE ( <seed> ) ]
```

The `sampling_method` can be either BERNOULLI or SYSTEM—these are provided with a standard PostgreSQL installation. More sampling methods are available as extensions. Both the sampling methods take one argument, which is a probability that a row will be selected, as a percentage. The difference between the two methods is that BERNOULLI implies a full table scan and the algorithm will decide for each individual row whether it should be selected or not.

The SYSTEM method does the same but on the level of blocks of rows. The latter is significantly faster, but the results are less accurate because of the different numbers of rows in different blocks. The REPEATABLE keyword is used to specify the seed value used by the random functions in the sampling algorithm. The results of queries with the same seed value is the same, as long as the data in the table doesn't change.

Sampling happens at the moment the data from a table is read, before any filtering, grouping, or other operations are performed.

To illustrate sampling, let's increase the number of records in the advertisement table by executing the following query:

```
car_portal=> INSERT INTO car_portal_app.advertisement
    (advertisement_date, car_id, seller_account_id)
  SELECT advertisement_date, car_id, seller_account_id
    FROM car_portal_app.advertisement;
INSERT 0 784
```

This simply duplicates the number of records in the table. If this is executed many times, the table will be pretty big. For the following example, that query was executed 12 more times. If we try to select the total count of records, it takes a fair bit of time:

```
car_portal=> \timing
Timing is on.
car_portal=> SELECT count(*) FROM car_portal_app.advertisement;
 count
---------
 6422528
(1 row)
Time: 394.577 ms
```

Now let's try sampling:

```
car_portal=> SELECT count(*) * 100
  FROM car_portal_app.advertisement TABLESAMPLE SYSTEM (1);
 ?column?
----------
 6248600
(1 row)
Time: 8.344 ms
```

The second query is much faster; however, the result is not very accurate. We multiply the `count` function by `100` because only one percent of the rows is selected.

If this query is performed several times, the results will always be different and, sometimes, can be quite different from the real `count` of rows in the table. To improve quality, the fraction of the rows that are selected can be increased:

```
car_portal=> SELECT count(*) * 10
  FROM car_portal_app.advertisement TABLESAMPLE SYSTEM (10);
 ?column?
----------
 6427580
(1 row)
Time: 92.793 ms
```

The time increased proportionally.

Set-returning functions

Functions in PostgreSQL can return not only single values, but also relations. Such functions are called **set-returning functions**.

This is a typical task for every SQL developer: generate a sequence of numbers, each in a separate record. This sequence or relation can have many use cases. For example, suppose you need to select data from the `car_portal` database to count the number of cars for each year of manufacture, from 2010 till 2015, and you need to show zero for the years where no cars exist in the system at all. A simple SELECT query from the only `car` table cannot be used to implement this logic. It isn't possible to count records that are not present in the table data.

That's why it would be useful if there was a table with the numbers from 2010 to 2015. Then it could be outer-joined to the results of the query.

You could create this table in advance, but that's not a very good idea, because the number of records for such a table wouldn't be known in advance, and if you created a very big table, it would be a waste of disk space in most cases.

There is a function, `generate_series`, that serves exactly this purpose: it returns a set of integers with the given start and stop values. The query for the example would be as follows:

```
car_portal=> SELECT years.manufacture_year, count(car_id)
  FROM generate_series(2010, 2015) as  years (manufacture_year)
    LEFT JOIN car_portal_app.car
      ON car.manufacture_year = years.manufacture_year
  GROUP BY years.manufacture_year
  ORDER BY 1;
 manufacture_year | count
------------------+-------
             2010 |    11
             2011 |    12
             2012 |    12
             2013 |    21
             2014 |    16
             2015 |     0
(6 rows)
```

In the preceding query, the `generate_series` function returns six integers from 2010 to 2015. This set has an alias: `years`. The `car` table is left-joined to this set of integers, and then all the years can be seen in the output result set.

It's possible to specify a step when calling `generate_series`:

```
car_portal=> SELECT * FROM generate_series(5, 11, 3);
 generate_series
-----------------
               5
               8
              11
(3 rows)
```

The `generate_series` function can also return a set of `timestamp` values:

```
car_portal=> SELECT * FROM generate_series(
  '2015-01-01'::date,
  '2015-01-31'::date,
  interval '7 days');
```

```
        generate_series
-------------------------------
 2015-01-01 00:00:00-05
 2015-01-08 00:00:00-05
 2015-01-15 00:00:00-05
 2015-01-22 00:00:00-05
 2015-01-29 00:00:00-05
(5 rows)
```

There are a couple of other set-returning functions designed to work with arrays:

- `generate_subscripts`: This generates numbers that can be used to reference the elements in a given array for the given dimension(s). This function is useful for enumerating the elements of an array in a SQL statement.
- `unnest`: This transforms a given array into a set or rows where each record corresponds to an element of the array.

Set-returning functions are also called **table functions**.

Table functions can return sets of rows of a predefined type, like `generate_series` returns a set of `int` or `bigint` (depending on the type of input argument). Moreover, they can return a set of abstract type records. This allows a function to return different numbers of columns depending on their arguments. SQL requires that the row structure of all input relations is defined so that the structure of the result set will also be defined. That's why table functions that return sets of records, when used in a query, can be followed by a definition of their row structure:

```
function_name (<arguments>) [AS] alias (column_name column_type [, ...])
```

The output of several set-returning functions can be combined together as if they were joined on the position of each row. The `ROWS FROM` syntax construct is used for this, as follows:

```
ROWS FROM (function_call [,...]) [[AS] alias (column_name [,...])]
```

The preceding construct will return a relation, therefore, it can be used in a `FROM` clause just like any other relation. The number of rows is equal to the largest output of the functions. Each column corresponds to the respective function in the `ROWS FROM` clause. If a function returns fewer rows than other functions, the missing values will be set to `NULL`:

```
car_portal=> SELECT foo.a, foo.b FROM
ROWS FROM (generate_series(1,3), generate_series(1,7,2)) AS foo(a, b);
 a | b
---+---
 1 | 1
```

```
 2 | 3
 3 | 5
   | 7
(4 rows)
```

Lateral subqueries

We discussed subqueries in `Chapter 5`, *SQL Language*. However, here, we'll go into detail about one specific pattern for using them.

It's very convenient to use subqueries in the select-list. They are used in `SELECT` statements, for example, to create calculated attributes when querying a table. Let's look at the `car_portal` database again. Suppose you need to query the `car` table and, for each car, you need to assess its age by comparing it with the age of other cars of the same model. Furthermore, you want to query the number of cars of the same model.

These two additional fields can be generated by scalar subqueries, as follows:

```
car_portal=> SELECT car_id, manufacture_year,
  CASE WHEN manufacture_year <= (
    SELECT avg(manufacture_year) FROM car_portal_app.car
      WHERE car_model_id = c.car_model_id)
    THEN 'old' ELSE 'new' END as age,
  (SELECT count(*) FROM car_portal_app.car
    WHERE car_model_id = c.car_model_id)
    AS same_model_count
  FROM car_portal_app.car c;
 car_id | manufacture_year | age | same_model_count
--------+------------------+-----+------------------
      1 |             2008 | old |                3
      2 |             2014 | new |                6
      3 |             2014 | new |                2
...
(229 rows)
```

The power of these subqueries is that they can refer to the main table in their `WHERE` clause. This makes them easy. It's also very simple to add more columns to the query by adding more subqueries. On the other hand, there's a problem here: performance. The `car` table is scanned by the database server once for the main query, and then it's scanned twice for *each* retrieved row, that is, for the `age` and `same_model_count` columns.

It's possible, of course, to calculate these aggregates once for each `car` model independently and then join the results with the `car` table:

```
car_portal=> SELECT car_id, manufacture_year,
    CASE WHEN manufacture_year <= avg_year THEN 'old'
      ELSE 'new' END as age,
    same_model_count
  FROM car_portal_app.car
    INNER JOIN (
      SELECT car_model_id, avg(manufacture_year) avg_year,
        count(*) same_model_count
      FROM car_portal_app.car
      GROUP BY car_model_id
    ) subq USING (car_model_id);
 car_id | manufacture_year | age | same_model_count
--------+------------------+-----+------------------
      1 |             2008 | old |                3
      2 |             2014 | new |                6
      3 |             2014 | new |                2
...
(229 rows)
```

The result is the same and the query is 20 times faster. However, this query is good only when retrieving many rows from the database. If you need to get information about only one car, the first query will be faster.

You can see that the first query could perform better if it were possible to select two columns in the same subquery in the select-list, but this isn't possible. Scalar queries can return only one column.

There is another way of using subqueries: it combines the advantages of the subqueries in the select-list, which can refer to the main table in their WHERE clause, with the subqueries in the FROM clause, which can return multiple columns. This can be done via lateral subqueries. Putting the LATERAL keyword before a subquery in the FROM clause makes it possible to reference any preceding item of the FROM clause from that subquery.

The query would be as follows:

```
car_portal=> SELECT car_id, manufacture_year,
    CASE WHEN manufacture_year <= avg_year THEN 'old'
      ELSE 'new' END as age,
    same_model_count
  FROM car_portal_app.car c,
    LATERAL (
      SELECT avg(manufacture_year) avg_year, count(*) same_model_count
        FROM car_portal_app.car
```

```
           WHERE car_model_id = c.car_model_id) subq;
   car_id | manufacture_year | age | same_model_count
  --------+------------------+-----+------------------
        1 |             2008 | old |                3
        2 |             2014 | new |                6
        3 |             2014 | new |                2
  ...
  (229 rows)
```

This query is approximately twice as fast as the first one, and is the best one to retrieve only one row from the car table.

The JOIN syntax is also possible with LATERAL subqueries, though in many cases, LATERAL subqueries have a WHERE clause that makes their records depend on other subqueries or tables, which effectively joins them.

When it comes to set-returning functions, it isn't necessary to use the LATERAL keyword. All functions that are mentioned in the FROM clause can already use the output of any preceding functions or subqueries:

```
car_portal=> SELECT a, b
  FROM generate_series(1,3) AS a, generate_series(a, a+2) AS b;
  a | b
 ---+---
  1 | 1
  1 | 2
  1 | 3
  2 | 2
  2 | 3
  2 | 4
  3 | 3
  3 | 4
  3 | 5
 (9 rows)
```

In the preceding query, the first function that has the a alias returns three rows. For each of these three rows, the second function is called, returning three more rows.

Advanced grouping

Databases are often used as a data source for any kind of reporting. In reports, it's quite common to display subtotals, totals, and grand totals that summarize the data rows in the same table, implying, in fact, grouping, and aggregation. Consider the following report, which displays the number of advertisements by car make and quarter, and displays the totals for each quarter (aggregating all makes), and the grand total. Here's how to select the data for the report:

```
car_portal=> SELECT to_char(advertisement_date, 'YYYY-Q') as quarter,
    make, count(*)
  FROM advertisement a
    INNER JOIN car c ON a.car_id = c.car_id
    INNER JOIN car_model m ON m.car_model_id = c.car_model_id
  GROUP BY quarter, make;
 quarter |      make      | count
---------+----------------+-------
 2014-4  | Peugeot        |    12
 2014-2  | Daewoo         |     8
 2014-4  | Skoda          |     5
 . . .
```

To make the subtotals, you would need to execute additional queries, as follows:

```
SELECT to_char(advertisement_date, 'YYYY-Q') as quarter, count(*)
 FROM advertisement a
 INNER JOIN car c ON a.car_id = c.car_id
 INNER JOIN car_model m ON m.car_model_id = c.car_model_id
 GROUP BY quarter;

SELECT count(*)
 FROM advertisement a
 INNER JOIN car c ON a.car_id = c.car_id
 INNER JOIN car_model m ON m.car_model_id = c.car_model_id;
```

The joins in these queries are redundant—they don't affect the results—but we leave them here to illustrate that the queries are actually the same as the first one, only the grouping makes the difference.

We could UNION them to produce the requested report, but PostgreSQL provides a better way of combining the three queries in a single one using a special construct, GROUP BY GROUPING SETS:

```
SELECT to_char(advertisement_date, 'YYYY-Q') as quarter, make, count(*)
FROM advertisement a
    INNER JOIN car c ON a.car_id = c.car_id
    INNER JOIN car_model m ON m.car_model_id = c.car_model_id
GROUP BY GROUPING SETS ((quarter, make), (quarter), ())
ORDER BY quarter NULLS LAST, make NULLS LAST;
quarter |      make       | count
--------+-----------------+-------
 2014-1 | Alfa Romeo      |     2
 2014-1 | Audi            |     5
...
 2014-1 | Volvo           |     9
 2014-1 |                 |   121       <- subtotal for the quarter 2014-1
 2014-2 | Audi            |    18
 2014-2 | Citroen         |    40
...
 2014-2 | Volvo           |    12
 2014-2 |                 |   266       <- subtotal for the quarter 2014-2
 2014-3 | Audi            |    11
...
 2015-1 | Volvo           |     4
 2015-1 |                 |    57       <- subtotal for the quarter 2015-1
        |                 |   784       <- grand total for the whole report
```

The GROUPING SETS ((quarter, make), (quarter), ()) construct makes the query work as a UNION ALL operation over the same query, repeated several times with different GROUP BY clause:

- GROUP BY quarter, make
- GROUP BY quarter—here, the make field will get the NULL value
- All the rows are grouped into a single group; both the quarter and make fields will get NULL values

Generally speaking, the GROUP BY clause takes not just expressions, but also **grouping elements**, which could be expressions or constructs, such as GROUPING SETS.

Other possible grouping elements are `ROLLUP` and `CUBE`:

- `ROLLUP (a, b, c)` is equivalent to `GROUPING SETS ((a, b, c), (a, b), (c), ())`
- `CUBE (a, b, c)` is equivalent to `GROUPING SETS ((a, b, c), (a, b), (a, c), (b, c), (a), (b), (c), ())`, which is all possible combinations of the argument expressions

It is also possible to use `CUBE` and `ROLLUP` inside `GROUPING SETS`, as well as combining different grouping elements in one `GROUP BY` clause, as follows:

GROUP BY a, CUBE (b, c)

This would be equivalent to `GROUP BY GROUPING SETS ((a, b, c), (a, b), (a, c), (a))`, which is basically a combination of the grouping elements.

Although the result of `GROUPING SETS` is the same as of `UNION ALL` operation over several queries with different `GROUP BY` clauses, in the background, it works differently from the `SET` operation. PostgreSQL will scan the tables and perform joining and filtering only once. This means that the use of these grouping techniques can help optimize the performance of your solutions.

The documentation for `GROUPING SETS` is available at `https://www.postgresql.org/docs/current/static/queries-table-expressions.html#QUERIES-GROUPING-SETS`.

Advanced aggregation

There are several aggregating functions that are executed in a special way.

The first group of such aggregating functions is called **ordered-set aggregates**. They take into account not just the values of the argument expressions, but also their order. They are related to statistics and calculate percentile values.

A percentile is the value of a group of numbers when the given percentage of other values is less than the percentile. For example, if a value is at the 95th percentile, this means that it's greater than 95 percent of the other values. In PostgreSQL, you can calculate a continuous or discrete percentile using the `percentile_cont` and `percentile_disc` functions, respectively.

A discrete percentile is one of the actual values of a group, while a continuous percentile is an interpolated value between two actual values. It's possible to calculate the percentile for a given fraction, or several percentile values for a given array of fractions.

For example, here is a query that calculates the distribution of the number of advertisements per car:

```
car_portal=> SELECT
    percentile_disc(ARRAY[0.25, 0.5, 0.75]) WITHIN GROUP (ORDER BY cnt)
  FROM (SELECT count(*) cnt
        FROM car_portal_app.advertisement
        GROUP BY car_id) subq;
 percentile_disc
-----------------
 {2,3,5}
(1 row)
```

The result means that there are, at most, 2 advertisements for 25 percent of the cars, 3 advertisements for 50 percent of the cars, and at most 5 advertisements for 75 percent of the cars in the database.

The syntax of the ordered-set aggregating functions differs from the normal aggregates and uses a special construct, WITHIN GROUP (ORDER BY expression). The expression here is actually an argument of a function. Here, not just the order of the rows but the values of the expressions affect the result of the function. In contrast to the ORDER BY clause of the SELECT query, only one expression is possible here and no references to the output column numbers are allowed.

Another ordered-set aggregating function is mode. It returns the most-frequently-appearing value of the group. If two values appear the same number of times, the first of them will be returned.

For example, the following query gets the ID of the most frequent car model from the database:

```
car_portal=> SELECT mode() WITHIN GROUP (ORDER BY car_model_id)
  FROM car_portal_app.car;
 mode
------
   64
(1 row)
```

To get the same result without this function would require a self-join or ordering and limiting the result. Both are more expensive operations.

Another group of aggregates that use the same syntax are the **hypothetical-set aggregating functions**. They are rank, dense_rank, percent_rank, and cume_dist. There are window functions with the same names. Window functions take no argument and return the result for the current row. Aggregate functions have no current row because they are evaluated for a group of rows. However, they take an argument: the value for the hypothetical current row.

For example, the rank aggregate function returns the rank of a given value in the ordered set as if that value existed in the set:

```
car_portal=> SELECT rank(2) WITHIN GROUP (ORDER BY a)
  FROM generate_series(1,10,3) a;
 rank
------
    2
(1 row)
```

In the preceding query, the 2 value doesn't exist in the output of generate_series (it returns 1..4..7..10). If it existed, it would take the second position in the output.

Another aggregate-function topic worth mentioning is the FILTER clause.

The FILTER clause filters the rows that are passed to the particular aggregating function based on a given condition. For example, suppose you need to count the number of cars in the database for each car model separately, for each number of doors. If you group the records according to these two fields, the result will be correct but not very convenient to use in reporting:

```
car_portal=> SELECT car_model_id, number_of_doors, count(*)
  FROM car_portal_app.car
  GROUP BY car_model_id, number_of_doors;
 car_model_id | number_of_doors | count
--------------+-----------------+-------
           47 |               4 |     1
           42 |               3 |     2
           76 |               5 |     1
           52 |               5 |     2
   . . .
```

A better query, which is suitable for reporting, can be created using CASE operators:

```
car_portal=> SELECT car_model_id,
    count(CASE WHEN number_of_doors = 2 THEN 1 END) doors2,
    count(CASE WHEN number_of_doors = 3 THEN 1 END) doors3,
    count(CASE WHEN number_of_doors = 4 THEN 1 END) doors4,
    count(CASE WHEN number_of_doors = 5 THEN 1 END) doors5
  FROM car_portal_app.car
  GROUP BY car_model_id, number_of_doors;
 car_model_id | doors2 | doors3 | doors4 | doors5
--------------+--------+--------+--------+--------
           43 |      0 |      0 |      0 |      2
            8 |      0 |      0 |      1 |      0
...
```

It does what's requested but it doesn't look very nice. The FILTER clause makes the query much clearer:

```
car_portal=> SELECT car_model_id,
 count(*) FILTER (WHERE number_of_doors = 2) doors2,
 count(*) FILTER (WHERE number_of_doors = 3) doors3,
 count(*) FILTER (WHERE number_of_doors = 4) doors4,
 count(*) FILTER (WHERE number_of_doors = 5) doors5
 FROM car_portal_app.car GROUP BY car_model_id;
 car_model_id | doors2 | doors3 | doors4 | doors5
--------------+--------+--------+--------+--------
           43 |      0 |      0 |      0 |      2
            8 |      0 |      0 |      1 |      0
           11 |      0 |      2 |      1 |      0
           80 |      0 |      1 |      0 |      0
...
```

Note that cars with a number of doors other than 2 to 5 will not be counted by the query.

Summary

In this chapter, we learned about some advanced SQL concepts and features, such as CTEs and window functions. These features, for example, allow us to implement a logic that wouldn't be possible otherwise, that is, recursive queries.

The other techniques explained here, such as the DISTINCT ON clause, grouping sets, the FILTER clause, and lateral subqueries, could be replaced by simple structures. However, that would require a lot of coding, and the result would be more complex and would work more slowly.

SQL can be used to implement very complicated logic. However, in difficult cases, queries can become overcomplicated and hard to maintain. Moreover, sometimes, it isn't possible to do certain things in pure SQL. In these cases, you need a procedural language to implement an algorithm. The next chapter will introduce one of them: PL/pgSQL.

Questions

1. What is a CTE?
2. Can one CTE use other CTEs?
3. Can a CTE reference itself?
4. How do we insert rows into several tables at once?
5. Is there a way to specify the order of execution of CTEs?
6. What is the difference between grouping and aggregation, and using window functions?
7. How do we calculate a moving average of a field for each row, taking three rows before and three rows after?
8. How do we calculate the difference between the value of a field in the current row and the average of the previous and the next rows for each row?
9. Can window functions be combined with aggregating functions?
10. What is the purpose of the DISTINCT ON clause?
11. How do we get a sample of data from a database table?
12. How do we get a sequence of numbers using a SELECT query?
13. Can a subquery (not a CTE) refer to another subquery?
14. How do we use several sets of expressions in a single GROUP BY clause?

Server-Side Programming with PL/pgSQL

7

The ability to write functions in PostgreSQL is an amazing feature. We can perform any task within the scope of the database server. These tasks may be directly related to data manipulation, such as data aggregation and auditing, or they may be used to perform miscellaneous services, such as statistics collection, monitoring, system information acquisition, and job scheduling. In this chapter, our focus will be on the PL/pgSQL language. PL/pgSQL is the default procedural language for PostgreSQL. As we mentioned previously, in `Chapter 4`, *PostgreSQL Advanced Building Blocks*, PL/pgSQL is installed in PostgreSQL by default.

PL/pgSQL has been influenced by the PL/SQL language, which is the Oracle stored procedural language. PL/pgSQL is a complete procedural language, with rich control structures and full integration with the PostgreSQL triggers, indexes, rules, user-defined data types, and operator objects. There are several advantages to using PL/pgSQL, as follows:

- It is easy to learn and use
- It has very good support and documentation
- It has very flexible result data types, and it supports polymorphism
- It can return scalar values and sets, using different return methods
- It can easily be integrated with SQL code
- It supports functions and procedures

The topics that will be covered in this chapter are as follows:

- The SQL language and PL/pgSQL – a comparison
- Functions and procedures – a comparison
- PostgreSQL function parameters
- The PostgreSQL PL/pgSQL control statements

- Function predefined variables
- Exception handling
- Dynamic SQL

The SQL language and PL/pgSQL – a comparison

As illustrated in Chapter 4, *PostgreSQL Advanced Building Blocks*, we can write functions in C, SQL, and PL/pgSQL. There are some pros and cons to each approach. You can think of an SQL function as a wrapper around a parameterized SELECT statement. SQL functions can be inlined into the calling subquery, leading to better performance. Also, since the SQL function execution plan is not cached as in PL/pgSQL, it is often better in performance than PL/pgSQL. Moreover, caching in PL/pgSQL can have some surprisingly bad side effects, such as the caching of sensitive timestamp values, as shown in the documentation at http://www.postgresql.org/docs/current/interactive/plpgsql-implementation.html. Finally, with the introduction of CTE, recursive CTE, window functions, and LATERAL JOINS, you can perform complex logic using only SQL. If function logic can be implemented in SQL, use an SQL function, instead of PL/pgSQL.

The PL/pgSQL function execution plan is cached; caching the plan can help to reduce execution time, but it can also hurt it if the plan is not optimal for the provided function parameters. From a functionality point of view, PL/pgSQL is much more powerful than SQL. PL/pgSQL supports several features that SQL functions cannot support, including the following:

- It provides the ability to raise exceptions and to raise messages at different levels, such as notice and debug.
- It supports the construction of dynamic SQL, using the EXECUTE command.
- It provides EXCEPTION handling.
- It has a complete set of assignment, control, and loop statements
- It supports cursors.
- It is fully integrated with the PostgreSQL trigger system. SQL functions cannot be used with triggers.

Functions and procedures – a comparison

In PostgreSQL 11, procedures were introduced. The main difference between functions and procedures is transaction control. Functions are explicitly run in a transaction, while a procedure can control transactions. In procedures, you can explicitly COMMIT and ROLLBACK a transaction. Functions can be called within SQL code, but procedures are executed via CALL statements. Finally, functions should have a return data type; if the function does not return anything, the VOID pseudo data type can be used.

Procedures have great benefits. Let's suppose that we would like to index all foreign keys. In this case, using a function is not very practical, because the indexes are created when the function completely finishes the execution. So, if an exception occurs in the middle of the execution, then all of the work is lost. In a stored procedure, we can create one index at a time, and we can keep iterating through all indexes until the procedure finishes the execution. To show the difference in transaction control, let's create a table inside of a function and procedure and deliberately cause an error, as follows:

```
CREATE PROCEDURE test_procedure_tx() AS $$
 BEGIN
 CREATE TABLE a (id int);
 COMMIT;
 CREATE INDEX a_id_idx ON a(id);
 SELECT 1/0;
 END;
$$ LANGUAGE plpgsql ;
CREATE FUNCTION test_function_tx() RETURNS VOID AS $$
 BEGIN
 CREATE TABLE a (id int);
 CREATE INDEX a_id_idx ON a(id);
 SELECT 1/0;
 END;
$$ LANGUAGE plpgsql ;
```

The following code executes the test_function_tx() function:

```
postgres=# SELECT test_function_tx();
ERROR: division by zero
CONTEXT: SQL statement "SELECT 1/0"
PL/pgSQL function test_function_tx() line 5 at SQL statement
postgres=# \d a
Did not find any relation named "a".
```

The following code executes the `test_procedure_tx()` procedure :

```
postgres=# call test_procedure_tx();
ERROR: division by zero
CONTEXT: SQL statement "SELECT 1/0"
PL/pgSQL function test_procedure_tx() line 6 at SQL statement
postgres=# \d a
 Table "public.a"
 Column | Type    | Collation | Nullable | Default
--------+---------+-----------+----------+---------
 id     | integer |           |          |
```

As shown in the preceding example, the a table was created when `test_procedure_tx` was executed. `test_function_tx` did not create the table, since the whole transaction was rolled back.

The syntax for creating functions and procedures is quite similar, and they share some common features, such as configuration parameters, authorization parameters, control statements, and iteration statements. We will focus on functions in the next sections. The synopsis for creating a procedure is as follows:

```
postgres=# \h CREATE PROCEDURE
Command: CREATE PROCEDURE
Description: define a new procedure
Syntax:
CREATE [ OR REPLACE ] PROCEDURE
 name ( [ [ argmode ] [ argname ] argtype [ { DEFAULT | = } default_expr ]
[, ...] ] )
 { LANGUAGE lang_name
 | TRANSFORM { FOR TYPE type_name } [, ... ]
 | [ EXTERNAL ] SECURITY INVOKER | [ EXTERNAL ] SECURITY DEFINER
 | SET configuration_parameter { TO value | = value | FROM CURRENT }
 | AS 'definition'
 | AS 'obj_file', 'link_symbol'
 } ...
```

In the following section, we will discuss function options and parameters. These options control the execution behavior of the functions and procedures.

PostgreSQL function parameters

In Chapter 4, *PostgreSQL Advanced Building Blocks*, we discussed the following function categories: immutable, stable, and volatile. In this section, we will continue by covering other function options. These options are not PL/pgSQL language-specific.

Function authorization related parameters

The first parameters are related to security; when functions are called, they are executed within a security context that determines their privileges. The following options control the function privileges context:

- SECURITY DEFINER
- SECURITY INVOKER

The default value for this option is SECURITY INVOKER, which indicates that the function will be executed with the privileges of the user that calls it. The SECURITY DEFINER functions will be executed using the privileges of the user that created it. For the SECURITY INVOKER functions, the user must have the permissions to execute the CRUD operations that the function implements; otherwise, the function will raise an error. The SECURITY DEFINER functions are very useful in defining triggers or for temporarily promoting the user to perform tasks only supported by the function.

To test these security parameters, let's create two dummy functions using the postgres user and execute them in different sessions, as follows:

```
CREATE FUNCTION test_security_definer () RETURNS TEXT AS $$
  SELECT format ('current_user:%s session_user:%s', current_user,
session_user);
$$ LANGUAGE SQL SECURITY DEFINER;

CREATE FUNCTION test_security_invoker () RETURNS TEXT AS $$
  SELECT format ('current_user:%s session_user:%s', current_user,
session_user);
$$ LANGUAGE SQL SECURITY INVOKER;
```

To test the functions, let's execute them using a session created by the postgres user, as follows:

```
$ psql -U postgres car_portal
psql (11.1 (Ubuntu 11.1-1.pgdg18.04+1))
Type "help" for help.
car_portal=# SELECT test_security_definer() , test_security_invoker();
          test_security_definer          | test_security_invoker
-----------------------------------------+-----------------------------
----------------
 current_user:postgres session_user:postgres | current_user:postgres
session_user:postgres
(1 row)
```

Now, let's use another session created by the `car_portal_app` user, as follows:

```
psql -U car_portal_app car_portal
psql (11.1 (Ubuntu 11.1-1.pgdg18.04+1))
Type "help" for help.

car_portal=> SELECT test_security_definer() , test_security_invoker();
                test_security_definer               |
test_security_invoker
----------------------------------------------------+--------------------
----------------------------------
 current_user:postgres session_user:car_portal_app  |
current_user:car_portal_app session_user:car_portal_app
(1 row)
```

The two functions, `test_security_definer` and `test_security_invoker`, are identical, except for the security parameter. When the two functions are executed by a `postgres` user, the results of the two functions are identical. This is simply because the user that created the function and the user that called it are the same user.

When the `car_portal_app` user executes the two preceding functions, the result of the `test_security_definer` function is `current_user:postgres` `session_user:car_portal_app`. In this case, `session_user` is `car_portal_app`, since it has started the session using a `psql` client. However, `current_user` that executes the `SELECT` statement is `postgres`.

Function planner related parameters

Function planner related parameters give the planner information about a function's execution cost. This helps the planner to generate a good execution plan. The following three parameters are used by the planner to determine the cost of executing the function, the number of rows that are expected to be returned, and whether the function pushes down when evaluating predicates:

- LEAKPROOF: LEAKPROOF means that the function has no side effects. It does not reveal any information about its argument. For example, it does not throw error messages about its argument. This parameter affects views with the `security_barrier` parameter.
- COST: This declares the execution cost per row; the default value for the C language function is 1, and for PL/pgSQL, it is 100. The cost is used by the planner to determine the best execution plan.

- ROWS: The estimated number of rows returned by the function, if the function is set-returning. The default value is `1000`.

To understand the effect of the `rows` configuration parameter, let's consider the following example:

```
CREATE OR REPLACE FUNCTION a() RETURNS SETOF INTEGER AS $$
   SELECT 1;
$$ LANGUAGE SQL;
```

Now, let's execute the following query:

```
car_portal=> EXPLAIN SELECT * FROM a() CROSS JOIN (Values(1),(2),(3)) as
foo;
                              QUERY PLAN
------------------------------------------------------------------------
 Nested Loop (cost=0.25..47.80 rows=3000 width=8)
   -> Function Scan on a (cost=0.25..10.25 rows=1000 width=4)
   -> Materialize (cost=0.00..0.05 rows=3 width=4)
         -> Values Scan on "*VALUES*" (cost=0.00..0.04 rows=3 width=4)
(4 rows)
```

The SQL function return type is `SETOF INTEGER`, which means that the planner expected more than one row to be returned from the function. Since the ROWS parameter is not specified, the planner uses the default value, which is `1000`. Finally, due to CROSS JOIN, the total estimated number of rows is `3000`, which is calculated as *3 x 1,000*.

In the preceding example, an incorrect estimation is not critical. However, in a real-life example, where we might have several joins, the error of row estimation will be propagated and amplified, leading to poor execution plans.

The COST function parameter determines when the function will be executed, as follows:

- It determines the function execution order
- It determines whether the function call can be pushed down

The following example shows how the execution order for functions is affected by the COST function. Let's suppose that we have two functions, as follows:

```
CREATE OR REPLACE FUNCTION slow_function (anyelement) RETURNS BOOLEAN AS $$
BEGIN
   RAISE NOTICE 'Slow function %', $1;
   RETURN TRUE;
END; $$ LANGUAGE PLPGSQL COST 10000;

CREATE OR REPLACE FUNCTION fast_function (anyelement) RETURNS BOOLEAN AS $$
```

```
BEGIN
  RAISE NOTICE 'Fast function %', $1;
  RETURN TRUE;
END; $$ LANGUAGE PLPGSQL COST 0.0001;
```

`fast_function` and `slow_function` are identical, except for the `cost` parameter:

```
car_portal=> EXPLAIN SELECT * FROM pg_language WHERE fast_function(lanname)
AND slow_function(lanname) AND lanname ILIKE '%sql%';
  QUERY PLAN
-----------------------------------------------------------------------
--------------------
 Seq Scan on pg_language (cost=0.00..101.05 rows=1 width=114)
 Filter: (fast_function(lanname) AND (lanname ~~* '%sql%'::text) AND
slow_function(lanname))
(2 rows)
car_portal=# EXPLAIN SELECT * FROM pg_language WHERE slow_function(lanname)
AND fast_function(lanname) AND lanname ILIKE '%sql%';
  QUERY PLAN
-----------------------------------------------------------------------
--------------------
 Seq Scan on pg_language (cost=0.00..101.05 rows=1 width=114)
 Filter: (fast_function(lanname) AND (lanname ~~* '%sql%'::text) AND
slow_function(lanname))
(2 rows)
```

The preceding two SQL statements are identical, but the predicates are shuffled. Both of the statements give the same execution plan. Notice how the predicates are arranged in the filter execution plane node. `fast_function` is evaluated first, followed by the ILIKE operator, and finally, `slow_function` is pushed. When you execute one of the preceding statements, you will get the following results:

```
car_portal=> SELECT lanname FROM pg_language WHERE lanname ILIKE '%sql%'
AND slow_function(lanname) AND fast_function(lanname);
NOTICE: Fast function internal
NOTICE: Fast function c
NOTICE: Fast function sql
NOTICE: Slow function sql
NOTICE: Fast function plpgsql
NOTICE: Slow function plpgsql
 lanname
---------
 sql
 plpgsql
(2 rows)
```

Notice that `fast_function` was executed four times and `slow_function` was only executed twice. This behavior is known as **short circuit** evaluation. `slow_function` is only executed when `fast_function` and the `ILIKE` operator have returned `true`.

 In PostgreSQL, the `ILIKE` operator is equivalent to the `~~*` operator, and `LIKE` is equivalent to the `~~` operator.

As we discussed in `Chapter 4`, *PostgreSQL Advanced Building Blocks*, views can be used to implement authorization, and they can be used to hide data from some users. The function `cost` parameter could be exploited in earlier versions of PostgreSQL to crack views; however, this has been improved by the introduction of the `LEAKPROOF` and `SECURITY_BARRIER` flags.

To be able to exploit the function `cost` parameter to get data from a view, several conditions should be met, some of which are as follows:

- The function `cost` should be very low.
- The function should be marked as `LEAKPROOF`. Note that only superusers are allowed to mark functions as `LEAKPROOF`.
- The `VIEW security_barrier` flag shouldn't be set.
- The function should be executed and not ignored due to short-circuit evaluation.

Meeting all of these conditions is very difficult. The following code shows a hypothetical example of exploiting views. First, let's create a view, alter the `fast_function` function, and set it as `LEAKPROOF`:

```
CREATE OR REPLACE VIEW pg_sql_pl AS SELECT lanname FROM pg_language WHERE
lanname ILIKE '%sql%';
ALTER FUNCTION fast_function(anyelement) LEAKPROOF;
```

To exploit the function, let's execute the following query:

```
car_portal=# SELECT * FROM pg_sql_pl WHERE fast_function(lanname);
NOTICE: Fast function internal
NOTICE: Fast function c
NOTICE: Fast function sql
NOTICE: Fast function plpgsql
 lanname
---------
 sql
 plpgsql
(2 rows)
```

In the preceding example, the view itself should not show c and internal. By exploiting the function cost, the function was executed before executing the lanname ILIKE '%sql%' filter , exposing information that will never be shown by the view.

Since only superusers are allowed to mark a function as LEAKPROOF, exploiting the function cost is not possible in newer versions of PostgreSQL.

Function configuration related parameters

PostgreSQL can be configured per session, as well as within a function scope. This is quite useful in particular cases, when we want to override the session settings in the function. The settings parameters can be used to determine resources (such as the amount of memory required to perform an operation such as work_mem), or they can be used to determine execution behavior, such as disabling a sequential scan or nested loop joins. Only parameters that have the context of the user can be used (referring to the settings parameters that can be assigned to the user session).

The SET clause causes the specified setting parameter to be set with a specified value when the function is entered; the same setting parameter value is reset back to its default value when the function exits. The parameter configuration setting can be set explicitly for the whole function or overwritten locally inside of the function, and it can inherit the value from the session setting using the CURRENT clause.

These configuration parameters are often used to tweak the function performance in the case of limited resources, legacy code, bad design, wrong statistics estimations, and so on. For example, let's suppose that a function behaves poorly due to database normalization. In this case, refactoring the database might be an expensive action to perform. To solve this problem, you can alter the execution plan by enabling or disabling some settings. Let's suppose that a developer would like to quickly fix the following statement, which uses an external merge sort method, without altering the work_mem session:

```
car_portal=# EXPLAIN (analyze, buffers) SELECT md5(random()::text) FROM
generate_series(1, 1000000) order by 1;
                                                                QUERY PLAN
--------------------------------------------------------------------------
-----------------------------------------------------------------
  Sort (cost=69.83..72.33 rows=1000 width=32) (actual
time=7324.824..9141.209 rows=1000000 loops=1)
    Sort Key: (md5((random())::text))
    Sort Method: external merge Disk: 42056kB
    Buffers: temp read=10114 written=10113
    -> Function Scan on generate_series (cost=0.00..20.00 rows=1000
width=32) (actual time=193.730..1774.369 rows=1000000 loops=1)
```

```
            Buffers: temp read=1710 written=1709
   Planning time: 0.055 ms
   Execution time: 9192.393 ms
  (8 rows)
```

The SELECT statement in the preceding example can be wrapped in a function, and the function can be assigned a specific work_mem, as follows:

```
CREATE OR REPLACE FUNCTION configuration_test () RETURNS TABLE(md5 text) AS
$$
 SELECT md5(random()::text) FROM generate_series(1, 1000000) order by 1;
$$ LANGUAGE SQL
SET work_mem = '100MB';
```

Now, let's run the function to see the results of the work_mem setting effect:

```
car_portal=# EXPLAIN (ANALYZE ,BUFFERS) SELECT * FROM configuration_test();
                                                      QUERY PLAN
-------------------------------------------------------------------------
----------------------------------------------------
 Function Scan on configuration_test (cost=0.25..10.25 rows=1000 width=32)
(actual time=7377.196..7405.635 rows=1000000 loops=1)
 Planning time: 0.028 ms
 Execution time: 7444.426 ms
(3 rows)

Time: 7444.984 ms
```

When the function is entered, work_mem is assigned a value of 100MB; this affects the execution plan, and the sorting is now done in the memory. The function's execution time is faster than the query. To confirm this result, let's change work_mem for the session, in order to compare the results, as follows:

```
car_portal=# set work_mem to '100MB';
SET
Time: 0.343 ms
car_portal=# EXPLAIN (analyze, buffers) SELECT md5(random()::text) FROM
generate_series(1, 1000000) order by 1;
                                                      QUERY PLAN
-------------------------------------------------------------------------
----------------------------------------------------
 Sort (cost=69.83..72.33 rows=1000 width=32) (actual
time=7432.831..7615.666 rows=1000000 loops=1)
   Sort Key: (md5((random())::text))
   Sort Method: quicksort Memory: 101756kB
   -> Function Scan on generate_series (cost=0.00..20.00 rows=1000
width=32) (actual time=104.305..1626.839 rows=1000000 loops=1)
 Planning time: 0.050 ms
```

```
Execution time: 7662.650 ms
(6 rows)

Time: 7663.269 ms
```

The PostgreSQL PL/pgSQL control statements

The PostgreSQL control statements are an essential part of the PL/pgSQL language; they enable developers to code very complex business logic inside of PostgreSQL.

Declaration statements

A **declaration statement** allows the developer to define variables and constants. The general syntax of a variable declaration is as follows:

```
name [ CONSTANT ] type [ COLLATE collation_name ] [ NOT NULL ] [ { DEFAULT
| := | = } expression ];
```

The description is as follows:

- name: The name should follow the naming rules that were discussed in Chapter 3, *PostgreSQL Basic Building Blocks*. For example, the name should not start with an integer.
- CONSTANT: The variable cannot be assigned another value after the initialization. This is useful in defining constant variables, such as PI.
- type: This type of the variable can be simple, such as an integer, user-defined data type, pseudo type, and record. Since a type is created implicitly when creating a table, you can use this type to declare a variable.
- NOT NULL: NOT NULL causes a runtime error to be raised if the variable is assigned a null. NOT NULL variables must be initialized.
- DEFAULT: This causes the initialization of the variable to be delayed until the block is entered. This is useful in defining a timestamp variable to indicate when the function is called, but not the function precompilation time.
- An expression is a combination of one or more explicit values, operators, and functions that can be evaluated to another value.

In PostgreSQL, the following two declarations are equivalent; however, the second declaration is more portable with Oracle. Additionally, it is more descriptive of the intent, and it cannot be confused with a reference to the actual table. This is the preferred type declaration style:

- `myrow tablename;`
- `myrow tablename%ROWTYPE;`

The PostgreSQL PL/pgSQL function body is composed of nested blocks, with an optional declaration section and a label. Variables are declared in the DECLARE section of the block, as follows:

```
[ <<label>> ]
[ DECLARE
    declarations ]
BEGIN
    statements
END [ label ];
```

The BEGIN and END keywords are not used to control the transaction behavior in this context, but only for grouping. The declaration section is used for declaring variables, and the label is used to give a name to the block, as well as to give fully qualified names to the variables. Finally, in each PL/pgSQL function, there is a hidden block labeled with a function name that contains predefined variables, such as FOUND. To understand the function block, let's take a look at the following code, which defines the factorial function in a recursive manner:

```
CREATE OR REPLACE FUNCTION factorial(INTEGER ) RETURNS INTEGER AS $$
BEGIN
  IF $1 IS NULL OR $1 < 0 THEN RAISE NOTICE 'Invalid Number';
    RETURN NULL;
  ELSIF $1 = 1 THEN
    RETURN 1;
  ELSE
    RETURN factorial($1 - 1) * $1;
END IF;
END;
$$ LANGUAGE 'plpgsql';
```

The block defines the variable scope; in our example, the scope of the argument variable, $1, is the whole function. Also, as shown in the example, there is no declaration section. To understand the scope between different code blocks, let's write the `factorial` function in a slightly different manner, as follows:

```
CREATE OR REPLACE FUNCTION factorial(INTEGER ) RETURNS INTEGER AS $$
  DECLARE
    fact ALIAS FOR $1;
  BEGIN
  IF fact IS NULL OR fact < 0 THEN
    RAISE NOTICE 'Invalid Number';
    RETURN NULL;
  ELSIF fact = 1 THEN
    RETURN 1;
  END IF;
  DECLARE
    result INT;
  BEGIN
    result = factorial(fact - 1) * fact;
    RETURN result;
  END;
END;
$$ LANGUAGE plpgsql;
```

The preceding function is composed of two blocks; the `fact` variable is an alias for the first argument. In the sub-block, the resulting variable is declared with a type integer. Since the `fact` variable is defined in the upper block, it can also be used in the sub-block. The resulting variable can only be used in the sub-block.

Assignment statements

An **assignment statement** is used to assign a value to a variable. Constants are assigned values at the time of declaration. The variable can be assigned an atomic value or a complex value, such as a record. Also, it can be assigned a literal value or a result of query execution.

The assignment :=, and =, operators are used to assign an expression to a variable, as follows:

```
variable { := | = } expression;
```

For the variable names, you should choose names that do not conflict with the column names. This is important when writing parameterized SQL statements. The = operator is used in SQL for equality comparisons; it is preferable to use the := operator, in order to reduce confusion.

In certain contexts, the operators = and := cannot be used interchangeably; it is important to pick the correct assignment operator for the following cases:

- When assigning a default value, you should use the = operator, as indicated in the documentation at http://www.postgresql.org/docs/current/interactive/sql-createfunction.html
- For named notations in a function call, you should use the := operator

The following example shows a case in which we cannot use = and := interchangeably:

```
CREATE OR REPLACE FUNCTION cast_numeric_to_int (numeric_value numeric,
round boolean = TRUE /*correct use of "=". Using ":=" will raise a syntax
error */)
RETURNS INT AS
$$
  BEGIN
  RETURN (CASE WHEN round = TRUE THEN CAST (numeric_value AS INTEGER)
  WHEN numeric_value>= 0 THEN CAST (numeric_value −.5 AS INTEGER)
  WHEN numeric_value< 0 THEN CAST (numeric_value +.5 AS INTEGER)
  ELSE NULL
  END);
END;
$$ LANGUAGE plpgsql;
```

To show how to call the cast_numeric_to_int function, let's execute the following code:

```
car_portal=# SELECT cast_numeric_to_int(2.3, round:= true);
 cast_numeric_to_int
---------------------
                   2
(1 row)

car_portal=# SELECT cast_numeric_to_int(2.3, round= true);
ERROR: column "round" does not exist
LINE 1: SELECT cast_numeric_to_int(2.3, round= true);
```

The assignment expression can be a single atomic value, such as $pi = 3.14$, or it can be a row, as shown in the following code snippet:

```
DO $$
  DECLARE
    test record;
  BEGIN
    test = ROW (1,'hello', 3.14);
    RAISE notice '%', test;
  END;
$$ LANGUAGE plpgsql;
```

```
DO $$
DECLARE
  number_of_accounts INT:=0;
BEGIN
  number_of_accounts:= (SELECT COUNT(*) FROM car_portal_app.account)::INT;
  RAISE NOTICE 'number_of accounts: %', number_of_accounts;
END; $$
LANGUAGE plpgsql;
```

There are other techniques for assigning values to variables from a query that returns a single row:

```
SELECT select_expressions INTO [STRICT] targets FROM ...;
 INSERT ... RETURNING expressions INTO [STRICT] targets;
 UPDATE ... RETURNING expressions INTO [STRICT] targets;
 DELETE ... RETURNING expressions INTO [STRICT] targets;
```

Often, expressions are column names, while targets are variable names. In the case of SELECT INTO, the target can be of the record type. The INSERT ... RETURNING query is often used to return the default value of a certain column; this can be used to define the ID of a primary key, using the SERIAL and BIGSERIAL data types, shown as follows:

```
CREATE TABLE test (
 id SERIAL PRIMARY KEY,
 name TEXT NOT NULL
 );
```

To show how to assign the result of a query to a variable, let's run the following code:

```
DO $$
  DECLARE
    auto_generated_id INT;
  BEGIN
    INSERT INTO test(name) VALUES ('Hello World') RETURNING id INTO
auto_generated_id;
    RAISE NOTICE 'The primary key is: %', auto_generated_id;
END
$$;
NOTICE: The primary key is: 1
DO
```

You can get the default value when inserting a row in plain SQL by using CTE, as follows:
```
WITH get_id AS (
INSERT INTO test(name) VALUES ('Hello World')
RETURNING id
) SELECT * FROM get_id;
```

Finally, you can use qualified names to perform assignments; in trigger functions, you can use NEW and OLD to manipulate the values of these records.

Conditional statements

PostgreSQL supports the IF and CASE statements, which allow for execution based on a certain condition. PostgreSQL supports the IF statement construct, as follows:

- IF ... THEN ... END IF
- IF ... THEN ... ELSE ... END IF
- IF ... THEN ... ELSIF ... THEN ... ELSE ... END IF

The CASE statement comes in two forms, as follows:

- CASE ... WHEN ... THEN ... ELSE ... END CASE
- CASE WHEN ... THEN ... ELSE ... END CASE

To understand the IF statement, let's suppose that we would like to convert the advertisement rank in to text, as follows:

```
CREATE OR REPLACE FUNCTION cast_rank_to_text (rank int) RETURNS TEXT AS $$
DECLARE
  rank ALIAS FOR $1;
  rank_result TEXT;
BEGIN
  IF rank = 5 THEN rank_result = 'Excellent';
  ELSIF rank = 4 THEN rank_result = 'Very Good';
  ELSIF rank = 3 THEN rank_result = 'Good';
  ELSIF rank = 2 THEN rank_result ='Fair';
  ELSIF rank = 1 THEN rank_result ='Poor';
  ELSE rank_result ='No such rank';
  END IF;
  RETURN rank_result;
END;
$$ Language plpgsql;
```

To test the function, run the following command:

```
SELECT n,cast_rank_to_text(n) FROM generate_series(1,6) as foo(n);
```

When any branch of the IF statement is executed due to the IF condition being met, then the execution control returns to the first statement after END IF, assuming that the RETURN statement is not executed inside of this branch. If none of the conditions are met for IF or ELSIF, then the ELSE branch will be executed. Also, note that you could nest all of the control structures; so, you could have an IF statement inside of another one.

The following code snippet implements the preceding function, using the CASE statement:

```
CREATE OR REPLACE FUNCTION cast_rank_to_text (rank int) RETURNS TEXT AS $$
DECLARE
   rank ALIAS FOR $1;
   rank_result TEXT;
BEGIN
   CASE rank
     WHEN 5 THEN rank_result = 'Excellent';
     WHEN 4 THEN rank_result = 'Very Good';
     WHEN 3 THEN rank_result = 'Good';
     WHEN 2 THEN rank_result ='Fair';
     WHEN 1 THEN rank_result ='Poor';
     ELSE rank_result ='No such rank';
   END CASE;
   RETURN rank_result;
END;$$ Language plpgsql;
```

In the CASE statement, if any branch of the case matches the selector, the execution of the case is terminated, and the execution control goes to the first statement after CASE. Moreover, in the previous form of CASE, we cannot use it to match NULL values, since NULL equality is NULL. To overcome this limitation, you should specify the matching condition explicitly, using the second form of the CASE statement, as follows:

```
CREATE OR REPLACE FUNCTION cast_rank_to_text (rank int) RETURNS TEXT AS $$
DECLARE
   rank ALIAS FOR $1;
   rank_result TEXT;
BEGIN
   CASE
     WHEN rank=5 THEN rank_result = 'Excellent';
     WHEN rank=4 THEN rank_result = 'Very Good';
     WHEN rank=3 THEN rank_result = 'Good';
     WHEN rank=2 THEN rank_result ='Fair';
     WHEN rank=1 THEN rank_result ='Poor';
     WHEN rank IS NULL THEN RAISE EXCEPTION 'Rank should be not NULL';
```

```
    ELSE rank_result ='No such rank';
  END CASE;
  RETURN rank_result;
END;
$$ Language plpgsql;
```

To test the function, use the following command:

```
SELECT cast_rank_to_text(null);
```

Finally, the CASE statement raises an exception if no branch is matched and the ELSE branch is not specified, as follows:

```
DO $$
DECLARE
  i int := 0;
BEGIN
  case WHEN i=1 then
    RAISE NOTICE 'i is one';
  END CASE;
END;
$$ LANGUAGE plpgsql;
ERROR: case not found
HINT: CASE statement is missing ELSE part.
CONTEXT: PL/pgSQL function inline_code_block line 5 at CASE
```

As shown earlier, PL/pgSQL supports declaration, assignment, and conditional statements. In addition to that, it supports code blocks. In the next section, we will demonstrate iterations.

Iterations

An **iteration** is used to repeat a block of statements in order to achieve a certain goal. With iteration, you often need to specify the starting point and the ending condition. In PostgreSQL, there are several statements for iterating through the results and for performing looping, including LOOP, CONTINUE, EXIT, FOR, WHILE, and FOR EACH.

Loop statements

The basic LOOP statement has the following structure:

```
[ <<label>> ]
LOOP
    statements
END LOOP [ label ];
```

To understand the LOOP statement, let's rewrite the factorial function, as follows:

```
DROP FUNCTION IF EXISTS factorial (int);
CREATE OR REPLACE FUNCTION factorial (fact int) RETURNS BIGINT AS $$
DECLARE
  result bigint = 1;
BEGIN
  IF fact = 1 THEN RETURN 1;
  ELSIF fact IS NULL or fact < 1 THEN RAISE EXCEPTION 'Provide a positive
integer';
  ELSE
    LOOP
      result = result*fact;
      fact = fact-1;
      EXIT WHEN fact = 1;
    END Loop;
  END IF;
  RETURN result;
END; $$ LANGUAGE plpgsql;
```

In the preceding code, the conditional EXIT statement is used to prevent infinite looping by exiting the LOOP statement. When an EXIT statement is encountered, the execution control goes to the first statement after the LOOP statement. To control the execution of the statements inside of the LOOP statement, PL/pgSQL also provides the CONTINUE statement, which works somewhat like the EXIT statement. Hence, instead of forcing termination, the CONTINUE statement forces the next iteration of the loop to take place, skipping any code in between.

The usage of the CONTINUE and EXIT statements, especially in the middle of a code block, is not encouraged, because it breaks the execution order, which makes the code harder to read and understand.

The WHILE loop statement

The WHILE statement keeps executing a block of statements while a particular condition is met. Its syntax is as follows:

```
[ <<label>> ]
WHILE boolean-expression LOOP
    statements
END LOOP [ label ];
```

The following example uses the while loop to print the days of the current month:

```
DO $$
DECLARE
 first_day_in_month date := date_trunc('month', current_date)::date;
 last_day_in_month date := (date_trunc('month', current_date)+ INTERVAL '1
MONTH - 1 day')::date;
 counter date = first_day_in_month;
BEGIN
 WHILE (counter <= last_day_in_month) LOOP
 RAISE notice '%', counter;
 counter := counter + interval '1 day';
 END LOOP;
END;
$$ LANGUAGE plpgsql;
```

The FOR loop statement

PL/pgSQL provides two forms of the FOR statement, and they are used to execute the following:

- Iterate through the rows returned by an SQL query
- Iterate through a range of integer values

The syntax of the FOR loop statement is as follows:

```
[ <<label>> ]
FOR name IN [ REVERSE ] expression1 .. expression2 [ BY expression ] LOOP
    statements
END LOOP [ label ];
```

The `name` parameter is the name of a local variable of the integer type. This local variable scope is the `FOR` loop. Statements inside of the loop can read this variable but cannot change its value. Finally, you can change this behavior by defining the variable in the declaration section of the outer block. `expression1` and `expression2` must be evaluated to integer values; if `expression1` equals `expression2`, then the `FOR` loop is run only once.

The `REVERSE` keyword is optional, and it is used to define the order in which the range will be generated (ascending or descending). If `REVERSE` is omitted, then `expression1` should be smaller than `expression2`; otherwise, the loop will not be executed. Finally, `BY` defines the steps between two successive numbers in the range. Note that the `BY` `expression` value should always be a positive integer. The following example shows a `FOR` loop iterating over a negative range of numbers in a reverse order; the following example will print the values $-1, -3, \ldots, -9$:

```
DO $$
BEGIN
   FOR j IN REVERSE -1 .. -10 BY 2 LOOP
       Raise notice '%', j;
   END LOOP;
END; $$ LANGUAGE plpgsql;
```

To iterate through the results of a set query, the syntax is different, as follows:

```
[ <<label>> ]
FOR target IN query LOOP
    statements
END LOOP [ label ];
```

`target` is a local variable in the outer block. Its type is not restricted to simple types, such as integer and text. However, its type might be a composite or a `RECORD` data type. In PL/pgSQL, you can iterate over a `CURSOR` result or a `SELECT` statement result. A cursor is a special data object that can be used to encapsulate a `SELECT` query and then to read the query result a few rows at a time. The following example shows all of the database names:

```
DO $$
DECLARE
   database RECORD;
BEGIN
   FOR database IN SELECT * FROM pg_database LOOP
     RAISE notice '%', database.datname;
   END LOOP;
END; $$;
----- output
NOTICE: postgres
NOTICE: template1
```

```
NOTICE: template0
....
DO
```

Returning from the function

The PostgreSQL return statement is used for terminating the function and for returning the control to the caller. The return statement has different forms, such as RETURN, RETURN NEXT, RETURN QUERY, and RETURN QUERY EXECUTE. The RETURN statement can return a single value or a set to the caller, as we will show in this chapter. In this context, let's consider the following anonymous function:

```
DO $$
BEGIN
  RETURN;
  RAISE NOTICE 'This statement will not be executed';
END
$$
LANGUAGE plpgsql;
--- output
DO
```

As shown in the preceding example, the function is terminated before the execution of the RAISE statement, due to the RETURN statement.

Returning voids

A void type is used in a function to perform some side effects, such as logging; the built-in function, pg_sleep, is used to delay the execution of a server process, in seconds, as follows:

```
postgres=# \df pg_sleep
                        List of functions
    Schema    | Name     | Result data type | Argument data types | Type
--------------+----------+------------------+---------------------+--------
 pg_catalog   | pg_sleep | void             | double precision    | normal
(1 row)
```

Returning a single row

PL/pgSQL can be used to return a single row from a function; an example of this type is the factorial function.

Some developers refer to PL/pgSQL and SQL functions that return a single-row, single-column scalar variable as **scalar functions**.

The RETURN type can be a base, composite, domain, pseudo, or domain data type. The following function returns a JSON representation of a certain account:

```sql
-- in sql
CREATE OR REPLACE FUNCTION car_portal_app.get_account_in_json (account_id
INT) RETURNS JSON AS $$
  SELECT row_to_json(account) FROM car_portal_app.account WHERE account_id
= $1;
$$ LANGUAGE SQL;

--- in plpgsql
CREATE OR REPLACE FUNCTION car_portal_app.get_account_in_json1 (acc_id INT)
RETURNS JSON AS $$
BEGIN
  RETURN (SELECT row_to_json(account) FROM car_portal_app.account WHERE
account_id = acc_id);
END;
$$ LANGUAGE plpgsql;
```

Returning multiple rows

Set returning functions (SRFs) can be used to return a set of rows. The row type can either be a base type, such as an integer, composite, table type, pseudo type, or domain type. To return a set from a function, the SETOF keyword is used to mark the function as an SRF, as follows:

```sql
-- In SQL
CREATE OR REPLACE FUNCTION car_portal_app.car_model(model_name TEXT)
RETURNS SETOF car_portal_app.car_model AS $$
  SELECT car_model_id, make, model FROM car_portal_app.car_model WHERE
model = model_name;
$$ LANGUAGE SQL;

-- In plpgSQL
CREATE OR REPLACE FUNCTION car_portal_app.car_model1(model_name TEXT)
RETURNS SETOF car_portal_app.car_model AS $$
BEGIN
  RETURN QUERY SELECT car_model_id, make, model FROM
car_portal_app.car_model WHERE model = model_name;
END;
$$ LANGUAGE plpgsql;
```

To test the previous functions, let's run them. Note the caching effect of `plpgsql` on the performance:

```
car_portal=> \timing
Timing is on.
car_portal=> SELECT * FROM car_portal_app.car_model('A1');
 car_model_id | make | model
--------------+------+-------
            1 | Audi | A1
(1 row)

Time: 1,026 ms
car_portal=> SELECT * FROM car_portal_app.car_model1('A1');
 car_model_id | make | model
--------------+------+-------
            1 | Audi | A1
(1 row)

Time: 0,546 ms
```

If the `return` type is not defined, you can do the following:

- Define a new data type and use it
- Use a return table
- Use output parameters and record the data type

Let's suppose that we would only like to return `car_model_id` and `make`; as in this case, we do not have a data type defined. The preceding function could be written as follows:

```
-- SQL
CREATE OR REPLACE FUNCTION car_portal_app.car_model2(model_name TEXT)
RETURNS TABLE (car_model_id INT , make TEXT) AS $$
   SELECT car_model_id, make FROM car_portal_app.car_model WHERE model =
model_name;
$$ LANGUAGE SQL;

-- plpgSQL
CREATE OR REPLACE FUNCTION car_portal_app.car_model3(model_name TEXT)
RETURNS TABLE (car_model_id INT , make TEXT) AS $$
BEGIN
   RETURN QUERY SELECT car_model_id, make FROM car_portal_app.car_model
WHERE model = model_name;
END;
$$ LANGUAGE plpgsql;
```

To test the `car_model2` and `car_model3` functions, let's run the following code:

```
car_portal=> SELECT * FROM car_portal_app.car_model2('A1');
 car_model_id | make
--------------+------
            1 | Audi
(1 row)


Time: 0,797 ms
car_portal=> SELECT * FROM car_portal_app.car_model3('A1');
ERROR: column reference "car_model_id" is ambiguous
LINE 1: SELECT car_model_id, make FROM car_portal_app.car_model WHE...
               ^
DETAIL: It could refer to either a PL/pgSQL variable or a table column.
QUERY: SELECT car_model_id, make FROM car_portal_app.car_model WHERE model
= model_name
CONTEXT: PL/pgSQL function car_model3(text) line 3 at RETURN QUERY
Time: 0,926 ms
```

Note that, in the preceding function, an error is raised, because `plpgsql` was confusing the column name with the table definition. The reason is that the return table is shorthand for writing `OUTPUT` parameters. To fix this, we need to rename the attribute names, as follows:

```
CREATE OR REPLACE FUNCTION car_portal_app.car_model3(model_name TEXT)
RETURNS TABLE (car_model_id INT , make TEXT) AS $$
BEGIN
   RETURN QUERY SELECT a.car_model_id, a.make FROM car_portal_app.car_model
a WHERE model = model_name;
END;
$$ LANGUAGE plpgsql;
car_portal=> SELECT * FROM car_portal_app.car_model3('A1');
 car_model_id | make
--------------+------
            1 | Audi
(1 row)
```

The preceding function can also be written using the `OUT` variables; actually, the return table is implemented internally, as indicated by the error with using the `OUT` variables, as follows:

```
CREATE OR REPLACE FUNCTION car_portal_app.car_model4(model_name TEXT, OUT
car_model_id INT, OUT make TEXT ) RETURNS SETOF RECORD AS $$
BEGIN
   RETURN QUERY SELECT a.car_model_id, a.make FROM car_portal_app.car_model
a WHERE model = model_name;
END;
$$ LANGUAGE plpgsql;
```

```
car_portal=> SELECT * FROM car_portal_app.car_model4('A1'::text);
 car_model_id | make
--------------+------
            1 | Audi
(1 row)
```

Function predefined variables

The PL/pgSQL functions have several special variables that are automatically created in the top-level block. For example, if the function returns a trigger, then several variables, such as NEW, OLD, and TG_OP, are created.

In addition to the trigger special values, there is a Boolean variable called FOUND. This is often used in combination with DML and PERFORM statements, in order to conduct sanity checks. The value of the FOUND variable is affected by the SELECT, INSERT, UPDATE, DELETE, and PERFORM statements. These statements set FOUND to true if at least one row is selected, inserted, updated, or deleted.

The PERFORM statement is similar to the SELECT statement, but it discards the result of the query. Finally, the EXECUTE statement does not change the value of the FOUND variable. The following examples show how the FOUND variable is affected by the INSERT and PERFORM statements:

```
DO $$
BEGIN
  CREATE TABLE t1(f1 int);

  INSERT INTO t1 VALUES (1);
  RAISE NOTICE '%', FOUND;

  PERFORM* FROM t1 WHERE f1 = 0;
  RAISE NOTICE '%', FOUND;
  DROP TABLE t1;
END;
$$LANGUAGE plpgsql;
--- output
NOTICE: t
NOTICE: f
```

In addition to the preceding query, you can get the last **object identifier (OID)** for an inserted row, as well as the affected number of rows, by using the INSERT, UPDATE, and DELETE statements, via the following commands:

```
GET DIAGNOSTICS variable = item;
```

Assuming that there is a variable called i, of the `integer` type, you can get the affected number of rows, as follows:

```
GET DIAGNOSTICS i = ROW_COUNT;
```

Exception handling

You can trap and raise errors in PostgreSQL by using the `EXCEPTION` and `RAISE` statements. Errors can be raised by violating data integrity constraints or by performing illegal operations, such as assigning text to integers, dividing an integer or float by zero, and out-of-range assignments. By default, any error occurrences inside of a PL/pgSQL function cause the function to abort the execution and roll back the changes. To be able to recover from errors, PL/pgSQL can trap the errors, using the `EXCEPTION` clause. The syntax of the `EXCEPTION` clause is very similar to PL/pgSQL blocks. Moreover, PostgreSQL can raise errors using the `RAISE` statement. To understand exception handling, let's consider the following helping function:

```
CREATE OR REPLACE FUNCTION check_not_null (value anyelement ) RETURNS VOID
AS
$$
BEGIN
  IF (value IS NULL) THEN RAISE EXCEPTION USING ERRCODE =
'check_violation'; END IF;
END;
$$ LANGUAGE plpgsql;
```

The `check_not_null` statement is a `polymorphic` function, which simply raises an error with `check_violation` `SQLSTATE`. Calling this function and passing the `NULL` value as an argument will cause an error, as follows:

```
car_portal=> SELECT check_not_null(null::text);
ERROR: check_violation
CONTEXT: PL/pgSQL function check_not_null(anyelement) line 3 at RAISE
Time: 0,775 ms
```

In order to properly determine when the exception is raised and why, PostgreSQL defines several categories of error codes. PostgreSQL error codes can be found at http://www. postgresql.org/docs/current/interactive/errcodes-appendix.html. For example, raising an exception by the user without specifying `ERRCODE` will set the `SQLSTATE` to P001, while a unique violation exception will set `SQLSTATE` to 23505.

Errors can be matched in the EXCEPTION clause, by either SQLSTATE or the condition name, as follows:

```
WHEN unique_violation THEN ...
WHEN SQLSTATE '23505' THEN ...
```

Finally, you can provide a customized error message and SQLSTATE when raising an exception, so that ERRCODE is five digits and/or uppercase ASCII letters (other than 00000), as follows:

```
DO $$
BEGIN
  RAISE EXCEPTION USING ERRCODE = '1234X', MESSAGE = 'test customized
SQLSTATE:';
  EXCEPTION WHEN SQLSTATE '1234X' THEN
    RAISE NOTICE '% %', SQLERRM, SQLSTATE;
END;
$$ LANGUAGE plpgsql;
```

The output from executing the preceding anonymous function is as follows:

```
NOTICE: test customized SQLSTATE: 1234X
DO
Time: 0,943 ms
```

To trap an exception, let's rewrite the factorial function, and let's suppose that the factorial function should return null if the provided argument is null:

```
DROP FUNCTION IF EXISTS factorial( INTEGER );
CREATE OR REPLACE FUNCTION factorial(INTEGER ) RETURNS BIGINT AS $$
DECLARE
  fact ALIAS FOR $1;
BEGIN
  PERFORM check_not_null(fact);
  IF fact > 1 THEN RETURN factorial(fact - 1) * fact;
  ELSIF fact IN (0,1) THEN RETURN 1;
  ELSE RETURN NULL;
  END IF;

  EXCEPTION
    WHEN check_violation THEN RETURN NULL;
    WHEN OTHERS THEN RAISE NOTICE '% %', SQLERRM, SQLSTATE;
END;
$$ LANGUAGE 'plpgsql';
```

To test the function handling exception, let's call the function and pass a NULL value to it, as follows:

```
car_portal=> \pset null 'null'
Null display is "null".
car_portal=> SELECT * FROM factorial(null::int);
 factorial
-----------
      null
(1 row)

Time: 1,018 ms
```

The factorial function did not raise an error, because the error is trapped in the EXCEPTION clause, and a NULL value is returned instead. Notice that the matching is performed by using the condition name, instead of SQLSTATE. The special condition name, OTHERS, matches any error; this is often used as a safe fallback when unexpected errors occur.

In handling exceptions, if SQLERRM and SQLSTATE are not deterministic enough to know the exception cause, you can get more information about the exception by using GET STACKED DIAGNOSTICS:

```
GET STACKED DIAGNOSTICS variable { = | := } item [ , ... ];
```

item is a keyword identifying a status value related to the exception. For example, the item keywords COLUMN_NAME, TABLE_NAME, and SCHEMA_NAME indicate the names of the column, table, and schema involved in the exception.

Dynamic SQL

Dynamic SQL is used to build and execute queries on the fly. Unlike a static SQL statement, a dynamic SQL statement's full text is unknown and can change between successive executions. These queries can be **DDL**, **DCL**, and **DML** statements. Dynamic SQL is used to reduce repetitive tasks. For example, you could use dynamic SQL to create table partitioning for a certain table on a daily basis, to add missing indexes to all foreign keys or to add data auditing capabilities to a certain table, without major coding effects. Another important use of dynamic SQL is to overcome the side effects of PL/pgSQL caching, as queries executed using the EXECUTE statement are not cached.

Dynamic SQL is achieved via the EXECUTE statement. The EXECUTE statement accepts a string, and simply evaluates it. The synopsis to execute a statement is as follows:

```
EXECUTE command-string [ INTO [STRICT] target ] [ USING expression [, ...]
];
```

Dynamic SQL is a very sharp knife, and should be treated carefully. Dynamic SQL, if not written carefully, can expose the database to SQL injection attacks. The next sections will demonstrate some uses of dynamic SQL.

Executing DDL statements in dynamic SQL

In some cases, you will need to perform operations at the database object level, such as tables, indexes, columns, and roles. For example, suppose that a database developer would like to vacuum and analyze a specific schema object, which is a common task after the deployment, in order to update the statistics. To analyze the car_portal_app schema tables, we could write the following script:

```
DO $$
DECLARE
  table_name text;
BEGIN
    FOR table_name IN SELECT tablename FROM pg_tables WHERE schemaname
='car_portal_app' LOOP
        RAISE NOTICE 'Analyzing %', table_name;
        EXECUTE 'ANALYZE car_portal_app.' || table_name;
    END LOOP;
END;
$$;
```

Executing DML statements in dynamic SQL

Some applications might interact with data in an interactive manner. For example, we might have billing data generated on a monthly basis. Also, some applications filter data on different criteria, as defined by the user. In such cases, dynamic SQL is very convenient. For example, in the car portal application, the search functionality is needed to get accounts using the dynamic predicate, as follows:

```
CREATE OR REPLACE FUNCTION car_portal_app.get_account (predicate TEXT)
RETURNS SETOF car_portal_app.account AS
$$
BEGIN
  RETURN QUERY EXECUTE 'SELECT * FROM car_portal_app.account WHERE ' ||
```

```
    predicate;
    END;
    $$ LANGUAGE plpgsql;
```

We can test how the function can be used to evaluate several predicates, as follows:

```
car_portal=> SELECT * FROM car_portal_app.get_account ('true') limit 1;
 account_id | first_name | last_name | email | password
------------+------------+-----------+-----------------+-------------------
---------------
          1 | James | Butt | jbutt@gmail.com |
1b9ef408e82e38346e6ebebf2dcc5ece
(1 row)
car_portal=> SELECT * FROM car_portal_app.get_account
(E'first_name=''James''');
 account_id | first_name | last_name | email | password
------------+------------+-----------+-----------------+-------------------
---------------
          1 | James | Butt | jbutt@gmail.com |
1b9ef408e82e38346e6ebebf2dcc5ece
(1 row)
```

Dynamic SQL and the caching effect

As we mentioned earlier, PL/pgSQL caches execution plans. This is quite good if the generated plan is expected to be static. For example, the following statement is expected to use an index scan, due to selectivity. In this case, caching the plan saves some time and increases performance:

```
SELECT * FROM account WHERE account_id =<INT>
```

In other scenarios, however, this is not true. For example, let's suppose that we have an index on the advertisement_date column, and we would like to get the number of advertisements since a certain date, as follows:

```
SELECT count (*) FROM car_portal_app.advertisement WHERE advertisement_date
>= <certain_date>;
```

In the preceding query, the entries from the `advertisement` table can be fetched from the hard disk, either by using the index scan or by using the sequential scan based on selectivity, which depends on the provided `certain_date` value. Caching the execution plan of such a query will cause serious problems; hence, writing the function as follows is not a good idea:

```
CREATE OR REPLACE FUNCTION car_portal_app.get_advertisement_count
(some_date timestamptz ) RETURNS BIGINT AS $$
BEGIN
  RETURN (SELECT count (*) FROM car_portal_app.advertisement WHERE
advertisement_date >=some_date)::bigint;
END;
$$ LANGUAGE plpgsql;
```

To solve the caching issue, we could rewrite the previous function, using either the SQL language function or the PL/pgSQL `execute` command, as follows:

```
CREATE OR REPLACE FUNCTION car_portal_app.get_advertisement_count
(some_date timestamptz ) RETURNS BIGINT AS $$
DECLARE
 count BIGINT;
BEGIN
 EXECUTE 'SELECT count (*) FROM car_portal_app.advertisement WHERE
advertisement_date >= $1' USING some_date INTO count;
 RETURN count;
END;
$$ LANGUAGE plpgsql;
```

Recommended practices for dynamic SQL usage

Dynamic SQL can cause security issues if it is not handled carefully; dynamic SQL is vulnerable to the SQL injection technique. SQL injection is used to execute SQL statements that reveal secure information or even destroy data in a database. A very simple example of a PL/pgSQL function that's vulnerable to SQL injection is as follows:

```
CREATE OR REPLACE FUNCTION car_portal_app.can_login (email text, pass text)
RETURNS BOOLEAN AS $$
DECLARE
  stmt TEXT;
  result bool;
BEGIN
  stmt = E'SELECT COALESCE (count(*)=1, false) FROM car_portal_app.account
WHERE email = \''|| $1 || E'\' and password = \''||$2||E'\'';
  RAISE NOTICE '%' , stmt;
  EXECUTE stmt INTO result;
```

```
    RETURN result;
END;
$$ LANGUAGE plpgsql;
```

The preceding function returns `true` if the email and the password match. To test this function, let's insert a row and try to inject some code, as follows:

```
car_portal=> SELECT car_portal_app.can_login('jbutt@gmail.com',
md5('jbutt@gmail.com'));
NOTICE: SELECT COALESCE (count(*)=1, false) FROM account WHERE email =
'jbutt@gmail.com' and password = '1b9ef408e82e38346e6ebebf2dcc5ece'
 can_login
-----------
 t
(1 row)

car_portal=> SELECT car_portal_app.can_login('jbutt@gmail.com',
md5('jbutt@yahoo.com'));
NOTICE: SELECT COALESCE (count(*)=1, false) FROM account WHERE email =
'jbutt@gmail.com' and password = '37eb43e4d439589d274b6f921b1e4a0d'
 can_login
-----------
 f
(1 row)

car_portal=# SELECT car_portal_app.can_login(E'jbutt@gmail.com\'--', 'Do
not know password');
NOTICE: SELECT COALESCE (count(*)=1, false) FROM car_portal_app.account
WHERE email = 'jbutt@gmail.com'--' and password = 'Do not know password'
 can_login
-----------
 t
(1 row)
```

Notice that the function returns `true` even when the password does not match the password stored in the table. This is simply because the predicate was commented, as shown by the `raise` notice:

```
SELECT COALESCE (count(*)=1, false) FROM account WHERE email =
'jbutt@gmail.com'--' and password = 'Do not know password'
```

To protect code against this technique, follow these practices:

- For parameterized dynamic SQL statements, use the `USING` clause.
- Use the `format` function with the appropriate interpolation to construct your queries. Note that `%I` escapes the argument as an identifier and `%L` as a literal.

- Use `quote_ident()`, `quote_literal()`, and `quote_nullable()` to properly format your identifiers and literal.

One way to write the preceding function is as follows:

```
CREATE OR REPLACE FUNCTION car_portal_app.can_login (email text, pass text)
RETURNS BOOLEAN AS
$$
DECLARE
  stmt TEXT;
result bool;
BEGIN
stmt = format('SELECT COALESCE (count(*)=1, false) FROM
car_portal_app.account WHERE email = %Land password = %L', $1,$2);
  RAISE NOTICE '%' , stmt;
  EXECUTE stmt INTO result;
  RETURN result;
END;
$$ LANGUAGE plpgsql;
```

Summary

PostgreSQL provides a complete programming language called PL/pgSQL, which is integrated with the PostgreSQL trigger system. The PL/pgSQL and SQL languages can be used to code very complex logic. You should use the SQL functions when possible. With the introduction of advanced query writing techniques, such as window functions and lateral joins, in PostgreSQL, we can write very complex logic using only the standard SQL language.

There are several parameters for controlling function behavior in PostgreSQL; these parameters are applicable to the PL/pgSQL and SQL functions, as well. For example, SECURITY DEFINER and SECURITY INVOKER define the execution security context and privileges. The functions' planner parameters help the planner to generate execution plans. These parameters are COST, LEAKPROOF, and ROWS. Configuration related parameters can also be applied to functions.

PL/pgSQL is a fully-fledged language; there are statements for assignments, conditionals, iterations, and exception handling. Functions can return the void pseudo type, scalar values, records, and so on. Also, functions support IN, OUT, and INOUT parameters.

The dynamic SQL technique enables developers to build SQL statements dynamically at runtime. We can create general purpose, flexible functions, because the full text of an SQL statement may be unknown at the time of compilation. Dynamic SQL needs careful handling, because it is exposed to SQL injection attacks.

In Chapter 8, *OLAP and Data Warehousing*, we will discuss modeling strategies for OLAP applications and some features that makes PostgreSQL a good candidate for OLAP applications. These features include SQL statements, such as the COPY statement, and data partitioning strategies via inheritance.

Questions

1. What are some concerns about using PL/pgSQL functions, as compared to SQL functions?
2. What's the difference between a function and procedure?
3. What's the difference between a security invoker and security definer ?
4. Write a function in pl/pgSQL to find the greatest common divisor, using iteration.
5. Write a function in pl/pgSQL to find the greatest common divisor, using recursion.
6. Write a function in SQL to find the greatest common divisor, using recursion.
7. How can polymorphism be achieved in pl/pgSQL?
8. What's the difference between return SETOF and return TABLE?
9. What's the meaning of dynamic SQL?
10. Why it is recommended to use the format function when writing functions and stored procedures?
11. Describe how functions can be used when defining triggers.

OLAP and Data Warehousing

A database usually performs the role of a storage component of a complex software solution. Depending on the type of the solution and what problem it aims to solve, the configuration of the database and the data structure can be different. It's common to configure a database and data structure in one of two ways: **online transaction processing (OLTP)** or **online analytical processing (OLAP)**.

In this chapter, we will discuss some features of PostgreSQL that help implement a data warehouse solution based on a PostgreSQL database, and theoretical concepts related to that, namely:

- **OLTP and OLAP**: their purpose and differences
- **Online analytical processing**: What it is and why it's special
- **Partitioning**: A way to physically organize and manage huge tables
- **Parallel query**: A feature that increases the speed of query execution
- **Index-only scans**: A way to improve performance by building indexes in the correct way

We will extend the `car_portal` database by adding another schema to the database, `dwh`, and creating some tables there. The schema itself and the sample data can be found in the attached media for this chapter, in `schema.sql` and `data.sql`, respectively. All the code examples can be found in the `examples.sql` file.

OLTP and OLAP

When a database works as a backend for an application, it implements an OLTP solution. This means that the database is supposed to perform a lot of small transactions on a regular basis. The car portal database we used as an example in previous chapters is an example of a typical OLTP data structure. The application working with this database executes a transaction each time a user does something: creates an account, modifies the password, enters a car into the system, creates or changes an advertisement, and so on. Each of these actions causes a transaction in the database that would create, change or delete a row/couple of rows in one or more tables. The more users work with the system, the more often the transactions are performed. The database should be able to handle the load, and its performance is measured by the number of transactions per second it can handle. The total amount of the data is usually not a concern.

The key characteristics of an OLTP database are as follows:

- A normalized structure
- A relatively small amount of data
- A relatively large number of transactions
- Each transaction is small, affecting one, or several, records in the database
- The users typically do all the operations on the data: select, insert, delete, and update

When a database is working as a data source for a reporting software and its data is used for analysis, it implements an OLAP solution. This implies the opposite of OLTP: a lot of data, but it's rarely changed. The number of queries is relatively small, but the queries are large and complex, and they usually read and aggregate many records. The performance of database solutions of this kind is measured by the amount of time the queries take. OLAP database solutions are often called **data warehouses**.

The OLAP databases normally have the following characteristics:

- A denormalized structure
- A relatively large amount of data
- A relatively small number of transactions
- Each transaction is big, affecting millions of records
- The users usually only perform SELECT queries

Online analytical processing

A company that runs such a car portal website could store the HTTP access log in a database table. This can be used to analyze user activity; for example, to measure the performance of the application, to identify the patterns in the users' behavior, or simply to collect statistics about which car models are most popular. This data would be inserted into the table and never changed, and maybe deleted only when it is too old. However, the amount of data would be much bigger than the actual business data in the car portal database, but the data would be accessed only from time to time by internal users to perform analysis and create reports.

These users are not expected to execute many queries per second—the opposite in fact, but those queries will be big and complex, therefore the time that each query can take matters.

Another thing about OLAP databases is that they aren't always up to date. As the analysis is performed on a basis of weeks and months (for example, comparing the number of requests in the current month with the previous month), it's not worth the effort to make the data of the very last second available in the data warehouse in real time. The data can be loaded into the data warehouse periodically; for example, daily or several times per day.

Loading data into a data warehouse

Let's consider the task of loading HTTP logs into the database and preparing them for analysis. Such tasks in data warehouse solutions are called **extract, transform, and load (ETL)**.

Suppose the HTTP server that runs the car portal application is writing access logs in files and they are recreated every day. Assuming that the server runs nginx, a popular HTTP server software, lines in such log files by default should look similar to this:

```
94.31.90.168 - - [01/Jul/2017:01:00:22 +0000] "GET / HTTP/1.1" 200 227 "-"
"Mozilla/5.0 (Windows NT 10.0; Win64; x64) AppleWebKit/537.36 (KHTML, like
Gecko) Chrome/55.0.2883.87 Safari/537.36"
```

It has the following fields, separated by a space: remote address, remote user, timestamp, access method and resource URL, status code, body size, bytes, HTTP referer, and HTTP user agent.

The setup process and configuration of an HTTP server is outside the scope of this book. However, it's worth mentioning that to make loading it into a PostgreSQL database easier, you should change the log file format. To make it contain comma-separated values, you should change the `log_format` directive in the configuration file, `nginx.conf`, to make it look like this:

```
log_format main '$time_local;$remote_addr;$remote_user;'
                '"$request";$status;$body_bytes_sent;'
                '"$http_referer";"$http_user_agent"'
```

Now the logs are produced as CSV files that contain the following lines:

```
01/Jul/2017:01:00:22 +0000;94.31.90.168;-;"GET / HTTP/1.1";200;227;"-
";"Mozilla/5.0 (Windows NT 10.0; Win64; x64) AppleWebKit/537.36 (KHTML,
like Gecko) Chrome/61.0.3163.79 Safari/537.36"
```

The file has the same fields as before, just the timestamp field is moved to the first position. All the fields are separated by a semicolon (;). In the database, there is a table named `dwh.access_log`, which has the following structure:

```
CREATE TABLE dwh.access_log
(
    ts timestamp with time zone,
    remote_address text,
    remote_user text,
    url text,
    status_code int,
    body_size int,
    http_referer text,
    http_user_agent text
);
```

PostgreSQL provides a way to load data into tables quickly, many rows at a time, instead of executing `INSERT` commands row by row. The `COPY` command loads data into a table. The data can be taken from a file that is located on the database server in a place accessible by the PostgreSQL server process or from a stream. The data by default should look like a tab-separated list of fields; with records separated by a new line. However, this is customizable. The command is not included in the SQL standard. Here is a simplified syntax diagram for this command:

```
COPY >table name> [(column [, ...])]
FROM { >file name> | STDIN | PROGRAM >command> } [[WITH] (>options>)]
```

Here, `options` is used to specify data format, delimiters, quotations, escape characters, and some other parameters. `STDIN` can be specified instead of the filename to copy the data from standard input. `PROGRAM` is used to take the data from the output of a shell command. The column list can be provided when the file does not have the data for all the columns or they are given in a different order.

The full description of all the options and parameters that the `COPY` command can take you can find in the documentation, here: `https://www.postgresql.org/docs/current/sql-copy.html`

To load the data into the database, you should copy the file to the server and then execute the following command:

```
COPY dwh.access_log FROM '/tmp/access.log';
```

This would load the contents of the file located at `/tmp/access.log` into the `dwh.access_log` table. However, this is not a good idea for several reasons:

- Only a superuser can execute the `COPY` command to read or write from files.
- As the PostgreSQL server process needs to access the file, it would be necessary to either place the file in the location where other database files are stored, or allow the PostgreSQL process to access other locations. Both may be considered issues from a security point of view.
- Copying the file to the server may be the issue by itself; it would be necessary to allow the user (or the application) to access the file system on the server or mount shared network locations to the server.

To avoid these issues, you should use the `COPY` command to load the data from a stream, namely standard input. To do so, it may be necessary to write an application that would connect to the database, execute the `COPY`, command, and then stream the data to the server. Luckily, the `psql` console can do this.

Let's try to load the `access.log` sample file that is provided in the attached media.

Suppose the file is located in the current directory. The database is running on localhost and the `car_portal_app` database user is allowed to connect. The following command will load the data from the file to the `dwh.access_log` table:

```
user@host:~$ psql -h localhost -U car_portal_app -d car_portal \
-c "COPY dwh.access_log FROM STDIN WITH (format csv, delimiter ';')" \
> access.log
COPY 15456
```

The `access.log` file is redirected to the input of the `psql` client. It executes the `COPY` command that loads the data from standard input. The output of the command is the word `COPY` followed by the number of rows copied.

The command will be the same on both Linux and Windows.

It's also possible to execute this operation interactively from the `psql` console. There's a `\copy` command provided by `psql`, which has a similar syntax to the SQL `COPY` command: `\copy dwh.access_log FROM 'access.log' WITH csv delimiter ';'`. In the background, it's still the same: on the server, the `COPY ... FROM STDIN` command is executed, and then `psql` reads the file and sends its contents to the server.

Using this approach, it's very easy to organize a simple ETL process. It may be executed once per day and would just execute the preceding command. The prerequisite for this would be setting up log rotation for the HTTP server to make sure that the same data is not loaded twice.

The `COPY` command can be used not only to load data into tables, but can also copy the data the other way around: from tables to files or to standard output. This feature can be used again in ETL processes that can be organized in the form of simple bash scripts, instead of complex software that would use high-level access to the database using JDBC or other APIs.

Here is an example of how to copy a data table from one server to another (supposing the structure of the table is identical):
```
$ psql -h server1 -d database1 -c "COPY table1 TO STDOUT"
| psql -h server2 -d database2 -c "COPY table2 FROM
STDIN"
```
Here, the first `psql` command will read the table and output it to standard output. This stream is piped to the second `psql` command that writes the data to the other table, taking it from standard input.

ETL can also include enriching the input raw data with additional attributes or preprocessing it to make it easier to query. For example, the entries could be mapped to the records in the `car_portal` database. Let's say API calls to `/api/cars/30` could be mapped to the record in the `car` table with `car_id = 30`. Such processing can be done in the database, as follows:

```
car_portal=> ALTER TABLE dwh.access_log ADD car_id int;
ALTER TABLE

car_portal=> UPDATE dwh.access_log
```

```
    SET car_id = (SELECT regexp_matches(url, '/api/cars/(d+)W'))[1]::int
    WHERE url like '%/api/cars/%';
UPDATE 2297
```

In a similar way, the `access_log` table can be enriched by another attribute and can be joined to other tables.

In real life, ETL is usually more complex. It would normally include checking whether the data being loaded exists already in the destination table and would clean it before loading. This will make the process idempotent. Additionally, the process could identify which data to load and locate the input data. For example, consider an ETL job that loads a dataset every day. If it has failed for some reason, when started the next day, it should detect the previous failure and load two sets of data instead of only one. Notifying the right systems or people in case of failure can also be done by the ETL process.

There are a lot of different ETL tools available on the market, and as open source software.

Data modeling for OLAP

It is usual to in a data warehouse to have a big table that constantly receives new data. That table contains information about business transactions, measurements, or events that are the object of analysis. Such table is usually called the **fact table**. The HTTP access log that we discussed in the previous section, *Loading data into a data warehouse*, plays the role of a fact table in those examples.

In many cases, it doesn't make too much sense to perform analytical queries on the fact table only. Grouping the data by `car_id` without knowing what the values in the `car_id` field actually mean is useless. Therefore, the `car` table should also be available in the data warehouse. The difference between this table and the fact table is that the data is always loaded into the fact table, but the `car` table is quite static. The number of records in this table is much smaller. The tables that are used to resolve IDs into names are called **lookup tables** or **dimension tables**. The `car` table has a reference `car_model_id` key that points to records in the `car_model` table, which is used to resolve the ID of the car model into the name of the car make and model.

The typical usage pattern for a fact table includes big `SELECT` queries that aren't executed very often, but read large numbers of records, sometimes millions or tens of millions. In this case, any additional operation performed by the server could cost a lot of time. This includes the joining of fact tables to dimension tables.

For this reason, it's quite common to denormalize the data. Practically, this means joining the source tables in advance and storing the result of the join in a table. For example, if the access log entries we discussed in the previous section, *Loading data into a data warehouse*, were mapped to `car_id` and the analytical task would imply calculating some statistics on car makes, this would mean we'd perform two joins: the `access_log` is joined to the `car` table, which would be joined to the `car_model` table. This can be expensive.

To save time, it could make sense to join the `car` and `car_model` tables and store the result in yet another table. This table would not be in a normal form because the same car model would appear in the table many times. This would consume some extra disk space, of course. However, this may be a good compromise to make, as querying the fact table would be faster when this new lookup table is joined instead of both `car` and `car_model`.

Alternatively, the `car_model_id` field could be created in the fact table and filled when data is loaded by the ETL process. This structure would also be denormalized, which consumes more disk space, but is easier to query.

A fact table can reference dimension tables. A dimension table in turn can have references to other dimension tables. This is called a **snowflake schema** in OLAP terminology. It could look like this:

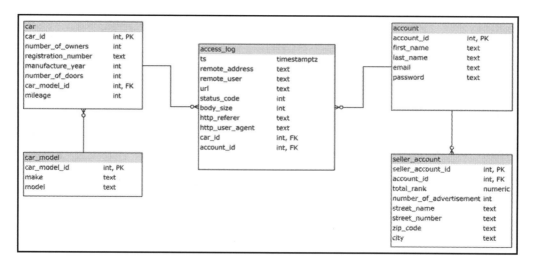

Snowflake data warehouse model

If the structure is denormalized and the dimension tables are not joined to each other, that is called a **star schema**. It could look like this:

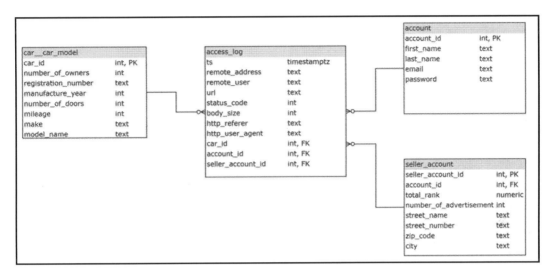

Star data warehouse model

There are advantages and disadvantages to both, and of course hybrid schemas that combine both star and snowflake models for different dimension tables are also possible. So usually, it's a trade-off between complexity, maintainability, and performance.

Aggregation

Storing individual entries in a data warehouse could be too expensive. The number of HTTP requests for a big web application could be huge, and nobody would care for the individual entries in such a dataset. The individual records are used to troubleshoot the system, but in this case it wouldn't make sense to keep them for longer than several days.

The table that contains the information about the HTTP API calls could have fields that contain the following information:

- The amount of bytes sent
- The response time
- The URL of the API endpoint
- the date and time of the request
- A user ID

In this case, the amount of bytes sent and the response time would be measures, and the URL of the API endpoint, HTTP status code, user ID, and date and time of the request are dimensions. The difference between them is that dimensions categorize the data, while measures themselves are the object of statistical analysis.

The data is grouped by the dimension fields, and the measure fields are aggregated. The meaningful aggregation functions for the measures in the example would be `sum` for the amount of bytes sent, and `avg` for the response time. Additionally, the total number of requests could be counted. For grouping, the date and time of the request could be truncated to hours. The result of this aggregation could be stored in the data warehouse. The amount of data in the aggregated table would be much smaller than individual entries would take, and therefore it would work much faster. The aggregation could be part of the ETL process.

When the amount of data is very large, it's possible to exchange granularity for performance. This means dropping one dimension in order to reduce the number of possible combinations of values in the grouping. For example, this could mean grouping by day instead of by hour, or removing the user ID from the table so that the number of rows will be reduced because all the users will be grouped together.

It may make sense to keep different levels of aggregation in different tables at the same time, and use the most suitable table for a particular report.

Partitioning

Data is constantly or periodically loaded into a data warehouse. The database can grow very big. The bigger it gets, the slower it works. The size of the database is limited by the capacity of the disk storage, so part of it needs to be deleted from time to time. Deletion from a very big table can also be quite slow.

The data that is newer is usually queried more often. Business users could check the reports of the last day every morning, of the last week every Monday, and of the last month at the beginning of the next month. It's common to compare the results of a time period with a corresponding previous period; for example, the current month as compared to the previous month, or to the respective month one year ago. It's unlikely that somebody would query ten-year-old data.

It would be nice to keep the newer, more-queried data in one relatively small table and the old data in a different table or tables, and for each report query only the table that has the data that is required. On the other hand, it would be quite complex to implement a reporting tool that would query different tables depending on the parameters of the query.

Declarative partitioning

PostgreSQL provides a way of keeping parts of table data in several different physical tables while using the same table name when querying them. This is called **partitioning**. Partitioning is implemented through the mechanism of table inheritance. This was mentioned in `Chapter 3`, *PostgreSQL Basic Building Blocks*. When a table inherits another table or tables, it's called a **child table**. The table that's inherited is a **parent table**. When the parent table is queried, the data from all the child tables is returned. In the context of partitioning, the parent table is called the **partitioned table** and the child tables are called **partitions**.

In older versions (before 10), PostgreSQL supported only basic partitioning, which required the following:

- Creating each partition table and defining the inheritance relationships with the parent table explicitly
- Creating `CHECK` constraints on the partitions to prevent data from being written to wrong partitions
- Defining triggers or rules on the parent table so that performing an `INSERT` into the parent table would lead to writing data to the partitions instead

- Maintaining those triggers to keep them up to date with a changing partition structure

All this was rather complicated and now PostgreSQL supports declarative partitioning. This implies only providing a specification of the partition structure. PostgreSQL will create all the necessary physical entities automatically. We will discuss declarative partitioning in this section, but basic partitioning with triggers and explicit inheritance is still possible and could be used in atypical cases.

To define partitions for a table, it's necessary to choose a **partition key**. The partition key is a field or an expression (or list of them) whose value will be used to identify the partition a record belongs to. In PostgreSQL, it's possible to define partitioning for a table using one of the three partitioning schemes: *range*, *list*, and *hash*. **Range partitioning** means that all the values of the partition key within a certain range will belong to a partition. **List partitioning** means that only a specific value or values of the partition key will belong to a partition. **Hash partitioning** means that rows that have the same hash value of the partition key will belong to the same partition.

When a partitioned table is queried with a WHERE clause that has a filter on the partition key, in many cases PostgreSQL is able to recognize that and perform a table scan on only the partition that has the data that's been requested.

Let's now define a partitioned data structure to store the data for the HTTP access log we imported in the *Loading data into a data warehouse* section. We will only use a subset of fields for simplicity.

Range partitioning is a good choice for data that has a date dimension. First, create the partitioned table, as follows:

```
CREATE TABLE dwh.access_log_partitioned
(
  ts timestamptz, url text,
  status_code int
)
PARTITION BY RANGE (ts);
```

This creates a table and defines the ts field as the partition key for a range partitioning scheme. This table doesn't have any partitions yet, but PostgreSQL knows that it's supposed to be partitioned, therefore no data can be physically stored in this table. To create a partition, we would need to create a new table and specify that it's a partition of the partitioned table.

Now, create partitions for the ranges of values of the `ts` field for July, August, and September 2018, as follows:

```
CREATE TABLE dwh.access_log_2018_07 PARTITION OF dwh.access_log_partitioned
FOR VALUES FROM ('2018-07-01') TO ('2018-08-01');

CREATE TABLE dwh.access_log_2018_08 PARTITION OF dwh.access_log_partitioned
FOR VALUES FROM ('2018-08-01') TO ('2018-09-01');

CREATE TABLE dwh.access_log_2018_09 PARTITION OF dwh.access_log_partitioned
FOR VALUES FROM ('2018-09-01') TO ('2018-10-01');
```

 The lower bound for a range partition is inclusive, and the upper bound is exclusive. In the preceding example, the `access_log_2018_07` partition will contain the records that satisfy the `ts >= '2018-07-01' AND ts > '2018-08-01'` predicate.

When such a structure is defined, it is possible to insert data into the `access_log_partitioned` parent table. Records will be automatically distributed into the correct partitions depending on the values of the partition key.

What if somebody tries to insert a record where the value of the partition key is outside any of the existing partition ranges? PostgreSQL will return an error, as follows:

```
car_portal=> INSERT INTO dwh.access_log_partitioned values ('2018-02-01',
'/test', 404);
 ERROR: no partition of relation "access_log_partitioned" found for row
 DETAIL: Partition key of the failing row contains (ts) = (2018-02-01
00:00:00+00).
```

To make it possible to insert such rows, we would need to create another partition for February. Alternatively, it's possible to create a partition for all rows whose partition key is greater than a certain value or below some value. To do this, the MAXVALUE and MINVALUE keywords are used. The following command will create a partition for all the records that are before July 1, 2018:

```
CREATE TABLE dwh.access_log_min PARTITION OF dwh.access_log_partitioned
FOR VALUES FROM (MINVALUE) TO ('2018-07-01');
```

It's possible to create a partition for records that don't fit any existing partition—we can use a **default partition**, as follows:

```
CREATE table dwh.access_log_default PARTITION OF dwh.access_log_partitioned
DEFAULT;
```

If there are records in the default partition, and a new partition is created so that any of those records would fit there, PostgreSQL will not allow us to create this new partition.

Sub-partitioning

PostgreSQL supports sub-partitioning. That means partitions can also be partitioned themselves.

The list-partition scheme can be used with fields that don't have too many distinct values and when the values are known in advance. We can use this scheme for the HTTP status code, and combine it with range partitioning as we did before. To create another partition for October 2018 and then further partition it for different values of the HTTP code, the following commands can be used:

```
CREATE TABLE dwh.access_log_2018_10 PARTITION OF dwh.access_log_partitioned
FOR VALUES FROM ('2018-10-01') TO ('2018-11-01')
PARTITION BY LIST (status_code);

CREATE TABLE dwh.access_log_2018_10_200 PARTITION OF dwh.access_log_2018_10
FOR VALUES IN (200);

CREATE TABLE dwh.access_log_2018_10_400 PARTITION OF dwh.access_log_2018_10
FOR VALUES IN (400);
```

We have now a partition for October that has two sub-partitions for the 200 and 400 HTTP status codes. Note that it won't be possible to insert other status codes into the table with such a configuration. It is, however, possible to give a list of values of the partition key when creating a partition.

Alternatively, it's possible to define the partitioning scheme not just on a field, but on an expression. Here, sub-partitions are created based on the first digit of the status code:

```
CREATE TABLE dwh.access_log_2018_11 PARTITION OF dwh.access_log_partitioned
FOR VALUES FROM ('2018-11-01') TO ('2018-12-01')
PARTITION BY LIST (left(status_code::text, 1));

CREATE TABLE dwh.access_log_2018_11_2XX PARTITION OF dwh.access_log_2018_11
FOR VALUES IN ('2');

CREATE TABLE dwh.access_log_2018_11_4XX PARTITION OF dwh.access_log_2018_11
FOR VALUES IN ('4');
```

Hash partitioning may be used with fields that have many distinct values or when they are not known in advance. As an example, let's create yet another partition for the access_log_partitioned table, for December 2018, and then define sub-partitioning using the hash-partitioning scheme:

```
CREATE TABLE dwh.access_log_2018_12 PARTITION OF dwh.access_log_partitioned
FOR VALUES FROM ('2018-12-01') TO ('2019-01-01')
PARTITION BY HASH (url);

CREATE TABLE dwh.access_log_2018_12_1 PARTITION OF dwh.access_log_2018_12
FOR VALUES WITH (MODULUS 3, REMAINDER 0);

CREATE TABLE dwh.access_log_2018_12_2 PARTITION OF dwh.access_log_2018_12
FOR VALUES WITH (MODULUS 3, REMAINDER 1);

CREATE TABLE dwh.access_log_2018_12_3 PARTITION OF dwh.access_log_2018_12
FOR VALUES WITH (MODULUS 3, REMAINDER 2);
```

The partitioning scheme in the previous example is based on the hash values of the url field. This is a text field, but the hash is an integer. The MODULUS keyword in the statements specifies the divisor by which the hash is to be divided. The remainder after the division will identify the partition, and the REMAINDER keyword is used to specify which value of the remainder will correspond to which partition. In the example, the modulus is 3, therefore three partitions will be necessary. The first partition, access_log_2018_12_1, will contain records whose hash value of the url field can be divided by 3 without a remainder. The second partition will contain records whose hash divided by 3 leaves a remainder of 1. The last partition will contain the records with the remainder of 2.

This will make the records distributed more or less equally over the three sub-partitions, assuming that the url field doesn't have values that appear much more often than other values.

The way hash partitioning is implemented in PostgreSQL is more complicated than in some other RDBMSes. For example, in Oracle, you should only specify the number of partitions and then the database will try to equally distribute data over all of them. The definition in PostgreSQL with MODULUS and REMAINDER gives more control over which fraction of data is to be stored in each partition. This can be used when changing the number of partitions to avoid migrating the whole table at once, and instead doing it per partition, one after another.

For example, if the amount of data for December 2018 grew too much and it became necessary to increase the number of sub-partitions from three to six, the following strategy could be used:

1. Detach one of the existing sub-partitions (convert a partition into a standalone table). Let's say the detached sub-partition had the remainder of 0.
2. Create another pair of sub-partitions with the modulus as 6 and the remainders as 0 and 3. Together, they will cover the hash values that the detached sub-partitions had.
3. Insert data from the detached sub-partitions into the main partitioned table. PostgreSQL will automatically redistribute the data into the proper sub-partitions.
4. Repeat these steps for the other two sub-partitions. The new remainder pairs will be (1, 4) and (2, 5).

This operation would still require us to copy a lot of data, but can be done per partition, which is better and faster than for the whole table.

The following is a summary of what we've covered so far:

- Range partitioning should be used when the data has a time dimension, and usually there are filters on a certain time range in queries. Partitioning will make it possible to keep the most recent data, which is usually queried more often, in a dedicated table, and the old data in other tables. Deleting the old data is very easy and can be done by removing old partitions.
- List partitioning should be used when there is a field with a small number of distinct values and this field is often used in queries to filter data.
- Hash partitioning should be used when there is no good way to structure data to make queries faster. Hash partitions, however, could be located, for example, on different hard disks, which will make concurrent access to them faster.
- Different partitioning schemes can be combined using sub-partitioning.

More complicated partitioning strategies are still possible using the traditional table-inheritance feature. This will require some manual effort to create tables, define an inheritance relationships, create check constraints to make PostgreSQL aware of which data is stored in which partition when necessary, and set up triggers or rules to distribute the records into proper partitions when inserted into the parent table.

It's possible to delete a partition by simply deleting the table. It's also possible to detach a partition from the parent table so that it's no longer a partition but just a standalone table:

```
car_portal=> ALTER TABLE dwh.access_log_partitioned
  DETACH PARTITION dwh.access_log_2018_11;
ALTER TABLE
```

It's also possible to make an existing table a partition of some other table:

```
car_portal=> ALTER TABLE dwh.access_log_partitioned
  ATTACH PARTITION dwh.access_log_2018_11
  FOR VALUES FROM ('2018-11-01') TO ('2018-12-01');
ALTER TABLE
```

Performance improvement

To illustrate the benefits of partitioning, let's see an example. First, create a non-partitioned table to compare the results, with the same structure as the partitioned one:

```
car_portal=> CREATE TABLE dwh.access_log_not_partitioned
  (LIKE dwh.access_log_partitioned);
CREATE TABLE
```

Insert the data into both the partitioned and non-partitioned tables, copying the contents of the dwh.access_log table 1,000 times, as follows:

```
car_portal=> INSERT INTO dwh.access_log_not_partitioned
SELECT ts, url, status_code FROM dwh.access_log, generate_series(1, 1000);
INSERT 0 15456000
car_portal=> INSERT INTO dwh.access_log_partitioned
SELECT ts, url, status_code FROM dwh.access_log, generate_series(1, 1000);
INSERT 0 15456000
```

Now let's count the number of records for the last 10 days of August, measuring the time the query takes, as follows:

```
car_portal=> \timing
Timing is on.

car_portal=> SELECT count(*) FROM dwh.access_log_not_partitioned
  WHERE ts >= '2018-08-22' AND ts > '2018-09-01';
 count
---------
 1712000
(1 row)
Time: 921.122 ms
```

```
car_portal=> SELECT count(*) FROM dwh.access_log_partitioned
  WHERE ts >= '2018-08-22' AND ts > '2018-09-01';
 count
---------
 1712000
(1 row)
Time: 336.221 ms
```

Querying the partitioned table was about three times quicker. That is because PostgreSQL knows which partition has the data for August and only scans that one. This is also visible in the execution plan:

```
car_portal=# EXPLAIN SELECT count(*) FROM dwh.access_log_partitioned
  WHERE ts >= '2018-08-22' AND ts > '2018-09-01';
                          QUERY PLAN
-----------------------------------------------------------------------
 Finalize Aggregate (cost=81063.45..81063.46 rows=1 width=8)
   -> Gather (cost=81063.23..81063.44 rows=2 width=8)
         Workers Planned: 2
         -> Partial Aggregate (cost=80063.23..80063.24 rows=1 width=8)
               -> Parallel Append (cost=0.00..80035.64 rows=11035 width=0)
                     -> Parallel Seq Scan on access_log_2018_08
                        (cost=0.00..79980.47 rows=11035 width=0)
                           Filter: ((ts >= '2018-08-22 00:00:00+00'
                           ::timestamp with time zone) AND (ts >
                           '2018-09-01 00:00:00+00'::timestamp with time
                           zone))
(7 rows)
```

The sequential scan was performed on the `access_log_2018_08` partition.

There is another small topic related to partitioning, which is how partitioning affects the process of changing the data in a table.

When records are inserted into a partitioned table, PostgreSQL will automatically distribute them into proper partitions based on their partition key. It's also possible to insert them directly into a partition. Deleting records from a partitioned table will effectively delete them from a partition. It's also possible to delete from a partition directly.

It's a common practice in data warehouse solutions to insert data into an independent table and then attach it as a partition to a partitioned table. Doing this might make huge numbers of records appear in a partitioned table in no time. The same can be done when a big deletion needs to be done: instead of deleting records, you could drop a partition.

If a partitioned table is being updated and the partition key changes for a row so that it needs to be moved to a different partition, PostgreSQL will perform that automatically.

If an index is created on a partitioned table, the same indexes will be automatically created on all the partitions.

Partitioning is described in detail in the PostgreSQL documentation: `https://www.postgresql.org/docs/current/static/ddl-partitioning.html`.

Parallel query

PostgreSQL creates a server process for each client connection. This means that only one CPU core will be used to perform all the work. Of course, when multiple connections are active, the resources of the server machine will be used intensively. However, in the data warehouse solutions, the number of concurrent sessions is usually not very large, but they tend to perform big complex queries. It makes sense to utilize multiple CPU cores to process the queries of a single client connection.

PostgreSQL supports a feature called **parallel query**, which makes it possible to use multiple CPUs for one query. Certain operations, such as table scans, joins, or aggregation, can be executed in several processes concurrently. The administrator can configure the number of workers that the PostgreSQL server will create for parallel query execution. When the query optimizer can detect a benefit from parallel execution, it will request some workers, and if they are available, the query (or a part of it) will be executed in parallel.

To see the benefits of the parallel query execution, let's consider an example using the HTTP access log table created in the *Loading data into a data warehouse* section. First, disable the parallel query feature for the current session by changing the `max_parallel_workers_per_gather` configuration parameter to zero. Note that this is not the total number of processes that performs the queries, but the number of *extra* processes. The main server process that serves the current client session is always there. The parameter is changed as follows:

```
car_portal=> SET max_parallel_workers_per_gather = 0;
SET
```

Assuming timing is still enabled, query the table:

```
car_portal=> SELECT count(*) FROM dwh.access_log_not_partitioned
  WHERE url ~ 'car';
 count
---------
 7030000
(1 row)
Time: 10876.095 ms (00:10.876)
```

Now, enable the parallel query again by setting `max_parallel_workers_per_gather` to `1`. This will effectively make the query execute in two parallel processes. Run the query again:

```
car_portal=> SET max_parallel_workers_per_gather = 1;
SET

car_portal=> SELECT count(*) FROM dwh.access_log_not_partitioned
  WHERE url ~ 'car';
 count
---------
 7030000
(1 row)
Time: 6435.174 ms (00:06.435)
```

The query is now almost twice as fast!

The query that we just saw is CPU-intensive because it uses a regular expression match in its WHERE clause. Otherwise, the hard disk would be a bottleneck and the effect of multiple CPUs being used wouldn't be that explicit.

Parallel query works for sequential table scans, bitmap heap scans, index scans and index-only scans, different kind of joins, and aggregation. PostgreSQL can scan different partitions of a partitioned table in parallel. It can also perform grouping and aggregation on different partitions separately in parallel, and then append the results. This will work if there is grouping by a partition key in the query.

More information on parallel query can be found in the PostgreSQL documentation: https://www.postgresql.org/docs/current/static/parallel-query.html.

Index-only scans

Indexes have already been described in `Chapter 4`, *PostgreSQL Advanced Building Blocks*. Simply speaking, indexes work like a glossary at the end of a book. When searching for a keyword in a book, to make it faster, you can look it up in the glossary and then go to the page specified. The glossary is alphabetically organized; that's why searching in it is fast.

Moreover, when you need to find out whether a keyword is present in the book, you don't have to go to the page – just looking in the glossary is enough.

PostgreSQL can do the same. If all the information that is needed for a query is contained in an index, the database won't perform the scan on the table data and will only use the index. This is called an **index-only scan**.

To demonstrate how it works, let's create an index for the `dwh.access_log_not_partitioned` table, as follows:

```
CREATE INDEX on dwh.access_log_not_partitioned (ts, status_code);
```

Now, suppose we want to find out when the first HTTP request that resulted in a `201` status code happened on August 1, 2018. The query will be as follows:

```
car_portal=> SELECT min(ts) FROM dwh.access_log_not_partitioned
  WHERE ts BETWEEN '2018-08-01' AND '2018-08-02' AND status_code = '201';
 min
------------------------
 2018-08-01 01:30:57+00
(1 row)
Time: 0.751 ms
```

The query took less than one millisecond. From the execution plan, it's clear that PostgreSQL didn't scan the table and performed an index-only scan:

```
car_portal=> EXPLAIN SELECT min(ts) FROM dwh.access_log_not_partitioned
  WHERE ts BETWEEN '2018-08-01' AND '2018-08-02' AND status_code = '201';
                          QUERY PLAN
-------------------------------------------------------------------------
 Result  (cost=4.23..4.24 rows=1 width=8)
   InitPlan 1 (returns $0)
     -> Limit  (cost=0.56..4.23 rows=1 width=8)
       -> Index Only Scan using
          access_log_not_partitioned_ts_status_code_idx on
          access_log_not_partitioned  (cost=0.56..135923.57 rows=37083
          width=8)
            Index Cond:  ((ts IS NOT NULL) AND (ts >=
            '2018-08-01 00:00:00+00'::timestamp with time zone)
```

```
                AND (ts >= '2018-08-02 00:00:00+00'::timestamp with time zone)
                AND (status_code = 201))
    (5 rows)
```

To see the benefit of applying this feature, let's switch it off and check the timing again, as follows:

```
car_portal=> SET enable_indexonlyscan = off;
SET

car_portal=> SELECT min(ts) FROM dwh.access_log_not_partitioned
  WHERE ts BETWEEN '2018-08-01' AND '2018-08-02' AND status_code = '201';
 min
------------------------
 2017-08-01 01:30:57+00
(1 row)
Time: 1.225 ms
```

Now the query is almost twice as slow. The execution plan is slightly different (though the total cost is the same):

```
car_portal=> EXPLAIN SELECT min(ts) FROM dwh.access_log_not_partitioned
  WHERE ts BETWEEN '2018-08-01' AND '2018-08-02' AND status_code = '201';
                        QUERY PLAN
---------------------------------------------------------------------------
 Result (cost=4.23..4.24 rows=1 width=8)
   InitPlan 1 (returns $0)
     -> Limit (cost=0.56..4.23 rows=1 width=8)
       -> Index Scan using access_log_not_partitioned_ts_status_code_idx on .
          access_log_not_partitioned (cost=0.56..135923.57 rows=37083
          width=8)
            Index Cond: ((ts IS NOT NULL) AND (ts >=
            '2018-08-01 00:00:00+00'::timestamp with time zone) AND (ts >=
            '2018-08-02 00:00:00+00'::timestamp with time zone) AND
            (status_code = 201))
(5 rows)
```

This feature can only work if all the fields that are referenced in a query are part of an index. There are two notes about this rule:

- Partial indexes support index-only scans if there is a filter condition in the WHERE clause of a query that is the same as in the definition of the index, even if the columns used in that condition are not the part of the index itself. Continuing with the previous example with the access log table, suppose there are a lot of queries for the specific status code 201. There might be a partial index that contains only data for that status code. Index-only scans are still possible if a query has a filter for that status code, because it's known that the index has all the data necessary for a query. Here's an example:

```
car_portal=> SET enable_indexonlyscan = off;
SET

car_portal=> CREATE INDEX ON dwh.access_log_not_partitioned (ts)
  WHERE status_code = 201;
CREATE INDEX

car_portal=> EXPLAIN SELECT min(ts)
  FROM dwh.access_log_not_partitioned
  WHERE ts BETWEEN '2018-08-01' AND '2018-08-02'
    AND status_code = '201';
                           QUERY PLAN
----------------------------------------------------------------
 Result  (cost=3.75..3.76 rows=1 width=8)
   InitPlan 1 (returns $0)
     -> Limit  (cost=0.43..3.75 rows=1 width=8)
       -> Index Only Scan using access_log_not_partitioned_ts_idx on
       access_log_not_partitioned  (cost=0.43..197571.22 rows=59591
       width=8)
         Index Cond: ((ts IS NOT NULL) AND (ts >=
         '2018-08-01 00:00:00+00'::timestamp with time zone) AND (ts
         >= '2018-08-02 00:00:00+00'::timestamp with time zone))
 (5 rows)
```

Note that PostgreSQL now uses a different index for the same query; that is, the new one created with a condition, because it is smaller and therefore is faster to be processed.

- PostgreSQL supports **covering indexes**. A covering index is an index that contains extra columns that aren't part of the index key. Consider the following example: for the access log table, it might be known that there are a lot of queries for url that have a filter condition on ts. But there are no filters on the url field itself. To make queries faster, it would make sense to create an index on the ts field and include the url field in the index to enable index-only scans. To save some space and build the index faster, it's rational not to make the url field part of the index key since no queries are expected to filter data based on the values of that column. The INCLUDE keyword of the CREATE INDEX command is used for this, as follows:

```
car_portal=> CREATE INDEX ON dwh.access_log_partitioned (ts)
   INCLUDE (url);
CREATE INDEX

car_portal=> EXPLAIN SELECT DISTINCT url
   FROM dwh.access_log_partitioned
   WHERE ts BETWEEN '2018-07-15' AND '2018-08-15';
                        QUERY PLAN
--------------------------------------------------------------
 HashAggregate (cost=289577.87..289579.87 rows=200 width=28)
   Group Key: access_log_2018_07.url
      -> Append (cost=0.00..276030.32 rows=5419021 width=28)
        -> Seq Scan on access_log_2018_07 (cost=0.00..128995.00
        rows=2932232 width=28)
           Filter: ((ts >= '2018-07-15 00:00:00+00'::timestamp with
           time zone) AND (ts >= '2018-08-15 00:00:00+00'::timestamp
           with time zone))
        -> Index Only Scan using access_log_2018_08_ts_url_idx on
        access_log_2018_08 (cost=0.43..119940.21 rows=2486789
        width=28)
           Index Cond: ((ts >= '2018-07-15 00:00:00+00'::timestamp
           with time zone) AND (ts >= '2018-08-15 00:00:00+00'
           ::timestamp with time zone))
```

The index was created on the partitioned table, and the filter condition in the query covers two partitions. PostgreSQL decided that it makes sense to do a sequential scan on the partition for July, but to perform an index-only scan on the partition for August.

Adding a column, or several columns into the INCLUDE list when creating an index will make these columns part of the index, but the index entries will not be ordered by the fields from the INCLUDE list.

For UNIQUE indexes, it also makes a logical difference, since they only enforce uniqueness of combinations of values of the fields that compose the key of the index, not considering the INCLUDE list.

In some cases, the optimizer may conclude that a sequential scan on the table will be cheaper, even if the index has all the data. This is usually true when a relatively large number of records are expected to be returned, and it would not make sense to scan the index and then look into the table for each entry found in the index.

Index-only scans have certain limitations due to how PostgreSQL maintains transaction isolation. For more information, see Chapter 10, *Transactions and Concurrency Control*. In short, PostgreSQL checks the visibility maps for the table to decide whether certain data should be visible to the current transaction. If it can't find this information there, checking the table data is necessary.

Not all index types support index-only scans. B-tree indexes always support them, GiST and SP-GiST support them only for certain operators, and GIN indexes don't support this feature.

This topic doesn't belong specifically to OLAP solutions. However, in data warehouses, it's common to create multiple indexes on different combinations of fields, and sometimes the same field could be included in several indexes. Understanding how index-only scans work can help you to design a better database structure.

More on index-only scans can be found in the PostgreSQL documentation: https://www.postgresql.org/docs/current/static/indexes-index-only-scans.html.

Summary

OLAP and data warehousing are both used in the context of specific database-design patterns, where a database is used for analysis and reporting. In contrast to OLTP, OLAP deals with bigger amounts of data and a smaller number of concurrent sessions and transactions, but the amount of changes within a transaction usually is bigger. The database structure is often denormalized to improve query performance. A database that is a part of an OLAP solution is often called a data warehouse.

In this chapter, we discussed structuring data in a data warehouse, how to load data there, and how to optimize the database performance by applying partitioning, and using parallel query execution and index-only scans.

In the next chapter, we will discuss the extended data types supported by PostgreSQL, such as arrays and JSON. These data types make it possible to implement complicated business logic using native database support.

Questions

1. What is OLAP and what is the difference between OLAP and OLTP?
2. What is ETL?
3. What are fact tables and dimension tables?
4. Why would we denormalize data in data warehouses?
5. What is the difference between dimensions and measures?
6. What is the purpose of partitioning?
7. What is a partition key?
8. Which partitioning schemes are supported by PostgreSQL? What are the typical use cases for each of them?
9. How do we implement sub-partitioning?
10. How do we utilize multiple CPU cores of the database server when executing a query?
11. What are index-only scans?
12. Is there a way to enable index-only scans for a field without building an index on that field?

Beyond Conventional Data Types

9

PostgreSQL can handle rich data types due to its powerful extensions. Data that doesn't fit the relational model inherently, such as semi-structured data, can be stored and manipulated, either using out-of-the-box data types or extensions. Also, the PostgreSQL community focuses not only on enhancing relational database features, but also on supporting rich data types, such as arrays, XMLs, hash stores, and JSON documents. The focus shift is a result of embracing changes in the software development process's life cycle, such as agile development methods, and supporting unknown and rapid software requirements.

Non-conventional data types allow PostgreSQL to store different data types, such as geographical, binary, and schemaless data, such as JSON documents and hash stores. PostgreSQL supports some of these data types out of the box, including JSON, JSONB, XML, array, byte, and BLOB. More data types are available via extensions, such as `hstore` and PostGIS.

JSON, JSONB, and `hstore` allow PostgreSQL to handle schemaless models, which in turn allow developers to make real-time adjustments to data in an automatic and transparent way. Using JSON, JSONB, and `hstore` allows developers to change the data structure without changing the table structure, using the `ALTER` command. Also, it allows them to have a flexible data model without using the **entity-attribute-value** (**EAV**) model, which is difficult to handle in the relational model. However, developers should take care when handling data integrity in the business logic to ensure that the data is clean and error-free.

In this chapter, the following data types will be covered:

- Array datatype
- Hstore datatype, which is used as a key/value store
- JSON datatype
- Full text search data types, including `tsquery` and `tsvector`

It would be nice to have a look at the PostGIS extension, knowing that PostGIS supports raster and vector formats, and provides very rich functions to manipulate data. Another interesting datatype is the range datatype, which can be used to define range intervals, such as a `daterange`.

Arrays

An array is a data structure that consists of a collection of elements (values or variables); the order of the elements in the array significant and each element in the array is identified by an index. The index of the array is often starts at 1, but in some programming languages, such as C and C++, the index starts at 0. Array elements should have the same type, such as `INT` or `TEXT`.

Multidimensional arrays are supported; the array type can be a base, enum, or composite type. Array elements should have only one data type. PostgreSQL arrays allow duplicate values as well as null values. The following example shows how to initialize a one-dimensional array and get the first element:

```
car_portal=> SELECT ('{red, green, blue}'::text[])[1] as red ;
 red
-----
 red
(1 row)
```

The array length, by default, isn't bound to a certain value, but this can be specified when using arrays to define a relation. By default, an array index, as shown in the preceding example, starts from index one; however, this behavior can be changed by defining the dimension when initializing the array, as follows:

```
car_portal=> WITH test AS (SELECT '[0:1]={1,2}'::INT[] as int_array)
    SELECT int_array, int_array[0] as first_element FROM test;
    int_array      | first_element
-------------------+-----
 [0:1]={1,2}       | 1
(1 row)
```

Arrays can be initialized using the `{}` construct. Another way to initialize an array is as follows:

```
car_portal=> SELECT array['red','green','blue'] AS primary_colors;
  primary_colors
------------------
 {red,green,blue}
(1 row)
```

PostgreSQL provides many functions to manipulate arrays, such as `array_remove` to remove a certain element. The following are some of the array functions:

```
car_portal=> SELECT
 array_ndims(two_dim_array) AS "Number of dimensions",
 array_dims(two_dim_array) AS "Dimensions index range",
 array_length(two_dim_array, 1) AS "The array length of 1st dimension",
 cardinality(two_dim_array) AS "Number of elements",
 two_dim_array[1][1] AS "The first element"
FROM
(VALUES ('{{red,green,blue}, {red,green,blue}}'::text[][])) AS
foo(two_dim_array);
-[ RECORD 1 ]--------------------+-----------
Number of dimensions | 2
Dimensions index range | [1:2][1:3]
The array length of 1st dimension | 2
Number of elements | 6
The first element | red
```

A common use case of arrays is to model multivalued attributes. For example, a dress can have more than one color, and a newspaper article can have several tags. Another use case is to model a hash store. This is achieved by having two arrays—one with the keys and another with the values—and the array index is used to associate the key with the value. For example, `pg_stats` uses this approach to store information about the common values histogram. The `most_common_vals` and `most_common_freqs` columns are used to list the most common values in a certain column and the frequencies of these most common values, respectively, as shown in the following example:

```
car_portal=> SELECT tablename, attname, most_common_vals, most_common_freqs
FROM pg_stats WHERE array_length(most_common_vals,1) < 10 AND schemaname
NOT IN ('pg_catalog','information_schema') LIMIT 1;
-[ RECORD 1 ]-----+----------------------------------------------------
tablename         | seller_account
attname           | zip_code
most_common_vals  | {10011,37388,94577,95111,99501}
most_common_freqs | {0.0136986,0.0136986,0.0136986,0.0136986,0.0136986}
```

Also, arrays can be used to facilitate coding and in performing some SQL tricks, such as passing several arguments to the function using the VARIADIC array option or performing loops using the generate_series function. This allows developers to perform complex tasks without using the PL/pgSQL language. For example, let's assume that we want to have at least one column as not null out of several columns. This, in reality, can be used to check for disjoint attributes or model inheritance.

Let's look at another example; let's assume that we have a table called vehicle that contains a vehicle's common attributes. Also, let's assume that we have several types of vehicles, such as trucks, cars, and sports cars. You could model this by having several columns that reference the car, truck, and sports car tables. To understand how you can use the VARIADIC function, let's model the vehicle inheritance example, as follows:

```
CREATE OR REPLACE FUNCTION null_count (VARIADIC arr int[]) RETURNS INT AS
$$
  SELECT count(CASE WHEN m IS NOT NULL THEN 1 ELSE NULL END)::int FROM
unnest($1) m(n)
$$ LANGUAGE SQL;
```

To use the preceding function, you need to add a check to the table, as follows:

```
CREATE TABLE public.car (
  car_id SERIAL PRIMARY KEY,
  car_number_of_doors INT DEFAULT 5
);
CREATE TABLE public.bus (
  bus_id SERIAL PRIMARY KEY,
  bus_number_of_passengers INT DEFAULT 50
);
CREATE TABLE public.vehicle (
  vehicle_id SERIAL PRIMARY KEY,
  registration_number TEXT,
  car_id INT REFERENCES car(car_id),
  bus_id INT REFERENCES bus(bus_id),
  CHECK (null_count(car_id, bus_id) = 1)
);
INSERT INTO public.car VALUES (1, 5);
INSERT INTO public.bus VALUES (1, 25);
```

When inserting a new row into the vehicle table, you should specify either car_id or bus_id, as follows:

```
car_portal=> INSERT INTO public.vehicle VALUES (default, 'a234', null,
null);
ERROR: new row for relation "vehicle" violates check constraint
"vehicle_check"
```

```
DETAIL: Failing row contains (1, a234, null, null).
Time: 1,482 ms
car_portal=> INSERT INTO public.vehicle VALUES (default, 'a234', 1, 1);
ERROR: new row for relation "vehicle" violates check constraint
"vehicle_check"
DETAIL: Failing row contains (2, a234, 1, 1).
Time: 0,654 ms
car_portal=> INSERT INTO public.vehicle VALUES (default, 'a234', null, 1);
INSERT 0 1
Time: 1,128 ms
car_portal=> INSERT INTO public.vehicle VALUES (default, 'a234', 1, null);
INSERT 0 1
Time: 1,217 ms
```

Note that to call the null_count function, we need to add VARIADIC to the function's argument, as follows:

```
car_portal=> SELECT * FROM null_count(VARIADIC ARRAY [null, 1]);
 null_count
------------
          1
(1 row)
```

Another trick is to generate the substring of a text; this comes in handy when you want to get the longest-prefix match. The longest-prefix match is very important in areas such as telecommunication, such as mobile operators or telephone companies. Longest-prefix matching is used to determine networks. The following example shows how we can achieve this:

```
CREATE TABLE prefix (
  network TEXT,
  prefix_code TEXT NOT NULL
);

INSERT INTO prefix VALUES ('Palestine Jawwal', 97059), ('Palestine
Jawwal',970599), ('Palestine watania',970597);

CREATE OR REPLACE FUNCTION prefixes(TEXT) RETURNS TEXT[] AS $$
  SELECT ARRAY(SELECT substring($1,1,i) FROM generate_series(1,length($1))
g(i))::TEXT[];
$$ LANGUAGE SQL IMMUTABLE;
```

The function prefixes will return an array with the prefix substring. To test whether the longest-prefix matching worked, let's get the longest prefix for the number 97059973456789 through the following code:

```
car_portal=> SELECT * FROM prefix WHERE prefix_code = any
(prefixes('97059973456789')) ORDER BY length(prefix_code) DESC limit 1;
     network         | prefix_code
--------------------+-------------
 Palestine Jawwal  | 970599
(1 row)
```

Common functions of arrays and their operators

Array operators are similar to other data type operators. For example, the = sign is used for equality comparison, and the || operator is used for concatenation. In the previous chapters, we saw some operators similar to &&, which returns true if the arrays are overlapping. Finally, the @> and <@ operators are used if an array contains or is contained by another array, respectively. The unnest function is used to return a set of elements from an array. This is quite useful when you want to use set operations on arrays, such as distinct, order by, intersect, or union. The following example is used to remove the duplicates and sort the array in ascending order:

```
SELECT array(SELECT DISTINCT unnest (array [1,1,1,2,3,3]) ORDER BY 1);
```

In the preceding example, the result of the unnest function is sorted and duplicates are removed using ORDER BY and DISTINCT, respectively. The array() function is used to construct the array from a set. Also, arrays can be used to aggregate the date. For example, if I want to get all the models of a certain make, array_agg can be used, as follows:

```
car_portal=> SELECT make, array_agg(model) FROM car_model group by make;
    make        | array_agg
---------------+----------------------------------------------------
 Volvo         | {S80,S60,S50,XC70,XC90}
 Audi          | {A1,A2,A3,A4,A5,A6,A8}
 UAZ           | {Patriot}
 Citroen       | {C1,C2,C3,C4,"C4 Picasso",C5,C6}
```

The array `ANY()` function is similar to the `IN` SQL construct and is used to compare containment, as shown in the following example:

```
car_portal=> SELECT 1 in (1,2,3), 1 = ANY ('{1,2,3}'::INT[]);
 ?column? | ?column?
----------+----------
 t        | t
(1 row)
```

The full list of arrays functions and operators is quite long; this can be found in the official documentation at `https://www.postgresql.org/docs/current/static/functions-array.html`. So far, we've looked at several functions, including `unnest`, `array_agg`, `any`, and `array_length`. The following list of functions is often used in daily development:

Function	Return type	Description	Example	Result
`array_to_string(anyarray, text [, text])`	text	Convert an array into a text-based array. You can specify the delimiter as well as the NULL value substitution.	`array_to_string(ARRAY[1, NULL, 5], ',', 'x')`	`'1,,x,5'`
`array_remove(anyarray, anyelement)`	anyarray	Remove all elements based on the element value.	`array_remove(ARRAY[1,2,3], 2)`	`{1,3}`
`array_replace(anyarray, anyelement, anyelement)`	anyarray	Replace all array elements equal to the given value with a new value.	`array_replace(ARRAY[1,2,5,4], 5, 3)`	`{1,2,3,4}`

Modifying and accessing arrays

An array element can be accessed via an index; if the array doesn't contain an element for this index, the NULL value is returned, as shown in the following example:

```
CREATE TABLE color(
  color text []
);
INSERT INTO color(color) VALUES ('{red, green}'::text[]);
INSERT INTO color(color) VALUES ('{red}'::text[]);
```

To confirm that NULL is returned, let's run the following code:

```
car_portal=> SELECT color [3] IS NOT DISTINCT FROM null FROM color;
 ?column?
----------
 t
 t
(2 rows)
```

Also, an array can be sliced by providing a lower and upper bound, as follows:

```
car_portal=> SELECT color [1:2] FROM color;
    color
-------------
 {red,green}
 {red}
(2 rows)
```

When updating an array, you could completely replace the array, get a slice, replace an element, or append the array using the concatenation operator (| |), as shown in the following example. The full set of array functions can be found at https://www.postgresql.org/docs/current/static/functions-array.html.

The following snippets show how to append and update array elements:

```
car_portal=> SELECT ARRAY ['red', 'green'] || '{blue}'::text[] AS append;
      append
------------------
 {red,green,blue}
(1 row)

Time: 0,848 ms
car_portal=> UPDATE color SET color[1:2] = '{black, white}';
UPDATE 2
car_portal=> table color ;
     color
```

```
--------------
 {black,white}
 {black,white}
(2 rows)
```

The `array_remove` function can be used to remove all the elements that are equal to a certain value, as follows:

```
car_portal=> SELECT array_remove ('{Hello, Hello, World}'::TEXT[],
'Hello');
 array_remove
--------------
 {World}
(1 row)
```

To remove a certain value based on an index, you can use the WITH ORDINALITY clause. So, let's assume that we want to remove the first element of an array; this can be achieved as follows:

```
car_portal=> SELECT ARRAY(SELECT unnest FROM unnest ('{Hello1, Hello2,
World}'::TEXT[]) WITH ordinality WHERE ordinality <> 1);
     array
----------------
 {Hello2,World}
(1 row)
```

Indexing arrays

The GIN index can be used to index arrays; standard PostgreSQL distributions have the GIN operator class for one-dimensional arrays. The GIN index is supported for the following operators:

- The **contains** operator, @>
- The **is contained by** operator, <@
- The **overlapping** operator, &&
- The **equality** operators, =

The following code shows how to create an index on the color column using the GIN function:

```
CREATE INDEX ON color USING GIN (color);
```

The `index` function can be tested by using the following code:

```
car_portal=> SET enable_seqscan TO off; -- To force index scan
SET
car_portal=> EXPLAIN SELECT * FROM color WHERE '{red}'::text[] && color;
                          QUERY PLAN
-------------------------------------------------------------------
---
 Bitmap Heap Scan on color (cost=8.00..12.01 rows=1 width=32)
   Recheck Cond: ('{red}'::text[] && color)
   -> Bitmap Index Scan on color_color_idx (cost=0.00..8.00 rows=1 width=0)
         Index Cond: ('{red}'::text[] && color)
(4 rows)
```

Mixing array data structures with `SET` data structures provides developers with great flexibility. Arrays are used in the PostgreSQL catalog systems in many scenarios, such as to store data statistics and data histograms. In the next section, we'll demonstrate the key-value store, also known as the hash store.

The hash store data structure

A hash store, also known as a key-value store, or associative array, is a famous data structure in modern programming languages, such as **Java**, **Python**, and **Node.js**. Also, there are dedicated database frameworks to handle this kind of data, such as the `Redis` database.

PostgreSQL has had a supported hash store, `hstore`, since PostgreSQL version 9.0. The `hstore` extension allows developers to leverage the best of both worlds. It increases the developer's agility without sacrificing the powerful features of PostgreSQL. Also, `hstore` allows the developer to model semi-structured data and sparse arrays in a relational model.

To create the `hstore`, you simply need to execute the following command as a superuser:

```
CREATE EXTENSION hstore;
```

The textual representation of `hstore` includes a zero or higher `key=> value` pair, followed by a comma. An example of the `hstore` data type is as follows:

```
SELECT 'tires=>"winter tires", seat=>leather'::hstore;
                  hstore
---------------------------------------------
 "seat"=>"leather", "tires"=>"winter tires"
(1 row)
```

You could also generate a single-value hstore using the hstore(key, value) function, as shown here:

```
SELECT hstore('Hello', 'World');
        hstore
------------------
 "Hello"=>"World"
(1 row)
```

Note that, in hstore, keys are unique, as shown in the following example:

```
SELECT 'a=>1, a=>2'::hstore;
   hstore
----------
 "a"=>"1"
(1 row)
```

In the car web portal, let's assume that the developer wants to support several other attributes, such as airbags, air conditioning, and power steering. The developer, in the traditional relational model, should alter the table structure and add new columns. Thanks to hstore, the developer can store this information using the key-value store without having to keep altering the table structure, as follows:

```
car_portal=# ALTER TABLE car_portal_app.car ADD COLUMN features hstore;
ALTER TABLE
```

One limitation of hstore is that it isn't a full document store, so it's difficult to represent nested objects in an hstore. The other problem is maintaining the set of keys, since an hstore key is case-sensitive:

```
car_portal=# SELECT 'color=>red, Color=>blue'::hstore;
                hstore
--------------------------------
 "Color"=>"blue", "color"=>"red"
(1 row)
```

The -> operator is used to get a value for a certain key. To append an hstore, the concatenation operator (||) can be used. Furthermore, the minus sign, -, is used to delete a key-value pair. To update an hstore, hstore can be concatenated with another hstore that contains the updated value. The following example shows how hstore keys can be inserted, updated, and deleted:

```
CREATE TABLE features (
        features hstore
);
```

The following example demonstrates the INSERT, UPDATE, and DELETE operations:

```
car_portal=# INSERT INTO features (features) VALUES
('Engine=>Diesel'::hstore) RETURNING *;
        features
--------------------
 "Engine"=>"Diesel"
(1 row)

INSERT 0 1
car_portal=# -- To add a new key
car_portal=# UPDATE features SET features = features || hstore ('Seat',
'Lethear') RETURNING *;
                  features
---------------------------------------
 "Seat"=>"Lethear", "Engine"=>"Diesel"
(1 row)

UPDATE 1
car_portal=# -- To update a key, this is similar to add a key
car_portal=# UPDATE features SET features = features || hstore ('Engine',
'Petrol') RETURNING *;
                  features
---------------------------------------
 "Seat"=>"Lethear", "Engine"=>"Petrol"
(1 row)

UPDATE 1
car_portal=# -- To delete a key
car_portal=# UPDATE features SET features = features - 'Seat'::TEXT
RETURNING *;
        features
--------------------
 "Engine"=>"Petrol"
(1 row)
```

The hstore datatype is very rich in functions and operators; there are several operators to compare hstore content. For example, the ?, ?&, and ?| operators can be used to check whether hstore contains a key, set of keys, or any of the specified keys, respectively. Also, an hstore can be cast to arrays, sets, and JSON documents.

An hstore data type can be converted into a set using the each (hstore) function, which allows the developer to use all the relational algebra set operators on hstore, such as DISTINCT, GROUP BY, and ORDER BY.

The following example shows how to get distinct `hstore` keys; these can be used to validate `hstore` keys:

```
car_portal=# SELECT DISTINCT (each(features)).key FROM features;
  key
--------
 Engine
(1 row)
```

To get `hstore` as a set, you can simply use each function again:

```
car_portal=# SELECT (each(features)).* FROM features;
  key    | value
--------+--------
 Engine | Petrol
(1 row)
```

Indexing an hstore

An `hstore` data type can be indexed using the `GIN` and `GIST` indexes, and picking the right index type depends on several factors, such as the number of rows in the table, available space, index search and update performance, and the queries pattern. To properly pick up the right index, it's good to perform benchmarking.

The following example shows the effect of using the `GIN` index to retrieve a record that has a certain key. The `?` operator returns `true` if `hstore` contains a key:

```
CREATE INDEX ON features USING GIN (features);
```

The `index` function can be tested by using the following code:

```
SET enable_seqscan to off;
car_portal=# EXPLAIN SELECT features->'Engine' FROM features WHERE features
? 'Engine';
                                    QUERY PLAN
-----------------------------------------------------------------------
---------
 Bitmap Heap Scan on features (cost=8.00..12.02 rows=1 width=32)
   Recheck Cond: (features ? 'Engine'::text)
   -> Bitmap Index Scan on features_features_idx (cost=0.00..8.00 rows=1
width=0)
         Index Cond: (features ? 'Engine'::text)
(4 rows)
```

If an operator isn't supported by the `GIN` index, such as the `->` operator, you can still use the B-tree index, as follows:

```
CREATE INDEX ON features ((features->'Engine'));
car_portal=# EXPLAIN SELECT features->'Engine' FROM features WHERE
features->'Engine'= 'Diesel';
                                QUERY PLAN
--------------------------------------------------------------------------
--------
 Index Scan using features_expr_idx on features (cost=0.12..8.14 rows=1
width=32)
   Index Cond: ((features -> 'Engine'::text) = 'Diesel'::text)
(2 rows)
```

The JSON data structure

JSON is a universal data structure that's human- and machine-readable. JSON is supported by almost all modern programming languages, embraced as a data interchange format, and heavily used in `RESTful` web services.

In this section, we'll compare JSON and XML, compare JSON and JSONB PostgreSQL data types, and explore JSON data format functions.

JSON and XML

XML and JSON are both used to define the data structure of exchanged documents. JSON grammar is simpler than that of XML, and JSON documents are more compact. JSON is easier to read and write. On the other hand, XML can have a defined data structure enforced by the **XML Schema Definition (XSD)** schema, and it also has namespace support, comments, **Extensible Stylesheet Language Transformations (XLST)**, and object-reference support. All in all, XML has more capabilities than JSON, but JSON is more compact, elegant, and easier to read.

Both JSON and XML have different usages as exchange formats. Based on personal experience, JSON is often used within the same organization or with web services and mobile applications due to its simplicity and compactness, while XML is used to define highly structured documents and formats to guarantee interoperability with data exchange between different organizations. For example, several **Open Geospatial Consortium (OGC)** standards, such as web map services, use XML as an exchange format with a defined XSD schema.

JSON data types for PostgreSQL

PostgreSQL supports two JSON data types, JSON and JSONB, both of which are implementations of RFC 7159. Both types can be used to enforce JSON rules. Both types are almost identical. However, JSONB is more efficient, as it stores JSON documents in a binary format and also supports indexes. JSONB is the successor of JSON. It was introduced in PostgreSQL 9.4.

When using JSON, it's preferable to have UTF-8 as the database encoding to ensure that the JSON type conforms to RFC 7159 standards. On the one hand, when storing data as a JSON document, the JSON object is stored in a textual format. On the other hand, when storing a JSON object as JSONB, the JSON primitive data types, mainly string, Boolean, and number, will be mapped to text, Boolean, and numeric, respectively.

The benefits of supporting the JSON data type

There are many use cases for storing and manipulating JSON data structures in relational databases, such as lack of requirements and performance requirements. In the case of a lack of requirements, you can easily extend JSON without changing the schema; this allows developers to make last-minute changes without creating new deployments. This approach is similar to the EAV model, with some advantages. Also, JSON could be used to solve some performance issues, such as complex joins, and it can help is solving some common issues when integrating PostgreSQL with ORM frameworks.

In addition, it makes sense to store the document exactly as it was generated by the source. This is helpful when storing the result of the rest API in the database from external sources. On the one hand, you don't need to convert the document back and forth using serializers and deserializers; on the other hand, the document state is reserved since no conversion is done.

Finally, JSON can be used as a data-transfer format. This allows the PostgreSQL data to be exposed to other systems easily.

Modifying and accessing JSON types

When casting text as a JSON type, the text is stored and rendered without any processing; it will preserve the whitespace, numeric formatting, and element's order details. JSONB doesn't preserve these details; the following example duplicates elimination in JSONB:

```
WITH test_data(pi) AS (SELECT '{"pi":"3.14", "pi":"3.14" }') SELECT
pi::JSON, pi::JSONB FROM test_data;
```

```
            pi               | pi
------------------------------+-----------------
 {"pi":"3.14", "pi":"3.14" } | {"pi": "3.14"}
(1 row)
```

JSON objects can contain other nested JSON objects, arrays, nested arrays, arrays of JSON objects, and so on. JSON arrays and objects can be nested arbitrarily, allowing the developer to construct complex JSON documents. The array elements in JSON documents can be of different types. The following example shows how to construct an account with the name as a text value, the address as a JSON object, and the rank as an array:

```
SELECT '{"name":"John", "Address":{"Street":"Some street", "city":"Some
city"}, "rank":[5,3,4,5,2,3,4,5]}'::JSONB;
                                                              jsonb
--------------------------------------------------------------------------------
------------------------------------
 {"name": "John", "rank": [5, 3, 4, 5, 2, 3, 4, 5], "Address": {"city":
"Some city", "Street": "Some street"}}
(1 row)
```

You could get the JSON object field as a JSON object or as text. Also, JSON fields can be retrieved using the index or the field name. The following table summarizes the JSON retrieval operators:

Return field as JSON	Return field as text	Description
->	->>	This returns a JSON field either using the field index or field name.
#>	#>>	This returns a JSON field that's been defined by a specified path.

To get the address and city from the JSON object we created before, you could use two methods, as follows (note that the field names of JSON objects are case-sensitive):

```
CREATE TABLE json_doc ( doc jsonb );
INSERT INTO json_doc SELECT '{"name":"John", "Address":{"Street":"Some
street", "city":"Some city"}, "rank":[5,3,4,5,2,3,4,5]}'::JSONB ;
```

To return the city from the previous JSON doc in TEXT format, you can use either the ->> or #>> operators, as follows:

```
SELECT doc->'Address'->>'city', doc#>>'{Address, city}' FROM json_doc WHERE
doc->>'name' = 'John';
 ?column?  | ?column?
-----------+-----------
 Some city | Some city
(1 row)
```

In older versions of PostgreSQL, such as 9.4, it was quite difficult to manipulate JSON documents. However, in the newer version, a lot of operators were introduced, such as || to concatenate two JSON objects, and – to delete a key-value pair. A simple approach to manipulating a JSON object in older versions of PostgreSQL is to convert it to text, use the regular expressions to replace or delete an element, and finally, cast the text to JSON again. To delete the rank from the account object, you can do the following:

```
SELECT (regexp_replace(doc::text, '"rank":(.*)]',','''))::jsonb FROM json_doc
WHERE doc->>'name' = 'John';
```

The `jsonb_set` and `json_insert` functions were introduced in PostgreSQL 9.5 and PostgreSQL 9.6, respectively. These functions allow us to amend a JSON object that we can insert into a JSON key-value pair:

```
car_portal=# update json_doc SET doc = jsonb_insert(doc,
'{hobby}','["swim", "read"]', true) RETURNING * ;
                                                                    doc
-----------------------------------------------------------------------
------------------------------------------------------------------

 {"name": "John", "rank": [5, 3, 4, 5, 2, 3, 4, 5], "hobby": ["swim",
"read"], "Address": {"city": "Some city", "Street": "Some street"}}
```

To amend an existing key-value pair, you can do the following:

```
car_portal=# update json_doc SET doc = jsonb_set(doc, '{hobby}','["read"]',
true) RETURNING * ;
 doc
-----------------------------------------------------------------------
----------------------------------------------------------

 {"name": "John", "rank": [5, 3, 4, 5, 2, 3, 4, 5], "hobby": ["read"],
"Address": {"city": "Some city", "Street": "Some street"}}
```

The following code shows how to delete a key-value pair:

```
car_portal=# update json_doc SET doc = doc -'hobby' RETURNING * ;
                                                        doc
-----------------------------------------------------------------------
------------------------------------------

 {"name": "John", "rank": [5, 3, 4, 5, 2, 3, 4, 5], "Address": {"city":
"Some city", "Street": "Some street"}}
```

The full list of JSON functions and operators can be found at https://www.postgresql.org/docs/current/static/functions-json.html.

Indexing a JSON data type

JSONB documents can be indexed using the GIN index, and the index can be used for the following operators:

- @>: Does the left JSON value contain the right value?
- ?: Does the key string exist in the JSON doc?
- ?&: Do any of the elements in the text array exist in the JSON doc?
- ?|: Do all the keys/elements in the text array exist in the JSON doc?

To see the effect of indexing on the json_doc table, let's create an index and disable the sequential scan, as follows:

```
CREATE INDEX ON json_doc(doc);
SET enable_seqscan = off;
```

We can use the following code to test the index function:

```
car_portal=# EXPLAIN SELECT * FROM json_doc WHERE doc @> '{"name":"John"}';
                              QUERY PLAN
-----------------------------------------------------------------------
--------------
 Index Only Scan using json_doc_doc_idx on json_doc (cost=0.13..12.16
rows=1 width=32)
    Filter: (doc @> '{"name": "John"}'::jsonb)
(2 rows)
```

> A JSON document can be converted into a set using the json_to_record() function. This is quite useful since we can sort and filter data like we do in normal tables. In addition, you can aggregate data from several rows and construct an array of JSON objects via the jsosn_agg() function.

RESTful APIs using PostgreSQL

It's convenient to provide an interface to share data that's commonly used by several applications via a RESTful API. Let's assume we have a table that's used by several applications; one way to make these applications aware of that table is to create a **Data Access Object (DAO)** for that table, wrap it in a library, and then reuse that library in those applications. This approach has some disadvantages, such as resolving library dependency and mismatching library versions. Also, deploying new versions of a library requires a lot of effort because applications using that library need to be compiled, tested, and deployed.

The advantage of providing a `RESTful` API interface for the PostgreSQL database is to allow easy access to data. Also, it allows the developer to utilize the microservice architecture, which leads to better agility.

There are several open source frameworks to set up a `RESTful` API interface for PostgreSQL, such as pREST (`https://github.com/prest/prest`), psql-api (`https://www.npmjs.com/package/psql-api`), and PostgREST (`http://postgrest.org/en/v5.2/`). For example, pREST could return a table using the following URI structure:

```
http://127.0.0.1:8000/DATABASE/SCHEMA/TABLE?_page=2&_page_size=10
(pagination, page_size 10 by default)
```

The `row_to_json ()`, `to_json()`, and `to_jsonb()` functions can be used to construct a JSON document from a relational row, as follows:

```
car_portal=# SELECT to_json (row(account_id, first_name, last_name, email))
FROM car_portal_app.account LIMIT 1;
                          to_json
----------------------------------------------------------------
 {"f1":1,"f2":"James","f3":"Butt","f4":"jbutt@example.com"}
(1 row)

car_portal=# SELECT to_json (account) FROM car_portal_app.account LIMIT 1;
                                                      to_json
-----------------------------------------------------------------------
-------------------------------------------------------------
{"account_id":1,"first_name":"James","last_name":"Butt","email":"jbutt@exam
ple.com","password":"1b9ef408e82e38346e6ebebf2dcc5ece"}
(1 row)
```

In the preceding example, the usage of the row (`account_id`, `first_name`, `last_name`, `email`) construct caused the `to_jsonb` function to be unable to determine the attribute names, and the names were replaced with `f1`, `f2`, and so on.

To work around this, you need to give a name to the row. This can be done in several ways, such as using subqueries or giving an alias to the result. The following example shows one way to resolve this issue, which is by specifying aliases using CTE:

```
WITH account_info(account_id, first_name, last_name, email) AS ( SELECT
account_id,first_name, last_name, email FROM car_portal_app. account LIMIT
1 ) SELECT to_json(account_info) FROM account_info;
 to_json
-----------------------------------------------------------------------
---------
{"account_id":1,"first_name":"James","last_name":"Butt","email":"jbutt@exam
ple.com"}
(1 row)
```

A PostgreSQL full-text search

PostgreSQL provides a full-text search capability, which is used to overcome SQL pattern-matching operators, including LIKE and ILIKE, boosting the performance of the text search. For example, even though an index on text using the text_pattern_op class is supported, this index can't be used to match a non-anchored text search.

Another issue with the traditional LIKE and ILIKE operators is the ranking based on similarity and natural language linguistic support. The LIKE and ILIKE operators always evaluate a Boolean value: either as TRUE or as FALSE.

In addition to ranking and non-anchored text-search support, PostgreSQL's full-text search provides many other features. The full-text search supports dictionaries, so it can support language, such as synonyms.

The tsquery and tsvector data types

The full-text search is based on the tsvector and tsquery data types. Here, tsvector represents a document in a normalized state and tsquery represents the query.

The tsvector data type

The `tsvector` datatype is a sorted list of distinct lexeme. A lexeme is the fundamental unit of a word. Simply speaking, you can think of a lexeme as the word's root without a suffix, inflectional forms, or grammatical variants. The following example shows casting text to a `tsvector`:

```
postgres=# SELECT 'A wise man always has something to say, whereas a fool
always needs to say something'::tsvector;
                                            tsvector
--------------------------------------------------------------------------
-----------------
 'A' 'a' 'always' 'fool' 'has' 'man' 'needs' 'say' 'say,' 'something' 'to'
'whereas' 'wise'
(1 row)
```

Casting a text to `tsvector` doesn't normalize the document completely, due to the lack of linguistic rules. To normalize the preceding example, you can use the `to_tsvector()` function, as follows:

```
postgres=# SELECT to_tsvector('english', 'A wise man always has something
to say, whereas a fool always needs to say something');
                                         to_tsvector
--------------------------------------------------------------------------
------------
 'alway':4,12 'fool':11 'man':3 'need':13 'say':8,15 'someth':6,16
'wherea':9 'wise':2
(1 row)
```

As shown in the preceding example, the `to_tsvector` function stripped some letters, such as s from `always`, and also generated the integer position of lexemes, which can be used for proximity ranking. The default text search config setting can be displayed as follows:

```
postgres=# SHOW default_text_search_config;
 default_text_search_config
----------------------------
 pg_catalog.english
(1 row)
```

The tsquery data type

The tsquery data type is used to search for a certain lexeme. A lexeme can be combined with the & (AND), | (OR), and ! (NOT) operators. Note that the NOT operator has the highest precedence, followed by AND and then OR. Also, parentheses can be used to group lexemes and operators to force a certain order. The following example shows how we can search for certain lexemes using tsquery, tsvector, and the match operator, @@:

```
car_portal=# SELECT 'A wise man always has something to say, whereas a fool
always needs to say something'::tsvector @@ 'wise'::tsquery;
 ?column?
----------
 t
(1 row)
```

tsquery also has the to_tsquery and plainto_tsquery functions to convert text into lexemes. plainto_tsquery provides a simple interface, while to_tsquery provides access to more features, such as Boolean operators and weight. Finally, to_tsquery requires a certain input format, otherwise it will throw a syntax exception:

```
postgres=# SELECT to_tsquery('english', 'wise & man'),
plainto_tsquery('english', 'wise man');
   to_tsquery    | plainto_tsquery
-----------------+-----------------
 'wise' & 'man'  | 'wise' & 'man'
(1 row)
```

Searching for phrases in tsquery is possible by using the followed by the tsquery operator, <->. This means that the result is matched if the two words are adjacent and in the given order:

```
car_portal=# SELECT to_tsvector('A wise man always has something to say,
whereas a fool always needs to say something') @@ to_tsquery('wise <->
man');
 ?column?
----------
 t
(1 row)
```

Pattern matching

Pattern matching is the act of checking a given sequence of words for the presence of the constituents of some pattern. There are several factors that affect the result of pattern matching, including the following:

- Text normalization
- Dictionary
- Ranking and weight
- How often query terms occur in the document
- Distance between the term's occurrence
- Document size

If the text isn't normalized, a text search might not return the expected result. The following examples show how pattern matching can fail with unnormalized text:

```
postgres=# SELECT 'elephants'::tsvector @@ 'elephant';
 ?column?
----------
 f
(1 row)
```

In the preceding query, casting elephants to `tsvector` and the implicit casting of elephant to the query doesn't generate normalized lexemes due to missing information about the dictionary. To add dictionary information, `to_tsvector` and `to_tsquery` can be used:

```
postgres=# SELECT to_tsvector('english', 'elephants') @@
to_tsquery('english', 'elephant');
 ?column?
----------
 t
(1 row)

postgres=# SELECT to_tsvector('simple', 'elephants') @@
to_tsquery('simple', 'elephant');
 ?column?
----------
 f
(1 row)
```

A full-text search supports pattern matching based on ranks. The `tsvector` lexemes can be marked with the A, B, C, and D labels, where D is the default and A has the highest rank. The set weight function can be used to assign a weight to `tsvector` explicitly, as follows:

```
postgres=# SELECT setweight(to_tsvector('english', 'elephants'),'A') ||
setweight(to_tsvector('english', 'dolphin'),'B');
        ?column?
---------------------------
 'dolphin':2B 'eleph':1A
(1 row)
```

For ranking, there are two functions: `ts_rank` and `ts_rank_cd`. The `ts_rank` function is used for standard ranking, while `ts_rank_cd` is used for the cover density ranking technique. Note that these functions are provided as examples since the relevancy concept is subject to business requirements:

```
ts_rank([ weights float4[], ] vector tsvector, query tsquery [,
normalization integer ]) returns float4
```

The following example shows the result of `ts_rank_cd` when used to search `eleph` and `dolphin`, respectively:

```
postgres=# SELECT ts_rank_cd
(setweight(to_tsvector('english','elephants'),'A') ||
setweight(to_tsvector('english', 'dolphin'),'B'), to_tsquery('english',
'eleph') );
 ts_rank_cd
------------
          1
(1 row)

postgres=# SELECT ts_rank_cd
(setweight(to_tsvector('english','elephants'),'A') ||
setweight(to_tsvector('english', 'dolphin'),'B'), to_tsquery('english',
'dolphin') );
 ts_rank_cd
------------
        0.4
(1 row)
```

`ts_rank` and `ts_rank_cd` also have an optional normalization parameter. This is used to control how the functions behave with regards to the document's size. For example, the probability of a term's occurrence in a big document is higher than a small document. So if the term occurs in both documents, the small document might be more relevant than the big document. The full description of the ranking functions can be found in the official documentation at `https://www.postgresql.org/docs/current/textsearch-controls.html`.

Ranking is often used to enhance, filter out, and order the result of pattern matching. In real-life scenarios, different document sections can have different weights. For example, when searching for a movie, the highest weight could be given to the movie title and main character, and less weight could be given to the summary of the movie's plot.

Full-text search indexing

`GIN` indexes are the preferred indexes for full-text searches. You can simply create an index on the document using the `to_tsvector` function, as follows:

```
CREATE INDEX ON <table_name> USING GIN (to_tsvector('english', <attribute
name>));
-- OR
CREATE INDEX ON <table_name> USING GIN (to_tsvector(<attribute name>));
```

The query that's predicated is used to determine the index definition, for example, if the predicate looks like `to_tsvector('english',..)@@ to_tsquey (..`, the first index will be used to evaluate the query.

`GIST` can be used to index `tsvector` and `tsquery`, while `GIN` can be used to index `tsvector` only. The `GIST` index is lossy and can return false matches, so PostgreSQL automatically rechecks the returned result and filters out false matches. False matches can reduce performance due to the records' random-access cost. The `GIN` index stores only the lexemes of `tsvector` and not the weight labels. Due to this, the `GIN` index could also be considered lossy if weights are involved in the query.

The performance of the `GIN` and `GIST` indexes depends on the number of unique words, so it's recommended to use dictionaries to reduce the total number of unique words. The `GIN` index is faster to search and slower to build, and requires more space than `GIST`. Increasing the value of the `maintenance_work_mem` setting can improve the `GIN` index's build time, but this doesn't work for the `GIST` index.

Summary

PostgreSQL is very rich in built-in data types and external extensions. It can be easily extended using the C and C++ languages. In fact, PostgreSQL provides an extension-building infrastructure, called PGXS, so that extensions can be built against an installed server. Some PostgreSQL extensions, such as PostGIS, require complete chapters of their own so that they can be discussed.

PostgreSQL provides a very rich set of data types, such as XML, `hstore`, JSON, and array. These data types can be used to ease the developer's life by not reinventing the wheel and utilizing their very rich set of functions and operators. Also, several PostgreSQL data types, such as `hstore` and JSON, can increase the developer's agility because the database's physical design isn't often amended.

PostgreSQL arrays are very mature; they have a rich set of operators and functions. PostgreSQL can handle multidimensional arrays with different base types. Arrays are useful when modeling multivalued attributes, as well as when performing several tasks that are difficult to achieve using only the pure relational model.

Hash store has been supported in PostgreSQL since version 9.0; it allows the developer to store key values in the data structure. Hash store is very useful when modeling semi-structured data, as well as at increasing the developer's agility.

Both JSON and XML documents are supported, allowing PostgreSQL to support different document-exchange formats. PostgreSQL provides several JSON functions to convert rows to JSON and vice versa. This allows PostgreSQL to server also `RESTful` web services easily.

PostgreSQL also supports full-text searches. A full-text search solves several problems related to linguistics, as well as non-anchored text-search performance, and enhances the end user's experience and satisfaction.

In the next chapter, we'll discuss the ACID properties and the relation between these properties in greater detail and concurrency controls. We'll also look at isolation levels and their side effects using SQL examples. Finally, we'll explore different locking methods, including pessimistic locking strategies, such as row locking and advisory locks.

Questions

1. What are the advantages and disadvantages of using rich data types? Consider the following comparison criteria: data consistency and sanity checks, performance, flexibility, and lack of requirements.

2. What's the difference between the JSON and JSONB data types?

3. What functions can be used to convert a row into JSON?

4. Hstore, JSON, and JSONB are candidates for storing a document in PostgreSQL. Which data type should be considered the default choice and why?

5. How can you sort and apply an aggregate function to an array?

6. In PostgreSQL, what's the equivalent of the `IN` set operator? Rewrite the `WHERE model IN ('Ford', 'VW')` expression using arrays.

7. Give a business use case for text search.

8. Explain the difference between `plainto_tsquery` and `to_tsquery` using examples.

9. Why is `GIN` preferable for indexing `ts_vector`?

Transactions and Concurrency Control

10

The relational model describes the logical unit of processing data as the *transaction*; transactions can be defined as a set of operations performed in sequence. Relational databases provide a locking mechanism to ensure the integrity of transactions.

In this chapter, we will focus on the basic concepts that guarantee the correct execution of transactions. Also, we will discuss concurrency control problems, locking systems, dead locks, and advisory locks.

In this chapter, we will be covering the following topics:

- Transactions
- Explicit locking
- Transaction in functions and procedure

The chapter will enable the developer to debug locking issues, thereby raising performance and increasing user satisfaction. Also, it will help developers to understand the difference between explicit locking and implicit locking, and it will allow them to create high-performance applications.

Transactions

A transaction is a set of operations that might include updating, deleting, inserting, and retrieving data. These operations are often embedded in a higher-level language, or can be explicitly wrapped in a transaction block using BEGIN and END statements. A transaction is successfully executed if all the operations with in the transaction are executed successfully. If an operation in a transaction fails, the effect of the partially executed operation on the transaction can be undone.

To control the beginning and end of a transaction explicitly, the BEGIN statement can be used to denote the start of the transaction, and the statements END or COMMIT to denote the end of the transaction. The following example shows how to explicitly execute an SQL statement in a transaction:

```
BEGIN;
CREATE TABLE employee (id serial primary key, name text, salary numeric);
COMMIT;
```

One use of transactions, other than ensuring data integrity, is to provide an easy way to undo changes to the database in development and testing modes. A transaction block can be combined with a SAVEPOINT statement to work with data interactively; a SAVEPOINT is a mark inside a transaction block where the state is saved. Savepoints undo parts of a transaction instead of the whole transaction. The following example shows how a SAVEPOINT can be used:

```
BEGIN;
UPDATE employee set salary = salary*1.1;
SAVEPOINT increase_salary;
UPDATE employee set salary = salary + 500 WHERE name ='john';
ROLLBACK to increase_salary;
COMMIT;
```

In the preceding example, the UPDATE employee set salary = salary*1.1; statement is committed to the database, while the UPDATE employee set salary = salary + 500 WHERE name ='john'; statement is rolled back.

All statements executed by PostgreSQL are transactional, even if you do not open a transaction block explicitly. For example, if you execute several statements without wrapping them in a transaction block, then each statement is executed in a separate transaction.

The transaction behavior can be controlled by the database driver and application frameworks, such as Java EE or Spring. For example, in JDBC, you can specify whether you would like to set the autocommit property or not.

Check your client tools to check whether BEGIN and COMMIT are issued automatically.

Transaction and ACID properties

A fundamental precept of relational databases is the concept of guaranteeing the **Atomicity, Consistency, Isolation,** and **Durability (ACID)** of its operations. This is referred to as ACID compliance.

A transaction is a logical execution unit and is indivisible, which means all-or-none, also known as **atomicity**; this statement holds true regardless of the reason for the failure. For example, a transaction might fail due to an error such as a mathematical error, the misspelling of a relation name, or even an operating system crash.

After the transaction is successfully committed, the transaction effect must persist even against hardware crashes; this property is referred to as **durability**. Furthermore, in a multi-user environment, several users can execute several transactions, and each transaction contains a set of actions or operations. Each transaction should be executed without interference from concurrently running transactions; this property is called **isolation**.

Finally, the **consistency** property is not a property of a transaction itself, but rather a desirable effect of transaction isolation and atomicity. Database consistency is concerned with business requirements, which are defined via rules, including triggers, constraints, and any combination thereof. If the database state is consistent immediately before executing a transaction, then the database state must also be consistent after executing the transaction. Database consistency is the responsibility of the developer who codes the transaction.

ACID properties are not easily met. For example, **durability** has heavy requirements because there are a lot of factors that might cause data loss, such as an operating system crash, power outage, or hard disk failure. Also, computer architecture is quite complex. For example, the data can flow through several layers of storage, such as memory, IO buffers, and the disk cache, until it is persisted on the hard disk.

By default, PostgreSQL uses `fsync`, which transfers all modified buffer cache pages to a file on the disk so that changes can be retrieved in the event of a system crash or reboot.

Transaction and concurrency

Concurrency can be defined as the interleaving of actions in time to give the appearance of simultaneous execution. Concurrency tries to solve several issues, including sharing global resources safely, and handling errors in multiple execution contexts.

Concurrency is pervasive in computing, occurring everywhere from low-level hardware design to worldwide access of shared data. Examples of concurrency handling can be found in instruction pipe lining in CPU micro-architecture and threading in operating system design. Even in our daily lives, we can encounter concurrency when using tools such as Git. A common scenario is when several developers are sharing the same code base, introducing conflicts, and finally resolving these conflicts by executing merges.

Concurrency and parallelism can be confused. Parallelism is distinguished by using extra computational units to do more work per unit time, while concurrency manages access to shared resources; hence, parallelism is often easier to handle. Concurrency is a more generalized form of parallelism, which can include time slicing as a form of virtual parallelism.

 Many databases utilize parallelism in addition to concurrency. PostgreSQL, in fact, has also utilized parallelism since version 9.6 to increase query performance. **Greenplum**, which is a fork of PostgreSQL, also uses **massively parallel processing** (**MPP**) to increase performance and to handle data warehousing loads.

A fundamental problem associated with concurrency is actions meddling with each other while accessing a shared global resource. No conflict will occur if developers do not write code in a concurrent manner, but rather in a serial manner, one after the other. However, in reality, this is not practical and causes a lot of delay in completing tasks.

Concurrency control coordinates the execution of concurrent transactions in a multi-user environment and handles potential problems, such as lost updates, uncommitted data, and inconsistent data retrieval.

Concurrency is a good selling point for PostgreSQL, because PostgreSQL is able to handle concurrency even on significant read and write activity. In PostgreSQL, write activity does not block read activity, or the other way around. PostgreSQL uses a technique called **Multi-Version Concurrency Control** (**MVCC**); this technique is also used by several commercial and non-commercial databases, such as Oracle, MySQL with InnoDB engine, Informix, Firebird, and CouchDB.

Note that MVCC is not the only way to handle concurrency in RDBMS; SQL Server uses another technique called **strong strict two-phase locking** (**SS2PL**).

MVCC in PostgreSQL

Accessing the same data at the same time for read and write purposes might cause an inconsistent data state or wrong reads. For example, the reader might get partially written data. The simplest technique for solving this is to lock the reader from reading the data until the writer finishes writing the data. This solution causes a lot of contention, hence the performance penalty, and causes the reader to wait until the writer is done with the job.

In MVCC, when the data is updated, a newer version of the data is created, and the original data is not overwritten. That means there are several versions of data, hence the name multi-version. Each transaction can access a version of the data based on the transaction isolation level, current transaction status, and tuple versions.

Each transaction in PostgreSQL is assigned to a transaction ID called **XID**. The XID is incremented whenever a new transaction is started. The transaction IDs are 4-byte unsigned integers, that is, around 4.2 billion compilations. New transaction assignments are based on a modular arithmetic function, which means the normal XID space is circular with no endpoint, and all transactions—around two billion—before a certain transaction are considered old and are visible to that particular transaction.

The following example shows how transaction IDs are incremented; note that, without opening an explicit transaction, each statement caused the XID to be incremented:

```
test=# SELECT txid_current();
 txid_current
--------------
          682
(1 row)

test=# SELECT 1;
 ?column?
----------
        1
```

```
 (1 row)

test=# SELECT txid_current();
 txid_current
--------------
          683

 (1 row)
test=# BEGIN;
BEGIN
test=# SELECT txid_current();
 txid_current
--------------
          684
 (1 row)

test=# SELECT 1;
 ?column?
----------
        1
 (1 row)
test=# SELECT txid_current();
 txid_current
--------------
          684
 (1 row)
```

 Due to the nature of transaction ID assignments, you need to be careful when handling them. First of all, never disable the vacuum process, otherwise your database will shut down due to a transaction wraparound issue. Also, when you have bulk insert and update, wrap the statements in an explicit transaction block. Finally, heavily updated tables might get bloated due to dead rows.

Internally, PostgreSQL assigns the transaction ID, which creates a tuple to xmin, and the transaction ID of the transaction deletes the tuple to xmax. The update is handled internally in MVCC as DELETE and INSERT and, in this case, another version of the tuple is created. PostgreSQL uses the information about the tuple's creation and deletion, transaction status, committed, in progress, and rolled back, isolation levels, and transaction visibility, to handle concurrency issues. The following example shows how transaction IDs are assigned to the tuple xmin column in the case of an insert scenario:

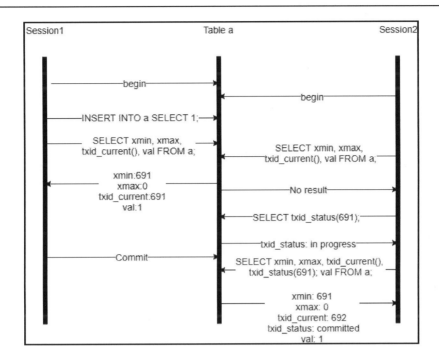

Transaction isolation levels

The transaction isolation levels define the type of locks acquired on the database objects, such as tables. Also, it defines the degree to which a transaction should be isolated from the data modifications made by any other transaction. A transaction isolation level can be set by the developer by invoking the following SQL statement:

```
SET TRANSACTION ISOLATION LEVEL { SERIALIZABLE | REPEATABLE READ | READ
COMMITTED | READ UNCOMMITTED}
```

The SET TRANSACTION ISOLATION LEVEL statement should be called inside a transaction block before any query, otherwise, it will have no effect. An alternative is to use the following syntax:

```
BEGIN TRANSACTION ISOLATION LEVEL { SERIALIZABLE | REPEATABLE READ | READ
COMMITTED | READ UNCOMMITTED}
```

Finally, you can change the whole default database isolation level to SERIALIZABLE as follows:

```
ALTER DATABASE <DATABASE NAME> SET DEFAULT_TRANSACTION_ISOLATION TO
SERIALIZABLE ;
```

As shown by the preceding SQL statement, the transaction isolation levels are as follows:

- SERIALIZABLE: The SERIALIZABLE isolation level is the strongest consistency level; it relieves the developer of the task of planning for concurrency effects. The cost of using the serialize isolation model is often performance. In the SQL standard, SERIALIZABLE is the default isolation model. In PostgreSQL, the default isolation model is READ COMMITTED.
- REPEATABLE READ: REPEATABLE READ is the second strongest transaction isolation level; it is similar to READ COMMITTED in that it allows only the reading of committed data. It also guarantees that any data read cannot be changed.
- READ COMMITTED: This is the default PostgreSQL model; it allows committed data to be read by the transaction. In this level, performance is favored over preciseness.
- READ UNCOMMITTED: This is the weakest transaction isolation level. It allows uncommitted data to be read.

> READ UNCOMMITTED is not supported in PostgreSQL and is treated as READ COMMITTED. PostgreSQL only supports three levels.

The transaction isolation level can be explained by having a look at the side effects of each level, which are as follows:

- **Dirty read**: A dirty read occurs when a transaction reads data from a tuple that has been modified by another running transaction and not yet committed. In PostgreSQL, this cannot happen since READ UNCOMMITTED is unsupported.
- **Nonrepeatable read**: A nonrepeatable read occurs when, during the course of a transaction, a row is retrieved twice and the values within the row differ between reads. A nonrepeatable read occurs in the READ COMMITTED isolation level and is often a result of updating a row several times with other transactions.
- **Phantom read**: A phantom read occurs when a new row (or rows) disappears from the time of the beginning of the transaction. This is often a result of committed inserts followed by committed deletes. A phantom read occurs when you select a set of rows several times and a different result is returned within the same transaction. A phantom read occurs in the READ COMMITTED and REPEATABLE READ levels based on the SQL standard definition. In PostgreSQL, a phantom read occurs only in READ COMMITTED.

- **Serialization anomaly**: The result of executing a group of transactions is inconsistent with all possible ordering of running these transactions. This can occur only in REPEATABLE READ.

 SQL standard allows phantom read in the REPEATABLE READ isolation level. In PostgreSQL, that is not allowed. That means that only a serialization anomaly can happen in REPEATABLE READ.

To understand different transaction isolation side effects, let's show the nonrepeatable read side effect; for that, we will use a test_tx_level table, which is defined as follows:

```
postgres=# CREATE TABLE test_tx_level AS SELECT 1 AS val;
SELECT 1
postgres=# TABLE test_tx_level ;
 val
-----
   1
(1 row)
```

To test repeatable read, the default transaction isolation model READ COMMITTED will be used; the **T** as in **T1** is used to indicate the execution time in ascending order, as follows:

	Session 1	Session 2

T1	`postgres=# BEGIN;`
	`BEGIN`
	`postgres=# SELECT * FROM test_tx_level ;`
	` val`
	`-----`
	`   1`
	`(1 row)`	

T2		`postgres=# BEGIN;`
		`BEGIN`
		`postgres=# UPDATE test_tx_level`
		`SET val = 2;`
		`UPDATE 1`
		`postgres=# COMMIT;`
		`COMMIT`

T3	`postgres=# SELECT * FROM test_tx_level ;`
	`val`
	`-----`
	`   2`
	`(1 row)`
	`postgres=# COMMIT;`
	`COMMIT`	

The `val` value has changed from 1 to 2 in **Session 1**. The changes that are committed by **Session 2** are reflected in **Session 1**. This is called a nonrepeatable read. Also notice that we have used `BEGIN` without specifying the transaction isolation level, and in this case, the default isolation level is used.

To check the phantom read, again, the default transaction isolation level will be used, as follows:

	Session 1	Session 2

T1	`postgres=# BEGIN;`
	`BEGIN`
	`postgres=# SELECT count(*) FROM`
	`test_tx_level;`
	`count`
	`-------`
	`  1`
	`(1 row)`	

T2		`postgres=# BEGIN;`
		`BEGIN`
		`postgres=# INSERT INTO`
		`test_tx_level SELECT 2;`
		`INSERT 0 1`
		`postgres=# COMMIT;`
		`COMMIT`

T3	`postgres=# SELECT count(*) FROM test_tx_level`
	`;`
	`  count`
	`-------`
	`   2`
	`(1 row)`
	`postgres=# COMMIT;`	

Phantom read and nonrepeatable read can occur, as shown in the preceding examples, in the `READ COMMITTED` transaction isolation level. The scope of nonrepeatable read is often a certain row or set of rows, while the scope of phantom read is all the table. Nonrepeatable read occurs when the transaction reads committed **updates** from another transaction, while phantom read happens as a result of committed **inserts** and **deletes**.

If we run the same preceding examples with the SERIALIZABLE and REPEATABLE READ isolation level, we will see that the result of **Session 1** is not affected by **Session 2**, as shown in the following example:

	Session 1	Session 2
| T1 | ```
BEGIN TRANSACTION ISOLATION LEVEL
SERIALIZABLE;
BEGIN
postgres=# SELECT count(*) FROM
test_tx_level;
 count
-------
     2
(1 row)
``` | |
| T2 | | ```
postgres=# BEGIN;
BEGIN
postgres=# INSERT INTO
test_tx_level SELECT 2;
INSERT 0 1
postgres=# COMMIT;
COMMIT
``` |
| T3 | ```
postgres=# SELECT count(*) FROM
test_tx_level;
 count
-------
     2
(1 row)
``` | |

In PostgreSQL versions prior to 9.1, PostgreSQL has only two transaction isolation levels. This changed with the introduction of PostgreSQL 9.1, where a true SERIALIZABLE transaction isolation model is submitted. The SERIALIZABLE transaction isolation level protects data against many anomalies, such as write skew. Write skew happens when two transactions read overlapping data, concurrently make updates, and finally commit the data. For example, let's assume we have a table containing ones and zeros; the first transaction wants to change the ones to zeros, and the second transaction wants to change the zeros to ones. If transactions are executed in a serial manner, we should get either ones or zeros based on which transaction is executed first. To demonstrate this anomaly, let's create a table, as follows:

```
postgres=# CREATE TABLE zero_or_one (val int);
CREATE TABLE
postgres=# INSERT INTO zero_or_one SELECT n % 2 FROM generate_series(1,10)
as foo(n) ;
INSERT 0 10
postgres=# SELECT array_agg(val) FROM zero_or_one ;
```
```

```
array_agg
-----------------------
 {1,0,1,0,1,0,1,0,1,0}
(1 row)
```

To see the effect of write skew, let's start two sessions with the REPEATABLE isolation level, as follows:

	Session 1	Session 2

T1	postgres=# BEGIN TRANSACTION ISOLATION LEVEL REPEATABLE READ ;
	BEGIN
	postgres=# UPDATE zero_or_one SET val = 1 WHERE val = 0;
	UPDATE 5	

T2		postgres=# BEGIN TRANSACTION ISOLATION LEVEL REPEATABLE READ ;
		BEGIN
		postgres=# UPDATE zero_or_one SET val =0 WHERE val =1;
		UPDATE 5
		postgres=# COMMIT;
		COMMIT

T3	postgres=# COMMIT; COMMIT	

Let's now have a look at the final result of the table, as follows:

```
postgres=# SELECT array_agg(val) FROM zero_or_one ;
        array_agg
-----------------------
 {1,1,1,1,1,0,0,0,0,0}
(1 row)
```

To see what happens in the serializable transaction mode, let's truncate the tables and rerun the example, as follows:

```
postgres=# truncate zero_or_one ;
TRUNCATE TABLE
postgres=# INSERT INTO zero_or_one SELECT n % 2 FROM generate_series(1,10)
as foo(n) ;
INSERT 0 10
```

	Session 1	Session 2

T1	`postgres=# BEGIN TRANSACTION ISOLATION LEVEL SERIALIZABLE ;`
	`BEGIN`
	`postgres=# UPDATE zero_or_one SET val = 1 WHERE val = 0;`
	`UPDATE 5`	

T2		`postgres=# BEGIN TRANSACTION ISOLATION LEVEL SERIALIZABLE ;`
		`BEGIN`
		`postgres=# UPDATE zero_or_one SET val =0 WHERE val =1;`
		`UPDATE 5`
		`postgres=# COMMIT;`

T3	`postgres=# COMMIT ;`
	`ERROR: could not serialize access due to read/write dependencies among transactions`
	`DETAIL: Reason code: Canceled on identification as a pivot, during commit attempt.`
	`HINT: The transaction might succeed if retried.`	

In the repeatable read isolation mode, both transactions were executed without an error; however, the end result was wrong. In the case of the serializable isolation level, when there is write skew, transactions will proceed until one transaction commits. The first committer wins and other transactions are rolled back. The first committer wins rule guarantees that we will make progress. Finally, note that only one transaction succeeded and the other failed. Also note the hint `The transaction might succeed if retried`, to see the final result, as follows:

```
postgres=# SELECT array_agg(val) FROM zero_or_one ;
        array_agg
----------------------
 {0,0,0,0,0,0,0,0,0,0}
(1 row)
```

More information on the `REPEATABLE READ` and `SERIALIZABLE` transaction isolation levels can be found on the **Serializable Snapshot Isolation (SSI)** wiki page at `https://wiki.postgresql.org/wiki/SSI`.

Explicit locking

In addition to MVCC locking, you can control locking explicitly when MVCC does not provide a desirable behavior. Generally speaking, PostgreSQL provides three locking mechanisms, which are as follows:

- Table-level locks
- Row-level locks
- Advisory locks

Table-level locks

Tables can be locked in several locking modes. The syntax of the LOCK statement is as follows:

```
LOCK [ TABLE ] [ ONLY ] name [ * ] [, ...] [ IN lockmode MODE ] [ NOWAIT ]

where lockmode is one of:

    ACCESS SHARE | ROW SHARE | ROW EXCLUSIVE | SHARE UPDATE EXCLUSIVE
    | SHARE | SHARE ROW EXCLUSIVE | EXCLUSIVE | ACCESS EXCLUSIVE
```

PostgreSQL locks the table implicitly when invoking an SQL command. It locks the table using the least restrictive mode to increase concurrency. When the developer desires a more restrictive lock, then the LOCK statement can be used.

Table locking modes

Table locks are often acquired automatically, but they can also be acquired explicitly with the LOCK command. The following is the list of locking modes:

- ACCESS SHARE: This mode is acquired by the SELECT statement.
- ROW SHARE: The SELECT FOR UPDATE and SELECT FOR SHARE commands acquire this lock.
- ROW EXCLUSIVE: The statements UPDATE, DELETE, and INSERT acquire this lock mode.

- SHARE UPDATE EXCLUSIVE: This mode is used to protect a table against concurrent schema changes. Acquired by VACUUM (without FULL), ANALYZE, CREATE INDEX CONCURRENTLY, CREATE STATISTICS, ALTER TABLE VALIDATE, and other ALTER TABLE variants.
- SHARE: This mode is used to protect a table against concurrent data changes. Acquired by CREATE INDEX (without CONCURRENTLY).
- SHARE ROW EXCLUSIVE: This mode protects a table against concurrent data changes, and is self-exclusive, so that only one session can hold it at a time. Acquired by CREATE COLLATION, CREATE TRIGGER, and many forms of ALTER TABLE.
- EXCLUSIVE: This is acquired by REFRESH MATERIALIZED VIEW CONCURRENTLY. This mode only allows reading data for the table.
- ACCESS EXCLUSIVE: This mode guarantees that the holder is the only transaction accessing the table in any way. Acquired by the DROP TABLE, TRUNCATE, REINDEX, CLUSTER, VACUUM FULL, and REFRESH MATERIALIZED VIEW (without CONCURRENTLY) commands. Many forms of ALTER TABLE also acquire a lock at this level. This is also the default lock mode for LOCK TABLE statements that do not specify a mode explicitly.

A very important thing to note for each mode is the list of modes that are in conflict with that specific mode. Transactions cannot hold locks on conflicting modes on the same table. The following table shows the list of lock modes and how the request lock mode is conflicting with the current lock mode:

Conflicting?	ACCESS SHARE	ROW SHARE	ROW EXCLUSIVE	SHARE UPDATE EXCLUSIVE	SHARE	SHARE ROW EXCLUSIVE	EXCLUSIVE	ACCESS EXCLUSIVE
ACCESS SHARE								yes
ROW SHARE							yes	yes
ROW EXCLUSIVE					yes	yes	yes	yes
SHARE UPDATE EXCLUSIVE				yes	yes	yes	yes	yes
SHARE			yes	yes		yes	yes	yes
SHARE ROW EXCLUSIVE			yes	yes	yes	yes	yes	yes
EXCLUSIVE		yes	yes	yes	yes	yes	yes	yes
ACCESS EXCLUSIVE	yes	yes	yes	yes	yes	yes	yes	yes

As shown in the preceding table, ACCESS EXCLUSIVE conflicts with ACCESS SHARE, which means you cannot perform the SELECT statement on a table if the table is locked in ACCESS EXCLUSIVE mode. Also, you cannot DROP a table if someone is reading it. Also note that you can execute SELECT statements in all other modes. Hence, the only mode where a SELECT statement can be blocked is the ACCESS EXCLUSIVE mode.

The following example shows what will happen in the case of dropping a table while another transaction is reading from it:

	Session 1	Session 2
T1	```BEGIN;``` ```BEGIN``` ```postgres=# SELECT COUNT(*) FROM test_tx_level ;``` ` count` `-------` `      3` `(1 row)` ```postgres=# SELECT mode, granted FROM pg_locks where``` ```relation ='test_tx_level'::regclass::oid;``` ` mode	granted`   `-----------------+---------`   ` AccessShareLock	t`   `(1 row)`	

T2		```BEGIN```
		 ```postgres=# DROP```
		 ```TABLE```
		 ```test_tx_level;```

T3	```postgres=# SELECT mode, granted FROM pg_locks where``` ```relation ='test_tx_level'::regclass::oid;``` ` mode	granted`   `---------------------+---------`   ` AccessShareLock	t`   ` AccessExclusiveLock	f`   `(2 rows)`	

The preceding example shows that the lock is acquired when the data is selected from the table in **Session 1** and they are not released. So, once a lock is acquired, the lock is normally held till the end of the transaction. The `pg_locks` table is very handy for understanding locks. It is often used to detect bottlenecks in high concurrency systems. The following view shows lock information in a human-friendly way:

```
CREATE OR REPLACE VIEW lock_info AS
SELECT
    lock1.pid as locked_pid,
    stat1.usename as locked_user,
    stat1.query as locked_statement,
    stat1.state as locked_statement_state,
    stat2.query as locking_statement,
    stat2.state as locking_statement_state,
    now() - stat1.query_start as locking_duration,
    lock2.pid as locking_pid,
```

```
        stat2.usename as locking_user
FROM pg_catalog.pg_locks lock1
        JOIN pg_catalog.pg_stat_activity stat1 on lock1.pid = stat1.pid
        JOIN pg_catalog.pg_locks lock2 on
(lock1.locktype,lock1.database,lock1.relation,lock1.page,lock1.tuple,lock1.
virtualxid,lock1.transactionid,lock1.classid,lock1.objid,lock1.objsubid) IS
NOT DISTINCT FROM
(lock2.locktype,lock2.DATABASE,lock2.relation,lock2.page,lock2.tuple,lock2.
virtualxid,lock2.transactionid,lock2.classid,lock2.objid,lock2.objsubid)
        JOIN pg_catalog.pg_stat_activity stat2 on lock2.pid = stat2.pid
WHERE NOT lock1.granted AND lock2.granted;
```

To see the output of the `lock_info` view, let's execute it as follows:

```
postgres=# SELECT * FROM lock_info ;
-[ RECORD 1 ]------------+------------------------------------------------
--------------------------
locked_pid               | 3736
locked_user              | postgres
locked_statement         | DROP TABLE test_tx_level;
locked_statement_state   | active
locking_statement        | SELECT mode, granted FROM pg_locks where
relation ='test_tx_level'::regclass::oid;
locking_statement_state  | idle in transaction
locking_duration         | 00:09:57.32628
locking_pid              | 3695
locking_user             | postgres
```

The view shows that the process 3736 tries to execute the DROP TABLE statement and is waiting for the transaction issued by the process ID 3695. Since the process 3695 is doing nothing at the time of running the preceding query, the state of the process is idle in transaction. Finally, the preceding view is a bit misleading, as it shows the locking statement is SELECT mode, granted .., which is not true. Simply, the pg_state_activity shows the last statement executed by the process. As we said earlier, once the lock is acquired, it is held by the transaction. So the process 3736 is waiting for the transaction started by process 3695 to finish.

Row-level locks

Row-level locking doesn't lock SELECT statements at all; they are used to lock UPDATE and DELETE statements. As in table-level locks, no two transactions can lock a row in the conflicting row-level lock mode. Row locking is useful in a scenario where the application inspects the value of the row before updating it. Another scenario is to lock users from updating an old value; for example, if you are editing a document, the application should forbid users from editing it. In PostgreSQL 9.5, the SKIP LOCKED option was introduced, which changes the behavior of row locking. The SKIP LOCKED option is useful in handling batch processing without introducing a high wait time, or handling queues and pools on the database's side.

Row-level lock modes

In older versions, as in PostgreSQL 9.3, there are only two locking modes, which are FOR UPDATE and FOR SHARE. FOR UPDATE is used to acquire an exclusive lock on the row and does not allow other transactions to update or delete it; FOR SHARE is less restrictive, allows other transactions to lock the ROW in FOR SHARE mode, and still does not allow other transactions to delete or update the row. FOR SHARE is used to handle a nonrepeatable read scenario in a READ COMMITTED transaction isolation level. For example, you could lock the row FOR SHARE and this will guarantee that the value will not change until the transaction is committed.

FOR SHARE does not handle the lost update problem, since FOR SHARE allows other transactions to lock the row in the same mode. To handle a lost update problem, FOR UPDATE can be used.

> Lost updates happen when two transactions try to update the same row concurrently. Refer to the deadlock section, which presents a lost update scenario.

PostgreSQL also provides the FOR NO KEY UPDATE, which is similar to FOR UPDATE, but the lock is weaker, and FOR KEY SHARE, which is again a weaker form of FOR SHARE. The row-level locking mode conflicts are given in the following table:

Conflicting?	FOR KEY SHARE	FOR SHARE	FOR NO KEY UPDATE	FOR UPDATE
FOR KEY SHARE				yes
FOR SHARE			yes	yes
FOR NO KEY UPDATE		yes	yes	yes
FOR UPDATE	yes	yes	yes	yes

To test row-level locking, let's truncate `test_tx_level` and populate a new record, as follows:

```
postgres=# truncate test_tx_level ;
TRUNCATE TABLE
postgres=# insert into test_tx_level Values(1), (2);
INSERT 0 2
```

To test for an updated row-level lock, perform the following operation:

	Session 1	Session 2

T1	`postgres=# BEGIN;`
	`BEGIN`
	`postgres=# SELECT * FROM test_tx_level`
	`WHERE val = 1 FOR update;`
	`  val`
	`-----`
	`    1`
	`(1 row)`	

T2		`postgres=# BEGIN;`
		`BEGIN`
		`postgres=# update test_tx_level SET`
		`val =2 WHERE val =1;`

Session 2 in the previous snippet is waiting for **Session 1,** since it has acquired a FOR UPDATE lock. The following query shows the locks information for the previous snippet:

```
postgres=# SELECT * FROM lock_info ;
-[ RECORD 1 ]-----+-------------------------------------------------------
locked_pid        | 3368
locked_user       | postgres
locked_statement  | update test_tx_level SET val =2 WHERE val =1;
state             | active
locking_statement | SELECT * FROM test_tx_level WHERE val = 1 FOR update;
state             | idle in transaction
locking_duration  | 00:04:04.631108
locking_pid       | 3380
locking_user      | postgres
```

Deadlocks

Deadlocks occur when two or more transactions each hold locks that the other wants. Using explicit locking can increase deadlocks. To simulate a deadlocks scenario, let's use FOR SHARE row-level locking, as follows:

	Session 1	Session 2

T1	`postgres=# begin;`
	`BEGIN`
	`postgres=# SELECT * FROM`
	`test_tx_level WHERE val = 1 FOR`
	`SHARE;`
	` val`
	`-----`
	`   1`
	`(1 row)`	

T2		`postgres=# begin;`
		`BEGIN`
		`postgres=# SELECT * FROM test_tx_level`
		`WHERE val = 1 FOR SHARE;`
		` val`
		`-----`
		`   1`
		`(1 row)`

T3	`postgres=# UPDATE test_tx_level` `SET val = 2 WHERE val=1;`	

T4		`postgres=# UPDATE test_tx_level SET val =`
		`2 WHERE val=1;`
		`ERROR: deadlock detected`
		`DETAIL: Process 3368 waits for`
		`ExclusiveLock on tuple (0,1) of relation`
		`139530 of database 13014; blocked by`
		`process 3380.`
		`Process 3380 waits for ShareLock on`
		`transaction 121862; blocked by process`
		`3368.`
		`HINT: See server log for query details.`

T5	`UPDATE 1`	

To avoid deadlocks, you should also ensure that the first lock acquired in a transaction is the most restrictive mode. For example, if **Session 1** has used FOR UPDATE, then **Session 2** will be blocked instead of failing due to deadlocks.

As mentioned previously, to avoid deadlocks, you can use a more restrictive mode. This forces other transactions to wait until the lock is removed. If the locking transaction is kept open for an extended period, that means the application will suffer a long delay.

Advisory locks

Advisory locks are application-enforced locks. Advisory locks are used to emulate pessimistic locking strategies. Advisory locks are acquired at session or transaction level and are released when the session ends or the transaction commits.

Advisory locks can be used to limit the concurrency to one process. For example, when the process starts, it tries to acquire a lock; if it acquires it successfully, it continues, otherwise it exits. Advisory locks enable the developers to treat the database system as a single user environment and relieves them of the complexity of the locking system.

Advisory locks are stored in memory, so you need to be careful not to exhaust the database cluster resources when using them. Finally, the full list of advisory locks can be found at https://www.postgresql.org/docs/current/static/functions-admin.html#functions-advisory-locks-table.

The following example, shows how to use advisory locks:

Session 1	Session 2
postgres=# SELECT pg_try_advisory_lock(1); pg_try_advisory_lock --------------------- t (1 row)	
	postgres=# SELECT pg_try_advisory_lock(1); pg_try_advisory_lock --------------------- f (1 row)

``
postgres=# select
pg_advisory_unlock(1);
 pg_advisory_unlock
-------------------- 	
 t
(1 row)
``	

	``
	postgres=# SELECT
	pg_try_advisory_lock(1);
	 pg_try_advisory_lock
	---------------------- 	
	 t
	(1 row)
	``

In the same session, you can acquire the same advisory lock several times. However, it should be released the same number of times as it has been acquired, for example:

```
SELECT pg_try_advisory_lock(1);
SELECT pg_try_advisory_lock(1);
-- To release
select pg_advisory_unlock(1);
select pg_advisory_unlock(1);
```

Transaction in functions and procedures

Prior to PostgreSQL 11, you could not control transactions explicitly inside a function. The function would always run within a transaction. This caused some difficulty in performing a number of development and administrative tasks. For example, a database administrator has performed bulk indexing inside a function, and, after a certain period of time, the administrator cancelled the function execution due to a time or performance constraint. In the preceding scenario, all work done is lost due to the nature of the transaction. From a development perspective, being able to control transactions inside a function is important because it allows the developers to control transactions based on business logic requirements.

PostgreSQL 11 provides a new feature, which is CREATE PROCEDURE. The procedure has a different transaction behavior than a function. Also, the procedure does not require to return a value. A stored procedure can be seen as a set of commands to be executed in a certain order, as follows:

```
CREATE TABLE test_tx_procedure (a int);
CREATE PROCEDURE test_tx_procedure()
 AS $$
 BEGIN
     FOR i IN 0..4 LOOP
```

```
            INSERT INTO test_tx_procedure (a) VALUES (i);
            IF i % 2 = 0 THEN
                    RAISE NOTICE 'i=%, txid=% will be committed', i,
    txid_current();
                    COMMIT;
            ELSE
                    RAISE NOTICE 'i=%, txid=% will be rolledback', i,
    txid_current();
                    ROLLBACK;
            END IF;
        END LOOP;
  END
  $$
  LANGUAGE PLPGSQL;
--- To test
postgres=# call test_tx_procedure();
NOTICE:  i=0, txid=858 will be committed
NOTICE:  i=1, txid=859 will be rolledback
NOTICE:  i=2, txid=860 will be committed
NOTICE:  i=3, txid=861 will be rolledback
NOTICE:  i=4, txid=862 will be committed
CALL
```

Summary

PostgreSQL provides several locking mechanisms to increase concurrency and performance, including implicit locking via MVCC, and explicit locking via table-level locks, row-level locks, and advisory locks.

The MVCC model is one of the biggest selling factors of PostgreSQL, since high performance can be achieved. In general, the MVCC model is suitable for most common database access patterns, and it is better to use the MVCC model instead of explicit locking where possible.

Using explicit locking via table-level or row-level locks enables the user to solve several data inconsistency issues. However, explicit locking, if not planned carefully, might increase the chances of having deadlocks. Finally, PostgreSQL provides advisory locks, which are used to emulate pessimistic locking strategies.

The next chapter covers the concepts of authentication and authorization. It describes PostgreSQL authentication methods and explains the structure of a PostgreSQL host-based authentication configuration file. It also discusses the permissions that can be granted to database building objects, such as schemas, tables, views, indexes, and columns. Finally, it shows how sensitive data, such as passwords, can be protected using different techniques, including one-way and two-way encryption.

Questions

1. Define the term transaction. What is the meaning of implicit transaction?
2. What are the functions of the following SQL commands: `BEGIN`, `END`, `COMMIT`, `ROLLBACK`, and `SAVEPOINT`?
3. Assuming you are working with an environment that does not support transactions, give a solution to mitigate the following scenario: A developer performed a bulk upload on a non-empty table, and during the upload, the power shut down. The developer would like to restore the initial state.
4. What is the difference between concurrency and parallelism? Does PostgreSQL support both?
5. What is MVCC? What negative impact does it have on the database design? How does PostgreSQL mitigate this impact?
6. List the transaction isolation levels. What is the default transaction isolation level in PostgreSQL?
7. List the side effects of each transaction isolation level and explain them briefly.
8. What are the levels of explicit locking?
9. What is the difference between the procedure and functions in PostgreSQL?

11
PostgreSQL Security

Data protection and security are essential for the continuity of business. Data protection is not recommended, but it is required by the legal system. Sensitive data, such as user information, email addresses, geographical addresses, and payment information, should be protected against any data breach. There are several other topics related to data security, such as data privacy, retention, and loss prevention.

There are several levels of data protection, often defined in the data protection policy and by the country's legal system. A data protection policy often defines data dissemination to other parties, users authorized to access the data, and so on. Data should be protected on different levels, including transferring and encrypting data on storage devices. Data security is a huge topic and often there are data security managers dedicated only to these tasks.

In this chapter, we will discuss the following topics:

- Authentication in PostgreSQL, including PostgreSQL host-based authentication and best practices
- Default access privileges and the privileges on the public schema
- Proxy authentication strategies
- PostgreSQL security levels, including database, schema, table, column, and row privileges
- Data encryption and decryption, including one-way and two-way encryption

Authentication in PostgreSQL

Authentication answers the question: Who is the user? PostgreSQL supports several authentication methods, including the following:

- **Trust**: Anyone who can connect to the server is authorized to access the database/databases as specified in the `pg_hba.conf` configuration file. Often used to allow connection using Unix domain socket on a single user machine to access the database. This method can also be used with TCP/IP, but it is rare to allow connection from any IP address other than the localhost.
- **Ident**: This works by getting the client's operating system user name from an ident server and then using it to access the database server. This method is recommend for closed networks where client machines are subject to tight controls by system administrators.
- **Peer**: This works in a similar manner to ident, but the client's operating system username is obtained from the kernel.
- **GSSAPI:** GSSAPI is an industry standard defined in RFC 2743. It provides automatic authentication (single sign-on).
- **Lightweight Directory Access Protocol (LDAP)**: The LDAP server is used only to validate the username/password pairs.
- **Password authentication**: There are three methods as follows:
    - **SCRAM-SHA-256**: The strongest authentication method, introduced in PostgreSQL 10. This method prevents password sniffing on untrusted connections. The default password authentication method is MD5 to use this feature, the configuration parameter `password_encryption` should be changed to `scram-sha-256`
    - **MD5**: MD5 has know limitations such as pre-computed lookup tables to crack password hashes. Also MD5 has only 4 billion unique hashes. Finally, MD5 computation is very fast, thus brute force password guessing does not require a lot of CPU resources. For new applications it is only recommended using scram-sha-256. Also, PostgreSQL provides the means to migrate from to scram-sha-256.
    - **Password**: This is not recommended to be used, since passwords are sent to the server in a clear text format.

There are other authentication methods not covered; the full list of supported authentication methods can be found at https://www.postgresql.org/docs/current/static/auth-methods.html.

To understand authentication, you need to have the following information:

- Authentication is controlled via a pg_hba.conf file, where **hba** stands for **host-based authentication**.
- It is good to know the default initial authentication settings shipped with PostgreSQL distribution.
- The pg_hba.conf file is often located in the data directory, but it can also be specified in the postgresql.conf configuration file.
- When changing the authentication, you need to send a **SIGHUP** signal, and this is done via several methods based on the PostgreSQL platform. Note that the user who sends the signal should be a superuser or the postgres, or a root system user on the Linux distribution; again, this depends on the platform. Here is an example of several ways to reload the PostgreSQL configuration:

  ```
  psql -U postgres -c "SELECT pg_reload_conf();"
  sudo service postgresql reload
  sudo /etc/init.d/postgresql reload
  sudo Kill -HUP <postgres process id>
  sudo systemctl reload postgresql-11.service
  ```

- The *order* of the pg_hba.conf records or entries is important. The session connection is compared with the pg_hba.conf records one by one until it is rejected or the end of the configuration file is reached.
- Finally, it is important to check the PostgreSQL log files to determine whether there are errors after configuration reload.

PostgreSQL pg_hba.conf

As in postgresql.conf, the pg_hba.conf file is composed of a set of records, lines can be commented using the hash sign, and spaces are ignored. The structure of the pg_hba.conf file record is as follows:

```
host_type database user [IP-address| address] [IP-mask] auth-method [auth-options]
```

The `host_type` part of this query can be the following:

- `Local`: This is used in Linux systems to allow users to access PostgreSQL using Unix domain socket connection.
- `Host`: This is to allow connections from other hosts, either based on the address or IP address, using TCP/IP with and without SSL encryption.
- `Hostssl`: This is similar to host, but the connection should be encrypted using SSL.
- `Hostnossl`: This is also similar to host, but the connection should not be encrypted.

The database part of the query is the name of the database that the user would like to connect to. For flexibility, you could also use a comma-separated list to specify several databases, or you could use `all` to indicate that the user can access all the databases in the database cluster. Also, the same user and same role values can be used to indicate that the database name is the same as the username, or the user is a member of a role with the same name as the database.

The user part of the query specifies the database user's name; again, the `all` value matches all users. The IP address, address, and IP subnet mask are used to identify the host from where the user tries to connect. The IP address can be specified using a **Classless Inter-Domain Routing** (**CIDR**) or dot decimal notation. Finally, the password authentication methods can be trust, MD5, reject, and so on.

The following are some typical examples of configuring a PostgreSQL authentication:

- **Example 1**: Any user on the PostgreSQL cluster can access any database using the Unix domain socket, as shown in the following database table:

#TYPE	DATABASE	USER	ADDRESS	METHOD
Local	all	all		trust

- **Example 2**: Any user on the PostgreSQL cluster can access any database using the local loop back IP address, as shown in the following database table:

#TYPE	DATABASE	USER	ADDRESS	METHOD
Host	all	all	127.0.0.1/32	trust
host	all	all	::1/128	trust

- **Example 3**: All connections that come from the IP address `192.168.0.53` are rejected, and the connections that come from the range `192.168.0.1/24` are accepted, as shown in the following database table:

```
#TYPE    DATABASE    USER     ADDRESS              METHOD
Host     all         all      192.168.0.53/32      reject
Host     all         all      192.168.0.1/24       trust
```

PostgreSQL provides a very convenient way to view the rules defined in the `pg_hba.conf` file by providing a view called `pg_hba_file_rules` as follows:

```
postgres=# SELECT row_to_json(pg_hba_file_rules, true) FROM
pg_hba_file_rules limit 1;
        row_to_json
-----------------------------
 {"line_number":84, +
  "type":"local", +
  "database":["all"], +
  "user_name":["all"], +
  "address":null, +
  "netmask":null, +
  "auth_method":"trust",+
  "options":null, +
  "error":null}
(1 row)
```

Listen addresses

The `listen_addresses` option is defined in `postgresql.conf`. The PostgreSQL `listen_addresses` connection setting is used to identify the list of IP addresses that the server should listen to from client applications. The `listen_addresses` are comma-separated lists of hostnames or IP addresses. Changing this value requires a server restart. In addition, the following should be noted:

- The default value is localhost which restricts direct connections to PostgreSQL cluster from network..
- Giving an empty list means that the server should accept only a Unix socket connection
- The value * indicates all

It is a common mistake for developers new to PostgreSQL to forget to change the `listen_address`. If a developer forgets to change it, and tries to connect to PostgreSQL using TCP/IP from the network, the following error will be raised:

```
Connection refused
Is the server running on host <host_ip> and accepting
TCP/IP connections on port 5432?
```

Authentication best practices

Authentication best practices depend on the whole infrastructure setup, the application's nature, the user's characteristics, data sensitivity, and so on. For example, the following setup is common for start-up companies: the database application, including the database server, is hosted on the same machine and only used from one physical location by intra company users.

Often, database servers are isolated from the world using firewalls; in this case, you can use the SCRAM-SHA-256 authentication method and limit the IP addresses so that the database server accepts connections within a certain range or set. Note that it is important not to use a superuser or database owner account to connect to the database, because if this account was hacked, the whole database cluster would be exposed.

If the application server—business logic—and database server are not on the same machine, you can use a strong authentication method, such as LDAP and Kerberos. However, for small applications where the database server and application are on the same machine, the SCRAM-SHA-256 authentication method and limiting the listen address to the localhost might be sufficient.

To authenticate an application, it is recommended to use only one user and try to reduce the maximum number of allowed connections using a connection pooling software to better tune the PostgreSQL resources. Another level of security might be needed in the application business logic to distinguish between different login users. For real-world users, LDAP or Kerberos authentication is more desirable.

Furthermore, if the database server is accessed from the outer world, it is useful to encrypt sessions using SSL certificates to avoid packet sniffing.

You should also remember to secure database servers that trust all localhost connections, as anyone who accesses the localhost can access the database server.

PostgreSQL default access privileges

By default, PostgreSQL users—also known as roles with the login option—can access the public schema. Additionally, note that the default PostgreSQL authentication policy allows users to access all databases from the localhost using peer authentication on a Linux system. Users can create database objects-tables, views, functions, and so on in the public schema of any database that they can access by default. Finally, the user can alter a number of settings relating to sessions such as work_mem.

The user cannot access other user objects in the public schema or create databases and schemas. However, the user can sniff data about the database objects by querying the system catalog. Unprivileged users can get information about other users, table structure, table owner, some table statistics, and so on.

The following example shows how test_user is able to get information about a table that is owned by a postgres user; to simulate this situation, let's create a test database as follows:

```
psql -U postgres -c 'CREATE ROLE test_user LOGIN;';
psql -U postgres -c 'CREATE DATABASE test;';
psql -U postgres -d test -c'CREATE TABLE test_permissions(id serial , name
text);'
```

test_user does not have permissions to access the table itself, but has permissions to access the system catalog. To see this, connect to the database using test_user, as follows:

```
test=# SET ROLE test_user;
SET
test=> \d
 List of relations
 Schema | Name                  | Type     | Owner
--------+-----------------------+----------+----------
 public | test_permissions      | table    | postgres
 public | test_permissions_id_seq | sequence | postgres
(2 rows)
test=> \du
                                 List of roles
 Role name | Attributes | Member of
-----------+---------------------------------------------------------------+--
---------
 postgres  | Superuser, Create role, Create DB, Replication, Bypass RLS |
{}
 test_user |                                                               |
{}
```

The user can also access functions that are created in the public schema by other users as long as this function does not access objects that the user cannot access.

For mistrusted languages, such as **plpythonu**, the user cannot create functions unless they are a superuser. If anyone who is not a superuser tries to create a function using the C language or **plpythonu**, an error will be raised.

To prevent the user from accessing the public schema, the public schema privileges should be revoked, as follows:

```
test=# SELECT session_user;
 session_user
--------------
 postgres
(1 row)
test=# REVOKE ALL PRIVILEGES ON SCHEMA PUBLIC FROM public;
REVOKE
test=# SET ROLE test_user;
SET
test=> CREATE TABLE b();
ERROR: no schema has been selected to create in
LINE 1: create table b();
```

 `test_user` has explicit privileges on the public schema; the user inherits these privileges from the public role.

For views, the view owner cannot execute a view unless they have permission to access the base tables used in the view. In the next section, we will demonstrate how to use the role system to define different levels of permissions. This is useful to protect the data.

Role system and proxy authentication

Often, when designing an application, a login role is used to configure database connections and connection tools. Another level of security needs to be implemented to ensure that the user who uses the application is authorized to perform a certain task. This logic is often implemented in application business logic.

The database's role system can also be used to partially implement this logic by delegating the authentication to another role after the connection is established or reused, using the SET SESSION AUTHORIZATION statement or SET ROLE command in a transaction block, as follows:

```
postgres=# SELECT session_user, current_user;
 session_user | current_user
--------------+--------------
 postgres     | postgres
(1 row)

postgres=# SET SESSION AUTHORIZATION test_user;
SET
postgres=> SELECT session_user, current_user;
 session_user | current_user
--------------+--------------
 test_user    | test_user
(1 row)
```

The SET ROLE requires a role membership, while SET SESSION AUTHORIZATION requires superuser privileges. Allowing an application to connect as a superuser is dangerous because the SET SESSION AUTHORIZATION and SET ROLE commands can be reset using the RESET ROLE and RESET SESSION commands, respectively, thereby allowing the application to gain superuser privileges.

To understand how the PostgreSQL role system can be used to implement authentication and authorization, we will use the role system and the car portal application. In the car portal application, several groups of users can be classified as web_app_user, public_user, registered_user, seller_user, and admin_user. The web_app_user is used to configure business logic connection tools; the public_user, registered_user, and seller_user are used to distinguish users. The public_user group can access only public information, such as advertisements, but cannot add ratings as registered_user nor create advertisements, since seller_user. admin_user is a super role to manage all of the application's content, such as filtering out spams and deleting the users that do not adhere to the website's policies. When the car web portal application connects to the database, the web_app_user user is used. After this, car_portal invokes the SET ROLE command based on the user class. This authentication method is known as **proxy authentication**.

The following examples demonstrates how a role system can be used to implement proxy authentication. The first step is to create roles and assign role memberships and privileges, as follows:

```
CREATE ROLE web_app_user LOGIN NOINHERIT;
CREATE ROLE public_user NOLOGIN;
GRANT SELECT ON car_portal_app.advertisement_picture,
car_portal_app.advertisement_rating , car_portal_app.advertisement TO
public_user;
GRANT public_user TO web_app_user;
GRANT USAGE ON SCHEMA car_portal_app TO web_app_user, public_user;
```

The NOINHERIT option for the web_app_user does not allow the user to inherit the permissions of role membership; however, web_app_user can change the role to public user, as in the following example:

```
$ psql car_portal -U web_app_user

car_portal=> SELECT * FROM car_portal_app.advertisement;
ERROR: permission denied for relation advertisement
car_portal=> SET ROLE public_user;
SET
car_portal=> SELECT * FROM car_portal_app.advertisement;
 advertisement_id | advertisement_date | car_id | seller_account_id
------------------+--------------------+--------+-------------------
(0 rows)

car_portal=> SELECT session_user, current_user;
 session_user | current_user
--------------+--------------
 web_app_user | public_user
(1 row)
```

PostgreSQL security levels

PostgreSQL has different security levels defined on PostgreSQL objects, including tablespace, database, schema, table, foreign data wrapper, sequence, domain, language, and large object. You can have a peek into different privileges by running the \h meta command in psql, as follows:

```
Command: GRANT
Description: define access privileges
Syntax:
GRANT { { SELECT | INSERT | UPDATE | DELETE | TRUNCATE | REFERENCES |
TRIGGER }
```

```
[, ...] | ALL [ PRIVILEGES ] }
ON { [ TABLE ] table_name [, ...]
      | ALL TABLES IN SCHEMA schema_name [, ...] }
TO role_specification [, ...] [ WITH GRANT OPTION ]
```

In the next section, we will address several security levels including database, entities (tables, views, and sequences), columns and rows.

Database security level

To disallow users from connecting to the database by default, you need to revoke the default database permissions from the public, as follows:

```
car_portal=# REVOKE ALL ON DATABASE car_portal FROM public;
REVOKE
car_portal=# \q
$ psql car_portal -U web_app_user
psql: FATAL: permission denied for database "car_portal"
DETAIL: User does not have CONNECT privilege.
```

To allow the user to connect to the database, the connect permissions should be granted, as follows:

```
postgres=# GRANT CONNECT ON DATABASE car_portal TO web_app_user;
GRANT
postgres=# \l car_portal
List of databases
-[ RECORD 1 ]-----+-----------------------------------
Name              | car_portal
Owner             | car_portal_app
Encoding          | UTF8
Collate           | en_US.UTF-8
Ctype             | en_US.UTF-8
Access privileges | car_portal_app=CTc/car_portal_app+
                  | web_app_user=c/car_portal_app
```

You could also revoke the default permissions from template databases to ensure that all newly created databases do not allow users to connect by default. If the database permissions are empty when using the l meta command, this indicates that the database has the default permissions.

Be careful when dumping and restoring your database using `pg_dump` and `pg_restore`. The database access privileges are not restored and need to be handled explicitly.

Schema security level

Users can CREATE or access objects in a schema; to allow a user access to a certain schema, the usage permissions should be granted, as seen in the following example:

```
GRANT USAGE ON SCHEMA car_portal_app TO web_app_user, public_user;
```

Object-level security

The database objects, such as tables, views, sequences, domain, data types, and functions can be secured by granting and revoking permissions. The permissions are different for each objects. For example, the sequence has USAGE permission, and the function has EXECUTE permission.

The table permissions are INSERT, UPDATE, DELETE, TRIGGER, REFERENCES, and TRUNCATE. You can also use the keyword ALL to grant all privileges at once, as follows:

```
GRANT ALL ON <table_name> TO <role>;
```

REFERENCES and TRIGGER permissions allow the creation of foreign key references to the table and triggers. Apart from this, you could use a comma-separated list for both tables and roles, or even grant permissions on all relations in a schema to a certain role.

Column-level security

PostgreSQL allows permissions to be defined on the column level. To explore this feature, let's create a table and role, as follows:

```
CREATE DATABASE test_column_acl;
\c test_column_acl
CREATE TABLE test_column_acl AS SELECT * FROM (values (1,2), (3,4)) as
n(f1, f2);
CREATE ROLE test_column_acl;
GRANT SELECT (f1) ON test_column_acl TO test_column_acl;
```

To check column permissions, let's try to get all the data from the table, as follows:

```
test_column_acl=# SET ROLE test_column_acl ;
SET
test_column_acl=> TABLE test_column_acl;
ERROR: permission denied for relation test_column_acl
test_column_acl=> SELECT f1 from test_column_acl ;
 f1
----
  1
  3
(2 rows)
```

Row-level security

Row-level security (RLS), also known as **row security policy**, is used to control access to the table rows, including INSERT, UPDATE, SELECT, and DELETE. Table truncate as well as referential integrity constraints, such as the primary key and unique and foreign keys, are not subject to row security. In addition to this, superusers bypass the row-level security. To enable row security, you need to use the ALTER statement for each table, as follows:

```
ALTER TABLE <table_name> ENABLE ROW LEVEL SECURITY
```

In order to use RLS, you need to define some polices on how a certain role or roles in the database can access a certain set of rows. For this reason, often, the role is embedded in the tables. The following sample code creates two users and a table, and enables RLS for that table:

```
CREATE DATABASE test_rls;
\c test_rls;
CREATE USER admin;
CREATE USER guest;
CREATE TABLE account (
 account_name NAME,
  password TEXT
  );
INSERT INTO account VALUES('admin', 'admin'), ('guest', 'guest');
GRANT ALL ON  account to admin, guest;
ALTER TABLE account ENABLE ROW LEVEL SECURITY;
```

By default, if no policy is defined, then the user will be restricted to access the rows, as follows:

```
test_rls=# SET ROLE admin;
test_rls=> table account;
 account_name | password
--------------+----------
(0 rows)
```

You could define a policy as follows:

```
CREATE POLICY account_policy_user ON account USING (account_name =
current_user);
test_rls=# SET ROLE admin;
test_rls=> Table account;
 account_name | password
--------------+----------
 admin        | admin
(1 row)
```

The preceding code simply matches each row `account_name` and `current_user` and, if the match returned is true, then the row is returned. Note that this policy is not restricted to a certain operation, so the policy is applicable for `INSERT`, `UPDATE`, and `DELETE` as well, as seen in the following code:

```
test_rls=# SET ROLE admin;
test_rls=> INSERT INTO account values('guest', 'guest');
ERROR: new row violates row-level security policy for table "account"
```

The syntax to create a policy is as follows:

```
CREATE POLICY name ON table_name
    [ FOR { ALL | SELECT | INSERT | UPDATE | DELETE } ]
    [ TO { role_name | PUBLIC | CURRENT_USER | SESSION_USER } [, ...] ]
    [ USING ( using_expression ) ]
    [ WITH CHECK ( check_expression ) ]
```

The create policy is very flexible; you can create policy for a certain operation or a certain condition, using any expression returning a Boolean value. `WITH CHECK` is used to validate newly inserted or updated rows. For example, we would like the users to see all the content of the account table but only modify their own rows, as follows:

```
CREATE POLICY account_policy_write_protected ON account USING (true) WITH
CHECK (account_name = current_user);

test_rls=# SET ROLE admin;
test_rls=> Table account;
```

```
account_name | password
--------------+----------
 admin        | admin
 guest        | guest
(2 rows)

test_rls=> INSERT INTO account values('guest', 'guest');
ERROR: new row violates row-level security policy for table "account"
```

The policies, by default, are *permissive policies*, which means that they are combined using the OR operator. Two polices were created as shown; one allows the users to see their own rows, and one allows the users to see all rows; in total, the user will be able to see all rows, as follows:

```
\d account
 Table "public.account"
 Column | Type | Collation | Nullable | Default
--------------+------+-----------+----------+---------
 account_name | name | | |
 password | text | | |
Policies:
 POLICY "account_policy_write_protected"
 USING (true)
 WITH CHECK ((account_name = CURRENT_USER))
 POLICY "account_user"
       USING ((account_name = CURRENT_USER))
```

Restrictive polices are supported in PostgreSQL; that is, the policies are combined using the AND logical operator. Let's now restrict table access based on working hours, as follows:

```
CREATE POLICY account_policy_time ON account AS RESTRICTIVE USING (
date_part('hour', statement_timestamp()) BETWEEN 8 AND 16 ) WITH CHECK
(account_name = current_user);
test_rls=# set role admin;
test_rls=# select now();
             now
-------------------------------
 2017-10-07 17:42:34.663909+02
(1 row)
test_rls=> table account;
 account_name | password
--------------+----------
(0 rows)
```

As seen in the example, no rows were returned due to adding the *restrictive policy*. The rows are filtered out by the expression; the filtering of rows is calculated using `admin` as the role, as follows:

Tuple	account_policy	account_policy_write_protected	account_policy_time	Final result
(admin,admin)	True	True	False	False
(guest,guest)	False	True	False	False

All the tuples or rows are filtered out because of the `account_policy_time` policy. In the preceding example, the final result for the tuple `(admin, admin)` is calculated as `True OR True AND False`, which evaluates to `False`.

Encrypting data

By default, PostgreSQL internally encrypts sensitive data, such as roles' passwords. However, database users can also encrypt and decrypt sensitive data using the `pgcrypto` extension.

PostgreSQL role password encryption

When creating a role with password and login options, you can see the role's details in the `pg_shadow` catalog relation. Note that it is not recommended to use the following format to create the password:

```
CREATE ROLE <role_name> <with options> PASSWORD 'some_password';
```

The `CREATE ROLE` statement can appear in `pg_stat_activity` as well as the server logs. All passwords stored in `pg_shadow` are encrypted with salt; finally, renaming an account will reset the password as follows:

```
postgres=# CREATE ROLE a password 'a'; ALTER ROLE a RENAME TO b;
CREATE ROLE
NOTICE: MD5 password cleared because of role rename
```

When creating a user with a password, it is recommended to use the `\password` psql client meta command because it ensures that the password does not appear in clear text form in the `psql` history command, server log files, or elsewhere. To change the password, you can invoke the meta command using a superuser role as follows:

```
postgres=#\password <some_role_name>
Enter new password:
Enter it again:
ERROR: role "<some_role_name>" does not exist
```

pgcrypto

The `pgcrypto` extension provides a cryptographic functionality. Data encryption and decryption consume hardware resources, so it is important to have a balance between data sensitivity and decryption complexity. There are two kinds of data encryption:

- One-way data encryption uses a function to generate a hash, which cannot be reversed. The resulting encrypted text often has a fixed length; for example, MD5 encryption generates 16 bytes of hashes. A good hash function should be quick to compute and not produce the same hash for a different input.
- Two-way data encryption allows the data to be encrypted and decrypted. `pgcrypto` comes with functions to support one-way and two-way encryption. It supports several hashing algorithms. `pgcrypto` can be installed using the CREATE EXTENSION command, as follows:

```
CREATE EXTENSION pgcrypto;
```

One-way encryption

In **one-way encryption**, retrieving data in a clear text form is not important. The encrypted text (digest) is used to verify that the user knows the secret text. One-way encryption is often used to store passwords. PostgreSQL supports out-of-the-box MD5 encryption; however, as MD5 can be cracked easily, MD5 could be used with salt, as seen in the preceding `pg_shadow` example.

The common scenario of validating a password is comparing the generated MD5 digest with the stored one, as follows:

```
CREATE TABLE account_md5 (id INT, password TEXT);
INSERT INTO account_md5 VALUES (1, md5('my password'));
SELECT (md5('my password') = password) AS authenticated FROM account_md5;
 authenticated
```

```
-----------------
 t
(1 row)
```

In PostgreSQL 11, new secure hash algorithms are supported (sha) out of the box, so it is better to use these functions instead of MD5 hashing, as follows:

```
postgres=# \df sha*
 List of functions
 Schema | Name | Result data type | Argument data types | Type
-------------+--------+------------------+---------------------+------
 pg_catalog | sha224 | bytea | bytea | func
 pg_catalog | sha256 | bytea | bytea | func
 pg_catalog | sha384 | bytea | bytea | func
 pg_catalog | sha512 | bytea | bytea | func
(4 rows)
postgres=# SELECT sha512('Hello World');
 sha512
----------------------------------------------------------------------
----------------------------------------------------------------
\x2c74fd17edafd80e8447b0d46741ee243b7eb74dd2149a0ab1b9246fb30382f27e853d858
5719e0e67cbda0daa8f51671064615d645ae27acb15bfb1447f459b
(1 row)
```

pgcrypto provides two functions to encrypt the password. These functions are crypt and gen_salt; also, the pgcrypto extension relieves the user from maintaining the salt. crypt and gen_salt can be used almost in the same way as MD5 to store the password, as follows:

```
CREATE TABLE account_crypt (id INT, password TEXT);
INSERT INTO account_crypt VALUES (1, crypt ('my password',
gen_salt('md5')));
INSERT INTO account_crypt VALUES (2, crypt ('my password',
gen_salt('md5')));
SELECT * FROM account_crypt;
 id | password
----+------------------------------------
  1 | $1$ITT7yisa$FdRe4ihZ9kep1oU6wBr090
  2 | $1$HT2wH3UL$8DRdP6kLz5LvTXF3F2q610
(2 rows)
SELECT crypt ('my password', password) = password AS authenticated FROM
account_crypt;
 authenticated
----------
 t
 t
(2 rows)
```

As shown in the example, the passwords' digest differ due to a differently generated salt. Also, note that salt does not need to be maintained. Finally, you could have a stronger password by tuning the salt generation. For example, you could use Blowfish hashing and specify the iteration count. Note that the more iteration counts there are, the slower the decryption, and the more time is subsequently required to break it, as shown in the following example:

```
\timing
SELECT crypt('my password', gen_salt('bf',4));
                             crypt
------------------------------------------------------------

 $2a$04$RZ5KWnI.IB4eLGNnT.37kuui4.Qi4Xh4TZmL7SOB6YW4LRpyZlP/K
(1 row)

Time: 1,801 ms

SELECT crypt('my password', gen_salt('bf',16));
                             crypt
------------------------------------------------------------

 $2a$16$/cUY8PX7v2GLPCQBCbnL6Ot1Fm4YACmShZaH1gDNZcHyAYBvJ.9jq
(1 row)

Time: 4686,712 ms (00:04,687)
```

Having a very fast algorithm to generate and compare hashes such as MD5 might be sometimes problematic. This will hackers to try more combinations is within a certain time period.

Two-way encryption

Two-way encryption is used to store sensitive information, such as payment information. pgcrypto provides two functions—mainly encrypt and decrypt—as shown in the following script:

```
test=# \df encrypt
                       List of functions
 Schema | Name    | Result data type | Argument data types | Type
--------+---------+------------------+---------------------+--------
 public | encrypt | bytea            | bytea, bytea, text  | normal
(1 row)

test=# \df decrypt
                       List of functions
 Schema | Name    | Result data type | Argument data types | Type
--------+---------+------------------+---------------------+--------
```

```
  public | decrypt | bytea              | bytea, bytea, text  | normal
(1 row)
```

The `encrypt` and `decrypt` functions require three arguments: the data to encrypt, the key, and the encryption algorithm. The following example shows how to `encrypt` and `decrypt` the `Hello World` string using the `aes` encryption algorithm:

```
test=# SELECT encrypt ('Hello World', 'Key', 'aes');
                encrypt
------------------------------------
 xf9d48f411bdee81a0e50b86b501dd7ba
(1 row)
test=# SELECT decrypt(encrypt ('Hello World', 'Key', 'aes'),'Key','aes');
         decrypt
--------------------------
 x48656c6c6f20576f726c64
(1 row)
test=# SELECT convert_from(decrypt(encrypt ('Hello World', 'Key',
'aes'),'Key','aes'), 'utf-8');
 convert_from
--------------
 Hello World
(1 row)
```

The preceding form of encryption has some limitations; for example, the statement can appear in `pg_stat_activity` or in the database server log, and thus, someone could get the key.

Two-way encryption can be achieved in two ways: symmetric and asymmetric encryption. The preceding example shows how symmetric encryption works, where there is a key used to `encrypt` and `decrypt` data. Asymmetric encryption uses public and private keys; the public key is used to `encrypt` the data, and the private key is used to `decrypt` it. Asymmetric encryption is more secure than symmetric encryption but harder to set up. To set up asymmetric encryption and decryption, you need to generate a public key via the `gpg` tool. Note that the `gpg` command asks for a passphrase; in this example, the passphrase should not be provided, and for simplicity, follow the default settings:

```
root@host:~# gpg --gen-key
```

Now, to extract the **public** and **private** keys, you could execute the following commands; note that if you use the `root` user to generate the key, you need to change ownership of the keys generated to the `postgres` user:

```
root@host:~# gpg --list-secret-key
/root/.gnupg/pubring.kbx
------------------------
```

```
sec  rsa3072 2019-01-27 [SC] [expires: 2021-01-26]
      0EE2255C86D09E727E6545F10F8061C2BDF98249
uid [ultimate] salah <juba@example.com>
ssb  rsa3072 2019-01-27 [E] [expires: 2021-01-26]


root@host:~# gpg -a --export
0EE2255C86D09E727E6545F10F8061C2BDF98249>/var/lib/postgresql/11/main/public
.key
root@host:~# gpg -a --export-secret-key
0EE2255C86D09E727E6545F10F8061C2BDF98249>/var/lib/postgresql/11/main/secret
.key
root@host:~# chown postgres.postgres /var/lib/postgresql/11/main/public.key
root@host:~# chown postgres.postgres /var/lib/postgresql/11/main/secret.key
```

The gpg option, `--list-secret-key`, is used to determine the key IDs, and the options, `--export-secret-key` and `--export`, are used to export the private and the public keys respectively. The `-a` option is used to dump the keys in copy and paste formats. On the PostgreSQL cluster, we need to run the dearmor function to change the secret key format. Also, the keys were moved to the database cluster folder for convenience purposes to use the `pg_read_file` function. After the generation of the keys, you could create a wrapper around `pgp_pub_encrypt` and `pgp_pub_decrypt` to hide the location of the keys, as follows:

```
CREATE OR REPLACE FUNCTION encrypt (text) RETURNS bytea AS
$$
BEGIN
  RETURN pgp_pub_encrypt($1, dearmor(pg_read_file('public.key')));
END;
$$ LANGUAGE plpgsql;
CREATE OR REPLACE FUNCTION decrypt (bytea) RETURNS text AS
$$
BEGIN
  RETURN pgp_pub_decrypt($1, dearmor(pg_read_file('secret.key')));
END;
$$ LANGUAGE plpgsql;
```

To test our functions, let's encrypt Hello World as follows:

```
test=# SELECT substring(encrypt('Hello World'), 1, 50);
                                               substring
----------------------------------------------------------------------
----------------------------
xc1c04c034db92a51d0b149a90107fe3dc44ec5dccc039aea2a44e1d811426583a265feb22f
68421355a3b4755a6cb19eb3fa
(1 row)
test=# SELECT decrypt(encrypt('Hello World'));
```

```
    decrypt
-------------
 Hello World
(1 row)
```

Summary

In this chapter, PostgreSQL security is tackled from the authorization, authentication, and data encryption aspects; however, you should also protect the code against SQL injection and other known security issues, such as function cost, and the security barrier options. PostgreSQL provides several authentication methods, such as password and trust. Also, it provides security levels on all database objects, including the database itself, schemas, tables, views, function, columns, and rows. Finally, you can also store sensitive data in the database in an encrypted format using the `pgcrypto` extension.

The next chapter will focus on the PostgreSQL system catalog and introduce several recipes to maintain the database. The recipes will be used to extract potential problems in the database, such as missing indexes, and introduce the solutions to tackle these problems.

Questions

1. Which configuration files need to be edited in order to allow a user to access the PostgreSQL from a remote machine using a password?
2. What are the authentication types supported by PostgreSQL?
3. Does the order of `pg_hba.conf` file entries matter?
4. When creating a table with a serial data type, which objects should be granted proper permissions?
5. List all the PostgreSQL access security levels.
6. What is the meaning of proxy authentication?
7. You need to allow a user to access only one set of rows of a table. Give two strategies to achieve this.
8. Why it is recommended to use the `\password psql` client toll?
9. What is the difference between one-way and two-way encryption?
10. What are the limitations of symmetric encryption? How can you overcome these limitations?

12
The PostgreSQL Catalog

The PostgreSQL system catalog and system administration functions can aid both developers and administrators to keep the database clean and performant. System catalogs can be used to automate several tasks, such as finding tables without indexes, finding dependencies between database objects, and extracting information about the database using health checks, such as table bloats, and database size. Information extracted from the system catalog can be employed in monitoring solutions and in dynamic SQL. This chapter will discuss some tasks that a developer and administrator need to execute on a daily basis, for example, cleaning up database data and unused objects, building an index automatically, and monitoring database objects access.

The following topics will be covered in this chapter:

- An overview of the system catalog
- System catalog for administrators
- Using system catalog for database cleanup
- using the system catalog for performance tuning
- Selective dump for a certain view dependency tree

The system catalog

PostgreSQL describes all database objects using the meta information stored in database relations. These relations hold information about tables, views, functions, indexes, **foreign-data wrappers (FDWs)**, triggers, constraints, rules, users, groups, and so on. This information is stored in the pg_catalog schema, and to make it more readable by humans, PostgreSQL also provides the information_schema schema, in which the meta information is wrapped and organized into views.

In the `psql` client, users can see exactly what is happening behind the scenes when a certain meta command is executed, such as `\z`, by enabling `ECHO_HIDDEN`. The `ECHO_HIDDEN` or `-E` switch allows users to study the system catalog tables of PostgreSQL. You need to run the following command:

```
postgres=# \set ECHO_HIDDEN
postgres=# \d
********* QUERY **********
SELECT n.nspname as "Schema",
  c.relname as "Name",
  CASE c.relkind WHEN 'r' THEN 'table' WHEN 'v' THEN 'view' WHEN 'm' THEN
'materialized view' WHEN 'i' THEN 'index' WHEN 'S' THEN 'sequence' WHEN 's'
THEN 'special' WHEN 'f' THEN 'foreign table' WHEN 'p' THEN 'table' WHEN 'I'
THEN 'index' END as "Type",
  pg_catalog.pg_get_userbyid(c.relowner) as "Owner"
FROM pg_catalog.pg_class c
     LEFT JOIN pg_catalog.pg_namespace n ON n.oid = c.relnamespace
WHERE c.relkind IN ('r','p','v','m','S','f','')
     AND n.nspname <> 'pg_catalog'
     AND n.nspname <> 'information_schema'
     AND n.nspname !~ '^pg_toast'
  AND pg_catalog.pg_table_is_visible(c.oid)
ORDER BY 1,2;
**************************
```

As seen in the preceding example, when the `\d` meta command is used, the query is sent to the database server backend. In addition to `ECHO_HIDDEN`, you can have a peek at the `information_schema` and `pg_catalog` views, as follows:

```
SELECT * FROM information_schema.views WHERE table_schema IN ('pg_catlog',
'information_schema');
```

The `pg_catalog` and `information_schema` schema contain hundreds of views, tables, and administration functions; for this reason, only some of the more common and heavily used catalog tables will be described.

The `pg_class` table is one of the main tables in `pg_catalog`; it stores information about various relation types, including tables, indexes, views, sequences, and composite types. The `relkind` attribute in `pg_class` specifies the relation type. The following characters are used to identify relations:

- `r`: Ordinary table
- `i`: Index
- `S`: Sequence
- `t`: TOAST table

- v: View
- m: Materialized view
- c: Composite type
- f: Foreign table
- p: Partitioned table
- I: Partitioned index

As this table is used to describe all relations, some columns are meaningless for some relation types.

You could think of **The Oversized-Attribute Storage Technique (TOAST)** as a vertical partitioning strategy. PostgreSQL does not allow tuples to span multiple pages where the page size is often 8 KB. Therefore, PostgreSQL stores, breaks, and compresses large objects into several chunks, and stores them in other tables called TOAST tables.

The relations are identified by object identifiers. These identifiers are used as primary keys in the pg_catalog schema, so it is important to know how to convert **object identifiers (OIDs)** into text to get the relation name. Also, note that the OIDs have types; for example, the regclass type is used to identify all relations stored in the pg_class, while the regprocedure type is used to identify functions. The following example shows how to convert a table name to OID and the other way around:

```
postgres=# SELECT 'pg_catalog.pg_class'::regclass::oid;
 oid
------
 1259
(1 row)
postgres=#SELECT 1259::regclass::text;
 text
----------
 pg_class
(1 row)
```

Another approach is to use pg_class and pg_namespace to get the oid as follows:

```
postgres=#SELECT c.oid FROM pg_class c join pg_namespace n ON
(c.relnamespace = n.oid) WHERE relname ='pg_class' AND nspname
='pg_catalog';
 oid
------
 1259
(1 row)
```

Another important table is `pg_attribute`; this table stores information about tables and other `pg_class` object columns. The `pg_index` table, as the name suggests, stores information about indexes. In addition, `pg_depend` and `pg_rewrite` are used to store information about dependent objects and rewrite rules for tables and views.

Another important set of tables and views are `pg_stat<*>` relations; these tables and views provide statistics regarding tables, indexes, columns, sequences, and so on. Information stored in these tables is highly valuable for debugging performance issues and usage patterns. The following query shows some of the static relations:

```
postgres=#SELECT relname, case relkind when 'r' then 'table' WHEN 'v' THEN
'VIEW' END as type FROM pg_class WHERE relname like 'pg_sta%' AND relkind
IN ('r','v') LIMIT 5 ;
        relname               | type
------------------------------+-------
 pg_statistic                 | table
 pg_stat_user_tables          | VIEW
 pg_stat_xact_user_tables     | VIEW
 pg_statio_all_tables         | VIEW
 pg_statio_sys_tables         | VIEW
```

System catalog for administrators

The following section introduces some functions and system information that are often used by database administrators. Some of these functions might be used on a daily basis, such as `pg_reload_conf()`, which is used to reload the database cluster after amending `pg_hba.conf` or `postgresql.conf`, and `pg_terminate_backend(pid)`, which is used to kill a certain process.

Getting the database cluster and client tools version

The PostgreSQL version allows the user to know the supported features and helps them to write compatible SQL queries for different versions. For example, the process ID attribute name in the `pg_stat_activity` view in PostgreSQL versions older than 9.2 is `procpid`; in PostgreSQL version 9.2, this attribute name is `pid`.

In addition, the version information provides compatibility information to client tools and the backend version. To get the database cluster, you can use the version function as follows:

```
postgres=# SELECT VERSION ();
                                                              version
-------------------------------------------------------------------------
-----------------------------------------
 PostgreSQL 11rc1 on x86_64-pc-linux-gnu, compiled by gcc (Ubuntu
 5.4.0-6ubuntu1~16.04.10) 5.4.0 20160609, 64-bit
(1 row)
```

It is also important to check the client tools version, be it pg_restore, pg_dumpall, or psql, in order to check its compatibility with the server. This can be done as follows:

```
$ pg_dump --version
pg_dump (PostgreSQL) 11.1 (Ubuntu 11.1-1.pgdg18.04+1)
```

The pg_dump utility generates dumps that can be restored on newer versions of PostgreSQL. Also, pg_dump can dump data from PostgreSQL versions older than its own version but, logically, not for a PostgreSQL server with a version newer than its own version.

Terminating and canceling user sessions

Database administrators often need to kill server processes for various reasons. For example, in certain scenarios, very slow queries running on the slave or master, which are configured using streaming replication, can break the replication.

Database connection can be terminated for several reasons, as follows:

- **The maximum number of connections is exceeded**: This happens in some cases where connections are misconfigured, such as when keeping IDLE connections open for a very long time, or when some sessions are opened but in a stale state.
- **Dropping the database**: You cannot drop a database if someone is connected to it. This is sometimes necessary in testing scenarios.
- **Very slow queries**: Very slow queries can have a cascading effect on streaming replication as well as other transactions.

PostgreSQL provides the `pg_terminate_backend(pid)` and `pg_cancel_backend(pid)` functions, while `pg_cancel_backend` only cancels the current query, and `pg_terminate_backend` kills the entire connection. The following query terminates all connections to the current database except the session connection:

```
SELECT pg_terminate_backend(pid) FROM pg_stat_activity WHERE datname =
current_database() AND pid <> pg_backend_pid();
```

The `pg_cancel_backend` function cancels the current query, but the application may run the same query again. The `pg_terminate_backend` function terminates the connection, and this can also be done via the `kill` Linux command using the SIGINT and SIGTERM signals. However, the `kill` command may be dangerous if you kill the PostgreSQL server process instead of a connection process. In addition to that, if the database administrator uses the SIGKILL signal or -9 in numeric notation, this will cause an emergency stop and put the server in recovery mode.

> It is recommended to avoid the `kill` command, and use the `pg_cancel_backend` and `pg_terminate_backend` functions provided to avoid human error.

When combining the `pg_stat_activity` view and the `pg_terminate_backend` function, you can achieve greater flexibility. For example, in streaming replication, you can detect queries that spend a lot of time on the slaves and thus cause a replication lag. Also, if a certain application is not configured properly and has a big number of idle connections, you can kill them to free memory and allow other clients to connect to the database.

Also, PostgreSQL allows for terminating the SQL statement due to timeouts. For example, in several cases, long running statements can have very bad side effects, such as blocking other statements. For example, blocking statements such as ALTER or CLUSTER commands can take a very long time, especially for large tables, and they lock other statements. Statement timeout can be set globally in `postgresql.conf`, or can be set to each session as follows:

```
SET statement_timeout to 1000;
SELECT pg_sleep(1001);
ERROR: canceling statement due to statement timeout
```

Defining and getting database cluster settings

The PostgreSQL configuration settings control several aspects of the PostgreSQL cluster. From an administration perspective, you can define the statement timeout, memory settings, connections, logging, vacuum, and planner settings. From a development point of view, these settings can help a developer optimize queries. You can use the `current_settings` function or the `show` statement for convenience, as follows:

```
SELECT current_setting('work_mem');
 current_setting
-----------------
 4MB
(1 row)

show work_mem;
 work_mem
----------
 4MB
(1 row)
```

In order to change a certain configuration value, you can simply use the SET command, as shown in the previous example. The SET command affects the whole session. In addition to that, the function `set_config(setting_name, new_value, is_local)` can be utilized. If `is_local` is `true`, the new value will only apply to the current transaction, otherwise to the current session, as follows:

```
SELECT set_config('work_mem', '8 MB', false);
```

The `set_config` function can raise an error if the setting cannot be set to the session context, such as the number of allowed connections and shared buffers, as follows:

```
SELECT set_config('shared_buffers', '1 GB', false);
ERROR: parameter "shared_buffers" cannot be changed without restarting the
server
```

In addition to `set_config`, PostgreSQL provides the ALTER SYSTEM command used to change PostgreSQL configuration parameters. The synopsis for the ALTER SYSTEM is as follows:

```
ALTER SYSTEM SET configuration_parameter { TO | = } { value | 'value' |
DEFAULT }
ALTER SYSTEM RESET configuration_parameter
ALTER SYSTEM RESET ALL
```

In case the setting value requires a system reload or restart, the setting will take effect after the system reload or restart, respectively.

The ALTER SYSTEM command requires superuser privileges. The ALTER SYSTEM command amends a file called postgresql.auto.conf. The ALTER SYSTEM name indicates that it has a global effect, and you need to reload the server configuration as follows:

```
postgres=# ALTER SYSTEM SET work_mem TO '8MB';
ALTER SYSTEM
postgres=# SHOW work_mem;
 work_mem
----------
 4MB
(1 row)

postgres=# SELECT pg_reload_conf();
 pg_reload_conf
----------------
 t
(1 row)

postgres=# SHOW work_mem;
 work_mem
----------
 8MB
(1 row)
```

The following command shows the content of postgresql.auto.conf:

```
$cat postgresql.auto.conf
# Do not edit this file manually!
# It will be overwritten by ALTER SYSTEM command.
work_mem = '8MB'
```

Finally, browsing the postgresql.conf file is a bit tricky due to the big number of PostgreSQL settings. Also, most settings have the default boot values. Therefore, getting the server configuration settings that are not assigned the default values in postgresql.conf can be easily done, as follows:

```
SELECT name, current_setting(name), source FROM pg_settings WHERE source IN
('configuration file');
            name           | current_setting                       |
source
---------------------------+---------------------------------------+----
----------------
 cluster_name              | 10/main                               |
configuration file
 DateStyle                 | ISO, DMY                              |
configuration file
```

Getting the database and database object size

Managing disk space and assigning table spaces to tables as well as databases requires knowledge of the size of the database and database objects. When performing a logical restore of a certain table, you could get information about the progress by comparing the original database table size to the one that is being restored. Finally, the database object size often gives information about bloats.

 Bloats are wasted disk space due to concurrent data manipulation. Heavily updated systems often get bloated due to the nature of MVCC. Bloats are often cleaned up by vacuum, so disabling the auto vacuum is not recommended.

To get the database size, you can get the `oid` database from the `pg_database` table and run the `du -h /data_directory/base/oid` Linux command. `data_directory` is the database cluster folder specified in the `postgresql.conf` configuration file.

 A quick look at the PostgreSQL cluster folders can be quite useful for familiarizing yourself with PostgreSQL's main concepts and operations, including configuration files. For example, to determine the creation date of a certain database, you could have a look at the `PG_VERSION` file creation date located in the database directory.

In addition to this, PostgreSQL provides the `pg_database_size` function to get the database size and the `pg_size_pretty` function to display the size in a human readable form, as follows:

```
SELECT pg_database.datname,
pg_size_pretty(pg_database_size(pg_database.datname)) AS size FROM
pg_database;
   datname       | size
-----------------+---------
 postgres        | 8093 kB
 template1       | 7481 kB
 template0       | 7481 kB
```

You can get the table size, including indexes, service relations, such as visibility map, free space map, and init, and TOAST tables, using the `pg_total_relation_size` function. If you are interested only in the table size, you can use the `pg_relation_size` function. This information helps manage table growth as well as tablespaces.

Take a look at the following query:

```
SELECT tablename,
pg_size_pretty(pg_total_relation_size(schemaname||'.'||tablename)) FROM
pg_tables LIMIT 2;
   tablename   | pg_size_pretty
---------------+----------------
 pg_statistic | 280 kB
 pg_type      | 184 kB
(2 rows)
```

Finally, to get the index size, you could use the pg_relation_size function, as follows:

```
SELECT indexrelid::regclass,
pg_size_pretty(pg_relation_size(indexrelid::regclass)) FROM pg_index LIMIT
2;
          indexrelid          | pg_size_pretty
------------------------------+----------------
 pg_toast.pg_toast_2604_index | 8192 bytes
 pg_toast.pg_toast_2606_index | 8192 bytes
(2 rows)
```

For simplicity, the psql tool also provides meta commands to get the size of the database, table, and index as follows:

- \l+: To list database information including size.
- \dtis+: The letters t, i, and s stand for table, index, and sequence, respectively. This meta command lists database objects, including tables, indexes, and sequences. The + is used to show the object size on the hard disk.

 The table size on the hard disk gives you hints about restoring the data progress of the table. Let's assume you are moving a table from one database to another using the copy command; you cannot see how many rows were inserted, but you can compare the two table sizes, which indicates your progress.

Cleaning up the database

Often, a database can contain several unused objects or very old data. Cleaning up these objects helps administrators perform a backup of images more quickly. From a development point of view, unused objects are noise because they affect the refactoring process.

In database applications, you need to keep the database clean, since unused database objects might hinder quick development due to those objects' dependencies. To clean the database, you need to identify the unused database objects, including tables, views, indexes, and functions.

Table statistics, such as the number of live rows, index scans, and sequential scans, can help identify empty and unused tables. Note that the following queries are based on statistics, so the results need to be validated. The pg_stat_user_tables table provides this information, and the following query shows empty tables by checking the number of tuples:

```
SELECT relname FROM pg_stat_user_tables WHERE n_live_tup= 0;
```

 All information based on PostgreSQL statistics is not one hundred percent bulletproof because the statistics might not be up to date.

To find the empty columns or unused columns, you can have a look at the null_fraction attribute of the pg_stats table. If the null_fraction equals one, then the column is completely empty, as follows:

```
SELECT schemaname, tablename, attname FROM pg_stats WHERE null_frac= 1 and
schemaname NOT IN ('pg_catalog', 'information_schema');
```

To find the useless indexes, two steps can be applied:

1. The first technique is to determine whether an index is duplicated or overlapped with another index
2. The second step is to assess whether the index is used based on the index statistics

The following query can be used to assess whether an index is used based on catalog statistics. Note that the constraint indexes—the unique constraints and primary keys—are excluded because we need these indexes even though they are not used, as follows:

```
SELECT schemaname, relname, indexrelname FROM pg_stat_user_indexes s JOIN
pg_index i ON s.indexrelid = i.indexrelid WHERE idx_scan=0 AND NOT
indisunique AND NOT indisprimary;
```

Overlapping index attributes can be used to identify duplicate indexes. The following SQL code compares the index attributes with each other and returns indexes that overlap attributes:

```
WITH index_info AS (
SELECT
    pg_get_indexdef(indexrelid) AS index_def,
    indexrelid::regclass
    index_name ,
    indrelid::regclass table_name, array_agg(attname order by attnum) AS
index_att
 FROM
     pg_index i JOIN
     pg_attribute a ON i.indexrelid = a.attrelid
GROUP BY
     pg_get_indexdef(indexrelid), indrelid, indexrelid
 ) SELECT DISTINCT
     CASE WHEN a.index_name > b.index_name THEN a.index_def ELSE b.index_def
END AS index_def,
     CASE WHEN a.index_name > b.index_name THEN a.index_name ELSE
b.index_name END AS index_name,
     CASE WHEN a.index_name > b.index_name THEN b.index_def ELSE a.index_def
END AS overlap_index_def,
     CASE WHEN a.index_name > b.index_name THEN b.index_name ELSE
a.index_name END AS overlap_index_name,
     a.index_att = b.index_att as full_match,
     a.table_name
 FROM
     index_info a INNER JOIN
     index_info b ON (a.index_name != b.index_name AND a.table_name =
b.table_name AND a.index_att && b.index_att );
```

To test the preceding query, let's create an overlapping index as follows and execute the query:

```
CREATE TABLE test_index_overlap(a int, b int);
CREATE INDEX ON test_index_overlap (a,b);
CREATE INDEX ON test_index_overlap (b,a);
```

The result of the preceding query is as follows:

```
-[ RECORD 1 ]-----+------------------------------------------------------
----------------------
index_def         | CREATE INDEX test_index_overlap_b_a_idx ON
test_index_overlap USING btree (b, a)
index_name        | test_index_overlap_b_a_idx
overlap_index_def | CREATE INDEX test_index_overlap_a_b_idx ON
test_index_overlap USING btree (a, b)
```

```
overlap_index_name| test_index_overlap_a_b_idx
full_match        | f
table_name        | test_index_overlap
```

Cleaning up unused views and functions is a little bit tricky. By default, PostgreSQL collects statistics about indexes and tables, but not functions. To enable statistics collection on functions, the `track_functions` setting needs to be enabled. The statistics on functions can be found in the `pg_stat_user_functions` table.

For views, there are no statistics collected unless the views are materialized. In order to assess whether a view is used, we need to do this manually. This can be done by rewriting the view and joining it with a function with a certain side effect. The joined function, for example, updates a table and increases the number of times the view is accessed, or raises a certain `log` message. To test this technique, let's write a simple function that raises a `log`, as follows:

```
CREATE OR REPLACE FUNCTION monitor_view_usage (view_name TEXT) RETURNS
BOOLEAN AS $$
BEGIN
 RAISE LOG 'The view % is used on % by % ', view_name, current_time,
session_user;
 RETURN TRUE;
END;
$$LANGUAGE plpgsql cost .001;
```

Now, let's assume that we want to drop the `dummy_view` view; however, there is uncertainty regarding whether a certain application depends on it, as follows:

```
CREATE OR REPLACE VIEW dummy_view AS
SELECT dummy_text FROM (VALUES('dummy')) as dummy(dummy_text);
```

To ensure that the view is not used, the view should be rewritten as follows, with the `monitor_view_usage` function used:

```
-- Recreate the view and inject the monitor_view_usage
CREATE OR REPLACE VIEW dummy_view AS
SELECT dummy_text FROM (VALUES('dummy')) as dummy(dummy_text) cross join
monitor_view_usage('dummy_view');
```

If the view is accessed, an entry in the `log` file should appear as follows:

```
$ tail /var/log/postgresql/postgresql-10-main.log
2017-10-10 16:54:15.375 CEST [21874] postgres@postgres LOG: The view
dummy_view is used on 16:54:15.374124+02 by postgres
```

Data cleanup

Cleaning up bloated tables and indexes can be done by invoking the VACUUM FULL statement for tables and REINDEX for indexes; VACUUM FULL requires exclusive lock, which means there will be an outage and the table is not accessible. There are third-party tools, such as pg_repack, which can help in solving such issues.

You can take a look at the Bucardo check_postgres Nagios plugin code at https:// bucardo.org/wiki/Check_postgres to understand how bloats in tables and indexes can be calculated. Another useful contribution module is pgstattuple, which contains many functions to get statistics about tuples. Refer to https://www.postgresql.org/docs/ current/pgstattuple.html.

Cleaning up data is an important topic; often, the data life cycle is not defined when creating a database application. This leads to tons of outdated data. Unclean data hinders several processes, such as database refactoring. Also, it can create side effects for all processes in the company, such as inaccurate report results, billing issues, and unauthorized access.

Several examples were introduced to determine unused objects, but that is not all. The data itself should be cleaned, and the data life cycle should be defined. For unclean data, there are several options; however, let's focus only on duplicated rows here, due to the missing unique and primary key constraints. The first step is to identify the tables that do not have unique and primary key constraints. This is quite easy using the information schema, as follows:

```
SELECT table_catalog, table_schema, table_name  FROM
information_schema.tables WHERE table_schema NOT IN
('information_schema','pg_catalog')
EXCEPT
SELECT table_catalog, table_schema, table_name FROM
information_schema.table_constraints WHERE
  constraint_type IN ('PRIMARY KEY', 'UNIQUE') AND table_schema NOT IN
('information_schema','pg_catalog');
```

The second step is to identify the tables that really contain duplicates; this can be done by aggregating the data in the table. To do this, let's create a table with some duplicates, as follows:

```
CREATE TABLE duplicate AS SELECT (random () * 9 + 1)::INT as f1 , (random
() * 9 + 1)::INT as f2 FROM generate_series (1,40);
SELECT count(*), f1, f2 FROM duplicate GROUP BY f1, f2;

 count | f1 | f2
-------+----+----
```

```
   2 | 7  | 4
   3 | 5  | 4
   2 | 2  | 6
(3 rows)
```

The tricky part is deleting the duplicates, as the rows are identical. To delete duplicates, a certain row needs to be marked to stay, and the rest need to be deleted. This can be achieved using the ctid column. In PostgreSQL, each row has a header, and the ctid column is the physical location of the row version within the table. Thus, the ctid column can be used as a temporary row identifier because this identifier may change after running maintenance commands such as CLUSTER.

To delete the duplicate, you can use the DELETE USING statement as follows:

```
SELECT ctid, f1, f2 FROM duplicate where (f1, f2) =(7,4)
  ctid   | f1 | f2
---------+----+----
 (0,11)  | 7  | 4
 (0,40)  | 7  | 4
(2 rows)
BEGIN;
DELETE FROM duplicate a USING duplicate b WHERE a.f1= b.f1 and a.f2= b.f2
and a.ctid > b.ctid;
SELECT ctid, f1, f2 FROM duplicate where (f1, f2) =(7,4);
  ctid   | f1 | f2
---------+----+----
 (0,11)  | 7  | 4
(1 row)
end;
```

Do not forget to use an explicit transaction block when manipulating data. This will allow you to rollback changes if you make an error.

There are several other approaches to clean up duplicate rows. For example, you can use the CREATE TABLE and SELECT DISTINCT statements to create a table with a unique set of rows. Then, you can drop the original table and rename the table created after the original table, as shown in the following example:

```
CREATE TABLE <tmp> AS SELECT DISTINCT * FROM <orig_tbl>;
DROP TABLE <orig_tbl>;
ALTER TABLE <tmp> RENAME TO <orig_tbl>;
```

Alternatively, you can speed up the performance by using the UNLOGGED table as follows:

```
CREATE UNLOGGED TABLE <tmp> AS SELECT DISTINCT * FROM <orig_tbl>;
DROP TABLE <orig_tbl>;
ALTER TABLE <tmp> RENAME TO <orig_tbl>;
ALTER TABLE <tmp> SET LOGGED;
```

Note that this approach might be faster than the approach represented in the preceding example. However, this technique may not work if there are other objects depending on the table that need to be dropped, such as views, and indexes.

If you are unfamiliar with the DELETE USING statement, here is another way to do the same trick using CTEs (however, note that the first query should be faster because it does not aggregate data and only scans the table once):

```
with should_not_delete as ( SELECT min(ctid) FROM duplicate group by f1, f2
)
    DELETE FROM duplicate WHERE ctid NOT IN (SELECT min FROM
should_not_delete);
```

Tuning for performance

High performance in PostgreSQL can be achieved by having good configuration settings and proper physical schemas, including indexes. Execution plans depend on the statistics gathered from the tables; fortunately, in PostgreSQL, you can control the behavior of the statistic collection.

For developers, it is important to get good performance. When handling foreign keys, there are two recommendations for increasing performance, which are as follows:

- **Always index foreign keys**: Indexing a table for foreign keys allows PostgreSQL to fetch data from the table using an index scan.
- **Increase the column statistic target on foreign keys**: This is also applicable to all predicates because it allows PostgreSQL to have a better estimation of the number of rows. The default statistic target is 100, and the maximum is 10,000. Increasing the statistics target makes the ANALYZE command slower.

Both of the preceding approaches require the identification of foreign keys. The pg_catalog.pg_constraint table can be used to look up table constraints. To get all foreign key constrains, you can simply run the following query:

```
SELECT * FROM pg_constraint WHERE contype = 'f';
```

Also, from the previous examples, we can see how to get overlapping indexes; you can combine information from both tables to get foreign keys that do not have indexes, as follows:

```
SELECT conrelid::regclass AS relation_name,
    conname AS constraint_name,
    reltuples::bigint AS number_of_rows,
    indkey AS index_attributes,
    conkey AS constraint_attributes,
    CASE WHEN conkey && string_to_array(indkey::text, ' ')::SMALLINT[] THEN
FALSE ELSE TRUE END as might_require_index
FROM pg_constraint JOIN pg_class ON (conrelid = pg_class.oid) JOIN
    pg_index ON indrelid = conrelid
WHERE
    contype = 'f';
```

Note that if `indkey` overlaps with `conkey`, we might not need to add an index; however, this should be validated by the usage pattern. Also, in the preceding example, the number of `reltuples` is selected, as this is an important factor in determining index creation, because performing sequential scans on big tables is quite costly. In addition to this, another option is to use the table statistics for sequential scans.

After identifying the foreign keys, you can use the CREATE INDEX command and ALTER TABLE to create indexes and alter default statistics, respectively.

Selective dump

When refactoring a certain view, including adding a new column or changing the column type, you need to refactor all the views that depend on this particular view. Unfortunately, PostgreSQL does not provide the means to create a logical dump of a dependent object.

PostgreSQL provides `pg_dump` to dump a certain database or a specific set of objects in a database. Also, in development, it is recommended that you keep the code in a Git repository.

 Plan your development cycle in advance, including development, testing, staging, and production. Use code versioning tools such as Git, and database migration tools such as Flyway, to define your processes. This will save you a lot of time.

Unfortunately, often the SQL code for legacy applications is not maintained in the version control system and in migration tools such as Flyway. In this case, if you need to change a certain view definition or even a column type, it is necessary to identify the affected views, dump them, and then restore them.

The first step is to identify the views to be dropped and restored. Depending on the task, you can write different scripts; a common pattern is to drop the views depending on a certain view, table, or table column. The base pg_catalog tables, pg_depend and pg_rewrite, store the dependency information and view rewriting rules. More human readable information can be found in information_schema.view_table_usage.

Let's assume that there are several views that depend on each other, as shown in the following diagram, and the base view **a** needs to be refactored, which means dropped and created:

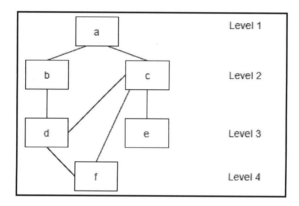

To generate this tree of dependency, you can execute the following queries:

```
CREATE TABLE test_view_dep AS SELECT 1;
CREATE VIEW a AS SELECT 1 FROM test_view_dep;
CREATE VIEW b AS SELECT 1 FROM a;
CREATE VIEW c AS SELECT 1 FROM a;
CREATE VIEW d AS SELECT 1 FROM b,c;
CREATE VIEW e AS SELECT 1 FROM c;
CREATE VIEW f AS SELECT 1 FROM d,c;
```

Now, to solve the dependency tree, a recursive query will be used, as follows:

```
CREATE OR REPLACE FUNCTION get_dependency (schema_name text, view_name
text) RETURNS TABLE (schema_name text, view_name text, level int) AS $$
WITH RECURSIVE view_tree(parent_schema, parent_view, child_schema,
child_view, level) as
(
```

```
    SELECT parent.view_schema, parent.view_name ,parent.table_schema,
parent.table_name, 1
    FROM information_schema.view_table_usage parent
    WHERE parent.view_schema = $1 AND parent.view_name = $2
    UNION ALL
    SELECT child.view_schema, child.view_name, child.table_schema,
child.table_name, parent.level + 1
    FROM view_tree parent JOIN information_schema.view_table_usage child ON
child.table_schema =                parent.parent_schema AND child.table_name
= parent.parent_view
)
SELECT DISTINCT
    parent_schema, parent_view, level
FROM (
  SELECT parent_schema, parent_view, max (level) OVER (PARTITION BY
parent_schema, parent_view) as max_level,level
  FROM view_tree) AS FOO
WHERE level = max_level
ORDER BY 3 ASC;
$$
LANGUAGE SQL;
```

In the preceding query, the inner part of the query is used to calculate dependency levels, while the outer part of the query is used to eliminate duplicates. The following shows the dependencies for the view a in the correct order. The result for executing the previous function for the view a is as follows:

```
SELECT * FROM get_dependency('public', 'a');
 schema_name | view_name | level
-------------+-----------+-------
 public      | a         | 1
 public      | b         | 2
 public      | c         | 2
 public      | d         | 3
 public      | e         | 3
 public      | f         | 4
(6 rows)
```

To dump the view's definition based on the defined level, you can use pg_dump with the -t option, which is used to dump a certain relation. So, to dump the views in the previous example, you can use the following trick in bash:

```
$relations=$(psql -t -c "SELECT string_agg (' -t ' ||
quote_ident(schema_name) || '.' || quote_ident(view_name), ' ' ORDER BY
level ) FROM get_dependency ('public'::text, 'a'::text)")
$echo $relations
-t public.a -t public.b -t public.c -t public.d -t public.e -t public.f
```

```
$pg_dump -s  $relations
 --
-- PostgreSQL database dump
--

-- Dumped from database version 10.0
-- Dumped by pg_dump version 10.0

SET statement_timeout = 0;
SET lock_timeout = 0;
SET idle_in_transaction_session_timeout = 0;
SET client_encoding = 'UTF8';
SET standard_conforming_strings = on;
SET check_function_bodies = false;
SET client_min_messages = warning;
SET row_security = off;

SET search_path = public, pg_catalog;

--
-- Name: a; Type: VIEW; Schema: public; Owner: postgres
--

CREATE VIEW a AS
 SELECT 1
   FROM test_view_dep;
...
```

The psql uses the -t option to return tuples only, and the string aggregate function is used to generate the list of views that need to be dumped based on the level order. In this case, we can guarantee the generation of a SQL script with the correct order of view creation.

Summary

Catalog tables provide invaluable information for maintaining and automating database administration tasks. For example, in the previous section, we were able to dump a tree of dependent objects in the correct order. In addition to that, you can automate daily task checks, such as bloats, locks, size, and database health. Also, by using the statistical table, we were able to detect unused indexes, as well as potential columns that require indexing, such as foreign key columns.

The PostgreSQL catalog contains meta information about PostgreSQL databases and objects. This information can be retrieved and manipulated using SQL statements. However, it is not recommended to manipulate the data directly in a catalog schema. PostgreSQL also provides a convenient way to extract data by providing user friendly information in `information_schema`.

With the help of the PostgreSQL catalog, you can write a complete book of recipes, and you can have recipes in your backlog for database cluster health, including memory consumption, idle connections, database size, and processes status. In addition to that, you can have recipes for handling roles and role membership, object permissions, lock detection, and streaming replication health.

The next chapter discusses several approaches to optimize performance. It presents PostgreSQL cluster configuration settings, which are used in tuning the whole cluster's performance. Also, it presents common mistakes in writing queries and discusses several approaches for increasing performance, such as using indexes or table partitioning, and constraint exclusion.

Questions

1. How can you display the queries that are generated by the `psql` client to the PostgreSQL server?
2. What is the purpose of the `pg_class` table? What is the difference between `pg_catalog` and `information_schema`?
3. What does the abbreviation TOAST stand for and what is it used for?
4. You work as an administrator and you would like to clean up unused indexes, What are the criteria you can use to find these indexes? Why is it important to monitor usage indexes?
5. Assume that you have a table with duplicate data due to the lack of unique and primary key constraints. Which column can be used to distinguish the rows?
6. Can a table have duplicate data even if it has a primary key?
7. What is the difference between the `pg_cancel_backend` and `pg_terminate_backend` functions?
8. Which is easier to find: unused tables or unused views? And why?
9. List the `contype` constraint types found in the `pg_constraint` table, and give the full name for each type.

13
Optimizing Database Performance

There are several aspects of optimizing database performance, such as hardware configuration, network settings, database configuration, rewriting SQL queries, and maintaining indexes. In this chapter, we'll focus only on basic configuration and rewriting queries.

Generally speaking, tuning database performance requires knowledge about the system's nature; for example, we need to know whether the database system can be used for **online analytical processing (OLAP)** or **online transactional processing (OLTP)**. The database system may be **IO-** or **CPU**-bound; these define the whole database cluster setup, such as the number of **CPU**s, **CPU** power, **RAID** configuration, amount of **RAM**, and the database cluster's configuration. Once the database server is configured, you could use a benchmark framework, such as `pgbench`, to calculate the number of **transactions per second (TPS)** for the database server setup.

The second step in optimizing database performance is carried out after the system is up and running, and often periodically. In this state, you could set up a monitoring system or log analysis, such as a `pgbadger`, **PostgreSQL Workload Analyzer (PoWA)**, or `pg_stat_statements`, to find slow queries, the most time-consuming queries, and so on.

To optimize a slow query, it should be analyzed first. If the query is poorly written, rewriting it might be enough. Otherwise, missing indexes can be created, server configuration settings can be amended, the physical structure can be refactored, and so on.

In this chapter, we'll cover the following topics:

- PostgreSQL configuration tuning
- Tuning performance for write
- Tuning performance for read
- Detecting problems in query plans
- Common mistakes in writing queries
- Table partitioning
- Query rewriting

PostgreSQL configuration tuning

PostgreSQL's default configuration values aren't suitable for a production environment; several default values are often undersized. In developing PostgreSQL applications, it's a good idea to have a test system that's configured very closely to a production environment to get accurate performance measures. In any PostgreSQL environment, the following configuration should be reviewed. For example, it's very useful to have a staging server similar in setup to the production server, especially the following properties:

- Server hardware or virtualization
- Operating system configuration and tweaks
- PostgreSQL version
- PostgreSQL configuration

Maximum number of connections

The maximum number of connections is an important parameter when configuring a database. Each client connection consumes memory, which also affects the total amount of memory that can be allocated for other purposes. The `max_connections` configuration parameter's default value is `100`; lowering this value allows the database administrator to increase the `work_mem` setting. In general, it's a good practice to use connection-pooling software to reduce the amount of memory used and increase performance, as killing and establishing a connection wastes time. There are a lot of connection-pooling tools, but the most mature ones are as follows:

- PgBouncer
- Pgpool-II

Also, you could use connection pooling on the business level. For example, for Java, there are many alternatives for connection pooling, such as Hikari, the Apache Tomcat connection pool, dbcp2, and c3p0.

Memory settings

There are several settings for controlling memory consumption and the way memory is consumed, and these settings are listed here:

- **Shared buffers (shared_buffers):** The amount of memory the database server uses for quick access to data. This amount of RAM is locked for the PostgreSQL server for reading and writing data. The default value for shared buffers is 128 MB; however, it's recommended to set it to around 25% of the total memory. Sometimes, increasing shared_buffers to a very high value leads to an increase in performance, because the database can be cached completely in the RAM. However, the drawback of increasing this value too much is that you can't allocate memory for CPU operations such as sorting and hashing.

- **Working memory (work_mem):** The amount of memory to be used by internal sort operations and hash tables. The default value is 4 MB; for CPU-bound operations, it's important to increase this value. The work_mem setting is linked with the number of connections and query complexity. If a query is complex and several parallel sort operations are forked, each operation will be allowed to use as much memory as this value specifies. Working memory is used to sort and hash, so it affects queries that use the ORDER BY, DISTINCT, UNION, and EXCEPT constructs. To test your working method, you could analyze a query that uses sort and take a look at whether the sort operation uses the memory or hard disk, as follows:

```
EXPLAIN ANALYZE SELECT n FROM generate_series(1,5) as foo(n) order
by n;
Sort (cost=59.83..62.33 rows=1000 width=4) (actual
time=0.075..0.075 rows=5 loops=1)
Sort Key: n
Sort Method: quicksort Memory: 25kB
-> Function Scan on generate_series foo (cost=0.00..10.00
rows=1000 width=4) (actual time=0.018..0.018 rows=5 loops=1)"
Total runtime: 0.100 ms
```

Disk settings

There are several hard disk settings that can boost I/O performance; however, this boost comes with a penalty. For example, the fsync setting forces each transaction to be written to the hard disk after each commit. Turning this off will increase performance, especially for bulk-upload operations. Disabling fsync can lead to serious problems, such as data consistency, in the case of power failure and crashes. A max_wal_size of a small value might lead to a performance penalty in write-heavy systems; on the other hand, increasing the max_wal_size setting to a high value will increase recovery time.

The recovery time is the amount of time required for the PostgreSQL cluster to start after a power failure, crash, or after promoting a stand-by server. PostgreSQL depends on WAL files to provide durability. That means all changes are written first to the log, also known as WAL files, and then to the data files. In the event of a crash, the server reads the WAL files (logs) in a specific order and applies the changes to the data files until all WAL files are processed; during this time, the server isn't responsive and is in recovery state.

In specific cases, such as bulk-upload operations, performance can be increased by altering hard-disk settings, changing the logging configuration to log minimal info, and disabling auto-vacuuming; however, after the bulk operation is over, you shouldn't forget to reset the server configurations and run the VACUUM ANALYZE command.

Planner-related settings

Effective cache size (effective_cache_size) should be set to an estimate of how much memory is available for disk caching in the operating system, and within the database, after taking into account what's used by the operating system and other applications. This value for a dedicated postgres server is around 50% to 70% of the total RAM.

Also, you could play with a planner setting, such as random_page_cost, to favor an Index Scan over sequential scans. The random_page_cost setting's default value is 4.0. In high-end SAN/NAS technologies, you could set this value to 3, and for SSD, you could use a random page cost of 1.5 to 2.5. The preceding list of parameters is minimal; in reality, you need to also configure the logging, checkpoint, WAL settings, and vacuum settings.

Note that some parameters can't be changed easily on production systems because they require a system restart, such as max_connections, shared_buffers, and fsync. In other cases, such as work_mem, it can be specified in the session, giving the developer the option of tuning queries that need specific work_mem.

Benchmarking is your friend

pgbench is a simple program used to execute a prepared set of SQL commands to calculate the average transaction rate (transactions per second). pgbench is an implementation of the **Transaction Processing Performance Council (TPC) TPC-B** standard. pgbench can also be customized with scripts. In general, when using a benching framework, you need to set it up on a different client to not steal the RAM and CPU from the tested server. Also, you should run pgbench several times with different load scenarios and configuration settings. Finally, in addition to pgbench, there are several open source implementations for different benchmarking standards, such as **TPC-C** and **TPC-H**. The pgbench synopsis is pgbench [options] dbname. The -i option is used to initialize the database with test tables, and the -s option determines the database scale factor, or simply the number of rows in each table.

A default output of pgbench using a default scale factor on a virtual machine with one CPU looks similar to the following:

```
$pgbench -i test_database
 creating tables...
 100000 of 100000 tuples (100%) done (elapsed 0.71 s, remaining 0.00 s).
 vacuum...
```

Finally, the pgbench manual pages (pgbench --help) explain the different query options.

Tuning performance for write

High write loads can have different patterns. For example, this can be a result of writing events to PostgreSQL or it can be a result of a bulk load from a database dump or an **ETL** job. You can tune PostgreSQL for high write loads by doing the following:

- **Hardware configuration**:
  - You should use RAID 1+0 instead of RAID 5 or 6. RAID 10 has a much better performance for heavy writes. Also, it's better to store transaction logs (pg_xlog) on a separate hard disk.
  - You can use SSD hard disks with **write-back cache** (**WBC**), which significantly increases write performance. Also make sure your SSDs can persist cached data on power failure.

- **PostgreSQL server setting**:
    - `fsync`: By default, `fsync` is on. This parameter makes sure that the database can be recovered in the event of a hardware crash. `fsync` makes sure that the data is actually written on the hard disk. You can disable this option if you can trust your hardware. Hardware failure might lead to corrupt data if this option is disabled.
    - `synchronous_commit` and `commit_delay`: When `synchronous_commit` is enabled by default, the transaction will wait until the WAL file is written to the hard disk to report `success` to the client. This will help to boost the performance of systems that have heavy, concurrent small transactions. `commit_delay` is used to delay WAL flushing in microseconds. Combining both will reduce the effect of `fsync`. Unlike disabling `fsync`, a hardware crash won't cause data to be corrupted, but might cause data to be lost.
    - `max_wal_size`: Increasing `max_wal_size` causes a performance gain special in heavy write loads. `max_wal_size` affects the checkpoint-triggering frequency. Setting this value very high causes a slow recovery in crash scenarios.
    - `wal_buffers`: This setting is disabled by default (auto-tuning). It's used to store WAL data that isn't written to a hard disk. Increasing this value helps a busy server with several concurrent clients. It's good to select a size around 3% of `shard_buffers` but not less than 64 KB. The maximum value of this setting shouldn't be more than the size of a WAL segment, which is typically 16 MB. If your system isn't tight in memory, it's good to set it to the maximum, that is 16 MB.
    - `maintenece_work_mem`: This setting doesn't directly affect the performance of data insertion, but it increases the performance of creating and maintaining indexes. Increasing the value of `maintenece_work_mem` increases the performance of the `INSERT` operation indirectly, especially if the target table has indexes.
    - **Other settings**: You can disable several other settings to increase performance, for example, logging and logging collection can increase performance if you're logging data heavily. Also, auto-vacuum can be disabled on bulk-load scenarios to not interrupt the loading process.

- **DDL and DML statements**:
  - In bulk-load scenarios, there are a lot of tricks to speed up performance. For example, you can disable triggers, indexes, and foreign keys on the table that you need to copy. Also, you can use an UNLOGGED table and then convert it into a logged table using ALTER TABLE <table name> SET LOGGED;.
  - For a heavy insert scenario, there are several common tricks. The first trick is to increase the batch size of each transaction. This is quite useful because it will decrease the delay caused by synchronous_commit. In addition, it will preserve transaction IDs; thus, less vacuum will be required to prevent transaction-ID wraparound. The second trick is to use the COPY command. The JDBC driver, CopyManager, can be used for this purpose. Finally, it's a good practice to use prepared statements. Prepared statements are faster to execute since the statements are precompiled on the PostgreSQL side.
- **External tools**: For bulk uploads, you can use pg_bulkload, which is quite fast.

To sum up, for a heavy write system, it's good to write to the hard disk in batches instead of single INSERT SQL statements. Also, it's better to use a COPY statement instead of an INSERT statement. Finally, you can parallelize statements using several sessions instead of one session. Starting from PostgreSQL 9.3, you can use COPY with the FREEZE option, which is used often for initial data loading. The FREEZE option violates the MVCC concept in PostgreSQL, which means the data is immediately visible to other sessions after it's loaded.

To test the effect of fsync, let's prepare a SQL script for pgbench, as follows:

```
$ cat test.sql
set aid random(1, 100000 * :scale)
set bid random(1, 1 * :scale)
set tid random(1, 10 * :scale)
set delta random(-5000, 5000)
BEGIN;
UPDATE pgbench_accounts SET abalance = abalance + :delta WHERE aid = :aid;
UPDATE pgbench_branches SET bbalance = bbalance + :delta WHERE bid = :bid;
INSERT INTO pgbench_history (tid, bid, aid, delta, mtime) VALUES (:tid,
:bid, :aid, :delta, CURRENT_TIMESTAMP);
END;
```

Now let's run `pgbench` before making any changes to test the system's base performance. Note that, in this test, all settings have default values:

```
$pgbench -t 1000 -c 15 -f test.sql
starting vacuum...end.
transaction type: test.sql
scaling factor: 1
query mode: simple
number of clients: 15
number of threads: 1
number of transactions per client: 1000
number of transactions actually processed: 15000/15000
latency average = 18.455 ms
tps = 812.801437 (including connections establishing)
tps = 813.032862 (excluding connections establishing)
```

To test the effect of disabling `fsync`, you can alter the system settings and restart the server as follows:

```
$ psql -U postgres << EOF
> ALTER SYSTEM RESET ALL;
> ALTER SYSTEM SET fsync to off;
> EOF
ALTER SYSTEM
ALTER SYSTEM

$sudo /etc/init.d/postgresql restart
[ ok ] Restarting postgresql (via systemctl): postgresql.service.

$ pgbench -t 1000 -c 15 -f test.sql
starting vacuum...end.
transaction type: test.sql
scaling factor: 1
query mode: simple
number of clients: 15
number of threads: 1
number of transactions per client: 1000
number of transactions actually processed: 15000/15000
latency average = 11.976 ms
tps = 1252.552937 (including connections establishing)
tps = 1253.082492 (excluding connections establishing)
```

To test the effect of `synchronous_commit` and `commit_delay`, you can alter the settings as follows:

```
$ psql -U postgres << EOF
> ALTER SYSTEM RESET ALL;
> ALTER SYSTEM SET synchronous_commit to off;
```

```
> ALTER SYSTEM SET commit_delay to 100000;
> EOF
ALTER SYSTEM
ALTER SYSTEM
ALTER SYSTEM
$ sudo /etc/init.d/postgresql restart
[ ok ] Restarting postgresql (via systemctl): postgresql.service.

$ pgbench -t 1000 -c 15 -f test.sql
starting vacuum...end.
transaction type: test.sql
scaling factor: 1
query mode: simple
number of clients: 15
number of threads: 1
number of transactions per client: 1000
number of transactions actually processed: 15000/15000
latency average = 12.521 ms
tps = 1197.960750 (including connections establishing)
tps = 1198.416907 (excluding connections establishing)
```

Tuning performance for read

PostgreSQL provides the means to figure out why a certain query is slow. Behind the scenes, PostgreSQL analyzes tables, collects statistics from them, and builds histograms using auto-vacuuming. Auto-vacuuming, in general, is used to recover disk space, update table statistics, and perform other maintenance tasks, such as preventing transaction-ID wraparound. Table statistics allow PostgreSQL to pick up an execution plan with the least cost. The least cost is calculated by taking into account the I/O and, naturally, the CPU cost. Also, PostgreSQL enables users to see the generated execution plan by providing the EXPLAIN command.

For beginners, it's extremely useful to write the same query in different ways and compare the results. For example, in some cases, the NOT IN construct can be converted to LEFT JOIN or NOT EXIST. Also, the IN construct can be rewritten using INNER JOIN as well as EXISTS. Writing the query in several ways teaches the developer when to use or avoid a certain construct and what the conditions that favor a certain construct are. In general, the NOT IN construct can sometimes cause performance issues because the planner can't use indexes to evaluate the query.

Another important issue is to keep tracking new SQL commands and features. The PostgreSQL development community is very active, and its contributions are often targeted toward solving common issues. For example, the LATERAL JOIN construct, which was introduced in PostgreSQL 9.3, can be used to optimize certain GROUP BY and LIMIT scenarios.

Explaining the command and execution plans

The first step in tuning PostgreSQL queries is to understand how to read the execution plans generated by the EXPLAIN command. The EXPLAIN command shows the execution plan of a statement and how data from tables is scanned; for example: a table might be scanned using an index or sequential scan. Also, it shows how tables are joined, the join method, and the estimated number of rows.

The EXPLAIN command also has several options; the ANALYZE option causes the statement to be executed and returns the actual time and number of rows. Finally, the EXPLAIN command can give insights into a buffer's usage and caching. The synopsis for the EXPLAIN command is as follows, where the option can be one of the following: ANALYZE, VERBOSE, COSTS, BUFFERS, TIMING, SUMMARY, or FORMAT :

```
\h EXPLAIN
Description: show the execution plan of a statement
Syntax:
EXPLAIN [ ( option [, ...] ) ] statement
EXPLAIN [ ANALYZE ] [ VERBOSE ] statement
```

To experiment with the EXPLAIN command, you can create a simple table and populate it with data, as follows:

```
postgres=# CREATE TABLE guru ( id INT PRIMARY KEY, name TEXT NOT NULL );
CREATE TABLE
postgres=# INSERT INTO guru SELECT n , md5 (random()::text) FROM
generate_series (1, 100000) AS foo(n);
INSERT 0 100000
postgres=# -- To update table statistics
postgres=# ANALYSE guru;
ANALYZE
```

To get the execution plan of selecting all the records for the table guru, you can use the EXPLAIN command, as follows:

```
postgres=# EXPLAIN SELECT * FROM guru;
 QUERY PLAN
-------------------------------------------------------------
```

```
Seq Scan on guru (cost=0.00..1834.00 rows=100000 width=37)
(1 row)
```

The execution plan is only a one-node sequential scan on the guru table, as shown in the preceding code. The number of rows is estimated correctly, as we analyzed the table after insertion. Auto-vacuum is important for keeping your database's statistics up to date.

Certainly, incorrect statistics mean poor execution plans. After database bulk operations, it's good to run the ANALYZE command to update the statistics. Also, you could control the data sampling performed with the ANALYZE command, using the following:

```
ALTER TABLE <table name> ALTER COLUMN <column name> SET STATISTICS
<integer>;
```

Increasing column statistics allows for a better estimation of rows, but also makes the auto-vacuum process slower. The cost is an estimation of the effort required to execute the query. In the preceding example, 0.00 is the cost to retrieve the first row, while 1834.00 is the cost to retrieve all rows, which is calculated as follows: (relpages * seq_page cost) + (reltuples * cpu_tuple_cost). The number of relation pages (relpages) and the number of rows in relation (reltuples) can be found in pg_class. seq_page_cost, and cpu_tuple_cost contains planner-related configuration settings. So, the cost of 1834 is calculated as shown in the following example:

```
postgres=# SELECT relpages*current_setting('seq_page_cost')::numeric +
reltuples*current_setting('cpu_tuple_cost')::numeric as cost FROM pg_class
WHERE relname='guru';
 cost
-------
 1834
(1 row)
```

For the simple case of a sequential scan, it's quite straightforward to calculate the cost. However, when a query involves predicates' evaluation, grouping, ordering, and joining, cost estimation becomes complicated. Finally, the width of 37 is the average width of the tuple in bytes. This information can be found in the pg_stats table. To execute and get the cost in real time, you could use EXPLAIN (ANALYZE) or EXPLAIN ANALYZE. The following example returns all the rows where the ID is between 10 and 20:

```
postgres=# EXPLAIN ANALYZE SELECT * FROM guru WHERE id >= 10 and id < 20;
                                      QUERY PLAN
-------------------------------------------------------------------------
-------------------------------------------------
 Index Scan using guru_pkey on guru (cost=0.29..8.51 rows=11 width=37)
(actual time=0.007..0.010 rows=10 loops=1)
   Index Cond: ((id >= 10) AND (id < 20))
```

```
        Planning time: 0.132 ms
        Execution time: 0.028 ms
        (4 rows)
```

In the preceding query, the planner got a very close estimation compared to the real values: it estimated 11 rows instead of 10. Also, the planner-generated execution plan now uses an `index scan` because we have used predicates. In the execution plan, you could also see other information, such as the number of loops and actual time. Note that the execution plan is four lines with different indentations. You should read the execution plan bottom-up and from the most to the least indented. `Index Cond: ((id >= 10) AND (id < 20))` is indented and belongs to the `Index Scan` node.

The `EXPLAIN (BUFFERS)` option shows the effect of caching and whether the cache is used and configured properly. To take a look at the complete effect of caching, you need to perform cold and hot testing. Also, you can control the format of the execution plan. The following example shows the effect of using the `BUFFERS` and `FORMAT` options' cold and hot testing. To do cold testing, let's `stop` and `start` the server, as follows:

```
$ sudo /etc/init.d/postgresql stop
$ sudo /etc/init.d/postgresql start
```

> Often, a PostgreSQL restart isn't enough to clean the cache. Note that PostgreSQL also utilizes the operating system buffers. In Ubuntu, you can clean the cache with the `echo 3 > /proc/sys/vm/drop_caches` command.

Now let's read the guru table:

```
postgres=# EXPLAIN (ANALYZE, FORMAT YAML, BUFFERS) SELECT * FROM guru;
            QUERY PLAN
--------------------------------
 - Plan: +
     Node Type: "Seq Scan" +
     Parallel Aware: false +
     Relation Name: "guru" +
     Alias: "guru" +
     Startup Cost: 0.00 +
     Total Cost: 1834.00 +
     Plan Rows: 100000 +
     Plan Width: 37 +
     Actual Startup Time: 0.016+
     Actual Total Time: 209.332+
     Actual Rows: 100000 +
     Actual Loops: 1 +
     Shared Hit Blocks: 0 +
     Shared Read Blocks: 834 +
```

```
        Shared Dirtied Blocks: 0 +
        Shared Written Blocks: 0 +
        Local Hit Blocks: 0 +
        Local Read Blocks: 0 +
        Local Dirtied Blocks: 0 +
        Local Written Blocks: 0 +
        Temp Read Blocks: 0 +
        Temp Written Blocks: 0 +
     Planning Time: 0.660 +
     Triggers: +
     Execution Time: 213.879
 (1 row)
```

To perform hot-testing, the query needs to be executed again, as follows:

```
postgres=# EXPLAIN (ANALYZE, FORMAT YAML, BUFFERS) SELECT * FROM guru;
          QUERY PLAN
--------------------------------
 - Plan: +
     Node Type: "Seq Scan" +
     Parallel Aware: false +
     Relation Name: "guru" +
     Alias: "guru" +
     Startup Cost: 0.00 +
     Total Cost: 1834.00 +
     Plan Rows: 100000 +
     Plan Width: 37 +
     Actual Startup Time: 0.009+
     Actual Total Time: 10.105 +
     Actual Rows: 100000 +
     Actual Loops: 1 +
     Shared Hit Blocks: 834 +
     Shared Read Blocks: 0 +
     Shared Dirtied Blocks: 0 +
     Shared Written Blocks: 0 +
     Local Hit Blocks: 0 +
     Local Read Blocks: 0 +
     Local Dirtied Blocks: 0 +
     Local Written Blocks: 0 +
     Temp Read Blocks: 0 +
     Temp Written Blocks: 0 +
   Planning Time: 0.035 +
   Triggers: +
   Execution Time: 14.447
 (1 row)
```

The first thing you can see is the execution time difference. The second execution time is around 93% less than the first execution time. This behavior is due to reading the data from memory instead of the hard disk, as we saw in the execution plan. For more details, have a look at `Shared Hit Blocks`, which simply means the data is found in the memory.

> Using `EXPLAIN (ANALYZE)` inside a transaction with rollback in the end allows us to test write queries with no real data modification.

Detecting problems in query plans

The `EXPLAIN` command can show why a certain query is slow, especially if the `BUFFER` and `ANALYZE` options are used. There are some hints that enable us to decide whether the execution plan is good or not; these hints are as follows:

- **The estimated row number in comparison with the actual rows**: This is important because this parameter defines the method of the query's execution. There are two cases: the estimated number of rows may either be overestimated or underestimated. An incorrect estimation affects the entire algorithm, which is used to fetch data from the hard disk, sort it, join it, and so on. In general, if the number of rows is overestimated, this affects performance, but not as much as if the number of rows is underestimated. On the one hand, if you perform a `Nested Loop` join on very big tables, the execution time will increase exponentially, assuming, for simplicity, that the `Nested Loop` join cost is **O (n^2)**. On the other hand, executing a `hashjoin` on a small table will reduce the query-execution speed, but the effect won't be devastating, as in the first case.
- **In-memory or in-disk sort operation**: When performing a sorting operation, such as `DISTINCT`, `LIMIT`, `ORDER`, or `GROUP BY`, if there's enough memory, this operation will be performed in the RAM, otherwise the hard disk will be used.
- **Buffer cache**: It's important to check how much data is buffered and dirtied. Reading data from buffers will increase performance.

To show an incorrect execution plan, let's confuse PostgreSQL planner by performing an operation on the ID column, as follows:

```
postgres=# EXPLAIN SELECT * FROM guru WHERE upper(id::text)::int < 20;
  QUERY PLAN
------------------------------------------------------------
  Seq Scan on guru (cost=0.00..3334.00 rows=33333 width=37)
  Filter: ((upper((id)::text))::integer < 20)
(2 rows)
```

In the preceding example, PostgreSQL planner isn't able to evaluate `upper(id::text)::int < 20` properly. Also, it can't use the `Index Scan` because there's no index that matches the column expression, and, in any case, the index won't be chosen here because of the high number of estimated rows. If this query were a subquery of another query, the error would be cascaded because it might be executed several times. We have artificially created this problem, but an incorrect number in row estimation is one of the most common issues. It might be the result of an incorrect auto-vacuum configuration. In big tables, it might be the result of small target statistics.

Finally, knowledge about different algorithms, such as the `Nested Loop` join, `hashjoin`, `Index Scan`, `Merge Join`, and bitmap `Index Scan` can be useful in detecting the root cause of performance degradation. In the following example, the effect of a `Nested Loop` join is examined on a big table. To check different algorithms on execution plans, let's execute the query without disabling the planner settings, as follows:

```
postgres=# EXPLAIN ANALYZE WITH tmp AS (SELECT * FROM guru WHERE id <10000)
SELECT * FROM tmp a inner join tmp b on a.id = b.id;
                                                             QUERY PLAN
----------------------------------------------------------------------------
----------------------------------------------------------------
  Merge Join (cost=2079.95..9468.28 rows=489258 width=72) (actual
time=8.193..26.330 rows=9999 loops=1)
    Merge Cond: (a.id = b.id)
    CTE tmp
      -> Index Scan using guru_pkey on guru (cost=0.29..371.40 rows=9892
width=37) (actual time=0.022..3.134 rows=9999 loops=1)
            Index Cond: (id < 10000)
    -> Sort (cost=854.28..879.01 rows=9892 width=36) (actual
time=6.238..8.641 rows=9999 loops=1)
        Sort Key: a.id
        Sort Method: quicksort Memory: 1166kB
        -> CTE Scan on tmp a (cost=0.00..197.84 rows=9892 width=36)
(actual time=0.024..5.179 rows=9999 loops=1)
    -> Sort (cost=854.28..879.01 rows=9892 width=36) (actual
time=1.950..2.658 rows=9999 loops=1)
        Sort Key: b.id
```

```
        Sort Method: quicksort Memory: 1166kB
        -> CTE Scan on tmp b (cost=0.00..197.84 rows=9892 width=36)
(actual time=0.001..0.960 rows=9999 loops=1)
 Planning time: 0.143 ms
 Execution time: 26.880 ms
(15 rows)
```

To test the `Nested Loop`, we need to disable other join methods, mainly `mergejoin` and `hashjoin`:

```
postgres=#set enable_mergejoin to off ;
SET
postgres=#set enable_hashjoin to off ;
SET
postgres=# EXPLAIN ANALYZE WITH tmp AS (SELECT * FROM guru WHERE id <10000)
SELECT * FROM tmp a inner join tmp b on a.id = b.id;
                                                    QUERY PLAN
------------------------------------------------------------------------
-------------------------------------------------------
 Nested Loop (cost=371.40..2202330.60 rows=489258 width=72) (actual
time=0.029..15389.001 rows=9999 loops=1)
    Join Filter: (a.id = b.id)
    Rows Removed by Join Filter: 99970002
    CTE tmp
      -> Index Scan using guru_pkey on guru (cost=0.29..371.40 rows=9892
width=37) (actual time=0.022..2.651 rows=9999 loops=1)
            Index Cond: (id < 10000)
    -> CTE Scan on tmp a (cost=0.00..197.84 rows=9892 width=36) (actual
time=0.024..1.445 rows=9999 loops=1)
    -> CTE Scan on tmp b (cost=0.00..197.84 rows=9892 width=36) (actual
time=0.000..0.803 rows=9999 loops=9999)
 Planning time: 0.117 ms
 Execution time: 15390.996 ms
(10 rows)
```

Notice the huge difference of execution between `Merge Join` and `Nested Loop` join. Also, as shown in the example, `Merge Join` requires a sorted list.

PostgreSQL is smart; the previous example can be written in SQL without using CTE. The previous example is written using CTE to demonstrate extreme scenarios when rows are underestimated. In the preceding example, even though hashjoin and Merge Join are disabled, PostgreSQL used Nested Loop with Index Scan to execute the query. In this case, instead of doing two loops, it was executed in one loop, which has increased the performance dramatically compared to the CTE example. The following code shows the execution plan for the previous query written without CTE:

```
EXPLAIN ANALYZE SELECT * FROM guru as a inner join guru b on a.id = b.id
WHERE a.id < 10000;
                                                    QUERY PLAN
----------------------------------------------------------------------
----------------------------------------------------------
 Nested Loop (cost=0.58..7877.92 rows=9892 width=74) (actual
time=0.025..44.130 rows=9999 loops=1)
    -> Index Scan using guru_pkey on guru a (cost=0.29..371.40 rows=9892
width=37) (actual time=0.018..14.139 rows=9999 loops=1)
          Index Cond: (id < 10000)
    -> Index Scan using guru_pkey on guru b (cost=0.29..0.76 rows=1
width=37) (actual time=0.003..0.003 rows=1 loops=9999)
          Index Cond: (id = a.id)
 Planning time: 0.123 ms
 Execution time: 44.873 ms
(7 rows)
```

If you have a very long and complex execution plan and it isn't clear where the bottleneck is, try to disable an algorithm that has exponential effects, such as Nested Loop join.

Common mistakes in writing queries

There are some common mistakes and bad practices that developers may fall into. For example, a relational database is based on set theory; new developers tend to think in the scope of row-level manipulation instead of set manipulation. In addition, a lot of people create poor physical designs because they aren't familiar with relational-database modeling. In this section, we'll cover common mistakes in writing queries. For modelling issues, it's recommended to have a look at normalization because normalization also can boost performance by reducing data size and enhance statistics. In general, there are several issues that might lead to bad performance:

- **Incorrect statistics**: This might happen if there are cross-correlations among predicates, or if the predicates have an immutable function.
- **Unnecessary data retrieval**: When there is unnecessary data, for example: selecting all rows and columns, even if only a subset is required.
- **Unnecessary data manipulation**: This is quite common, such as applying sorting to the data when not required.

Unnecessary operations

There are different ways to introduce extra operations, such as hard-disk scans, sorting, and filtering. For example: some developers often use DISTINCT even if it isn't required, or they don't know the difference between UNION, UNION ALL, EXCEPT, and EXCEPT ALL. This causes slow queries, especially if the expected number of rows is high. The following two queries are equivalent simply because the table has a primary key, but the one with DISTINCT is much slower:

```
postgres=# \timing
Timing is on.
postgres=# SELECT * FROM guru;
Time: 85,089 ms
postgres=# SELECT DISTINCT * FROM guru;
Time: 191,335 ms
```

Another common mistake is to use DISTINCT with UNION, as in the following query:

```
postgres=# SELECT * FROM guru UNION SELECT * FROM guru;
Time: 267,258 ms
postgres=# SELECT DISTINCT * FROM guru UNION SELECT DISTINCT * FROM guru;
Time: 346,014 ms
```

Unlike UNION ALL, the UNION statement eliminates all duplicates in the final result set. Due to this, there's no need to do sorting and filtering several times.

Another common mistake is to use ORDER BY in a view definition. If ORDER BY is used when selecting data from the view, it also introduces unnecessary sort operations, as in the following query:

```
postgres=# CREATE OR REPLACE VIEW guru_vw AS SELECT * FROM guru order by 1
asc;
CREATE VIEW
Time: 42,370 ms
postgres=#
postgres=# SELECT * FROM guru_vw;
Time: 132,292 ms
```

In the preceding examples, retrieving data from the view takes 132 ms, while retrieving data from the table directly takes only 85 ms.

Misplaced or missing indexes

Missing indexes on column expressions causes a full-table scan. There are several cases where indexes can help to increase performance. For example: it's a good practice to index foreign keys. To test this case, let's create a table and populate it as follows:

```
CREATE TABLE success_story (id int, description text, guru_id int
references guru(id));
INSERT INTO success_story (id, description, guru_id) SELECT n,
md5(n::text), random()*99999+1 from generate_series(1,200000) as foo(n) ;
```

Now, to get a certain guru success_story, you can write a query that joins both guru and success_story tables, as follows:

```
postgres=# EXPLAIN ANALYZE SELECT * FROM guru inner JOIN success_story on
guru.id = success_story.guru_id WHERE guru_id = 1000;
                                                    QUERY PLAN
--------------------------------------------------------------------------
-------------------------------------------------
 Nested Loop (cost=0.29..4378.34 rows=3 width=78) (actual
time=0.030..48.011 rows=1 loops=1)
   -> Index Scan using guru_pkey on guru (cost=0.29..8.31 rows=1 width=37)
(actual time=0.017..0.020 rows=1 loops=1)
         Index Cond: (id = 1000)
   -> Seq Scan on success_story (cost=0.00..4370.00 rows=3 width=41)
(actual time=0.011..47.987 rows=1 loops=1)
         Filter: (guru_id = 1000)
```

```
                Rows Removed by Filter: 199999
   Planning time: 0.114 ms
   Execution time: 48.040 ms
  (8 rows)
```

Note that the `success_story` table was sequentially scanned. To fix this, an index can be created on the foreign key, as follows:

```
postgres=# CREATE index on success_story (guru_id);
CREATE INDEX
postgres=# EXPLAIN ANALYZE SELECT * FROM guru inner JOIN success_story on
guru.id =success_story.guru_id WHERE guru_id = 1000;
 QUERY PLAN
-----------------------------------------------------------------------------
--------------------------------------------------------------
 Nested Loop (cost=4.74..24.46 rows=3 width=78) (actual time=0.023..0.024
rows=1 loops=1)
  -> Index Scan using guru_pkey on guru (cost=0.29..8.31 rows=1 width=37)
(actual time=0.010..0.010 rows=1 loops=1)
  Index Cond: (id = 1000)
  -> Bitmap Heap Scan on success_story (cost=4.44..16.12 rows=3 width=41)
(actual time=0.009..0.010 rows=1 loops=1)
  Recheck Cond: (guru_id = 1000)
  Heap Blocks: exact=1
  -> Bitmap Index Scan on success_story_guru_id_idx (cost=0.00..4.44 rows=3
width=0) (actual time=0.006..0.006 rows=1 loops=1)
  Index Cond: (guru_id = 1000)
  Planning time: 0.199 ms
  Execution time: 0.057 ms
```

Note the execution time difference between timings after the index has been created. The execution time was reduced from 48 ms to around `0.057 ms`.

Text searches can also benefit from indexes. In several cases, you need to search case-insensitive data, such as search and login. For example: you could log into an account using the login name as case-insensitive. This could be achieved using lowercase or uppercase matching. To test this, let's create another function, as follows, as the md5 hashing only generates lowercase text:

```
CREATE OR REPLACE FUNCTION generate_random_text ( int ) RETURNS TEXT AS
 $$
 SELECT
string_agg(substr('0123456789abcdefghijklmnopqrstuvwxyzABCDEFGHIJKLMNOPQRST
UVWXYZ', trunc(random() * 62)::integer + 1, 1), '') FROM
 generate_series(1, $1)
 $$
 LANGUAGE SQL;
```

To create a table with a lowercase and uppercase login, execute the following SQL code:

```
CREATE TABLE login as SELECT n, generate_random_text(8) as login_name FROM
generate_series(1, 1000) as foo(n);
CREATE INDEX ON login(login_name);
VACUUM ANALYZE login;
```

The `generate_random_text()` function is used to generate random text of a certain length. Let's assume that we want to check whether an entry exists in table one; we could do this as follows:

```
postgres=# EXPLAIN SELECT * FROM login WHERE login_name = 'jxaG6gjJ';
                                 QUERY PLAN
--------------------------------------------------------------------------
--------
 Index Scan using login_login_name_idx on login (cost=0.28..8.29 rows=1
width=13)
    Index Cond: (login_name = 'jxaG6gjJ'::text)
(2 rows)
```

As seen in the preceding example, an `Index Scan` is used, as there is an index on `login_name`. Using functions on constant arguments also causes the index to be used if this function isn't volatile, as the optimizer evaluates the function as follows:

```
postgres=# EXPLAIN SELECT * FROM login WHERE login_name =
lower('jxaG6gjJ');
                                 QUERY PLAN
--------------------------------------------------------------------------
--------
 Index Scan using login_login_name_idx on login (cost=0.28..8.29 rows=1
width=13)
    Index Cond: (login_name = 'jxag6gjj'::text)
(2 rows)
```

Using functions on columns, as stated in the preceding example, causes a sequential scan, as shown in the following query:

```
postgres=# EXPLAIN SELECT * FROM login WHERE lower(login_name) =
lower('jxaG6gjJ');
 QUERY PLAN
-----------------------------------------------------
 Seq Scan on login (cost=0.00..21.00 rows=5 width=13)
 Filter: (lower(login_name) = 'jxag6gjj'::text)
(2 rows)
```

Note that, here, the number of rows returned is also five, as the optimizer can't evaluate the predicate correctly. To solve this issue, simply add an index, as follows:

```
postgres=# CREATE INDEX ON login(lower(login_name));
CREATE INDEX
postgres=# analyze login;
ANALYZE
postgres=# EXPLAIN SELECT * FROM login WHERE lower(login_name) =
lower('jxaG6gjJ');
                              QUERY PLAN
----------------------------------------------------------------------
---
 Index Scan using login_lower_idx on login (cost=0.28..8.29 rows=1
width=13)
   Index Cond: (lower(login_name) = 'jxag6gjj'::text)
(2 rows)
```

Also, text indexing is governed by the access pattern. In general, there are two ways to index text: using an index with `opclass`, which allows you to perform an anchored text search, or using `tsquery` and `tsvector`:

```
postgres=# CREATE INDEX on login (login_name text_pattern_ops);
CREATE INDEX
postgres=# EXPLAIN ANALYZE SELECT * FROM login WHERE login_name like 'a%';
                                            QUERY PLAN
----------------------------------------------------------------------
----------------------------------------------------
 Index Scan using login_login_name_idx1 on login (cost=0.28..8.30 rows=1
width=13) (actual time=0.019..0.063 rows=19 loops=1)
   Index Cond: ((login_name ~>=~ 'a'::text) AND (login_name ~<~ 'b'::text))
   Filter: (login_name ~~ 'a%'::text)
 Planning time: 0.109 ms
 Execution time: 0.083 ms
(5 rows)

Time: 0,830 ms
```

Finally, if you'd like to have an anchored case-insensitive search, you can combine the `lower` and `text_pattern_ops` functions, as follows:

```
postgres=# CREATE INDEX login_lower_idx1 ON login (lower(login_name)
text_pattern_ops);
CREATE INDEX
postgres=# EXPLAIN ANaLYZE SELECT * FROM login WHERE lower(login_name) like
'a%';
                                            QUERY PLAN
----------------------------------------------------------------------
----------------------------------------------------
```

```
 Bitmap Heap Scan on login (cost=4.58..11.03 rows=30 width=13) (actual
time=0.037..0.060 rows=30 loops=1)
   Filter: (lower(login_name) ~~ 'a%'::text)
   Heap Blocks: exact=6
   -> Bitmap Index Scan on login_lower_idx1 (cost=0.00..4.58 rows=30
width=0) (actual time=0.025..0.025 rows=30 loops=1)
        Index Cond: ((lower(login_name) ~>=~ 'a'::text) AND
(lower(login_name) ~<~ 'b'::text))
 Planning time: 0.471 ms
 Execution time: 0.080 ms
(7 rows)
```

Using CTE when not mandatory

Common table expressions (CTEs) allow developers to write very complex logic. Also, a CTE can be used in several places to optimize performance. However, using a CTE may be problematic in the case of a predicate pushdown, as PostgreSQL doesn't optimize beyond CTE boundaries; each CTE runs in isolation. To understand this limitation, let's have a look at the following two dummy equivalent examples and note the difference between their performance:

```
\o /dev/null
\timing
postgres=# SELECT * FROM guru WHERE id = 4;
Time: 0,678 ms
postgres=# WITH gurus as (SELECT * FROM guru) SELECT * FROM gurus WHERE id
= 4;
Time: 67,641 ms
```

Using the PL/pgSQL procedural language consideration

The PL/pgSQL language caching is an amazing tool to increase performance; however, if the developer isn't careful, it may lead to bad execution of their plans. For example: let's assume that we want to wrap the following query in a function:

```
SELECT * FROM guru WHERE id <= <predicate>;
```

In this example, we shouldn't cache the execution plan, since the execution plan might differ depending on the predicate value. For example, if we use a value of 1 as the predicate, the execution planner will favor an `Index Scan`. However, if we use the 90,000 predicate, the planner will favor the use of a sequential scan. Due to this, caching the execution of this query is wrong. However, consider that the preceding select statement is as follows:

```
SELECT * FROM guru  WHERE id = <predicate>;
```

In this case, it's better to cache it, as the execution plan is the same for all the predicates due to the index on the ID column. Also, exception handling in PL/pgSQL is quite expensive, so you should be careful when using this feature.

Cross-column correlation

Cross-column correlation can cause an incorrect estimation of the number of rows, as PostgreSQL assumes that each column is independent of other columns. In reality, there are a lot of examples where this isn't true. For example, you could find patterns where the first and last names in certain cultures are correlated. Another example is the country and language preference of clients. To understand cross-column correlation, let's create a table called client, as follows:

```
CREATE TABLE client (
    id serial primary key,
    name text,
    country text,
    language text
);
```

To test the cross-correlation statistics, the following sample data is generated as follows:

```
INSERT INTO client(name, country, language) SELECT generate_random_text(8),
'Germany', 'German' FROM generate_series(1, 10);
 INSERT INTO client(name, country, language) SELECT
generate_random_text(8), 'USA', 'English' FROM generate_series(1, 10);
 VACUUM ANALYZE client;
```

If you want to get users where language is German and country is Germany, you'll end up with an incorrect estimation of rows, as both columns are correlated, as follows:

```
postgres=# EXPLAIN SELECT * FROM client WHERE country = 'Germany' and
language='German';
                              QUERY PLAN
---------------------------------------------------------------------------
```

```
   Seq Scan on client (cost=0.00..1.30 rows=5 width=26)
      Filter: ((country = 'Germany'::text) AND (language = 'German'::text))
(2 rows)
```

Note that the number of estimated rows is 5 instead of 10, which is calculated as follows: *estimated number of rows = total number of rows * selectivity of country * selectivity of language*, thus, *the estimated number of rows = 20 * .5 * .5 = 5*. Prior to PostgreSQL 10, a simple way to correct the number of rows is to change the physical design of the table and combine both fields into one, as follows:

```
CREATE TABLE client2 (
    id serial primary key,
    name text,
    client_information jsonb
);
 INSERT INTO client2(name, client_information) SELECT
generate_random_text(8),'{"country":"Germany", "language":"German"}' FROM
generate_series(1,10);
 INSERT INTO client2(name, client_information) SELECT
generate_random_text(8),'{"country":"USA", "language":"English"}' FROM
generate_series(1, 10);
 VACUUM ANALYZE client2;
```

In the preceding example, `jsonb` is used to wrap the `country` and `language`; the explain plan gives the correct estimation of the number of rows, as follows:

```
postgres=# EXPLAIN SELECT * FROM client2 WHERE client_information =
'{"country":"USA","language":"English"}';
                                QUERY PLAN
------------------------------------------------------------------------
----------
  Seq Scan on client2 (cost=0.00..1.25 rows=10 width=60)
     Filter: (client_information = '{"country": "USA", "language":
"English"}'::jsonb)
(2 rows)
```

With cross-column statistics, you don't need to change the physical structure to overcome an incorrect number of rows estimated for correlated columns. However, you need to inform the planner about these dependencies. To extend the statistics, run the following statement:

```
CREATE STATISTICS stats (dependencies) ON country, language FROM client;
```

To view the new `statistic` object, you need to first analyze the table and then query the `pg_catalog` schema, as follows:

```
postgres=# analyze client;
ANALYZE
Time: 5,007 ms
postgres=# SELECT stxname, stxkeys, stxdependencies FROM pg_statistic_ext
WHERE stxname = 'stats';
 stxname | stxkeys | stxdependencies
---------+---------+-------------------------------------------------
 stats   | 3 4     | {"3 => 4": 1.000000, "4 => 3": 1.000000}
(1 row)

Time: 0,671 ms
```

The `stxkey` column contains information about the column's locations in the original table, in this case, 3 and 4. `stxdependencies` defines the correlation dependencies; in our case, we have 100% dependency between the `language` and `country` and vice versa. Finally, let's rerun the previous query to see whether the extended statistics helped to solve the cross-column statistics:

```
postgres=# EXPLAIN SELECT * FROM client WHERE country = 'Germany' and
language='German';
 QUERY PLAN
------------------------------------------------------------------------
 Seq Scan on client (cost=0.00..1.30 rows=10 width=26)
   Filter: ((country = 'Germany'::text) AND (language = 'German'::text))
(2 rows)
```

As shown, the estimated number of rows is now 10, which is much better than 5. In the next section, we'll discuss some physical tuning techniques, such as table partitioning.

Table partitioning

Table partitioning is used to increase performance by physically arranging data in the hard disk based on a certain grouping criteria. There are two techniques for table partitioning:

- **Vertical table partitioning**: The table is divided into several tables to decrease the row size. This allows a faster sequential scan on divided tables, as a relation page holds more rows. To explain, let's assume that we want to store pictures for each client in the database by adding a column of the byte or blob type to the client table. Now, since we have a table that might contain a big row, the number of rows per page is reduced. To solve this, you can create another table that references the client table, as follows:

  ```
  CREATE TABLE client_picture (
  id int primary key,
  client_id int references client(id),
  picture bytea NOT NULL
  );
  ```

- **Horizontal table partitioning**: This is used to decrease the whole table size by splitting rows over multiple tables; it's supported by table inheritance and the constraint exclusion. In horizontal table partitioning, the parent table is often a proxy, while the child tables are used to store actual data. Table inheritance can be used to implement horizontal table partitioning, whereas constraint exclusion is used to optimize performance by only accessing the child tables that contain the required data when performing a query. Table partitioning has evolved a lot in PostgreSQL; it started with table inheritance, and now PostgreSQL supports declarative partitioning. For more information on this topic, have a look at Chapter 13, *Optimizing Database Performance*.

Constraint exclusion limitations

Sometimes, constraint exclusion fails to kick in, leading to very slow queries. There are limitations on constraint exclusion, which are as follows:

- The constraint exclusion setting can be disabled
- Constraint exclusion doesn't work if the where expression isn't written in the equality or range manner

- Constraint exclusion doesn't work with non-immutable functions, such as CURRENT_TIMESTAMP, so if the predicate in the WHERE clause contains a function that needs to be executed at runtime, the constraint exclusion won't work
- A heavily-partitioned table might decrease performance by increasing planning time

Let's assume that we want to partition a table based on a text pattern, such as pattern LIKE 'a%'. This can be achieved by rewriting the LIKE construct using range equality, such as pattern >='a ' and pattern < 'b'. So, instead of having a check constraint on a child table using the LIKE construct, you should have it based on ranges. Also, if a user performs a SELECT statement using the LIKE construct, the constraint exclusion won't work.

Query rewriting

Writing a query in several ways enables the developer to detect some issues in coding best practices, planner parameters, and performance optimization. The example of returning the guru IDs, names, and the count of success_stories can be written as follows:

```
postgres=# \o /dev/null
postgres=# \timing
Timing is on.
postgres=# SELECT id, name, (SELECT count(*) FROM success_story where
guru_id=id) FROM guru;
Time: 144,929 ms
postgres=# WITH counts AS (SELECT count(*), guru_id FROM success_story
group by guru_id) SELECT id, name, COALESCE(count,0) FROM guru LEFT JOIN
counts on guru_id = id;
Time: 728,855 ms
postgres=# SELECT guru.id, name, COALESCE(count(*),0) FROM guru LEFT JOIN
success_story on guru_id = guru.id group by guru.id, name ;
Time: 452,659 ms
postgres=# SELECT id, name, COALESCE(count,0) FROM guru LEFT JOIN ( SELECT
count(*), guru_id FROM success_story group by guru_id )as counts on guru_id
= id;
Time: 824,164 ms
postgres=# SELECT guru.id, name, count(*) FROM guru LEFT JOIN success_story
on guru_id = guru.id group by guru.id, name ;
Time: 454,865 ms
postgres=# SELECT id, name, count FROM guru , LATERAL (SELECT count(*) FROM
success_story WHERE guru_id=id ) as foo(count);
Time: 137,902 ms
postgres=# SELECT id, name, count FROM guru LEFT JOIN LATERAL (SELECT
```

```
count(*) FROM success_story WHERE guru_id=id ) AS foo ON true;
Time: 156,294 ms
```

In the previous example, using LATERAL gave the best performance results, while CTE and joining a subquery gave the worst performance. Note that the result shown here might be different on other machines due to hardware specifications. LATERAL is very powerful at optimizing queries that require limiting the results, such as *give me the top-ten stories for each journalist*. Also, LATERAL is very useful when joining table functions.

Summary

There are several aspects to tuning the performance of PostgreSQL. These aspects are related to hardware configuration, network settings, and PostgreSQL configuration. PostgreSQL is often shipped with a configuration that isn't suitable for production. Due to this, you should at least configure the PostgreSQL buffer settings, RAM settings, the number of connections, and logging. Note that several PostgreSQL settings are correlated, such as the RAM settings and the number of connections. In addition, you should take great care with settings that require a server restart, because these are difficult to change in the production environment. Often, PostgreSQL produces a good execution plan if the physical structure of a database is normalized and the query is written properly. However, this isn't always the case. To overcome performance issues, PostgreSQL provides the EXPLAIN utility command, which can be used to generate execution plans. The EXPLAIN command has several options, such as ANALYZE and BUFFERS. Also, you should know the limitations of PostgreSQL to write good queries, such as cross-column statistics, CTE execution boundaries, and PL/pgSQL features. You should also know the exact difference between different SQL statements and how they're executed, such as UNION, UNION ALL, and DISTINCT. Furthermore, you should learn how to rewrite the same query in different ways and compare the performance of each.

Finally, you should know the limitation of PostgreSQL. There are some limitations for CTE, constraint exclusion, and cross-column statistics. In addition, you should consider the caching behavior of PL/pgSQL.

The next chapter will cover some aspects of the software-testing process and how it can be applied to databases. Unit tests for databases can be written as SQL scripts or stored as functions in a database.

Questions

1. What's the difference between hot and cold testing?
2. What's the `psql` meta-command that shows the execution time?
3. What's the difference between the `EXPLAIN` and `EXPLAIN ANALYZE` commands?
4. Why don't we need to use `DISTINCT` with `UNION` ?
5. How can CTE be used to enhance performance? What's the limitation of CTEs?
6. What are the general partitioning strategies for big tables?
7. How we can tune statistics gathering for a certain column?
8. Let's assume we want to get the top three gurus based on the number of success stories, write a SQL query in two different ways.
9. What's the limitation of constraint exclusion?
10. What's the problem with cross-column correlation, and how can it be solved?

14
Testing

Software testing is the process of analyzing program components, programs, and systems with the intention of finding errors in them, and to determine or check their technical limits and requirements.

The database is a specific system that requires special approaches for testing. This is because the behavior of database software components (views, stored procedures, or functions) may depend not only on their code, but also on the data. In many cases, functions are not immutable. This means that executing them again with the same parameters can produce different results.

That is why we should use specific techniques to test database modules. PostgreSQL provides some features that can help developers and testers in doing this.

In software architecture, the database is usually found at the lowest level. User interface components display information and pass commands to backend systems. The backend systems implement business logic and manipulate data. The data is modeled and stored in a database. This is the reason why, in many cases, changes in the database schema affect many other software components. Changes are necessary when businesses develop. New tables and fields are created, old ones are removed, and the data model evolves.

Developers should make sure that when changing the database structure, they do not break existing applications and they can use the new structures properly.

In this chapter, some techniques for testing database objects are discussed. They can be applied when implementing changes in the data structure of complex systems and when developing database interfaces.

The following topics will be covered in this chapter:

- Unit testing
- Database abstraction interfaces

Technical requirements

The examples in this chapter can be executed in the same database we have already used, `car_portal`, but they do not depend on the objects in that database. To create the database, use the `schema.sql` script and `data.sql` to fill it with sample data. All the code samples are provided in the `examples.sql` file.

The code samples in the chapter are written based on the assumption that the user executing the commands is able to connect to a PostgreSQL server and is allowed to create databases.

The way we will define a remote server connection using the `postgres_fdw` extension in the section *Data differences*, require that the user is able to connect to the database using the `host` authentication type without a password. To achieve that please add two lines in the beginning of the configuration file `pg_hba.conf`, as follows:

```
host  all  car_portal,car_portal_new  127.0.0.1/32 trust
host  all  car_portal,car_portal_new  ::1/128      trust
```

After that PostgreSQL server needs to be restarted. Refer to the `Chapter 11`, *PostgreSQL security* for details.

Unit testing

Unit testing is a process in software development that makes it possible to find errors in various components or modules in an application. In databases, those components are stored procedures, functions, triggers, and so on. A view definition, or even the SQL code of queries that applications use, can also be the subject of unit testing.

The idea behind unit testing is that for every module of a software system, such as a class or a function, there is a set of tests that invokes that module with a certain input data and checks whether the outcome of the invocation matches the expected result.

If the function being tested does not have any side-effects, meaning that it does not change any data or state of a component outside of the function, it is called a **pure function**. Mathematical functions are pure functions. In a database, `IMMUTABLE` functions are usually pure functions. Such functions are easy to test with unit tests because the only thing that needs to be done is to call the function with specific input parameters and verify the result. In other cases, when there are side-effects and they need to be tested, it can significantly increase the complexity of testing.

When a function or module being tested needs to interact with other components, those components become part of the testing process. Alternatively, they can be emulated by the test framework. The emulation of a component during testing is called **mocking**.

Unit tests should cover all the possible execution paths of the code under test. This can be achieved when the tests imply the invocation of the tested code with all possible logical combinations of values of the input parameters. If the tested module is supposed to be able to react to invalid data, the tests should include that as well. An example can be testing a function that divides two numbers. There must be a test when the divisor is not zero to check whether the division itself is correct, and there must be a test when the divisor is zero to check whether the function correctly reacts to that.

The execution of tests should be automated, which makes it possible to run the tests each time the source code changes. This is important when the modules being tested have side effects, because a change in one module might break other modules. Testing all the modules, even if their source code did not change, to discover such issues is called **regression testing**.

 There is a technique in software development called **test-driven development**. This approach means writing tests at the beginning, and then writing as little code as possible to make the tests pass. The tests should reflect the functional requirements for a module being developed. In the end, the developer will have working code that is covered with tests and good, formally-defined functional requirements for the module.

Specificity of unit testing in databases

In databases, it's uncommon to have pure functions. In most cases, the return value depends on the data in the database or, in the case of trigger functions, the function changes the data and returns nothing at all. In other words, functions in the database often produce side effects. Moreover, they are not usually idempotent, which means that when executed several times with the same parameters, they can produce different results.

Therefore, a testing framework should be able to create test data in the database, run tests, and then validate the changes in the data. Furthermore, the testing framework could also be required to manage the transactions in which the tests are executed. The easiest way to do all of that is by writing the tests as SQL scripts. In many cases, it is convenient to wrap them into stored procedures or functions. These procedures can be put in the same database where the components being tested were created.

Testing functions can take test data from a table that iterates through the records. There could be many testing functions, and one managing function that executes them one by one and then formats the result protocol.

Let's create a simple example. Suppose there is a table in the database, and a function performing an action on the data in the table:

```
car_portal=> CREATE TABLE counter_table(counter int);
CREATE TABLE
car_portal=> CREATE FUNCTION increment_counter() RETURNS void AS $$
BEGIN
    INSERT INTO counter_table SELECT count(*) FROM counter_table;
END;
$$ LANGUAGE plpgsql;
CREATE FUNCTION
```

The table contains only one integer field. The function counts the number of records in the table, and inserts that number in the same table. So, subsequent calls of the function will cause the insertion of the numbers 0, 1, 2, and so on, into the table. Suppose we want to test this functionality. The test procedure can be as follows:

```
CREATE PROCEDURE test_increment() AS $$
DECLARE
  c int; m int;
BEGIN
  RAISE NOTICE '1..2';
  -- Test 1. Call the increment function
  BEGIN
    PERFORM increment_counter();
    RAISE NOTICE 'ok 1 - Call increment function';
  EXCEPTION WHEN OTHERS THEN
    RAISE NOTICE 'not ok 1 - Call increment function';
  END;
  -- Test 2. The results are correct
  BEGIN
    SELECT COUNT(*), MAX(counter) INTO c, m FROM counter_table;
    IF NOT (c = 1 AND m = 0) THEN
      RAISE EXCEPTION 'Test 2: wrong values in output data';
    END IF;
    RAISE NOTICE 'ok 2 - Results are correct';
  EXCEPTION WHEN OTHERS THEN
    RAISE NOTICE 'not ok 2 - Results are correct';
  END;
  ROLLBACK;
END;
$$ LANGUAGE plpgsql;
```

The preceding stored procedure works in the following way:

1. Each test in the test scenario is executed in its own `BEGIN`, `EXCEPTION`, and `END` block. This makes it possible to continue testing even if one of the tests fails.

2. The first test runs the `increment_counter()` function. The test is considered successful if the function is executed without any error. The test is considered unsuccessful if an exception of any kind occurs.

3. The second test selects the data from the table and checks whether it matches the expected values. If the data is wrong, or if the select statement fails for any reason, the test fails.

4. The result of testing is reported to the console by the `RAISE NOTICE` command. The output format follows the **Test Anything Protocol (TAP)** specification, and can be processed by a test harness (external testing framework), such as Jenkins.

5. The procedure rolls back the transaction to return the database to the state it was in before the execution of the test.

If we run the test procedure, we will get the following protocol:

```
car_portal=> CALL test_increment();
NOTICE: 1..2
NOTICE: ok 1 - Call increment function
NOTICE: ok 2 - Check first record
CALL
```

The test is successful!

Suppose the requirements have been changed, and it is now necessary to add another field to the table to record the time when a value was inserted:

```
car_portal=> ALTER TABLE counter_table ADD insert_time timestamp with time
zone NOT NULL;
ALTER TABLE
```

After the change, we should run the test again to see whether the function still works:

```
car_portal=> CALL test_increment();
NOTICE: 1..2
NOTICE: not ok 1 - Call increment function
NOTICE: not ok 2 - Check first record
```

The test fails. This happens because the `increment_counter()` function does not know about the new field. The function should also be changed:

```
car_portal=> CREATE OR REPLACE FUNCTION increment_counter() RETURNS void AS
$$
BEGIN
  INSERT INTO counter_table SELECT count(*), now() FROM counter_table;
END;
$$ LANGUAGE plpgsql;
CREATE FUNCTION
```

Now the tests are successful again:

```
car_portal=> CALL test_increment();
NOTICE: 1..2
NOTICE: ok 1 - Call increment function
NOTICE: ok 2 - Check first record
```

The preceding test procedure is not perfect. First, it does not check whether the `increment_counter()` function actually counts the records. The test will succeed even if the `increment_counter()` function just inserts the constant value of zero in the database. To fix this, the test procedure should run the tested function at least twice and check the new data.

Secondly, if the test fails, it would be good to know the exact reason for the failure. The testing procedure could get this information from PostgreSQL using the GET STACKED DIAGNOSTICS command, and show it with RAISE NOTICE.

The improved version of the test procedure code is available in the attached media in the `examples.sql` file. It's too big to put here.

It's a very good practice to have unit tests for database components in a complicated software system when a database is shared by several services. Any development in the database on behalf of one of those services can cause others to break. Sometimes, it's not clear which service uses which object in the database and how they are used. That's why it is essential to have unit tests that emulate the usage of the database by each of the external services. And when developers work on changes to the data structure, those tests should be executed to check whether the whole system can work with the new structure.

The tests could be run in a newly-created testing environment. In that case, the install script should include some code to create testing data. Alternatively, the tests could be executed in a copy of the production database. The test script could also contain some cleanup code.

Unit test frameworks

The example in the previous section has more drawbacks. For example, if the function being tested raises warnings or notices, they will spoil the test protocol. Moreover, the testing code is not clean; the same pieces of code are repeated several times, those BEGIN, and END blocks are bulky, and the resulting protocol is not formatted very well. All these tasks could be automated using any of the **unit test frameworks**.

There is no unit test framework that comes out of the box with PostgreSQL, but there are several available from the community.

One of the most commonly-used ones is pgtap (http://pgtap.org/). It is available in the PGDG apt repository for Debian and Ubuntu Linux distributions (https://www.postgresql.org/about/news/1432/). Alternatively, one can download it from GitHub (https://github.com/theory/pgtap/), and then compile and install it in the test database. The installation in a Linux system is quite easy and described well in the documentation. To compile and install the framework, the postgresql-server-dev-11 package must be installed. To install the framework in a particular database, you will need to create an extension in PostgreSQL, as follows:

```
car_portal=> CREATE EXTENSION pgtap;
CREATE EXTENSION
```

The tests are written as SQL scripts and can be run in batches by the pg_prove utility, provided with pgtap. There is also a way to write tests as stored functions using PL/pgSQL.

The pgtap framework provides the user with a set of helper functions that are used to wrap the testing code. They also write the results into a temporary table, which is used later to generate the testing protocol. For example, the ok() function reports a successful test if its argument is true, and a failed test if not. The has_relation() function checks whether the specified relation exists in the database. There are about a hundred of these functions.

The test scenario that was described in the preceding section can be implemented in the following script using pgtap:

```
-- Isolate test scenario in its own transaction
BEGIN;
-- report 2 tests will be run
SELECT plan(5);
-- Validate the schema
SELECT has_table('counter_table');
SELECT has_column('counter_table', 'counter');
SELECT has_function('increment_counter');
```

```
-- Test 1. Call the increment function
SELECT lives_ok('SELECT increment_counter()','Call increment function');
-- Test 2. The results are correct
SELECT is( (SELECT ARRAY [COUNT(*), MAX(counter)]::text FROM
counter_table), ARRAY [1, 0]::text,'The results are correct');
-- Report finish
SELECT finish();
-- Rollback changes made by the test
ROLLBACK;
```

The code is much cleaner now. This script is available in the attached media in the pgtap.sql file. This is how it looks when the file is executed in the psql console. To make the test protocol look more compact, the Tuples only mode is switched on:

```
car_portal=> \t
Tuples only is on.
car_portal=> \i pgtap.sql
BEGIN
 1..5
 ok 1 - Table counter_table should exist
 ok 2 - Column counter_table.counter should exist
 ok 3 - Function increment_counter() should exist
 ok 4 - Call increment function
 ok 5 - The results are correct
ROLLBACK
```

Another unit test framework worth mentioning is plpgunit. The tests are written as functions in PL/pgSQL. They use the provided helper functions to perform tests; for example, assert.is_equal() checks whether two arguments are equal. The helper functions format the results of the tests and display them on the console. The unit_tests.begin() managing function runs all the testing functions, logs their output into a table, and formats the results protocol.

The advantage of plpgunit is its simplicity—it is very lightweight and easy to install, and there is only one SQL script that you need to execute to get the framework in your database.

The plpgunit framework is available in GitHub at https://github.com/mixerp/plpgunit.

Schema difference

When you work on changes in the database schema for an application, it is sometimes necessary to determine the difference between the old and the new structure. This information could be used in the documentation or can be analyzed to check whether the changes might have an undesired impact on other applications using the same database. The differences can be found using conventional command-line utilities.

For example, suppose someone changed the structure of the car portal database. First, let's create another database that will contain the updated schema. Assuming that the user can access the database running on localhost and is allowed to create databases and connect to any databases, the following command will create a new database using the old one as a template:

```
user@host:~$ createdb -h localhost car_portal_new -T car_portal \
-O car_portal_app
```

Now there are two identical databases. Connect to the new one and change the schema of the new database by adding a field to the `car_portal_app.car` table, as follows:

```
user@host:~$ psql -h localhost car_portal_new
 psql (11.0)
 Type "help" for help.
 car_portal_new=# ALTER TABLE car_portal_app.car
  ADD insert_date timestamp with time zone DEFAULT now();
ALTER TABLE
```

Now the structure of these two databases is different. To find the difference, dump the schema of both databases into files:

```
user@host:~$ pg_dump -h localhost -s car_portal > old_db.sql
user@host:~$ pg_dump -h localhost -s car_portal_new > new_db.sql
```

The `old_db.sql` and `new_db.sql` files that would be created after executing the preceding commands are available in the attached media. It is easy to compare these files using conventional utilities. On Linux, it can be done with the `diff` command:

```
user@host:~$ diff -U 7 old_db.sql new_db.sql
--- old_db.sql 2017-09-25 21:34:39.217018000 +0200
+++ new_db.sql 2017-09-25 21:34:46.649018000 +0200
@@ -351,15 +351,16 @@
 CREATE TABLE car (
 car_id integer NOT NULL,
 number_of_owners integer NOT NULL,
 registration_number text NOT NULL,
 manufacture_year integer NOT NULL,
```

```
    number_of_doors integer DEFAULT 5 NOT NULL,
    car_model_id integer NOT NULL,
-  mileage integer
+  mileage integer,
+  insert_date timestamp with time zone DEFAULT now()
    );
```

On Windows, this can be done with the `fc` command:

```
c:dbdumps>fc old_db.sql new_db.sql
Comparing files old_db.sql and new_db.sql
***** old_db.sql
 car_model_id integer NOT NULL,
 mileage integer
);
***** new_db.sql
 car_model_id integer NOT NULL,
 mileage integer,
 insert_date timestamp with time zone DEFAULT now()
);
*****
```

Both make it visible that one line of the schema dump has changed and another one was added. There are many more convenient ways to compare files; for example, using text editors, such as Vim or Notepad++.

In many cases, it is not enough to just see the difference in the schema. It could also be necessary to synchronize the schema of the two databases. There are commercial products that can do this, such as *EMS DB Comparer* for PostgreSQL.

Database-abstraction interfaces

When a big database is shared between many applications, it's sometimes hard to understand which of them is using which schema objects, and what would happen if the database schema changes. On the other hand, when a database is big and complex, changing the data structure is a constant process: business requirements change, new features get developed, and refactoring the database itself for the sake of normalization is quite normal.

In that case, it makes sense to build the whole system using a layered architecture. The physical data structure is located in the first layer. Applications do not access it directly.

Moving upward from the bottom, the second layer contains components that abstract logical entities from their physical implementation. These structures play the role of data-abstraction interfaces. There are several ways to implement them. They can be created in the database as functions or stored procedures. In that case, applications will work with the data by invoking them. Another approach is using updatable views. In that case, applications can access the logical entities with conventional SQL statements.

Alternatively, this interface can be implemented outside the database as a set of lightweight services that process the requests of high-level systems, perform queries, and make changes to the database. Each approach has its own benefits and drawbacks; consider the following, for example:

- Database functions keep the database-abstraction logic in the database and they are easy to test, but they hide the logical model and sometimes it could be difficult to integrate them with high-level applications
- Updatable views expose the relational model (although they do not have foreign keys), but the implementation of logic that goes beyond simple `INSERT`, `UPDATE`, or `DELETE` functions can be very complex and counterintuitive
- Microservices working outside of the database are more difficult to implement and test, but could provide additional functionally, such as providing access to the data using the HTTP REST API

At the top layer are the applications that implement business logic. They do not care about the physical structure of the data and interact with the database through the data abstraction interfaces.

This approach reduces the number of agents that access the physical data structures. It makes it easier to see how the database is used, and can be used. The database documentation should contain the specification of these interfaces. So the database developer, when working on refactoring the database schema, should only make sure that the interfaces follow the specification, and until they do, the rest of the database is free to change.

The existence of these interfaces makes it easier to develop unit tests: it's clear what to test and how, as the specification is given. With test-driven development, the tests themselves will play the role of the interface specification.

Data differences

The easiest way to create a database-abstraction interface is to use views to access the data. In this case, if we want to change the table structure, it can be done without changing the code of the external applications.

The only thing necessary is to update the definitions of the interface views. Moreover, if we wanted to, for example, remove a column from a table that is used in a view, PostgreSQL will not allow this. This way, the objects in the database that are used by applications will be protected from undesired changes.

Nevertheless, if the database structure was changed and the view definitions were updated accordingly, it's important to check whether the new views return the same data as the old.

Sometimes, it's possible to implement the new version of the view in the same database. In this case, we just need to create a copy of the production database in the test environment, or prepare a test database that contains all possible combinations of the attributes of the business entities. Then the new version of the view can be deployed with a different name. The following query can then be used to see whether the new view returns the same data:

```
WITH
  n AS (SELECT * FROM new_view),
  o AS (SELECT * FROM old_view)
SELECT 'new', * FROM (SELECT * FROM n EXCEPT ALL SELECT * FROM o) a
UNION ALL
SELECT 'old', * FROM (SELECT * FROM o EXCEPT ALL SELECT * FROM n) b;
```

Here, new_view and old_view refer to the names of the respective relations. The query returns no rows if both views return the same result.

However, this works only when both views are in the same database, and the old view works as it worked before the refactoring. If the structure of underlying tables changes, the old view cannot work as it did before and the comparison is not applicable. This problem can be solved by creating a temporary table from the data returned by the old view before refactoring, and then comparing that temporary table with the new view.

This can also be done by comparing the data from different databases—the old one before refactoring, and the new one. We can use external tools to do so. For example, data from both of the databases can be dumped into files using psql, and then these files can be compared using diff (this will work only if the rows have the same order). There are also some commercial tools that provide this functionality.

Another approach is to connect the two databases, perform queries, and compare the results inside the database. This might seem complicated, but in fact, it's the fastest and most reliable way. There are a couple of methods to connect two databases—through the dblink (database link) or postgres_fdw (foreign data wrapper) extensions.

Using the dblink extension may seem easier than using postgres_fdw, and it allows you to perform different queries for different objects. However, this technology is older, and uses a syntax that is not standard-compliant and has performance issues, especially when big tables or views are queried.

On the other hand, postgres_fdw requires you to create an object in the local database for each object in the remote database that is going to be accessed, which is not that convenient. However, this makes it easy to use the remote tables together with the local tables in queries, and it's faster.

In the example in the previous section, *Schema difference*, another database, car_portal_new, was created from the original car_portal database, and another field was added to the car_portal_app.car table.

Let's try to find out whether that operation caused changes in the data. The following would need to be implemented:

1. Connect to the new database as a superuser:

    ```
    user@host:~$ psql -h localhost -U postgres car_portal_new
    psql (11.0)
    Type "help" for help.
    car_portal_new=#
    ```

2. Create an extension for the foreign data wrapper. The binaries for the extension are included in the PostgreSQL server package:

    ```
    car_portal_new=# CREATE EXTENSION postgres_fdw;
    CREATE EXTENSION
    ```

3. Once the extension has been created, create a server object and a user mapping:

    ```
    car_portal_new=# CREATE SERVER car_portal_original
      FOREIGN DATA WRAPPER postgres_fdw
      OPTIONS (host 'localhost', dbname 'car_portal');
    CREATE SERVER
    car_portal_new=# CREATE USER MAPPING FOR CURRENT_USER SERVER
    car_portal_original;
    CREATE USER MAPPING
    ```

4. Create a foreign table and check whether it's possible to query it:

```
car_portal_new=# CREATE FOREIGN TABLE car_portal_app.car_orignal
(
  car_id int,
  number_of_owners int,
  registration_number text,
  manufacture_year int,
  number_of_doors int,
  car_model_id int,
  mileage int
)
SERVER car_portal_original OPTIONS (table_name 'car');
CREATE FOREIGN TABLE
car_portal_new=# SELECT car_id FROM car_portal_app.car_orignal
LIMIT 1;
 car_id
---------
      1
(1 row)
```

Now the table that is, in fact, in a different database can be queried as if it was a normal table. It can be used in joins, filtering, grouping—everything that you would do in SQL will work. To compare the data, the same query can be used as in the example we just saw for the old and new views:

```
car_portal_new=# WITH n AS (
  SELECT car_id, number_of_owners, registration_number, manufacture_year,
    number_of_doors, car_model_id, mileage
  FROM car_portal_app.car),
o AS (SELECT * FROM car_portal_app.car_orignal)
SELECT 'new', * FROM (SELECT * FROM n EXCEPT ALL SELECT * FROM o) a
UNION ALL
SELECT 'old', * FROM (SELECT * FROM o EXCEPT ALL SELECT * FROM n) b;
 ?column? | car_id | number_of_owners | registration_number |
manufacture_year | number_of_doors |  car_model_id | mileage
----------+--------+------------------+---------------------+---------------
----+-----------------+
---------------+----------
(0 rows)
```

The result is empty. This means that the table data in both databases is the same.

A foreign data wrapper can be used not only for comparing database tables, but also for distributing data over several databases and then querying them. This will be discussed in Chapter 16, *Scalability*.

Performance testing

Here's an important question regarding a database system: how fast is it? How many transactions can it handle per second, and how much time does a particular query take to execute? The performance of a database was covered in Chapter 13, *Optimizing Database Performance*. Here, we will only discuss the task of measuring it.

The psql meta-command, \timing, is used to measure the time of execution of a particular SQL command. Once timing is enabled, psql shows the execution time for each command:

```
car_portal=> \timing
Timing is on.
car_portal=# SELECT count(*) FROM car_portal_app.car;
 count
-------
 229
(1 row)
Time: 0.643 ms
```

Usually, that is enough to understand which query is faster and whether you are on the right way when working on making a query faster. However, you cannot rely on this timing when it comes to estimating the number of requests that the server can handle per second. This is because the time for a single query depends on many random factors, such as the current load of the server and the state of the cache.

PostgreSQL provides a special utility that connects to the server and runs a test script many times to collect performance metrics. It is called pgbench. By default, pgbench creates its own small database and executes a sample SQL script in it, emulating a load pattern of an **online transaction-processing application (OLTP)**. This is already enough to understand how powerful the database server is, and how changes to the configuration parameters affect the performance.

To get more specific results, we should prepare a test database that has a size comparable to the database in production. A test script, which contains the same or similar queries that the production system performs, should also be prepared.

For example, let's assume the car portal database is used by a web application. The typical usage scenario is to query the car table to get the number of records and then query it again to retrieve the first 20 records, which fit into a page on the screen. The following is the test script:

```
SELECT count(*) FROM car_portal_app.car;
SELECT * FROM car_portal_app.car INNER JOIN car_portal_app.car_model
USING (car_model_id) ORDER BY car_id LIMIT 20;
```

It is saved in a file called `test.sql`, available in the attached media, which will be used by pgbench.

It is necessary to initialize the sample data for pgbench (assuming that the database is running on the same machine and the current user can access the database):

```
user@host:~$ pgbench -h localhost -i car_portal
NOTICE: table "pgbench_history" does not exist, skipping
NOTICE: table "pgbench_tellers" does not exist, skipping
NOTICE: table "pgbench_accounts" does not exist, skipping
NOTICE: table "pgbench_branches" does not exist, skipping
creating tables...
100000 of 100000 tuples (100%) done (elapsed 0.17 s, remaining 0.00
s).
vacuum...
set primary keys...
done.
```

The test can now be started, as follows:

```
user@host:~$ pgbench -h localhost -f test.sql -T 60 car_portal
starting vacuum...end.
transaction type: test.sql
scaling factor: 1
query mode: simple
number of clients: 1
number of threads: 1
duration: 60 s
number of transactions actually processed: 143152
latency average = 0.419 ms
tps = 2385.858977 (including connections establishing)
tps = 2386.037643 (excluding connections establishing)
```

As you can see, the performance is about 2.4 thousand transactions per second, which is more than enough for a small car portal application. However, pgbench was running on the same machine as the database server, and they shared the same CPU. On the other hand, network latency was minimal.

To get more realistic statistics, pgbench should be started on the machine where the application server is installed, and the number of connections in use should match the configuration of the application server. Usually, for such simple queries, the network connection and transmit times play a bigger role than database processing.

pgbench allows a user to specify the number of connections it establishes to the database server. Moreover, it provides the functionality to generate random queries to the database. So, it can be quite useful to assess database performance and tune database server configurations.

Summary

In this chapter, we covered some aspects of software testing and how it applies to databases.

Unit-testing techniques can be used when developing code in a database, such as functions or triggers. Test-driven development is a very good approach to software development. Unit testing in databases has its own specificity. Unit tests for databases could be written as SQL scripts or stored functions in the database. There are several frameworks that help to implement unit tests and process the results of testing.

Another aspect of testing the database software is to compare data in the same database or between databases to test the results of refactoring the data model. This can be done via SQL queries, and sometimes requires establishing connections between databases. Connections between databases can be established via foreign data wrapper objects or database links.

Database schemas can be compared quite simply using command-line tools provided with PostgreSQL and operating systems. Additionally, there are more advanced software products that do this as well.

pgbench is a utility provided with PostgreSQL that can be used to assess the performance of a database system.

In the next chapter, we will continue talking about integrating PostgreSQL with other software and will discuss how to use the database in Python applications.

Questions

1. What is unit testing?
2. What are pure functions and side effects?
3. What is special about testing database functions or stored procedures?
4. How can we automate unit testing in databases?
5. What is test-driven development?
6. How can we compare the database schemas of two databases?
7. What is the purpose of database-abstraction layers?
8. How can we compare data in different databases?
9. How can we test database performance?

15
Using PostgreSQL in Python Applications

A database is a storage component of a software solution. However, it does not just store information; it also ensures consistency when the data is properly modeled in relational structures. Additionally, a database can implement more complicated logic related to consistency, which goes beyond normalization, with triggers and rules. Of course, business logic can also be fulfilled by a database with functions written in PostgreSQL in PL/pgSQL or other languages supported by the DBMS. Implementation of business logic in a database is questionable from an architecture point of view, but this is outside the scope of this book.

Nevertheless, the tasks related to interaction with users or I/O cannot be performed by the database. External applications do this. In this chapter, you will learn how to connect and interact with a database from an external application written in Python.

Python is a language that is very easy to learn and also quite powerful. It has huge support from the community and a lot of modules that extend the functionality of the standard library. It's very expressive, which is to say that humans can easily read and understand code written in Python. On the other hand, it's an interpreted language, which makes it quite slow compared to a compiled language, such as C or Java. Python is dynamically-typed. This can be convenient, but also error-prone.

The following topics will be covered in this chapter:

- Python DB-API 2.0
- Low-level access to databases using Psycopg 2

- Alternative drivers for PostgreSQL
- The concept of object-relational mapping and its implementation with `SQLAlchemy`

Technical requirements

To proceed with this chapter, you need to have a basic understanding of object-oriented programming. If you want to try the examples, you will need to install Python. The examples were made with Python 3.5, but they should also work in newer versions.

For Windows, you can download the installer package from `https://www.python.org/`. Simply let it install the software in the default location, and make sure that you also install `pip`, which is the installer for additional modules. Make sure that the location where Python is installed is included in the `PATH` system variable. To enter the Python shell, type `python` in the command line. Alternatively, there is an interactive Python shell available from the **Start** menu, called IDLE.

Python is available in standard repositories for many Linux distributions. Run `sudo apt-get install python3.5 python3-pip` to install Python and `pip`. To enter the Python shell, type `python3` in the command line.

In the examples, we will use the same database, `car_portal`, as we did in the other chapters. The scripts to create the database and fill it with sample data are available in the enclosed media in the `schema.sql` and `data.sql` files. The examples will work as they are if the database server is running on `localhost` and the `car_poral_app` user is allowed to connect to the `car_portal` database without a password (using the `trust` authentication method). In other cases, you may need to change the connection parameters in the sample script files.

Python DB-API 2.0

PostgreSQL is not the only relational database, and of course it's not the only one you can use with Python. There is an API in Python that is designed to unify the way applications work with databases. It's called the **Python Database API**. By the time this book was written, it already had the second revision of its specification, defined in the **Python Enhancement Proposal (PEP)** 249. The specification of the Python DB-API 2.0 is available at `https://www.python.org/dev/peps/pep-0249/`.

The API defines the following objects that are used when connecting to a database and interacting with it:

- **Connection**: Implements the logic of connecting to the database server, authenticating, and managing transactions. A connection is created by calling the `connect()` function with a number of parameters, which can differ depending on the database and the driver that is used.

- **Cursor**: Represents a cursor in the database. It's an object that is used to manage the context of executing a SQL command. For example, it is used to execute a `SELECT` query and to fetch rows one by one or in bulk, and in some implementations, to seek to a different position in the result set. A cursor is created by calling the `cursor()` method of a connection object.

- **Exceptions**: The API defines a hierarchy of different exceptions that may occur during execution. For example, there is an exception class, `IntergrityError`, which is supposed to be raised when the database reports an integrity-constraint violation. It's a subclass of `DatabaseError`.

Using the API makes it easy to switch between different database drivers or event databases. It also standardizes the logic and therefore makes it understandable and maintainable by others. However, details may differ between database drivers.

As an example, here is a small program in Python that uses the `psycopg2` module; it selects some data from the database, and prints it to the console (how to install Psycopg 2 will be explained in the next *Low-level database access with Psycopg 2* section):

```python
#!/usr/bin/python3
from psycopg2 import connect

conn = connect(host="localhost", user="car_portal_app",
 dbname="car_portal")

with conn.cursor() as cur:
 cur.execute("SELECT DISTINCT make FROM car_portal_app.car_model")
 for row in cur:
 print(row[0])

conn.close()
```

The program is available in the `print_makes.py` file in the enclosed code bundle.

There are several Python modules for PostgreSQL. We will take a closer look at the following:

- psycopg2: This is one of the most-commonly used; it utilizes the native PostgreSQL library, libpq, which makes it quite efficient, but less portable.
- pg8000: This is the pure Python driver and does not depend on libpq.
- asyncpg: This is an asynchronous driver. It uses binary protocol to talk to the database to achieve great performance, but does not implement the DB-API.

Low-level database access with Psycopg 2

Psycopg 2 is one of the most popular PostgreSQL drivers for Python. It is compliant to the Python's DB-API 2.0 specification. It is mostly implemented in C and uses the libpq library. It is thread-safe, which means that you can share the same connection object between several threads. It can work both with Python 2 and Python 3.

The official web page of the library is located at http://initd.org/psycopg/.

The psycopg2 driver can be installed with pip on Linux from the command line, as follows:

```
user@host:~$ sudo pip3 install psycopg2
[sudo] password for user:
Collecting psycopg2
  Downloading psycopg2-2.7.3.1-cp35-cp35m-manylinux1_x86_64.whl (2.6MB)
  100% |████████████████████████████████| 2.6MB 540kB/s
Installing collected packages: psycopg2
Successfully installed psycopg2-2.7.3.1
```

On Windows, use the following commands:

```
C:Users\User>python —m pip install psycopg2
Collecting psycopg2
  Downloading psycopg2-2.7.3.1-cp35-cp35m-win_amd64.whl (943kB)
  100% |##############################| 952kB 1.1MB/s
Installing collected packages: psycopg2
Successfully installed psycopg2-2.7.3.1
```

Let's take a closer look at the Python program from the previous *Python DB-API 2.0* section. We will go line by line to understand what is happening:

```
#!/usr/bin/python3
```

This is called a **shebang** or **hashbang** line: the `#!` characters followed by a path will indicate that the file is actually a script that is supposed to be interpreted by the specified interpreter. This makes it possible to make the file executable in Linux and simply run it. In Windows, the shebang line is not used by the shell. However, it doesn't hurt to have it in the script to make the script portable. In this case, the shebang line indicates that Python 3 is supposed to be used.

The program starts with importing an external function, as follows:

```
from psycopg2 import connect
```

Here, the `psycopg2` module is imported and the `connect()` function will be available in the current namespace. Alternatively, the `import psycopg2` expression could be used, but that would make the module itself imported to the namespace and the function would be called using the expression, as follows: `psycopg.connect()`.

The connection to the database is established in this line. The `connect()` function returns the `connection` object and the `conn` variable refers to it:

```
conn = connect(host="localhost", user="car_portal_app",
               dbname="car_portal")
```

The `cursor()` method of the connection is used to create a cursor object:

```
with conn.cursor() as cur:
```

The `with ... as` construct is used to create a **context manager** in Python. This is a very convenient technique used to allocate and release resources. In our case, the cursor is created—the `cur` variable refers to it, but when the execution leaves the with-block, the cursor will be automatically closed. This will happen no matter how the execution leaves the block, whether it's as normal or an exception is raised.

The `SELECT DISTINCT make FROM car_portal_app.car_model` query is executed, and the cursor now represents the context of the query execution:

```
cur.execute("SELECT DISTINCT make FROM car_portal_app.car_model")
```

Note that this line and the two following lines are indented. In Python, indentation is used to indicate nested lines of code. In our case, this line and the two following lines are inside the `with`-block created earlier. Indentation in Python is used instead of curly brackets, as in Java or C. Indentation of four spaces should be used according to the *Style Guide for Python Code*.

Refer to the documentation for details: `https://www.python.org/dev/peps/pep-0008/`.

The following two lines are also a part of the with-block:

```
for row in cur:
    print(row[0])
```

The first line of the two defines a `for` loop that will iterate over the records, returned by the cursor `cur` object. The records in the body of the loop are referred to by the `row` variable. The second line prints the first field of the record to the console. The `row` variable is of the `tuple` type, which works here as a zero-based array that contains the record's data, and the `row[0]` expression returns the value of the first field.

The following closes the database connection:

```
conn.close()
```

Note that this line is not indented, which means that the execution has left the `with` block and therefore, the cursor is also closed implicitly.

Now let's consider some of the aspects of the usage of Psycopg 2 in more detail.

Connecting to a database

Connections to databases are handled by the objects of the `connection` class. These objects represent database sessions in the application. The objects are created using the `connect()` function from the `psycopg2` module. This way of creating connections is defined by the **DB-API 2.0**.

To specify the location and authenticate in the database, a connection string can be used, such as this:

```
conn = connect("host=db_host user=some_user dbname=database "
               "password=$ecreT")
```

Alternatively, named parameters can be used, such as this:

```
conn = connect(host="db_host", user="some_user", dbname="database",
               password="$ecreT")
```

Here, the connection would be established to the database named `database`, located at the `db_host` server as the `some_user` user identified by the password, `$ecreT`.

Optionally, the `connect()` function can take two parameters: `connection_factory` and `cursor_factory`. They can be used to specify a custom function that would create connections or cursors. This feature can be used to extend the default functionality; for example, if you want to log all the SQL queries that are executed by the application, a customized `cursor` class could be a good solution.

The connection object returned by the `connect()` function is assigned to the `conn` variable in the preceding examples. The object is used to create cursor objects to execute queries and manage the database session. The most common methods of the `connection` class are as follows:

- `commit()`: This is used to commit the current transaction in the database. By default, Psycopg 2 will open a transaction before executing any command. For this reason, there is no method to explicitly begin a transaction.
- `rollback()`: This is used to roll back the current transaction.
- `close()`: This is used to disconnect from the database and close the `connection`.
- `cancel()`: This is used to cancel a current command. This can be executed from a different thread. This method is not defined in the DB-API 2.0.

There are also a number of methods used to perform two-phase commit. The **two-phase commit protocol** is an algorithm that is used when several systems should perform a commit or a rollback action together, in a coordinated way. There are more fields (some of them are read-only) and methods of the `connection` class that can be used to check the state of the connection, set and get its properties, manage the transaction isolation level, and perform other operations.

An object of the `connection` class can be instantiated with the context manager syntax, as follows:

```
with connect(host="db_host", user="some_user", dbname="database",
             password="$ecreT") as conn:
    cur = conn.cursor()
    ...
```

After the execution leaves the `with`-block, the connection will be closed automatically, regardless of whether the program continued normally or an exception was raised.

When a connection is established in a `with`-block, if the execution continues normally, the transaction will be committed before closing the connection. If an exception is raised, the transaction will be rolled back.

Connection pooling

Establishing a connection to a database can be quite expensive. It implies the connection on the network level and handshaking, authentication, and allocating server resources for the new session. Imagine a web application that would connect to a database for each request from users, perform a query, and disconnect. It could take milliseconds, but when the number of requests is huge, in total it can take a lot of time. If these requests are processed simultaneously, it can happen that too many connections are created and the database server is overloaded because each connection consumes resources from the server, and even if the sessions do nothing, the number of them is always limited.

In web applications (and not only there), it's a common practice to create a fixed number of database connections once and reuse them for different tasks. When there are more tasks than the number of connections, they should be blocked until there is a free connection. This is called **connection pooling**. The benefits of using connection pooling are as follows:

- No time spent connecting to the database as the connections are created in advance
- The number of connections is limited, which makes it easier to manage server resources

Psycopg 2 offers a connection-pooling feature with a simple API. There are three different implementations:

- **Simple connection pool**: Designed to be used in single-threaded applications
- **Threaded connection pool**: For multithreaded applications
- **Persistent connection pool**: Designed to work with Zope, a web application server

 Unfortunately, Psycopg 2 does not support blocking when trying to get a connection from a pool that is already exhausted, which is why one should be careful when using this connection pool. It also doesn't support the context manager syntax, which makes it less convenient to use.

In the attached media, there is an example script, called `psycopg2_pool.py`, that shows you how to use the connection pool provided by Psycopg 2. It's too big to include here. We will return to this topic later when another library, `SQLAlchemy`, is described.

Executing SQL commands

Suppose that the connection is established and there is a `conn` variable that refers to the instance of the `connection` class. To execute an SQL command, it's necessary to create a cursor object that will represent the context of the command. Cursors are created by calling the `connection.cursor()` method of a connection, as follows:

```
cur = conn.cursor()
```

Now the `cur` variable refers to the cursor object. Optionally, the `cursor()` method can take the following parameters:

- `name`: When specified, the cursor will represent a server-side cursor. When not, it is a client-side cursor. The difference between client-side and server-side cursors is that the first would usually download the whole result set and store it in memory, and the last would ask the server to give the data in portions when the application is ready to process it.
- `cursor_factory`: This is used to create non-standard cursors.
- `scrollable`: This only works with server-side cursors. When set to `True`, the cursor will be able to scroll back when iterating over the result set.
- `withhold`: This only works with server-side cursors. When set to `True`, the cursor will be able to fetch data even after the transaction commit (but not after rollback).

After a cursor is created, the `cursor.execute()` method should be used to execute a SQL command, such as to select rows or to delete records. For this, the following code can be used:

```
cur.execute("SELECT * FROM car_portal_app.car_model")
cur.execute("DELETE FROM car_portal_app.car_model " \
            "WHERE car_model_id = 2")
```

To use query parameters, specify the placeholders in the query using the `%s` sequence, and then pass the list of their values as a second argument to the `cursor.execute()` method. For example, to insert a record into a table, the following code would be used:

```
new_make = "Ford"
new_model = "Mustang"
sql_command = "INSERT INTO car_portal_app.car_model (make, model) " \
    "VALUES (%s, %s)"
cur.execute(sql_command, [new_make, new_model])
```

Here, **positional notation** was used, meaning that the order of the parameter values must be the same as the order of the parameters' placeholders in the query string. Note the backslash at the end of the third line in the preceding example. It is used to separate long lines of code and tells the Python interpreter that the expression continues on the following line.

Psycopg 2 also supports named notation for specifying parameter values. In this case, the placeholders should contain their names in parentheses between the percent sign (%) and the s character. The parameter values should be given as a dictionary mapping the values to the names. The same example could look like this:

```
new_make = "Ford"
new_model = "Mustang"
sql_command = "INSERT INTO car_portal_app.car_model (make, model) " \
    "VALUES (%(make)s, %(model)s)"
cur.execute(sql_command, {"model": new_model, "make": new_make})
```

Executing SQL commands with parameters might seem more complicated than including the values directly in the SQL code, like this:

```
new_make = "Ford"
new_model = "Mustang"
sql_command = "INSERT INTO car_poral_app.car_model (make, model) " \
    "VALUES ('" + new_make + "', '" + new_model + "')"
cur.execute(sql_command)
```

However, this is wrong! Never put data directly into the SQL command. This can lead to a serious security issue. Imagine if the value of the new_model variable was a single quote character, '. Then the SQL that is sent to the server will look like INSERT INTO car_portal_app.car_model (make, model) VALUES ('Ford', '''), which is obviously wrong. This command will simply not work, causing the database to raise an exception. In a web application, this could crash the server or make it possible to retrieve secret data. If parameters were used, Psycopg 2 would take care that this ' character is properly inserted into the table as if it was a valid car model name.

This misbehavior is called **SQL injection**.

The same cursor object can be used multiple times to execute several queries. However, cursors are not thread-safe. This means the same cursor should not be used by multiple threads. Different cursors should be created in this case. The connection object is thread-safe though.

There is a sample script that inserts a record into the car_model table in the psycopg2_insert_data.py file in the attached media.

Reading data from a database

When a query that returns a dataset is executed in a cursor, this data can be made available in the application. This is not only about SELECT queries, but also any data-changing query that has a RETURNING clause.

Suppose there is a cursor that has executed a query, as follows:

```
cur = conn.cursor()
cur.execute("SELECT make, model FROM car_portal_app.car_model")
```

The cursor object provides several ways to retrieve the data:

- Use the object as an iterator:

    ```
    for record in cur:
        print("Make: {}, model: {}".format(record[0], record[1]))
    ```

    Here, record is a tuple and the values of the fields can be accessed using the square-bracket syntax, specifying the number of the field (zero-based).

- Invoke the cursor.fetchone() method to get a record. A subsequent call will return the next record. When no more records are available, the method returns None:

    ```
    while True:
        record = cur.fetchone()
        if record is None:
            break
        print("Make: {}, model: {}".format(record[0], record[1]))
    ```

- Invoke the curosr.fetchmany() method to get a set of records. The method can take a parameter that specifies the number of records to retrieve. Otherwise, the number of records can be specified in the cursor.arraysize field. Subsequent calls to this method will return the next set of records. When there are no more records, the method returns an empty set. Here is an example:

    ```
    while True:
        records = cur.fetchmany()
        if len(records) == 0:
            break
        print(records)
    ```

After the data is retrieved and processed in the application, it's better to close the cursor. This will happen automatically if the cursor was created in a `with`-block. If cursors are not closed explicitly, they will eventually be removed by the garbage collector or when the database connection is closed, but they will consume system resources until then.

There is a sample script that uses all three methods in the `psycopg_query_data.sql` file in the attached media.

The COPY command

Psycopg 2 is able to execute the `COPY` command to quickly retrieve big amounts of data from the database or to store data in the database. The `copy_to()` and `copy_from()` methods of the `cursor` class are used, respectively, to copy data to a file-like object from a database table, and from a file-like object to a database table. There is another method, `cursor.copy_expert()`, that provides more advanced functionality with all the flexibility that the `COPY` command provides.

The `cursor.copy_to()` method takes the following parameters:

- `file`: A file-like object that will receive the data. It can be a file or a `StringIO` object, or any other object that supports the `write()` method.
- `table`: The name of the table to copy.
- `sep`: A column separator. By default, it is the tabulation character.
- `null`: A textual representation of NULLs.
- `columns`: A list of columns to copy from the table.

The records in the object referred by the `file` parameter will be separated by a newline. Here is an example of applying the `cursor.copy_to()` method, assuming the cursor is already created and assigned to the `cur` variable:

```
import io
with io.StringIO() as s:
    cur.copy_to(table='car_portal_app.car_model', file=s)
    print(s.getvalue())
```

This will print the contents of the table `car_portal_app.car_model` to the console as if the `COPY car_portal_app.car_model TO STDOUT;` command was executed in `psql`.

The `cursor.copy_from()` method takes the same parameters and yet another parameter `size` specifying the size of the buffer used to read from the `file` object. The `file` object must support the `read()` and `readline()` methods. Here is an example of how to write a record to the `car_portal_app.car_model` table using the `COPY` command, assuming the cursor is already created and assigned to the variable `cur`:

```
import io
with io.StringIO('Teslat\tModel-X\n) as s:
    cur.copy_from(table='car_portal_app.car_model', file=s,
                  columns=['make', 'model'])
```

In the attached media, there is a script in the file named `psycopg2_copy_data.py` that uses these two methods to copy data to and from the database.

Asynchronous access

In the preceding examples, the `cursor.execute()` method will block the program for the time a query is executing in the database. When the query is long, the program can be blocked for a long time, which sometimes is not a desired behavior. Psycopg 2 provides a way to execute queries asynchronously. Basically, it means that the Python program can do something else while a long query is being executed by the database server.

To use this feature, the database connection should be created as an asynchronous one. This is done by passing the `async=1` argument to the `connect()` function. The process of connection itself is also asynchronous. Now the Python program should be made to wait until the connection is established. This can be done using the `connection.poll()` method and Python's `select()` function, which is a wrapper for a corresponding system call. This is quite complicated and is outside the scope of this book. Luckily, Psycopg 2 provides a helper function that can be used to block the execution and wait for an asynchronous operation to finish. The function is named `psycopg2.extras.wait_select(conn)`, where `conn` is a parameter used to pass the database-connection object.

Here is a simplified example of how to use an asynchronous connection and perform a SELECT query:

```
from psycopg2 import connect
from psycopg2.extras import wait_select

aconn = connect(host="localhost", user="car_portal_app",
                dbname="car_portal", async=1)
wait_select(aconn)
acur = aconn.cursor()
# Supposing the following query takes a lot of time
acur.execute("SELECT DISTINCT make FROM car_portal_app.car_model")
# Do something else here
# ...
# When done with other tasks wait until the query is finished
wait_select(aconn)
for row in acur:
   print(row[0])
acur.close()
aconn.close()
```

More advanced examples of asynchronous execution are available in the attached media in the `print_makes_async.py` script.

More information about asynchronous operations with Psycopg 2 can be found in the documentation at `http://initd.org/psycopg/docs/advanced.html#asynchronous-support`.

Alternative drivers for PostgreSQL

In this section, we will take a closer look at two other PostgreSQL libraries for Python. The first one, `pg8000`, also implements the DB-API 2.0. This makes it very similar to Psycopg 2. The difference is that it's not dependent on the `libpq` library, and is written entirely in Python. This makes the library very lightweight, and applications that would use it are easily portable.

The second one, `asyncpg`, doesn't implement the Python DB-API. It uses a binary protocol to communicate with a PostgreSQL database and asynchronous API in the applications. This makes it possible to create very fast database applications that perform a great amount of commands in a short time.

pg8000

To install the `pg8000` library, you should use `pip` in the same way as with Psycopg 2. Here is an example of how it looks in Windows:

```
c:Usersuser>python -m pip install pg8000
Collecting pg8000
 Downloading pg8000-1.11.0-py2.py3-none-any.whl
Collecting six>=1.10.0 (from pg8000)
 Downloading six-1.11.0-py2.py3-none-any.whl
Installing collected packages: six, pg8000
Successfully installed pg8000-1.11.0 six-1.11.0
```

In Linux, execute the `pip3 install pg8000` command. The output will be very similar.

As the library also implements the DB-API 2.0, it is used almost in the same way as Psycopg 2.

Here is a small program that connects to the database, and queries and prints to the console the list of car makes entered into the system:

```
#!/usr/bin/python3

from pg8000 import connect

conn = connect(host="localhost", user="car_portal_app",
            database="car_portal")
query = "SELECT make, model FROM car_portal_app.car_model"
with conn.cursor() as cur:
    cur.execute(query)
    for record in cur:
        print("Make: {}, model: {}".format(record[0], record[1]))

conn.close()
```

The only difference from using Psycopg 2 here is the name of the module that is imported in the beginning. There are some differences in functions that are not part of the DB-API 2.0—for example, the COPY command is executed in `pg8000` by invoking the `cursor.execute()` method. Database data types are converted into Python data types slightly differently. `pg8000` does not offer an asynchronous API, and it does not have connection pools.

The main benefit of using `pg8000` module over `psycopg2` is that it does not have any dependencies on PostgreSQL drivers or libraries that would need to be installed in the system. The main drawback is performance. Depending on what is being done, `pg8000` can be significantly slower.

An example of using pg8000 to query data from a database is available in the pg8000_query_data.py file in the attached code bundle.

asyncpg

Another library, asyncpg, doesn't implement the Python DB-API. Instead, it provides an asynchronous API that is supposed to be used with asyncio, a Python library used to write concurrent code. It's outside the scope of this book to cover asynchronous programming, so we will only provide and explain a couple of simplified examples.

To install the library, use pip, just as in the previous sections. To install asyncpg on Windows, execute the python -m pip install asyncpg command. On Linux, the command will be pip3 install asyncpg.

As mentioned before, asynchronous execution implies firing a task and, while it is executing, doing something else. The asyncio.connect() function that is used to connect to the database is asynchronous. Functions that are used to execute queries or close the connection are also asynchronous.

There is a concept of callbacks in asynchronous programming. A **callback function** is a function belonging to your application that is executed automatically when a certain event happens. Here is an example of using a callback function that reacts on messages from the database:

```python
import asyncio
import asyncpg

async def main():
    conn = await asyncpg.connect(host='localhost', user='car_portal_app',
                                 database='car_portal')
    conn.add_log_listener(lambda conn, msg: print(msg))
    print("Executing a command")
    await conn.execute('''DO $$ BEGIN RAISE NOTICE 'Hello'; END; $$;''')
    print("Finished execution")
    await conn.close()

asyncio.get_event_loop().run_until_complete(main())
```

If you are not familiar with asynchronous features of Python, to understand the preceding code, you need to know the following keywords and expressions:

- async: Used to indicate that the function defined after it is a **coroutine**, which means that it's asynchronous and should be executed in a special way.

- `await`: Used to execute coroutines synchronously. Basically, when a coroutine function is called with the `await` statement, it's working as a normal function and the execution will continue only when the function returns.
- `lambda`: Defines an inline function. In the preceding example, the `lambda conn, msg: print(msg)` expression defines a function with two parameters, `conn` and `msg`, that prints the value of `msg` (`conn` is ignored). Lambda expressions are not specific to asynchronous programming, but they are very convenient to use as simple callbacks.

The preceding script executes a piece of code in the database written in PL/pgSQL. This code is doing nothing but generating a NOTICE. This code is executed asynchronously in the database. Although the script waits for the `conn.execute()` function to finish, the callback function is triggered immediately when NOTICE is raised. You may add some delays into the DO expression by calling the `pg_sleep()` function to see that.

In the last line of the code sample, the `main()` function is invoked. The function is defined as a coroutine, that is why it's not possible to simply call it. In the example, the expression in the last line invokes the function and waits until it finishes.

A more explicit example is available in the enclosed code bundle in the `asyncpg_raise_notice.py` file.

The benefit of using `asyncpg` over `psycopg2` is performance. The developers of `asyncpg` claim that it is about three times faster than `psycopg2`. It doesn't require any PostgreSQL libraries present in the system. It's asynchronous, which makes it possible to develop very efficient applications.

The drawback is that it is quite complicated to develop and debug asynchronous code. It does not comply with the DB-API 2.0 and, for this reason, other libraries that use this database-abstraction API could not use `asyncpg`. It is a relatively new software. There is not that much information or many examples available yet.

Object-relational mapping with SQLAlchemy

The libraries described earlier provide low-level access to databases. A developer must understand how databases work and must know SQL to use them. On the other hand, when a database is just a storage component in the software solution and all the business logic is found in high-level applications, developers of such applications should concentrate on business logic, instead of implementing the interaction with a database that deals with individual queries.

In high-level applications, the business objects are represented as classes and their instances. Methods of these classes represent business methods. The tasks of saving the state of the object in the database and loading it don't belong to business methods.

There is a concept of **object-relational mapping (ORM)** in software development. It concerns a software layer that represents records that are stored in a database table as instances of a class in a high-level application. When instances of such a class are created, the records are inserted into the table. When the instances are modified, the records are updated.

There is a library for Python named SQLAlchemy that implements ORM and can work with many different databases. It can also work with PostgreSQL.

SQLAlchemy consists of two major components: *Core* and *ORM*. Core is responsible for the interaction with the database and performing SQL commands. ORM works on top of Core and implements object-relational mapping. Both of them are briefly described in the following sections.

To get more information about SQLAlchemy, refer to the official website at `https://www.sqlalchemy.org/`.

The installation of SQLAlchemy is similar to the other libraries described in this chapter. To install the library with `pip`, execute the following in Windows:

```
> python -m pip install sqlalchemy
```

In Linux, type the following:

```
$ sudo pip3 install sqlalchemy
```

Now, SQLAlchemy is installed and can be used in Python programs.

Main components of SQLAlchemy

SQLAlchemy works on top of the DB-API. It can use `psycopg2` to connect to PostgreSQL or any other driver that implements the API, such as `pg8000`. There are several components that belong to the Core of SQLAlchemy:

- **Dialects**: Used to communicate with a particular database driver. SQLAlchemy has several dialects for different databases, such as Oracle, MS SQL Server, PostgreSQL, and MySQL. Each of the dialects of SQLAlchemy requires the respective Python library to be installed.

- **Connection-pooling component**: Responsible for establishing connections to databases using a dialect, managing connection pools, and providing a connection API to the Engine.
- **Engine**: Represents the database for other components that perform SQL commands. It's the starting point for an application that is using SQLAlchemy.
- **SQL expression language**: An abstraction layer that translates high-level API calls to SQL that engine could execute.
- **Schema and types**: Objects that define a logical data model. They are used by ORM or can be used directly with SQL expression language to manipulate the data.

ORM stands on top and uses the Core components. It implements the representation of database records as instances of classes that define business entities. ORM also manages relationships between the classes that are implemented as foreign keys in the database, though this is not mandatory.

Connecting to a database and retrieving data with SQL expression language

The SQL expression language component can be used to manipulate data in the database.

To connect to a database, it is necessary to first create an `engine` object. This is done with the `create_engine()` function, as follows:

```
from sqlalchemy import *

engine = create_engine(
    "postgresql+pg8000://car_portal_app@localhost/car_portal",
    echo=True)
```

Here, a connection string was used. It has a format `dialect[+driver]://user:password@host/dbname`. The `echo` parameter is set to `True`. This tells SQLAlchemy to log every SQL statement that was executed for debugging purposes. In the preceding example, the `pg8000` driver is used to connect to the database (assuming it's also installed with `pip`). Note that the application doesn't connect to the database at this point. It has created a connection pool and, once SQLAlchemy needs to execute a command, a connection from the pool will be requested. When there is no existing connection, it will be established.

Next, the `MetaData` >object needs to be created. This is an object that keeps the information about data structures the application is dealing with:

```
metadata = MetaData()
```

Now, we need to define the table that we want to work with:

```
car_model = Table('car_model', metadata,
                Column('car_model_id', Integer, primary_key=True),
                Column('make', String),
                Column('model', String),
                schema='car_portal_app')
```

Now, the `metadata` knows about the table's data structure. However, no interaction with the database has happened so far.

It's possible to implement the logical structure defined in metadata in the database by invoking `metadata.create_all(engine)`. It's also possible to load a physical data structure into a `MetaData` object, which is called **reflection**. Here, the definition of the `car` table is loaded into the `metadata` object:

```
car = Table('car', metadata, schema='car_portal_app', autoload=True,
            autoload_with=engine)
```

To get the structure of the `car` table, `engine` needs to connect to the database and execute some queries to different `pg_catalog` tables.

Now let's get data from the database. To do this, it's necessary to obtain a connection object by executing the `engine.connect()` method, which will take a connection from the connection pool. The application already connected to the database when it was retrieving the information about the `car` table. The same connection will be reused now:

```
conn = engine.connect()
```

The `conn` variable refers to the connection object.

An object of the `Select` type is used to define a query. It is created using the `select()` function. The `connection.execute()` method is used to run the query, as follows:

```
query = select([car_model])
result = conn.execute(query)
```

The result is an object of the `ResultProxy` class, which represents a cursor. It can be used as an iterator to get the records:

```
for record in result:
    print(record)
```

To insert new data, the following code can be used:

```
ins = car_model.insert()
conn.execute(ins, [
    {'make': 'Jaguar', 'model': 'XF'},
    {'make': 'Jaguar', 'model': 'XJ'}])
```

The logic is similar. At first, the object of the `Insert` type is created. Then it is used in the `conn.execute()` method. The method takes the list of parameters for the query to be executed. SQLAlchemy is smart enough to understand that two records are inserted here and the values for the `make` and `model` fields are provided in the list of dictionaries.

No SQL code has been written yet. However, SQLAlchemy is executing SQL commands in the background because this is the only language that the database can understand. SQLAlchemy provides an easy way to check which SQL statement stands behind each high-level object. Simply print it! `print(ins)` will print this to the console:

```
INSERT INTO car_portal_app.car_model (car_model_id, make, model)
VALUES (:car_model_id, :make, :model)
```

It's possible to filter results when querying the data using the SQL expression language. The object that represent a query provides a `where()` method, which is used for the filtering. There are a lot of operators and functions defined in SQLAlchemy that represent SQL operators and expressions. Here, we use the `==` operator to filter rows:

```
query = select([car_model]).where(car_model.c.make == "Jaguar")
```

This query will return only the Jaguar models.

These objects also have the `order_by()` and `group_by()` methods, which implement the corresponding SQL clauses.

The library can do a lot more already with the SQL expression language. For example, it can join tables, use subqueries, perform set operations (`UNION`), and even execute window functions. You can learn more about SQL expression language from the tutorial at `http://docs.sqlalchemy.org/en/latest/core/tutorial.html`.

A sample script that performs the operations described in this section can be found in the attached media in the `sqlalchemy_sql_expression_language.py` file.

ORM

Even though SQL expression language already provides a good level of abstraction, it still operates with a physical data model, not with business entities.

ORM makes it possible to map business entities, that a Python application deals with, to data structures in the database. To show this, let's create a Car class and define the mapping.

When using ORM, we describe the database structure and, at the same time, define the classes that represent business entities. This is done using a system named declarative. In SQLAlchemy, this system is initiated by creating a class that is then used as a base class for other classes:

```
from sqlalchemy.ext.declarative import declarative_base
Base = declarative_base()
```

Now the high-level class that will represent cars can be defined as follows:

```
class Car(Base):
    __tablename__ = "car"
    __table_args__ = {'schema': 'car_portal_app'}
    car_id = Column(Integer, primary_key=True)
    registration_number = Column(String, nullable=False)
    def __repr__(self):
        return "Car {}: '{}'".format(self.car_id, self.registration_number)
```

Only two fields are defined here to save space. However, to emphasize that this is a business entity and not just a definition of a data structure, a custom representation method is defined in the class. It will be called when a text representation of an instance of the class is requested, for example, to print it. You can find the complete code of the class in the enclosed code bundle in the sqlalchemy_orm.py file.

To query the data from the database and get some instances of the defined class in the application, it's necessary to create an object of the Session class. This class implements a session, which is a dialogue with a database that is related to the current business operation the application is performing. If the application accesses several objects in the same operation, the same session is used. For example, the car portal application could query cars and corresponding car models in the same session if a user is searching for a car. At the same time, another user could create a user account. This will be done in a different session. In many cases, one session is bound to one transaction in the database.

The session is created as follows: first, create a `Session` class that is bound to the `engine` object that was created before, and then instantiate an object of that class:

```
from sqlalchemy.orm import sessionmaker
Session = sessionmaker(bind=engine)
session = Session()
```

The `session` object is used to query the data. It's done in a way, that is similar to querying using the SQL expression language and, in fact, the same operators and methods are used when building a query. Let's create a query to retrieve the first five cars with the smallest IDs:

```
query = session.query(Car).order_by(Car.car_id).limit(5)
```

When this query is used to retrieve data, it actually returns instances of the `Car` class:

```
for car in query.all():
    print(car)
```

Note that when the objects are printed, the custom text representation is used, which was defined in the class. This is the output on console:

```
Car 1: 'MUWH4675'
Car 2: 'VSVW4565'
Car 3: 'BKUN9615'
...
```

Let's update one of the cars. To get the first object of the `Car` class that the `query` returns, use the `query.first()` method:

```
car = query.first()
```

To change its licence plate, simply change the value of the field:

```
car.registration_number = 'BOND007'
```

The attribute of that instance is now changed. ORM knows that this instance is mapped to the database row with `car_id` = 1 and it will perform an UPDATE in the database.

Finally, to commit the transaction and close the `session`, the following methods need to be invoked:

```
session.commit()
session.close()
```

Relational databases are all about relations and relationships. ORM cares about relationships too. The `car` table has a `car_model_id` field, which points to a record in the `car_model` table.

Logically, it means that the `Car` class has the `car_model` attribute. The physical implementation (namely, another table) does not matter for the business logic.

Please note: in the following examples, the `Car` class will be redefined. SQLAlchemy doesn't provide an easy way to redefine classes that were mapped to database tables. That means if you used to type the code in the Python console, you should close it and start again, import the `sqlalchemy` module, initialize the `engine`, and create the `Base` and `Session` classes, as follows:

```
from sqlalchemy import *
from sqlalchemy.ext.declarative import declarative_base
from sqlalchemy.orm import sessionmaker

engine = create_engine(
    "postgresql+pg8000://car_portal_app@localhost/car_portal",
    echo=True)
Base = declarative_base()
Session = sessionmaker(bind=engine)
```

To implement the relationship, let's create another class that will represent car models, `Car_model`. It should be defined before the `Car` class, as follows:

```
class Car_model(Base):
    __tablename__ = "car_model"
    __table_args__ = {'schema': 'car_portal_app'}
    car_model_id = Column(Integer, primary_key=True)
    make = Column(String)
    model = Column(String)
```

Now define the `Car` class. Add the two new attributes and redefine the __repr__ method, as follows:

```
from sqlalchemy.orm import relationship

class Car(Base):
    __tablename__ = "car"
    __table_args__ = {'schema': 'car_portal_app'}
    car_id = Column(Integer, primary_key=True)
    registration_number = Column(String, nullable=False)
    car_model_id = Column(Integer, ForeignKey(Car_model.car_model_id))
    car_model = relationship(Car_model)
    def __repr__(self):
```

```
        return "Car {}: {} {}, '{}'".format(
            self.car_id, self.car_model.make, self.car_model.model,
            self.registration_number)
```

Now, perform the same query, as we did before defining the relationship, as follows:

```
session = Session()
query = session.query(Car).order_by(Car.car_id).limit(5)
for car in query.all():
    print(car)
```

The following will be printed to the console:

```
Car 1: Peugeot 308, 'BOND007'
Car 2: Opel Corsa, 'VSVW4565'
Car 3: Citroen C3, 'BKUN9615'
...
```

ORM can also be used to create new objects and save them in the database and delete them. To create a new car model, the following code is used:

```
new_car_model = Car_model(make="Jaguar", model="XE")
session = Session()
session.add(new_car_model)
session.commit()
session.close()
```

The following code is used to delete a car model:

```
session = Session()
old_car_model = session.query(Car_model).filter(
    and_(Car_model.make == "Jaguar", Car_model.model == "XE")).one()
session.delete(old_car_model)
session.commit()
session.close()
```

SQLAlchemy provides you with a very powerful and flexible API to work with entities that are mapped to database tables. Relationships can be set up in a way that would, for example, when a car model is deleted, also delete all the cars of that model, this is called cascade delete. The Car_model could have a cars attribute that would represent a list of instances of Car of that model. It's possible to make SQLAlchemy join the car_model table with the car table when entities of Car are retrieved from the database, to make it work faster.

The sample script that shows how to manipulate data using SQLAlchemy ORM API is available in the enclosed media in the sqlalchemy_orm.py file.

Summary

Databases are often used as storage components in complex software solutions. Even if they could implement complex logic in triggers and functions, there is still a necessity for external applications to implement user interfaces. It's quite common to separate storage logic from business logic. In this case, the business logic is also performed in external applications.

In this chapter, you learned how to connect to a PostgreSQL database from applications written in Python. There are several libraries for Python that provide different programming interfaces for developers. Some of them implement the standard Python DB-API and some don't. There are implementations of ORM for Python that work well with PostgreSQL.

The `psycopg2`, `pg8000`, and `asyncpg` low-level libraries were described in this chapter. They make it possible to connect to a database from a Python application and execute SQL commands to retrieve or modify data.

Another library, SQLAlchemy, was described in the last section of the chapter. SQLAlchemy provides an object-relational mapping functionality that eases the implementation of business logic by mapping business entities to database tables. This makes it possible for a developer to concentrate on the business logic instead of low-level database interaction. Although developers must know what's happening in the systems they work with and be aware of how databases work, using ORM frameworks removes the necessity of writing SQL code.

In the next chapter, you will learn how to use multiple PostgreSQL servers together to achieve greater performance or high availability, or both. This will make the software solution scalable and able to grow as the business using it grows.

Questions

1. What is the difference between low-level access to a database and object-relation mapping in the context of a Python application?
2. What is the Python DB-API?
3. What is the difference between `psycopg2` and `pg8000`?
4. In `psycopg2`, what are `connection` and `cursor`?

5. Is there a way to execute a `COPY` command from a Python application?
6. What's special about `asyncpg`?
7. How does SQLAlchemy connect to a database?
8. What are the benefits of using ORM when manipulating objects in the database?

16
Scalability

In this chapter, we will discuss the problem of **scalability**. This term means the ability of a software system to grow as the business using it grows. PostgreSQL provides some features that help you to build a scalable solution but, strictly speaking, PostgreSQL itself is not scalable. It can effectively utilize the following resources of a single machine:

- It uses multiple CPU cores to execute a single query faster with the parallel query feature
- When configured properly, it can use all available memory for caching
- The size of the database is not limited; PostgreSQL can utilize multiple hard disks when multiple tablespaces are created; with partitioning, the hard disks could be accesses simultaneously, which makes data processing faster

However, when it comes to spreading a database solution to multiple machines, it can be quite problematic because a standard PostgreSQL server can only run on a single machine. That's why, in this chapter, we will talk not only about PostgreSQL itself, but about a bigger solution that could be based on top of PostgreSQL.

In particular, the following topics will be covered:

- The problem of scalability and the CAP theorem
- Data replication in PostgreSQL, including physical replication and logical replication
- Different scaling scenarios and their implementation in PostgreSQL

 This topic is very large and itself deserves a dedicated book. That's why we will not describe the practical recipes too much, but rather discuss the concepts so that you can get an understanding of possible options and then learn particular topics yourself.

Technical requirements

The examples for the chapter require setting up multiple database instances, which is why we'll use Docker compositions to set up and implement sample scenarios. If you aren't familiar with Docker, refer to the documentation at `https://docs.docker.com/get-started/`. To run the examples, you will need to install `docker engine` and `docker-compose`.

The examples are also based on the `car_portal` database that we have used throughout the whole book.

The problem of scalability and the CAP theorem

The requirement for a system to be scalable means that a system that supports a business now, should also be able to support the same business with the same quality of service as it grows. Let's say a database can store 1 GB of data and effectively process 100 queries per second. What if with development of the business, the amount of data being processed grows 100 times? Will it be able to support 10,000 queries per second and process 100 GB of data? Maybe not now, and not in the same installation. However, a scalable solution should be ready to be expanded to be able to handle the load as soon as it is needed.

Usually, scalability comes together with the distributed architecture of a system. If the database was able to utilize the power of multiple computers, then in order to scale it, we would need to add more machines to the cluster. There are solutions that do this. In fact, many NoSQL databases (even if they provide a SQL interface) are distributed systems. One of the most spectacular examples of a scalable solution is Cassandra—a distributed NoSQL database. There are clusters of tens of thousands of nodes, operating petabytes of data and performing hundreds of millions of operations per day. This could never be possible with a single server.

On the other hand, these systems are less flexible in functionality. Simply speaking, Cassandra provides key-value storage and does not provide consistency in the sense of ACID principles. PostgreSQL, by contrast, is a relational database management system that supports big concurrent isolated transactions and integrity constraints.

There is a theorem in computer science that was formulated by Eric Brewer in 2000, called the **CAP theorem**, stating that a distributed data storage system can support only two of the following three features:

- **Consistency (defined differently from the ACID principles)**: Any read operation always returns the most current state of the data, regardless of which node was queried
- **Availability**: Any request to the system is always successful (but the result may not be consistent)
- **Partition-tolerance**: A system can survive even if some parts of it are not available, or if a cluster is separated

The theorem is named for the first letters of these features: **CAP**. It says that all three features are not possible at the same time. Let's consider a distributed system running on multiple nodes. We may expect that it should tolerate the unavailability of some nodes. To achieve consistency, the system has to be able to coordinate all reads and writes, even if they happen on different nodes. To guarantee availability, the system needs to have copies of the same data on different nodes and to keep them in sync. In this definition, these two features cannot be achieved at the same time when some nodes are not available.

Cassandra provides availability and partition tolerance, so it is **cAP**:

- **Not consistent**: It is possible that a read operation performed on one node does not see the data written on another node until the data is replicated to all the nodes that are supposed to have it. This will not block the read operation.
- **Available**: Read and write operations are always successful.
- **Partition-tolerant**: If a node breaks, it does not break the whole database. When the broken node is returned to the cluster, it receives the missing changes in the data automatically.

We can increase the consistency level when working with Cassandra to make it absolutely consistent, but in this case, it will not be partition-tolerant.

Relational databases that comply with the ACID principles are consistent and available. PostgreSQL is **CAp**:

- **Consistent**: Once a session commits a transaction, all other sessions can immediately see the results. The intermediate states of data are not visible.
- **Available**: When the database is running, all the queries will succeed if they are correct.

- **Not partition-tolerant**: If we make part of the data unavailable, the database will stop working. However, strictly speaking, PostgreSQL is not a distributed system, therefore network partitioning is not applicable here.

For example, for banking operations, consistency is required. If money is transferred from one account to another, we expect that either both accounts' balances are updated, or none. If, for some reason, the application that performs the transfer crashes after it has updated one of the accounts, the whole transaction will be canceled and the data will return to the previous consistent state. Availability of the data is also important. Even if the transaction is committed, what if the hard disk fails and the whole database is lost? Therefore, all the operations have to be replicated into backup storage and the transaction can only be considered successful when it is consistent and also durable. A money transfer in a bank can take some time because consistency is extremely important; performance has a lower priority.

If an online banking system is not available for a while because they need to restore a database from a backup, the customers can tolerate the inconvenience because they do not want to lose their money.

On the other hand, if someone *likes* a picture on Instagram, the system tracks this action in the context of the picture and also in the context of the user who *likes* it. If any of the two operations fails, the data will be not consistent, but that is not critical. This does not mean that the data Instagram operates is less valuable. The requirements are different. There are millions of users and probably billions of pictures and nobody wants to wait when using the service. If likes are not displayed correctly, it does not matter too much, but if the whole system is not available for some time to be recovered to a consistent state after a failure, users may decide to leave.

This means different solutions for different business requirements, but unfortunately, there is a natural limitation making it impossible to achieve everything at once.

Data replication in PostgreSQL

In scenarios where it is required to achieve better performance, it is quite common to set up more servers that would handle additional load and copy the same data to them from a master server. In scenarios where high availability is required, this is also a typical solution to continuously copy the data to a standby server so that it could take over in case the master server crashes.

Transaction log

Before explaining how to set up data replication, let's quickly look at how PostgreSQL handles changes in data at the lower level.

When PostgreSQL processes a command that changes the data in the database, it writes the new data on disk to make it persistent. There are two locations on disk where the data is written (the paths are given for Linux Debian; in other operating systems the locations might be different):

- The data files are located in by default at `/var/lib/postgresql/11/main/base`. Here, the data is stored—tables, indexes, temporary tables, and other objects. The size of this directory is only limited by the size of the disk.
- The transaction log is located by default at `/var/lib/postgresql/11/main/pg_wal`. Here, the log of most recent changes in the data files is stored. Its size is limited in the configuration and by default is around 1 GB.

The same data is always written in both locations. This may seem redundant, but there is a reason for this.

Imagine there is a transaction that inserts a record with a text value, `test`, into a big table, and it so happens that the server crashes in the middle of the transaction. The letters `te` are written to disk and the rest was lost. When the database is started again, it would not be able to tell whether the record is corrupted, because it would not know whether it is the word `test` or only the letters `te` that was supposed to be the value of the field. OK, this can be solved using checksums. How would the database find the corrupted record? It would be very expensive to validate the checksums for the whole database after every unexpected restart.

The solution for this is that before writing data into the data files, PostgreSQL always writes it into the transaction log. The **transaction log** (also called the **write-ahead log**) is a list of changes made by PostgreSQL to a data file. The transaction log appears as a set of 16 MB files (called **WAL-files**) located in the `pg_wal` subdirectory under the PostgreSQL database path. Each file contains a lot of records that basically indicate which data file should be changed in which way. Only when the transaction log is saved on disk does the database write the data to the data files. When the transaction log is full, PostgreSQL deletes the oldest segment of it to reuse disk space, but first, it will make sure that the data is written to the data files. The transaction log is relatively small, and the server is able to go through it after an unexpected shutdown.

Now, after a system failure, the following will happen after restart:

- If the system crashed during the writing of the transaction log, PostgreSQL will identify that the log record is incomplete because the checksum will not match. It would discard this log record and perform a rollback of the transactions that were writing the data into that record.
- If the system crashed during writing to the data files but the transaction log is not corrupted, PostgreSQL will go through the transaction log, validate that the content is written into the data files, and correct the data files when necessary. There is no need to scan all the data files because it knows from the transaction log which part of which data file was supposed to be changed and how.

The process of replaying the transaction log is called recovery, and this is what the database always does after an unexpected restart. If you had a full transaction log from the time a database server was initialized until the current time, then it would be possible to recover the state of the database to any point in time in the past. This is, in fact, possible. PostgreSQL can be configured to archive the transaction log somewhere, instead of deleting old WAL files. This archive can be then used to perform a **point-in-time recovery** of the database on another machine.

Physical replication

The transaction log entries can be taken from one database server, the master server, and applied to the data files on another server, the standby server. In this case, the standby server will then have the exact replica of the database of the master server. The process of transferring transaction log entries and applying them on another server is called **physical replication**. It is called physical because the transaction log recovery works on the level of data files, and the database replica on the standby server will be exact byte copy of the master database.

Physical replication works for the entire database cluster for all the databases. When a new database is created, this is reflected in the transaction log, and therefore replicated to the standby server.

The standby server can be configured to allow read-only queries; in this case, it would be called **hot standby**.

Log shipping replication

One of the ways to set up physical replication is to constantly ship new WAL files from the master server to the standby and apply them there to have the synchronized copy of the database. This scenario is called **log shipping**.

To set up log shipping, the following actions should be taken:

- On the master server, do the following:
    - Make sure that the WAL files have enough information for replication—in the postgresql.conf file set the wal_level configuration parameter to replica or logical.
    - Enable archiving of the WAL files by setting the archive_mode configuration parameter to on.
    - Make PostgreSQL archive the WAL files to a safe location specified using the archive_command configuration parameter. PostgreSQL will apply this OS command to every WAL file that needs to be archived. This command can, for example, compress the file and copy it to a network drive. If the command is empty but archiving of WAL files is enabled, those files will be accumulated in the pg_wal folder.

- On the standby server, do the following:
    - Restore the base backup taken from the master server. The easiest way to do it is to use the pg_basebackup tool. The command, executed on the standby machine, may look like this:

    ```
    postgres@standby:~$ pg_pasebackup -D
    /var/lib/postgresql/11/main -h master -U postgres
    ```

    Here is a detailed description of the command: https://www.postgresql.org/docs/current/static/app-pgbasebackup.html.

    - Create a recovery.conf file in the data directory. This file is used to configure how the server should perform the recovery and whether it should work as a standby server. To set up the server as a standby server, at least the following two lines should be included in the file:

    ```
    standby_mode = on
    restore_command = 'cp /wal_archive_location/%f %p'
    ```

The value of the `restore_command` parameter will depend on the location of the WAL archive. It is an OS command that copies a WAL file from the WAL archive location to the location of the transaction log in the data directory. More about `recovery.conf` can be found at `https://www.postgresql.org/docs/current/static/recovery-config.html`.

When all of this is set up and both servers are started, the master server will copy all the WAL files to the archive location, and the standby server will take them from there and replay them over its base backup. This process will continue until the `standby_mode =` on line in the `recovery.conf` file. No transactions will be possible on the standby server, but it can be configured for read-only access.

If the master server crashes and it is necessary to switch to the standby server, it should be promoted. This means that it should stop the recovery and allow read-write transactions. To do this, simply remove the `recovery.conf` file and restart the server. After this, the standby server becomes the new master. It would make total sense to make the old master a standby after it's back in service, to keep the cluster redundant. In that case, the preceding steps should be repeated, with the servers switching roles. Never start the master server as a master if the standby was promoted—it could cause differences in the replicas and eventual data loss!

The benefits of replication implemented via log shipping are as follows:

- It is relatively easy to set up.
- There is no need to connect the standby server and the master server.
- The master does not know that there is a standby and does not depend on it.
- The number of standby servers can be greater than one. In fact, a standby can be used as a master for other standby servers. This would be called cascading replication.

On the other hand, there are also some problems:

- It's necessary to provide a network location for the WAL archive, which both master and standby can access. This implies the involvement of a third entity. It's possible to archive the WAL files directly to the standby server, but then the setup would not be symmetrical and in case of failure of the master and promotion of the standby, the setup of the new standby will be a bit more complex.

- The standby can replay a WAL file only after it is archived. This happens only when the file is complete, meaning it reached the size of 16 MB. That means the latest transactions performed on the master may not be reflected on the standby, especially if the transactions on the master are small and do not happen very often. In that case it may happen that the backup database doesn't have the recent transactions and its state is behind the master database. In the case of master failure, some data could be lost.

Streaming replication

There is another physical replication scenario that can work on top of log shipping or without log shipping at all: **streaming replication**. Streaming replication implies a connection between the standby and the master servers. The master would send all transaction log entries directly to the standby. By doing this, the standby will have all the recent changes without waiting for the WAL files to be archived.

To set up streaming replication, in addition to the steps mentioned previously, the following should be done on the master:

1. A database role for replication should be created in the database, like this:

   ```
   postgres=# CREATE USER streamer REPLICATION PASSWORD 'secret';
   CREATE USER
   ```

2. Connections for this user should be allowed in the pg_hba.conf file to the virtual database called replication, like this:

   ```
   host      replication     streamer    172.16.0.2/32    md5
   ```

3. On the standby server, add the primary_conninfo parameter to the recovery.conf file, which will set up the connection from the standby to the master, as follows:

   ```
   primary_conninfo = 'host=172.16.0.1 port=5432 user=streamer
   password=secret'
   ```

This is already enough. If the WAL archive was enabled and configured, the log shipping scenario will be performed first, until all the WAL files from the archive are applied to the backup database. When there are no more files, the standby server will connect to the master server and start receiving new WAL entries directly from the master. If that connection breaks or if the standby is restarted, the process will start again.

It's possible to set up streaming replication without the WAL archive at all. The master server by default stores last 64 WAL files in the `pg_wal` folder. It can send them to the standby when necessary. The size of each file is 16 MB. This means that, as long as the amount of changes in the data files is less than 1 GB, the streaming replication is able to replay these changes in the backup database without using the WAL archive.

Additionally, PostgreSQL provides a way to make the master server aware of which WAL files were processed by the standby and which were not. If the standby is slow (or simply disconnected), the master will not delete the files that are not yet processed, even if the number of them is greater than 64. This is done by creating a replication slot on the master. Then the standby will use the replication slot and the master will keep track of which of the WAL files were processed for this replication slot.

To use this feature, the following should be done on the master:

- Create the replication slot on the master by executing the `pg_create_physical_replication_slot()` function in the database:

```
postgres=# SELECT * FROM
pg_create_physical_replication_slot('slot1');
 slot_name | lsn
-----------+-----
 slot1     |
(1 row)
```

- Make sure the `max_replication_slots` configuration parameter in the `postgresql.conf` file is big enough.

And make the following change on the standby server:

- Add the `primary_slot_name` parameter to the `recovery.conf` file:

```
primary_slot_name = 'slot1'
```

After this, the master will not delete the WAL files that are not received by the standby even if the standby is not connected. When the standby connects again, it will receive all the missing WAL entries and the master will delete the old files.

The benefits of streaming replication over log shipping are as follows:

- The lag between the backup and the master is smaller because the WAL entries are sent immediately after the transactions are finished on the master, without waiting for the WAL files to be archived

- It's possible to set up the replication without WAL archiving at all, therefore there's no need to set up network storage or another common location for the master and the standby

Synchronous replication

Streaming replication is asynchronous by default. This means that if a user commits a transaction on the master, it gets the confirmation of the commit immediately, and the replication will happen only afterward. In case the master crashes right after a commit and the WAL records were not sent yet, the data will be lost, although the user has seen the commit was successful.

When high availability is a requirement in the sense that no data loss is acceptable, streaming replication can be set to synchronous mode.

To enable it on the master, in the `postgresql.conf` file, the `synchronous_standby_names` configuration parameter should be set to the name that identifies the standby server, for example, `synchronous_standby_names = 'standby1'`.

Then on the slave, the same name should be used in the connection string in the `recovery.conf` file, as follows:

```
primary_conninfo = 'host=172.16.0.1 port=5432 user=streamer password=secret application_name=standby1'
```

After this is done, the master server will wait for the standby, confirming that it has received and processed every WAL record before confirming the commit request. This will make commits slightly slower, of course. If the standby server is disconnected, all the transactions on the master will be blocked. It will not fail though; rather, it will only wait until the standby is connected again. The read-only queries will work normally.

The benefit of the synchronous replication is that it is guaranteed that if a transaction is finished and the commit command returned, the data is replicated to the standby server. The drawback is the performance overhead and the dependency of the master on the standby.

There is a Docker composition in the attached media that implements a streaming replication setup. To try it on Linux, change the directory to `streaming_replication` and bring up the composition by executing the `docker-compose up` command:

```
user@host:~/learning_postgresql/scalability/streaming_replication$ docker-
compose up
```

```
Creating network "streamingreplication_default" with the default driver
Creating streamingreplication_master_1
Creating streamingreplication_standby_1
Attaching to streamingreplication_master_1, streamingreplication_standby_1
...
```

Now there are two database instances running in two Docker containers—master and standby. Synchronous replication is already enabled. The database on the master is empty. The log output from both servers will be printed in that Terminal window. Open another Terminal window, change the directory to streaming_replication, connect to the master container, start a psql console, and create the car_portal database:

```
user@host:~/learning_postgresql/scalability/streaming_replication$ docker-
compose exec master bash
root@master:/# psql -h localhost -U postgres
psql (11.0)
SSL connection (protocol: TLSv1.2, cipher: ECDHE-RSA-AES256-GCM-SHA384,
bits: 256, compression: off)
Type "help" for help.
postgres=# \i schema.sql
...
car_portal=> \i data.sql
...
```

Now the database is created on the master and it's already replicated to the standby. Let's check that. Exit the shell session in the master container, connect to the container standby container, start psql, and run some queries:

```
user@host:~/learning_postgresql/scalability/streaming_replication$ docker-
compose exec standby bash
root@standby:/# psql -h localhost -U car_portal_app car_portal
psql (11.0)
SSL connection (protocol: TLSv1.2, cipher: ECDHE-RSA-AES256-GCM-SHA384,
bits: 256, compression: off)
Type "help" for help.
car_portal=> SELECT count(*) FROM car;
 count
-------
 229
(1 row)
car_portal=> UPDATE car set car_id = 0;
ERROR: cannot execute UPDATE in a read-only transaction
```

The data is replicated but it is read-only; the server that is running in recovery mode does not allow any changes.

To stop the Docker composition, switch to the Terminal window where the PostgreSQL log output is printed, and press *Ctrl* + *C*. Then execute `docker-compose down`. This will remove the Docker containers.

Failover procedures

The primary purpose of physical replication is high availability. That means in the case of a failure of the master server, the standby can take its role and become a new master. This is called **failover**. As mentioned in the *Log shipping replication* section, to promote the standby and make it a new master, we would need to delete the `recovery.conf` file and restart the server. It's important not to use the old master anymore, otherwise, the new master and the old master would have different data.

After the failover, the solution is not redundant anymore. The old standby has taken the role of a new master, but the old master is broken. It does not become a new standby. Database administrators need to set up a new standby by installing a new server, or making the old master a new standby. Until then, the systems are in a degenerate state.

In many cases, there is a mechanism that would automatically migrate the server's IP address to the current master server so that applications wouldn't need to care about failovers and require configuration changes.

PostgreSQL does not provide any automatic failover or common-IP capabilities. Depending on the setup and the requirements, the solutions could be very different and usually, third-party software is used for that. A good example of such software is `Patroni`, which is a software solution that manages a cluster of PostgreSQL servers, and automatically performs failover and sets up a new standby server. Documentation about Patroni can be found at `https://patroni.readthedocs.io/en/latest/`.

More on this topic can be found in the PostgreSQL documentation, at `https://www.postgresql.org/docs/current/static/high-availability.html`.

Logical replication

Physical data replication has a small disadvantage—it requires an identical configuration of the servers that are in sync. Simply speaking, the data has to be placed at the same locations on the filesystem. Another thing is that every change in the data files will be replicated, even if that doesn't change the data itself. For example, this happens when the VACUUM command is executed on the master that removes dead tuples from tables, or the CLUSTER command that rearranges rows.

Even if an index is created on a table, it's not the `CREATE INDEX` command that's sent to the standby, but the contents of the data file with the index data. This can create excessive load on the network and can become a bottleneck for a system under heavy load.

Logical replication, which does not send the results of SQL commands, but the commands themselves, is an alternative to physical replication. In this case, the amount of data sent over a network can be much smaller and the servers don't need to be identical. What's more, the data structure on the servers doesn't need to be the same.

For example, if you were to execute an SQL command, such as `INSERT INTO table_a (a, b) VALUES (1, 2)`, on the master and this command is replicated to the standby server, it's not a problem when the table has more columns on the standby than `a` and `b`. The SQL is correct, therefore it can be executed; the extra columns will get their default values.

PostgreSQL supports logical replication. The way it works makes it possible for the same server to receive some data from one server and send data to another server. That's why when talking about logical replication, there is no master and standby; there is the **publisher**—the server that sends the data, and the **subscriber**—the one that receives it. The same server can be both publisher and subscriber for different tables or sets of tables, and a subscriber can receive data from multiple publishers.

Logical replication works on the level of individual tables or sets of tables. It is also possible to set it up for all the tables in a database, and this will be automatically enabled for any new tables. However, logical replication does not affect other schema objects, such as sequences, indexes, or views.

To set up logical replication, the following actions should be performed on the publisher side:

1. Create a database role for replication or enable `REPLICATION` for the existing user:

   ```
   postgres=# ALTER USER car_portal_app REPLICATION;
   ALTER USER
   ```

2. Allow this user to connect to the `replication` virtual database in the `pg_hba.conf` file:

   ```
   host     replication     car_portal_app     172.16.0.2/32     md5
   ```

3. Set the `wal_level` configuration parameter to `logical` in `postgresql.conf`. This is necessary to make PostgreSQL write enough information for logical replication into WAL files.

4. Make sure that the value of the `max_replication_slots` configuration parameter is equal to or greater than the number of subscribers that are supposed to connect to this publisher server.

5. Set the `max_wal_senders` configuration parameter to be more or equal to the value of the `max_replication_slots` parameter.

6. Create a publication object. A publication is a named set of tables. When it is created, the server will track changes to the data in these tables to send them to any subscriber that would use the publication. The CREATE PUBLICATION SQL command is used for it; here is an example that would create a publication for all the tables in the `car_portal` database:

```
car_portal=> CREATE PUBLICATION car_portal FOR ALL TABLES;
CREATE PUBLICATION
```

On the subscriber side, a subscription has to be created. A subscription is a special object that stands for a connection to an existing publication on the publisher server. The CREATE SUBSCRIPTION command is used for this, as shown in the following example:

```
car_portal=# CREATE SUBSCRIPTION car_portal CONNECTION 'dbname=car_portal
host=publisher user=car_portal_app' PUBLICATION car_portal;
CREATE SUBSCRIPTION
```

The tables to replicate are defined in the publication. The tables should be created in advance on the subscriber side. In the preceding example, the `car_portal` subscription connects to a `car_portal` publication, which publishes all the tables in the database. Therefore, the same tables should also exist on the subscriber side.

Once the subscription is created, the replication will start automatically. At first, by default, PostgreSQL will replicate the whole table and after that, it will replicate the changes asynchronously, after they happen on the publisher side. If any of the servers are restarted, the connection will be re-established automatically. If the subscriber is offline for some time, the publisher will remember all the pending changes and they will be sent to the subscriber once it is connected again. This functionality is implemented using replication slots, in a similar way to streaming replication.

Logical replication can be treated as if the all the data-changing SQL commands, which are performed on the published tables were sent to the subscriber. The subscriber would then apply the commands in its database to the same tables. This happens at the level of SQL, not at the low level of the physical replication. This allows the subscriber to have different data structures; as long as the SQL commands can be executed, it will work.

Logical replication doesn't affect sequences. It doesn't apply any DDL commands, such as `ALTER TABLE`. The subscriber, when applying the commands it receives, respects primary keys, `UNIQUE` and `CHECK` constraints on the target tables, but it ignores `FOREIGN KEY` constraints.

Logical replication can be set up to be synchronous in the same way as streaming replication. To do it, on the publisher, set the subscriber name in the `synchronous_standby_names` configuration parameter in `postgresql.conf`, and on the subscriber, specify this name in the connection string when executing the `CREATE SUBSCRIPTION` command.

Logical replication has the following benefits over physical replication:

- It's simple to set up
- It can be very flexible:
    - It does not require an identical database schema on the two servers, and does not require an identical setup of the servers in general
    - The same server can work as a subscriber and publisher at the same time
    - The same table can be used in multiple subscriptions, so it would collect the data from several servers
    - A publication can be configured to replicate only certain types of operations (`INSERT` and `DELETE`, but not `UPDATE`, for example)
    - The target table on the subscriber is accessible for writing
- Logical replication can be used with different major versions of PostgreSQL
- It doesn't require any third-party software or hardware, and works out of the box in PostgreSQL
- The changes in data on the physical level (such as `VACUUM` or `CLUSTER`) are not replicated

On the other hand, flexibility brings complexity. When implementing logical replication, the following should be kept in mind:

- Logical replication does not respect foreign keys, so it can bring the target database into an inconsistent state.
- When the schema changes on the publisher side, the replication can suddenly break if the schema on the subscriber is not compatible.
- Logical replication only replicates changes from publisher to subscriber. If somebody changes the data directly on the subscriber, the replication will not bring the tables back in sync.
- Only tables are replicated; other schema objects are not. This can be an issue when auto-incremented fields that are based on sequences are used in the databases.

There is a sample Docker composition in the attached media that implements a logical replication scenario. To try it, change directory to `logical_replication` and run `docker-compose up`. This will bring up two instances of PostgreSQL—`publisher` and `subscriber`. Create the `car_portal` database on `publisher`, and create a publication. `subscriber` also has the database but it is still empty. Now, in another Terminal, start a `bash` shell on `subscriber`, open `psql`, and run the following commands:

```
user@host:~/learning_postgresql/scalability/logical_replication$ docker-
compose exec subscriber bash
root@subscriber:/# psql -h localhost -U postgres car_portal
psql (11.0)
SSL connection (protocol: TLSv1.2, cipher: ECDHE-RSA-AES256-GCM-SHA384,
bits: 256, compression: off)
Type "help" for help.
car_portal=# CREATE SUBSCRIPTION car_portal CONNECTION 'dbname=car_portal
host=publisher user=car_portal_app' PUBLICATION car_portal;
psql:subscriber.sql:2: NOTICE: created replication slot "car_portal" on
publisher
CREATE SUBSCRIPTION
```

At this moment, there will be a lot of output in the first Terminal window telling you that all the tables in the `car_portal` database were replicated to the subscriber. Now let's query the data on the subscriber:

```
car_portal=# select count(*) from car_portal_app.car;
 count
-------
 229
(1 row)
```

Replication works! Now you may open a session in the `publisher` container, start `psql`, and insert some data into the publisher's database. Then check how it's replicated to the subscriber.

There is another example in the `logical_replication_multi_master` directory that shows how the same table can get changes from two different publishers. To try it, open a terminal, change the directory to `logical_replication_multi_master` and bring up the Docker composition with `docker-compose up`. This will create three containers: `subscriber`, `publisher_a`, and `publisher_b`. The publications are already created in both publishers for the `car_portal.car_model` table. But there is no subscription yet.

To see how multi-master replication can work, open another terminal, navigate to the `logical_replication_multi_master` directory, start a bash session in the subscriber container, open psql (connecting as user `postgres`), and import the `subscriber.sql` file, as follows:

```
user@host:~/learning_postgresql/scalability/logical_replication_multi_maste
r$ docker-compose exec subscriber bash
root@subscriber:/# psql -h localhost -U postgres car_portal
psql (11.0)
SSL connection (protocol: TLSv1.2, cipher: ECDHE-RSA-AES256-GCM-SHA384,
bits: 256, compression: off)
Type "help" for help.
car_portal=# \i subscriber.sql
SET
ALTER TABLE
psql:subscriber.sql:3: NOTICE: created replication slot "car_model_a" on
publisher
CREATE SUBSCRIPTION
psql:subscriber.sql:4: NOTICE: created replication slot "car_model_b" on
publisher
CREATE SUBSCRIPTION
```

This will disable create two subscriptions. Now you can connect to both publishers and try to insert data in the `car_portal.car_model` table, and then select from the table in the subscriber to make sure that the records from both publishers are replicated. The primary key was removed (the `ALTER TABLE` output is the indication of that), which is why it is possible to replicate records with the same IDs.

Note that if the `TRUNCATE TABLE` command is executed on one of the publishers, it'll be replicated to the subscriber and wipe the whole table, also removing the records copied from the other publisher. This is why it is the command itself that is replicated, not the physical changes that were made to the data.

More about logical replication can be found in the PostgreSQL documentation at `https://www.postgresql.org/docs/current/static/logical-replication.html`.

Building a scalable PostgreSQL solution

Replication can be used in many scaling scenarios. Its primary purpose is to create and maintain a backup database in case of system failure. This is especially true for physical replication. However, replication can also be used to improve the performance of a solution based on PostgreSQL. Sometimes, third-party tools can be used to implement complex scaling scenarios.

Scaling for heavy querying

Imagine there's a system that's supposed to handle a lot of read requests. For example, there could be an application that implements an HTTP API endpoint that supports the auto-completion functionality on a website. Each time a user enters a character in a web form, the system searches in the database for objects whose name starts with the string the user has entered. The number of queries can be very big because of the large number of users, and also because several requests are processed for every user session. To handle large numbers of requests, the database should be able to utilize multiple CPU cores. In case the number of simultaneous requests is really large, the number of cores required to process them can be greater than a single machine could have.

The same applies to a system that is supposed to handle multiple heavy queries at the same time. You don't need a lot of queries, but when the queries themselves are big, using as many CPUs as possible would offer a performance benefit—especially when parallel query execution is used.

In such scenarios, where one database cannot handle the load, it's possible to set up multiple databases, set up replication from one master database to all of them, making each them work as a hot standby, and then let the application query different databases for different requests. The application itself can be smart and query a different database each time, but that would require a special implementation of the data-access component of the application, which could look as follows:

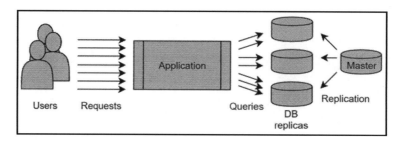

Another option is to use a tool called **Pgpool-II**, which can work as a load-balancer in front of several PostgreSQL databases. The tool exposes a SQL interface, and applications can connect there as if it were a real PostgreSQL server. Then Pgpool-II will redirect the queries to the databases that are executing the fewest queries at that moment; in other words, it will perform load-balancing:

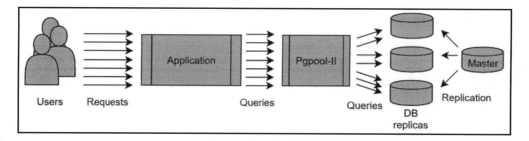

More information about Pgpool-II can be found at http://www.pgpool.net.

Yet another option is to scale the application together with the databases so that one instance of the application will connect to one instance of the database. In that case, the users of the application should connect to one of the many instances. This can be achieved with HTTP load-balancing:

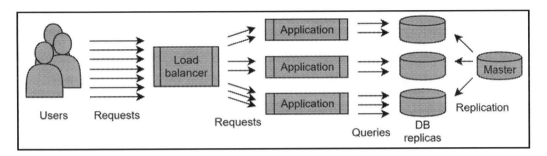

Data sharding

When the problem is not the number of concurrent queries, but the size of the database and the speed of a single query, a different approach can be implemented. The data can be separated into several servers, which will be queried in parallel, and then the result of the queries will be consolidated outside of those databases. This is called **data sharding**.

PostgreSQL provides a way to implement sharding based on table partitioning, where partitions are located on different servers and another one, the master server, uses them as foreign tables. We discussed partitioning in Chapter 08, *OLAP and Data Warehousing*, and foreign tables in Chapter 14, *Testing*. When performing a query on a parent table defined on the master server, depending on the WHERE clause and the definitions of the partitions, PostgreSQL can recognize which partitions contain the data that is requested and would query only these partitions. Depending on the query, sometimes joins, grouping, and aggregation could be performed on the remote servers. PostgreSQL can query different partitions in parallel, which will effectively utilize the resources of several machines. Having all this, it's possible to build a solution when applications would connect to a single database that would physically execute their queries on different database servers depending on the data that is being queried.

It's also possible to build sharding algorithms into the applications that use PostgreSQL. In short, applications would be expected to know what data is located in which database, write it only there, and read it only from there. This would add a lot of complexity to the applications.

Another option is to use one of the PostgreSQL-based sharding solutions available on the market or open source solutions. They have their own pros and cons, but the common problem is that they are based on previous releases of PostgreSQL and don't use the most recent features (sometimes providing their own features instead).

One of the most popular sharding solutions is **Postgres-XL** (`https://www.postgres-xl.org/`), which implements a shared-nothing architecture using multiple servers running PostgreSQL. The system has several components:

- **Multiple data nodes**: Store the data
- **A single global transaction monitor** (**GTM**): Manages the cluster, provides global transaction consistency
- **Multiple coordinator nodes**: Supports user connections, builds query-execution plans, and interacts with the GTM and the data nodes

Postgres-XL implements the same API as PostgreSQL, therefore the applications don't need to treat the server in any special way. It is ACID-compliant, meaning it supports transactions and integrity constraints. The `COPY` command is also supported.

The main benefits of using Postgres-XL are as follows:

- It can scale to support more reading operations by adding more data nodes
- It can scale for to support more writing operations by adding more coordinator nodes
- The current release of Postgres-XL (at the time of writing) is based on PostgreSQL 10, which is relatively new

The main downside of Postgres-XL is that it does not provide any high-availability features out of the box. When more servers are added to a cluster, the probability of the failure of any of them increases. That's why you should take care with backups or implement replication of the data nodes themselves.

Postgres-XL is open source, but commercial support is available.

Another solution worth mentioning is **Greenplum** (`http://greenplum.org/`). It's positioned as an implementation of a massive parallel-processing database, specifically designed for data warehouses. It has the following components:

- **Master node**: Manages user connections, builds query execution plans, manages transactions
- **Data nodes**: Store the data and perform queries

Greenplum also implements the PostgreSQL API, and applications can connect to a Greenplum database without any changes. It supports transactions, but support for integrity constraints is limited. The `COPY` command is supported.

The main benefits of Greenplum are as follows:

- It can scale to support more reading operations by adding more data nodes.
- It supports column-oriented table organization, which can be useful for data-warehousing solutions.
- Data compression is supported.
- High-availability features are supported out of the box. It's possible (and recommended) to add a secondary master that would take over in case a primary master crashes. It's also possible to add mirrors to the data nodes to prevent data loss.

The drawbacks are as follows:

- It doesn't scale to support more writing operations. Everything goes through the single master node and adding more data nodes does not make writing faster. However, it's possible to import data from files directly on the data nodes.
- It uses PostgreSQL 8.4 in its core. Greenplum has a lot of improvements and new features added to the base PostgreSQL code, but it's still based on a very old release; however, the system is being actively developed.
- Greenplum doesn't support foreign keys, and support for unique constraints is limited.

There are commercial and open source editions of Greenplum.

Scaling for many numbers of connections

Yet another use case related to scalability is when the number of database connections is great. We mentioned connection pooling in `Chapter 15`, *Using PosgreSQL in Python Applications*, and discussed how necessary and beneficial it is. However, when a single database is used in an environment with a lot of microservices and each has its own connection pool, even if they don't perform too many queries, it's possible that hundreds or even thousands of connections are opened in the database. Each connection consumes server resources and just the requirement to handle a great number of connections can already be a problem, without even performing any queries.

If applications don't use connection pooling and open connections only when they need to query the database, and close them afterwards, another problem could occur. Establishing a database connection takes time—not too much, but when the number of operations is great, the total overhead will be significant.

There is a tool, named **PgBouncer** (https://PgBouncer.github.io/), that implements a connection-pool functionality. It can accept connections from many applications as if it were a PostgreSQL server and then open a limited number of connections towards the database. It would reuse the same database connections for multiple applications' connections. The process of establishing a connection from an application to PgBouncer is much faster than connecting to a real database, because PgBouncer doesn't need to initialize a database backend process for the session.

PgBouncer can create multiple connection pools that work in one of the three modes:

- **Session mode**: A connection to a PostgreSQL server is used for the lifetime of a client connection to PgBouncer. Such a setup could be used to speed up the connection process on the application side. This is the default mode.
- **Transaction mode**: A connection to PostgreSQL is used for a single transaction that a client performs. That could be used to reduce the number of connections at the PostgreSQL side when only a few translations are performed simultaneously.
- **Statement mode**: A database connection is used for a single statement. Then it is returned to the pool and a different connection is used for a next statement. This mode is similar to the transaction mode, though more aggressive. Note that multi-statement transactions are not possible when statement mode is used.

Different pools can be set up to work in different modes.

It's possible to let PgBouncer connect to multiple PostgreSQL servers, thus working as a reverse proxy.

The way PgBouncer could be used is represented in the following diagram:

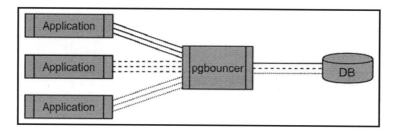

PgBouncer establishes several connections to the database. When an application connects to PgBouncer and starts a transaction, PgBouncer assigns an existing database connection to that application, forwards all SQL commands to the database, and delivers the results back. When the transaction is finished, PgBouncer will dissociate the connections, but not close them. If another application starts a transaction, the same database connection could be used. Such a setup requires configuring PgBouncer to work in transaction mode.

Summary

In this chapter, we discussed the problem of building scalable solutions based on PostgreSQL utilizing the resources of several servers. There is a natural limitation for such systems—basically, there is always a compromise between performance, reliability, and consistency. It's possible to improve one aspect, but others will suffer.

PostgreSQL provides several ways to implement replication that would maintain a copy of the data from a database on another server or servers. This can be used as a backup or a standby solution that would take over in case the main server crashes. Replication can also be used to improve the performance of a software system by making it possible to distribute the load on several database servers.

In some cases, the functionality of replication provided by PostgreSQL isn't enough. There are third-party solutions that work around PostgreSQL, providing extra features, such as PgBouncer, which works as a connection pool, or Pgpool-II, which can work as a load balancer. There are also more complex solutions, based on the code of PostgreSQL, that store different parts of data on different nodes and query them simultaneously. They implement a multi-server distributed database solution that can operate very large amounts of data and handle a huge load. We mentioned Postgres-XL and Greenplum, but there is more, both commercial and open source.

This was the last practical topic we'll discuss in this book. We hope we managed to arouse your interest in databases, and PostgreSQL specifically. In the last chapter, we'll provide guidance on where to go next to learn more about PostgreSQL and its surrounding technologies, so you can become a database professional and develop and implement efficient software solutions for your needs.

Questions

1. What does it mean for a software solution to be scalable?
2. What does the CAP theorem say about a distributed storage solution?
3. Which features, in the context of the CAP theorem, does PostgreSQL support?
4. What is the Write-Ahead Log?
5. How is WAL used when performing database recovery and replication?
6. What is streaming replication?
7. What is a failover process?
8. What is a hot standby?
9. What is the difference between physical replication and logical replication?
10. How can replication help in distributing the load over several database servers?
11. What is data sharding?

Further reading

For more information on the topics covered in this chapter, check out these other books by Packt Publishing:

- *PostgreSQL Replication, Second Edition* by Hans-Jürgen Schönig offers a great explanation of how PostgreSQL replication features work internally, and provides a lot of practical examples of how to use them
- *PostgreSQL High Availability Cookbook, Second Edition* by Shaun M. Thomas provides comprehensive hand-on recipes on how to build highly-available database solutions based on PostgreSQL using its replication capabilities

17
What's Next?

At the end of a book, it makes sense to look back at what was discussed in the chapters to understand where to go next.

The book is intended to be an introduction to PostgreSQL for beginners, those who didn't have any experience with this RDBMS before, or who knew nothing about relational databases. The topic is quite vast and complex and, for this reason, even an entry-level book could not be simple.

In this chapter, we will summarize the topics we've covered in this book, and try to provide some tips and point the reader in the right direction for further learning.

 First of all, if you are going to continue working with PostgreSQL, it makes sense have a link to its official documentation at `https://www.postgresql.org/docs/current/static/index.html`. The documentation is also available in French, Japanese, and Russian at `https://www.postgresql.org/docs/manuals/`.

At `https://www.postgresql.org/docs/manuals/`, you can find links to many books on PostgreSQL, including this one.

Fundamentals

We started with a general introduction to the theory of relational algebra, relational databases, and data modeling. This was discussed in `Chapter 1`, *Relational Databases*.

Normalization

Normalization is a process of restructuring a relational database in order to bring its tables into one of the **normal forms**. There are several normal forms that define requirements to the structure of a table or, strictly speaking, a relation.

For example, a relation is in **first normal form (1NF)** only when each of its attributes contains a single value. To understand this concept, think about a table that contains a phone book where each record corresponds to a person. If a person has more than one telephone number, they all would be stored in a singe field, comma-separated, as follows:

```
SELECT person, phones FROM contacts;
    person    |            phones
--------------+--------------------------------
 John Smith   | +1-254-4556-44587
 George Brown | +49-151-7151515, +49-123-4595246
 Alex Snow    | +7-90256-45698
```

This would not be a table in 1NF. However, if such a record were split into several rows, so that each of them contains only one phone number, the table would get into 1NF, as follows:

```
SELECT person, phone FROM contacts;
    person     |       phone
---------------+-------------------
 John Smith    | +1-254-4556-44587
 George Braun  | +49-151-7151515
 George Braun  | +49-123-4595246
 Alex Snowman  | +7-90256-45698
```

The benefit of bringing such a table into 1NF is that after the change, the values of that field could be used directly to call that person. Originally, it wouldn't have been possible to call; we would need first to determine whether the value in the field is a single number or a list, and if it's a list, it would be necessary to split it into individual numbers and then make the calls. This implies additional complexity and could lead to errors, while having the relation in 1NF would prevent that.

There are more requirements to defining the first normal form. For example, a relation must not imply any ordering of records or columns, and there must be no duplicated rows.

Second normal form (2NF) requires that a relation is already in 1NF and there is no attribute that would be in a functional dependency of a subset of any candidate key. To explain it, let's consider a phonebook table again. Suppose the table contains not only phone numbers but also addresses. If the table is already in 1NF, it's a given that if a person has more than one number, each will be stored in a separate record. But that would mean that the person's address should be duplicated in each of these records, as follows:

```
SELECT person, phone, address FROM contacts;
    person     |       phone        |             address
---------------+--------------------+---------------------------------
 John Smith    | +1-254-4556-44587  | 123, Green Road, Jacksonville +
               |                    | Mississippi 45678
 George Braun  | +49-151-7151515    | Gruenerweg 7, 12345 Darmstadt
 George Braun  | +49-123-4595246    | Gruenerweg 7, 12345 Darmstadt
 Alex Snowman  | +7-90256-45698     | Moscow, Kuznetsova st. 15-183
```

How do we guarantee that the address is the same in all of these records? And what if a person had several addresses? In this example, the telephone number is a dependency of the person. The address is also a dependency of the person, but not of the number. This contradiction violates the requirements of 2NF. To bring the model to 2NF, the table should be split into two, and the address should be taken out into a different table, as follows:

```
SELECT person, address FROM contacts_address;
    person     |            address
---------------+---------------------------------
 John Smith    | 123, Green Road, Jacksonville +
               | Mississippi 45678
 George Braun  | Gruenerweg 7, 12345 Darmstadt
 Alex Snowman  | Moscow, Kuznetsova st. 15-183
(3 rows)

SELECT person, phone FROM contacts_phone;
    person     |       phone
---------------+--------------------
 John Smith    | +1-254-4556-44587
 George Braun  | +49-151-7151515
 George Braun  | +49-123-4595246
 Alex Snowman  | +7-90256-45698
(4 rows)
```

Further normalization is also possible, and would be recommended; for example, creating a separate table with data, such as name and date of birth date, and making the tables with phone numbers and addresses reference that table by ID. Normalization can ease the validation of data consistency, simplify data processing, and save some disk space.

The theory of normal forms was first proposed by Edgar F. Codd in 1970. It was developed later by him and other computer scientists. In fact, Codd invented the relational model for data management and developed a theoretical foundation for modern relational database-management systems.

There are more normal forms—11, in fact. It isn't always practical to get extreme and try to normalize a database up to the strictest normal form, but being aware of them is essential to develop a good data model. Keeping a data model normalized is a way to provide data integrity and consistency, and simplifies processing the data at the end.

Normalization is not the only way to improve a data model. Also, it cannot prevent all the errors or conflicts in the data because real life is usually more complex than any data model that tries to describe it. However, the great achievement of Codd, and others who developed the relational theory, is the proposal of a strict and formal measure that describes the quality of a data model, and normalization as a way to improve that quality.

Denormalization

One of the very typical use cases for a database is to work as a storage component of a reporting solution. Such databases are often called **data warehouses**. Chapter 8, *OLAP and Data Warehousing*, was dedicated to that topic and explains the major concepts of these solutions and how to implement them using PostgreSQL.

In Chapter 8, *OLAP and Data Warehousing*, we briefly discussed ideas of denormalization, which is the opposite process of normalization. It is common for OLAP solutions to optimize the database structure for the sake of performance. Normalized data structures usually have a lot of relations and a lot of relationships defined between them. In data warehouses, it's quite typical that the data is loaded once and then never changed. However, the task of searching and retrieving the data is happening very often and usually it requires reading a lot of information. To reduce the number of joins during querying, it often makes sense to join tables in advance and store the result in a bigger table.

As an example of a topic related to OLAP that was not covered in this book, let's look at slowly-changing dimensions. Consider a big fact table showing information about company's sales. One of the dimensions of this table could be a customer. It can be a multi-level dimension, and one of the levels could be the customer's city. This structure would make it possible to analyze sales data over time per city. What if a customer moves from one city to another? If the information about the city is taken from the customer's properties, it could appear that all the sales history has now changed, since the customer is now in a different city, but the fact table only references *the customer*, not *the customer at a point in time in the past*.

There are different possible solutions for this problem: decouple the dimensions of city and customer, and then write the city directly to the fact table (that would be denormalization) or introduce a time-range attribute in the customer table and keep several versions of the data of the same customer at different times.

A lot of theoretical work was done in this area. The first important names in this field are Bill Inmon and Ralph Kimball. Their approaches to modeling OLAP data structures are similar, but not the same, and the implementation of a data model would depend on particular requirements. In any case, anyone working on a data warehouse would benefit from getting familiar with their work.

NoSQL databases

There are cases when classical relational structures are not enough. In `Chapter 9`, *Beyond Conventional Data Types*, we explain how to make a PostgreSQL database multidimensional via use of arrays, and how to use the features that are usually offered by NoSQL databases, such as storing and indexing JSON data. In this chapter, we talked about the PostgreSQL full-text search—a powerful feature often used by web applications.

Still, PostgreSQL is a relational database. It's designed to work with relations and relationships. These NoSQL features are provided on top of the relational basement. For this reason, PostgreSQL cannot be a perfect choice as a storage component for data that is not relational in nature. A developer working on a data-intensive solution should be aware of possible options to make educated decisions on which technology to use.

There is no formal definition of the term "NoSQL". Sometimes, it refers to a data storage technology that's not relational, and therefore, SQL is not applicable. Sometimes, NoSQL is treated as Not only SQL, meaning that a technology supports SQL or a language that is very similar, offering something more at the same time.

There are a lot of non-relational data management systems. They can be grouped based on the type of data they store, how they store data, and how they provide access to it, in the following categories:

- **Document stores**: These deal with documents that are usually represented as JSON or XML objects. The store system validates the incoming documents, stores them, and provides capabilities for searching and retrieving documents or parts of them. PostgreSQL can also store JSON or XML data, but those systems are designed specifically for this purpose. They are often distributed and can be scaled much more easily than PostgreSQL. Some of them offer the HTTP API out of the box and therefore can be used as a backend systems for web applications without any intermediate software layer. Some examples include MongoDB, Amazon DynamoDB, and Couchbase.

- **Key-value stores**: Their functionality may seem primitive; they operate with associative arrays or hash tables. Data entries in such structures are identified by a key, and can be found, modified, or deleted when the key is given. You may treat a PostgreSQL table with a primary key in a similar way. However, those specialized systems being designed specifically for this purpose can do the task much faster, or at a larger scale. In many cases, such systems work as in-memory database. They are mostly used as caching backends in different software solutions. Examples of key-value stores are Redis and Memcached. Amazon DynamoDB and Cassandra can also work as a key-value store.

- **Time series databases**: These store data that has a time dimension. They provide a lookup functionality and aggregation where time is either used as a search criterium or in grouping and aggregation. Such systems are often used as a storage backend for monitoring systems that collect metrics from applications or sensor data. Again, relational databases, such as PostgreSQL, could also store this data in a table and index its rows by `time` column; however, specialized solution could offer more than conventional SQL. For example, you could start a query that would provide new data in real time, constantly, until cancelled. The most popular time series databases are InfluxDB, Graphite, Prometheus, and Druid.

- **Wide-column stores**: These store data in tables; and different records of the same table can have different fields. This structure can be used to store semi-structured data like document stores do, or as key-value stores. They could also be treated as multidimensional key-value stores. Unstructured data is difficult to store in a relational database, especially when performance is a requirement. Specialized wide-column stores can do it very efficiently. As mentioned in `Chapter 16,` *Scalability,* Cassandra can handle huge clusters with thousands of servers, without a single point of failure. Of course, such solutions require a special approach to data modeling. Examples of wide-column stores are Cassandra, HBase, and Accumulo. Some cloud providers also offer them as a service, such as Microsoft Azure, Cosmos DB, or Google Cloud Bigtable.

- **Search engines**: These are different systems, that process and store different kinds of data, but their common goal is to provide efficient search capabilities, including pattern matching, full-text search, or fuzzy search. They often provide the HTTP API and could be used directly in web applications without a backend layer. The most popular search systems are Elasticsearch, Splunk, and Solr.
- **Object-oriented databases**: These provide a persistence layer for applications written in an object-oriented programming language. We discussed object-relational mapping in `Chapter 15`, *Using PostgreSQL in Python Applications*. ORM means converting class instances used in an application to records in a database table. Object-oriented database are usually integrated with an object-oriented programming language, which makes it possible to store and manipulate objects directly in the database without a mapping layer.

PostgreSQL supports **Atomicity, Consistency, Isolation, and Durability (ACID)** properties. Leaving aside complicated theory, it could be said that PostgreSQL supports transactions. We can open a transaction and start making changes to the data. Until the transaction is committed, these changes are not visible to others. If the transaction is committed, it's guaranteed that all the changes are written on disk and will not be lost. It cannot happen that a part of the transaction is written, and another part is not; it's always all or nothing. `Chapter 10`, *Transactions and Concurrency Control* explains that in detail.

Most of the NoSQL databases don't support those principles mainly because they are not relational, and those concepts aren't applicable there. Their definitions of a transaction, or consistency, could be very different from PostgreSQL's definitions.

As you may have noticed, many of the NoSQL capabilities and features could also be implemented in PostgreSQL. Going this way instead of using a specialized solution has its benefits and drawbacks. The main benefit is that PostgreSQL provides transactions and may enforce data integrity, when applicable. The main drawbacks are that special systems are often faster and, in many cases, they can be scaled better and more easily than PostgreSQL.

Working with PostgreSQL software

In `Chapter 2`, *PostgreSQL in Action*, we discussed the history and main features of PostgreSQL. We also learned how to install PostgreSQL.

A database should be secure. From `Chapter 10`, *PostgreSQL Security*, you learned how to use PostgreSQL features that help to protect data from unauthorized access and control the ways the database is being accessed. This chapter provides some best practice recipes.

A big concern of developers of any software solution is performance. Making it work faster is important—we don't need to explain why. PostgreSQL is a complicated system with a huge amount of configuration parameters. Chapter 13, *Optimizing Database Performance*, we learn how to configure PostgreSQL to make it work faster, with different kinds of load patterns.

The PostgreSQL server

The topics mentioned in the introduction to this section are first related to the installation and configuration of the PostgreSQL server. We already provided enough information about installing the server software on different operating systems and starting to work with PostgreSQL.

But if you want to go further and learn more about the PostgreSQL server administration tasks, you might need to look deeper into the following topics:

- **Server administration in general**: PostgreSQL works on top of an operating system and relies a lot on the file system caching functionality that accelerates I/O operations.

- **Virtualization and OS-level virtualization (containers)**: Nowadays, it's normal to run server software in the cloud, on virtual machines, or inside containers. PostgreSQL can run in a virtual machine as well as in a containerized virtual environment, and the task of automation of deploying database servers gets more common.

- **Disk system setup**: Depending on the size of the database and load patterns (OLTP or OLAP, more reads or more writes, how often a parallel query is used, or how often a sequential table scan is performed), it may make sense to keep different parts of a database on different physical disks. It may be worth considering using HDD or SSD for different tablespaces to achieve optimal balance between performance and cost.

- **IT security**: As mentioned in Chapter 10, *Transactions and Concurrency Control*, PostgreSQL can be integrated with LDAP servers or software that implements the GSS-API. To use these features properly, a database administrator should understand how those technologies work.

- **Replication and cluster management**: Having a cluster of two PostgreSQL servers, a master and a standby, is a common redundant setup that aims for high availability. To be able to manage the cluster, you would need to understand how to set up a shared IP address and make it always associated with the current master server. Similar functionality can also be achieved with a TCP proxy solution. You would also need to be able to set up log shipping when necessary.

- **Version control**: When you have servers deployed automatically or a cluster of servers, it's convenient to keep configuration files in a version-control system to be able to track changes and keep the files identical on all the machines where it is needed.

There are software products that can be used together with PostgreSQL to help to set up and manage a single database server or a cluster of servers. Some of them have been mentioned in the book:

- **Patroni** (`https://patroni.readthedocs.io/en/latest/`): This is used to set up and manage a high-availability cluster. Can perform automatic failover of a standby server, and convert the former master into a new standby. Can manage a cluster with multiple standby nodes. Can be used in a cloud environment, for example Kubernetes.
- **HAProxy** (`http://www.haproxy.org/`): Working as a TCP proxy, this can be used to provide a single entry point to a high-availability cluster of several nodes. It can be used together with Patroni.
- **Corosync** (`http://corosync.github.io/corosync/`) **and Pacemaker** (`http://clusterlabs.org/pacemaker/`): These can be used to set up automatic failover for a high-availability cluster. These applications can monitor PostgreSQL servers, detect a failure, and promote the standby. They can also manage a shared-IP solution to switch the common entry point to the new master.
- **rsync** (`https://rsync.samba.org/`): This is used to copy and synchronize files over a network. Can be used for WAL shipping.
- **Docker** (`https://www.docker.com/`): This performs operating-system-level virtualization; it is used to run software in isolated containers to abstract them from a particular configuration of a server. This is similar to running applications in a virtual machine, but more lightweight and easier to set up. Using Docker containers makes it possible to automate and standardize the deployment of different kinds of software. It's especially useful during testing since it makes it possible to quickly bring up big compositions of several services working together and talking to each other as if each of them was running on a dedicated server.
- **PgBouncer** (`https://pgbouncer.github.io/`): This is used for connection pool for PostgreSQL. Can be used in front of a database server to reduce the load related to establishing database connections in case of a large number of client systems.

- **Pgpool-II** (`http://www.pgpool.net`): Connection pool, load-balancing, and replication-software layer, and can be used to set up a PostgreSQL cluster for high availability, providing replication, and automated failover. It can also be used to scale a database to read redirecting connections to one of the standby nodes and distribute the load.

- **PL/Proxy** (`https://plproxy.github.io/`): A data-sharding solution for PostgreSQL-based functions; can be used to set up a cluster of PostgreSQL servers, distribute data over them, and query them simultaneously to achieve better performance. PostgreSQL 11 already includes a big part of this functionality with the parallel query, partitioning, and allowing remote partitions, but PL/Proxy still can help in special cases.

PostgreSQL client software

First of all, the main and most commonly used PostgreSQL client is the `psql` console. We've used it in the examples throughout this book, but we haven't explained all of its features. In fact, it deserves its own chapter. To master PostgreSQL, it's essential to be able to use `psql` well. We introduced `psql` in `Chapter 2`, *PostgreSQL in Action*, and described some of its key features.

What's worth mentioning again is its backslash meta-commands. The tool supports over a hundred of them, each providing a different functionality, such as the following:

- Querying the database system catalog to list databases, roles, schemas, tables, views, and types
- Describing a database object, for example, to get a list of fields of a table, a view definition, or a function's source code
- Managing query execution, such as measuring execution time, redirecting the output to a file, or formatting the output as HTML
- Scripting functionality, such as executing a file in the current `psql` interactive session, including a file into another script, conditionally executing parts of a script, or using variables in a script
- Managing a database connection and user session, such as connecting to a different database or changing user's password
- Customizing the behavior and appearance of `psql` itself, such as switching between a columnar or expanded representation mode, changing the command prompt, or formatting the query output

To continue learning about `psql`, please refer to the documentation at `https://www.postgresql.org/docs/current/static/app-psql.html`.

There are other great client and server tools that are provided by the PostgreSQL community:

- **pgAdmin 4**: A database-server management tool. It has a web-based user interface. It provides access databases displaying schema objects in a tree-like view, allowing you to modify the schema, manage user-access rights, and execute SQL queries. It also can show database statistics and show the current database status and metrics graphs. Documentation and download links for pgAdmin 4 can be found at `https://www.pgadmin.org/`.
- **pgAgent**: A scheduler that can run and manage jobs, such as SQL scripts, OS scripts, and other jobs related to data and database management. pgAdmin also provides a UI to manage these jobs.

- More information about pgAgent can be found at `https://www.pgadmin.org/docs/pgadmin4/dev/pgagent.html`.

Working with data in PostgreSQL databases

We discussed the topics of setting up a PostgreSQL server or cluster of servers, now we will talk about the data itself.

We discussed a lot about the ways of how to model data, and manipulate it in a database, and in this section, we will do a short recap and point to the topics you might need to take a closer look.

PostgreSQL schema objects

From Chapter 3, *PostgreSQL Basic Building Blocks*, we learned about the base hierarchy of PostgreSQL objects: databases, roles, and tablespaces. Tables, the main objects that we use to define a data model, were introduced there. We started working on the car portal database—a sample database supposed to be used by a hypothetical car web-portal application. This database was used as a base for code examples throughout this book. Chapter 4, *PostgreSQL Advanced Building Blocks* introduced other data objects available in PostgreSQL, such as views, indexes, and functions. In these two chapters, we started learning about SQL and **data definition language** (DDL), which is used to create and modify those data objects.

We mentioned custom data types in Chapter 4, *PostgreSQL Advanced Building Blocks*. PostgreSQL provides a very powerful and flexible system of custom data types, functions, and operators. We described domains, composite types, and enum types. It is also possible to create new scalar base types, by providing the following:

- Functions used to convert the new type to and from a string, to be able to use it in queries
- Functions used to convert the new type to and from its binary representation, used in copy operations, for example
- Type-modifier functions that would allow us to perform additional validation, such as specifying precision and scale for numeric types
- An analyze function used to collect statistics for columns of the new type
- Other parameters that would be used to control how the data is stored on disk, used by indexing, or typecasting

Those new types can be used in tables, of course, in composite types, and arrays.

It's possible to create custom operators that would be able to perform transformations of operands of different types, as well as unary operators. It's also possible to define custom aggregation functions. Also, PostgreSQL allows us to create custom cast operators that convert data from one type to another.

All this enables developers to create data structures that would fit almost any complicated business logic naturally, which makes PostgreSQL closer to object-oriented databases.

Continuing on this topic, it's worth mentioning the geometry types that are supported by PostgreSQL out of the box, such as points, lines, circles, and polygons. These types can be used to store two-dimensional spatial data. Indexing and integrity constraints are supported with these types as well.

More about data types can be found in the PostgreSQL documentation at `https://www.postgresql.org/docs/current/static/datatype.html`.

To generate values for auto-incremented fields in PostgreSQL, you should define those fields as `IDENTITY` columns. PostgreSQL will implicitly create sequences to support the auto-increment functionality. It's also possible to create sequences explicitly, as schema objects. They are normally used to concurrently generate unique ID values. If a value is received from a sequence, the same value will never be returned again, even if the transaction that requested it rolls back, unless the sequence is explicitly reset.

Foreign tables, server objects, and user mappings are used to access one PostgreSQL database from another. Foreign tables behave just like normal tables, and can be used in joins and written to. We introduced them briefly in the `Chapter 14`, *Testing* and `Chapter 16`, *Scalability*. PostgreSQL tries to optimize operations with foreign tables. For example, in a query with a `GROUP BY` clause, PostgreSQL could push the grouping to the remote server instead of requesting all the raw data and do grouping locally.

 For more about the foreign data wrapper that you can find in the addendum to the PostgreSQL documentation, check out `https://www.postgresql.org/docs/current/static/postgres-fdw.html`.

PostgreSQL stores meta-information, or in other words, information about the database itself, in the same database in a special area called system catalog. It can be queried in a normal way with SQL, like any table or view. `Chapter 12`, *The PostgreSQL Catalog*, is dedicated to that topic. Each database by default also contains a special schema named `information_schema`, which contains a set of views that provide user-friendly access to the system catalog tables.

PostgreSQL uses statistics that describe data contained in tables and their columns to build execution plans for queries. For example, if there is an index on a table but the table is very small, it doesn't make sense to use the index because this would end up being more expensive than reading the whole table. The database will not count rows before executing each query. Instead, it keeps estimated statistics about all the tables, updating them from time to time.

It's possible to access those statistics, which can be used for troubleshooting, to find out why an index was not used by the optimizer, for example.

Information about the current state of a database server can also be retrieved in similar way. For example, the `pg_stat_activity` view shows information about current client connections.

 More information on this topic can be found at `https://www.postgresql.org/docs/current/static/monitoring-stats.html`.

PostgreSQL offers many extension modules that bring additional functionality to a database. We mentioned some already, such as the foreign data wrapper, which is one of the extensions. Here are a few more:

- `file_fdw`: Enables us to query CSV files using SQL as if they were normal tables
- `hstore`: Brings the `hstore` data type and related functions and operators, as discussed in `Chapter 9`, *Beyond Conventional Data Types*
- `tablefunc`: Creates several functions that return tables and can, for example, perform a pivot operation in a table, which converts rows to columns and columns to rows by applying certain rules
- `seg`, `ltree`, `cube`, `citext`: These and some other provides extended data types and functions and operators to work with them

 Please refer to their respective pages in the documentation to learn more: `https://www.postgresql.org/docs/current/static/contrib.html`.

Working with data

The `Chapter 5`, *SQL Language* and `Chapter 6`, *Advanced Query Writing* were dedicated to the other part of SQL: **data manipulation language (DML)**. It's essential to know SQL when working with any relational database, not only PostgreSQL. This language is used to create, modify, and remove data from a database. And of course, it's used to retrieve data. The power of PostgreSQL comes from its ability to understand SQL queries of any complexity and execute them efficiently. But even the best database algorithms can't know the data better than the people who created it, therefore it is very important to know SQL and be able to compose good queries.

In many cases, the capabilities of SQL are not enough. Sometimes, SQL's declarative nature makes it impossible to implement complex logic in a way that is understandable by people, which is crucial for maintainability. Other times, it makes more sense to perform data processing tasks on the server instead of retrieving the data to the application side and then putting it back after processing. PostgreSQL provides a way to implement functions in the database. `Chapter 7`, *Server-Side Programming with PL/pgSQL*, explains how to do it.

Testing is another concern that is sometimes undervalued. Testing database solutions or their parts is explained in `Chapter 14`, *Testing*. It also provides some practical examples and techniques that are not directly related to testing, but could help identifying and solving problems.

We didn't discuss an interesting feature of PostgreSQL: notification events. Several applications connected to a PostgreSQL server can communicate with each other by creating notification events and listening to them. This is done using the `NOTIFY` and `LISTEN` commands.

 You can find more information in the documentation at `https://www.postgresql.org/docs/current/static/sql-notify.html`.

PostgreSQL as a component of a software solution

Going outside databases to the area of applications that use databases, in `Chapter 15`, *Using PostgreSQL in Python Applications*, we learned how to connect to a PostgreSQL database and work with data from a Python application. Several approaches were discussed, such as using low-level access with native SQL queries, or using object-relational mapping and manipulating business entities on a high level.

We used Python because it is very explicit and easy to learn. But if you prefer other programming languages, you might want to learn how to interact with PostgreSQL using them.

For JVM-based languages, such as Java, Scala, or Kotlin, it's common to interact with databases using the **Java Database Connectivity (JDBC)** interface. PostgreSQL provides a driver for this. Using JDBC functions and objects directly is a low-level approach. It's also possible and quite common to use ORM features provided by a library named Hibernate. And nowadays, it's normal to use frameworks such as Spring and Spring Boot, which also use Hibernate, and abstract the database access code from the application logic.

There are a lot of different books and other resources about Spring, Hibernate, and JDBC.

There is another commonly used API that provides database access, named **Open Database Connectivity** (**ODBC**). It is mostly used in Windows applications, but also available on Linux. There are several ODBC drivers for PostgreSQL, provided by the community and as commercial products.

Yet another database API that is used by .NET applications is ADO.NET. There are drivers for PostgreSQL available.

In the next chapter, Chapter 16, *Scalability*, we discussed the problem of using several PostgreSQL servers together to achieve results that aren't possible with only one machine. One of these goals would be to provide high-availability features by making the data storage redundant. Another task it to make the whole solution faster by utilizing the resources of several machines simultaneously.

This topic of scalability is mostly related to the subject of setting up the PostgreSQL server, virtualization, and using third-party software to manage a cluster of PostgreSQL servers. Some technologies were mentioned, and we have provided some links. However, it's worth mentioning the two solutions that use PostgreSQL in their core: Greenplum and Postgres-XL. They both follow the concept of **massive parallel processing** (**MPP**).

MPP is a way of executing a big data processing task by separating them into smaller parts, executing them in parallel with different processors, and then combining the results.

Hadoop and Spark are a couple of solutions that do a similar thing, to process big amounts of data they separate a processing task into sub-tasks and execute them in parallel.

Hadoop is a big project, combining several components and providing a whole stack of technologies making it possible to implement MPP applications. For a few years, the terms big data and Hadoop were synonymous. One of the components of Hadoop is MapReduce. It's used to split a processing task into smaller parts, execute them on different nodes, and then merge the results.

Spark is a distributed computation engine used for the real-time processing of huge amounts of data by many processing nodes.

PostgreSQL-based solutions are different from Hadoop and Spark (and from many other big data engines) because they still implement a relational database concept and support SQL and transactions. They support ACID principles, at least partially.

 To learn more about Greenplum and Postgres-XL, refer to the documentation at `https://greenplum.org/` and `https://www.postgres-xl.org/`.

Summary

In this final chapter, we did a brief review of all the topics covered in this book. However, the point was to show the areas that were not fully described or not mentioned at all and direct the readers in their further learning.

PostgreSQL is an easy-to-use, though complicated, database management system. It's very flexible, powerful, and it can be extended, so it can be applied to many different kinds of solutions. Not all aspects of using this system could be fully covered by a beginner-level book, so in this chapter, we let the readers discover areas and technologies that they can explore in more depth, which would enable them to use PostgreSQL most efficiently in the ways that interest them.

We hope we've provided enough information for you to be able to start using PostgreSQL, and to continue learning about this great system and databases in general.

Other Books You May Enjoy

If you enjoyed this book, you may be interested in these other books by Packt:

Mastering PostgreSQL 11, Second Edition
Hans-Jürgen Schönig

ISBN: 978-1-78953-781-9

- Get to grips with advanced PostgreSQL 11 features and SQL functions
- Make use of the indexing features in PostgreSQL and fine-tune the performance of your queries
- Work with stored procedures and manage backup and recovery
- Master replication and failover techniques
- Troubleshoot your PostgreSQL instance for solutions to common and not-so-common problems
- Perform database migration from MySQL and Oracle to PostgreSQL with ease

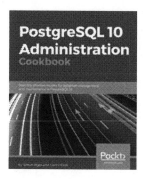

PostgreSQL 10 Administration Cookbook
Simon Riggs, Bob Gianni Ciolli

ISBN: 978-1-78847-492-4

- Get to grips with the newly released PostgreSQL 10 features to improve database performance and reliability
- Manage open source PostgreSQL versions 10 on various platforms.
- Explore best practices for planning and designing live databases
- Select and implement robust backup and recovery techniques in PostgreSQL 10
- Explore concise and clear guidance on replication and high availability
- Discover advanced technical tips for experienced users

Leave a review - let other readers know what you think

Please share your thoughts on this book with others by leaving a review on the site that you bought it from. If you purchased the book from Amazon, please leave us an honest review on this book's Amazon page. This is vital so that other potential readers can see and use your unbiased opinion to make purchasing decisions, we can understand what our customers think about our products, and our authors can see your feedback on the title that they have worked with Packt to create. It will only take a few minutes of your time, but is valuable to other potential customers, our authors, and Packt. Thank you!

Index